# THE CHAMBERLAIN LITANY

# THE CHILDREN OF JOSEPH CHAMBERLAIN

Joseph Chamberlain
b.1836, d.1914

m.1861 Harriet Kenrick          m.1868 Florence Kenrick          m.1888 Mary Endicott
b1835, d.1863                        b.1847, d.1875                        b.1864, d.1957

Beatrice                              Neville
b.1862, d.1918                     b.1869, d.1940

Austen                                        m.1911 Anne de Vere Cole,
b.1863, d.1937                                   b.1883, d.1967

m.1906 Ivy Dundas                          Dorothy
b.1878, d.1941                           b.1912, d.1992

Joseph                                     Frank
b.1907, d.1979                          b.1914, d.1966

Diane                               Ida
b.1911, d.1999                  b.1870, d.1943

Lawrence                          Hilda
b.1917, d.2003                  b.1872, d.1967

Ethel
b.1873, d.1905

m. 1900 Lionel Richards
b.1868, d.1954

Hilda Mary
b.1901, d.1993

# The Chamberlain Litany

*Letters within a Governing Family
from Empire to Appeasement*

PETER T. MARSH

HAUS BOOKS
London

to Amanda, Mary and Susan
who draw families together

First published in Great Britain in 2010 by
Haus Publishing Ltd
70 Cadogan Place
London SW1X 9AH
www.hauspublishing.com

Copyright © Peter T. Marsh, 2010

The moral right of the author has been asserted

A CIP catalogue record for this book is available from the British Library

ISBN 978-1-906598-63-1

Typeset in Garamond by MacGuru Ltd
info@macguru.org.uk
Printed in the UK by CPI William Clowes Beccles NR34 7TL

Previous page: *The Chamberlains at Highbury during Neville's exile.*

# List of Illustrations

# Acknowledgements

My greatest debt as I conclude this book is to the Chamberlain family, past and present: to Joseph's children who wrote such enthralling letters to each other, to their children who collected the letters assiduously for safekeeping in the University of Birmingham Library, and to their children's children who have encouraged me to write the statesmen's story as the sisters saw it. I am particularly indebted to Neville's daughter-in-law Roma Chamberlain and his grandson James Lloyd for permission to reproduce photographs in their possession. I am also deeply grateful to Susan Worrall, Director of Special Collections at the University of Birmingham for permission to reproduce photographs and quote from the Chamberlain papers and for years of patient assistance from her predecessor, Christine Penney, and the staff of the Heslop Room, particularly Martin Killeen and Philippa Bassett. Aside from a lifetime of professional indebtedness to other historians, I must single out for special praise Robert Self whose editing of the letters of Austen and Neville to Ida and Hilda after the death of their father remains a treasure-trove for historians of 20th-century Britain. I have received stimulating encouragement along the way from colleagues and students in the University of Birmingham's Department of History, through the National Trust's Barber Lectures, from Arnold Whittall, Geoffrey Best, Andrew Adonis, friends and associates at the Reform Club, and the most sparkling of publishers, Barbara Schwepcke. Andrew Jones is a very acute as well as heartening critical reader: I only wish I had known this sooner. Olivia Richmond kindly showed me over The Bury House in Hampshire, the centre of Chamberlain family correspondence for twenty-five years. But how can I ever thank Amanda Cadman who has made the first decade of this century the happiest and most fulfilling time of my life?

# Contents

*Ida and Hilda in their forties*

*Prologue*

# As the Sisters Saw It

Families are formative in the upbringing of most people. But for the children of Joseph Chamberlain the family remained formative throughout their lives. They remained close through the letters they wrote to each other whenever they were separated. And separated they often were, by schooling, apprenticeships and the demands of work, during travels, eventually tending their stricken father, and by the break-up of the family household after his death. Their uneasiness at separation from each other was accentuated by the early death of their mothers – for there were two – in childbirth, and by the ensuing remoteness of their always enthralling father.

Their letters to each other are of more than private interest because the family was further held together by its absorption in the family business of politics and public service. The children of Joseph Chamberlain grew up at the centre of Britain's political life at the height of its imperial might. Joe, as he was known from the back-to-back houses of Birmingham to Windsor Castle, was the pivotal British statesman of the age. After his stroke, his two sons took up central positions in public life, though they never matched his originating power. The Chamberlains thus produced three leading statesmen within two generations, an achievement unrivalled in British history. One or other of these men was of major importance in British politics throughout the sixty-five years covered in this book, from the death of Joseph's second wife in 1875 until the death of her son Neville in 1940.

And it was not just the men who mattered. Joe's daughters participated on the same basis as his sons in the political conversation that rolled around the dinner table once his third wife, Mary, overcame his remoteness. Three of his four daughters devoted themselves to the public in education, voluntary services, and local government. The women in the family also sustained the correspondence that kept them all together. Mary developed a correspondence with Austen, Joseph's elder son, which grew in political importance after Joe's stroke. The women Austen and Neville married played lesser but still significant parts in the family letter-writing.

But the crucial contributors were Joe's daughters: Beatrice, his first child, born in 1862, sister of Austen who was born the next year, and the younger sisters of Neville, who was born in 1869: Ida born in 1870, Hilda in 1872 and Ethel in 1873. Though children of Joseph's first two wives, they never thought of each other as half-brothers or half-sisters. Beatrice was the mentor of the family and wrote to both her brothers in instructive as well as endearing terms. Ida, Hilda and Ethel joined her in writing to Neville during his exile in the Bahamas, whipping up waves of correspondence, which they all saved. Their letters to each other returned to full flood during Joseph's convalescence in France after a stroke on his seventieth birthday until his death on the eve of the First World War. Soon afterwards Ida and Hilda set up home together in Hampshire. There they formed the keystone in the arch of Chamberlain family communication, writing weekly to their brothers, collecting their replies, and keeping them in touch with each other.

Historians have long known that Neville's letters to his sisters provide a singularly revealing record of his thinking, particularly over appeasement and the agreement he reached with Hitler at Munich. Robert Self assembled exemplary editions, first of Austen's and then of Neville's letters to Ida and Hilda after the death of their father. But scarcely any attention has been paid to the letters from the sisters that elicited this massive response, nor to the quarter-century of correspondence among Joseph's children before his death. Nor have the letters exchanged over half a century between Austen and Neville been put together. Everyone knows that letters are shaped by both writer and recipient. And the Chamberlains knew that their letters to each other were passed around the family. These were family letters. But the very volume of the Chamberlain family letters – altogether there are some ten thousand – has deterred investigation.

The correspondence of Joseph's Chamberlain's children makes full sense only when read in its entirety. There are great advantages in doing so. These letters show us how Joe's children interpreted their world to each other. As they told each other about their activities week by week, their letters amount to an autobiography of the family. The Chamberlains picked up a pen as effortlessly as we now pick up a telephone, and they expressed themselves with similar ease. Reading these letters is like eavesdropping. The Chamberlains recoiled from expressing their feelings – and to this extent the correspondence is non-revelatory. But politics was their conversational meat and drink – that and gardening, the other passion that united the Chamberlains. Their letters are long, each usually covering many sides of paper. They incorporate the experience of two generations, spilling into a third. And they were meticulously preserved, often numbered to make sure that each received its response.

Gradually Austen, Neville, Ida and Hilda became aware that their correspondence was acquiring historical importance. When Austen retired from office, he turned the letters to his father and stepmother which he had written before the First World War into a book on the politics of that time.[1] Neville sent weekly letters to Ida and Hilda not just as an account of his activities but to win their understanding and endorsement. The daughters of Joseph Chamberlain were almost as strong-minded as his sons, and their approval carried the stamp of the family. Ida and Hilda saw in Neville's letters an explanation of the policies he adopted as Prime Minister, an explanation that they hoped would form the basis for a history of those years. Neville did not share that hope. But he knew, as the war that he struggled to avert finally broke out, that his sisters were keeping his letters safe in the strong room of their bank. A generation later the grandchildren of Joseph Chamberlain gathered all the family letters – his and those of his sons and daughters – and deposited them alongside their political papers in the university which he founded.

In an attempt to see the Chamberlains' world as they saw it, this book relies primarily upon information they provided in their letters. That information covered the wider world as well as the nuclear family. The other statesmen who forwarded or frustrated the ambitions of the Chamberlains bulk large in the family correspondence: Arthur Balfour, Andrew Bonar Law, David Lloyd George, Stanley Baldwin, Winston Churchill. But these men appear in this study as the Chamberlains saw them. This book's reliance upon what the Chamberlains wrote to each other has, therefore, some obvious drawbacks as well as dividends. It does not provide a balanced account of Britain in the period when the Chamberlains were politically prominent – though it provides some corrective balance to the prevailing Churchillian interpretation. Nor can it serve on its own as a study of international relations during these years. Furthermore, correspondence within a close-knit family is unlikely to portray its members in an unbecoming light. But so anxious were Joseph's children to secure each other's understanding that they exposed their weaknesses as well as their accomplishments. Their letters contained revelations that still haunt the historical record.

There were strands of tragedy in the solidarity of the Chamberlain family. The

---

1 *Politics From Inside: An epistolary chronicle, 1906–1914* (London: Cassell, 1936)

family letters began in an attempt to deal with the death in childbirth of the only mother any of Joseph's children knew. The correspondence brightened over the next thirty years, deepening the delight the family took in keeping together. But the Chamberlain men refused to listen to criticism, even within the family, of the policies they prized. Moreover, the enthusiastic response of the sisters to the main achievements of their father and brothers stiffened the men's disregard of criticism outside the family.

An undercurrent of anxiety at the thought of failure also ran through the family story, particularly for Neville. Both Austen and Neville disappointed their father; Neville in his school days, and Austen much later when he failed to seize the leadership of his party when it was within his grasp. Neville failed in his first assignments both in business and in national, though not local, politics. Neither son matched Joseph's achievements. When Neville appeared to do so, on becoming Prime Minister and keeping the peace with Hitler at Munich, it proved to be a terrible illusion.

The Chamberlains were in many ways an ordinary family. Joseph was the only truly original figure among them. But he focused his children's attention on politics and dedicated them to public service, placing them in an extraordinary position. He also imbued them with his understanding of the roots of public wellbeing, an understanding based on his early discovery of the social as well as economic benefits that could be derived from the manufacturing industry. Neville and his sisters brought that understanding to bear with great effect in the local and national governance of Britain. But Joseph's vision proved hard to apply throughout the British Empire, which became his supreme concern. And it proved tragically misleading in the international arena. Among Joe's children, only Austen acquired some understanding of great power politics: and Austen allowed that understanding to be overridden by his loyalty to his family. All the children of Joseph Chamberlain followed doggedly in his footsteps and interpreted their public service in his terms.

Eventually Hilda, the youngest of the surviving children, turned her family's story into a kind of litany, a set of repetitive sentences about how the Chamberlain men secured ultimate victory for each other over their adversaries. Beginning with her father before turning to Austen and Neville, Hilda sang of victory but only after repeated setbacks. Each of the three, as she saw it, was betrayed by a colleague. But each son then managed to complete the mission of his predecessor. Joseph's crusade for imperial preference and tariff reform was frustrated by his party leader, Balfour. Austen was betrayed by the subsequent leaders of the party, Bonar Law and Baldwin. Neville was traduced by the First World War Prime Minister, Lloyd George. But soon after that war, Austen as Chancellor inched Britain towards his father's goal of tariff protection. A decade later Neville secured a good deal of the imperial tariff reform for which his father had fought and died. At the same time, Baldwin denied Austen the opportunity to consolidate the work of European peacemaking which he had begun with the Locarno treaties. But Neville carried Austen's quest for European peace to apparent triumph at Munich. There Hilda's song reached its exultant climax.

But Hilda had not reckoned with the last and greatest of the Chamberlains' adversaries, Winston Churchill. Neville's achievement at Munich was discredited by the outbreak of the war that he had struggled to avert. He was driven from power and soon died, replaced by Churchill with resounding success. Churchill's achievement, not only during the war but afterwards in writing its history, forced Hilda to change her interpretation of the Chamberlains' story from a song of praise to a lament.

*Part I*

# SETTING THE PACE

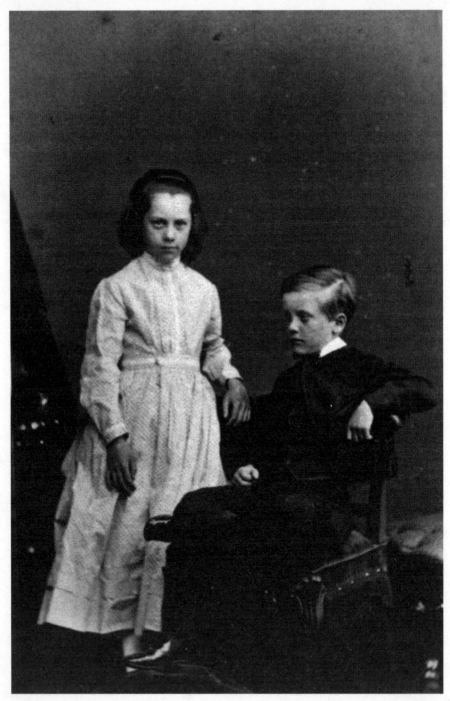

*Beatrice standing tall over Austen*

# I

# Munich Tulips

'I can't tell you how much we have enjoyed your Munich tulips,' Ida wrote to Neville after Hitler completed his takeover of Czechoslovakia: 'They at least have proved no disappointment.'[1] These tulips were among the gifts showered on Neville the previous October in gratitude for saving Europe from war through the accord he reached with Hitler at Munich. Gifts had poured in from every corner of Europe except from Czechoslovakia, which Neville had shorn of its defensive perimeter to satisfy Hitler's demand to incorporate into the German Reich all lands peopled by Germans. From the Netherlands had come '4000 tulips 500 hyacinths 500 daffodils and 1000 crocuses. So,' Neville told his sisters, 'if you would like some you can make your choice'.[2] But when the bulbs bloomed that spring, they brought to the minds even of Neville's supportive, indeed cocooning, sisters the shattered glory of the Munich agreement. That agreement destroyed Neville's reputation and tarnished the family name.

In her phrase 'Munich tulips', Ida encapsulated the two passions, as well as the tragedy, which the Chamberlains shared. One passion was for gardening, a love they had learned from their father Joseph. From Joseph they also imbibed their other passion: for governing. Both of Joe's sons distinguished themselves in government. Austen, the elder, held a succession of high offices, culminating in the Foreign Office where he won the Nobel Peace Prize. Neville became Prime Minister, the ultimate goal in British politics which eluded his father and brother. And

---

1 Ida to Neville Chamberlain, 18 May 1939, The Bury House, NC18/2/1127
2 Neville to Ida, 24 Oct.1938, Chequers, in Robert Self, ed., *The Neville Chamberlain Diary Letters*, IV, 358

though only the men of the family attained such prominence, the women of the family were also deeply involved in the work of government. Beatrice, the eldest, made a name for herself in education, in war work, and on the public platform. Ida did likewise in local government; and her younger sister Hilda became a leader in the formative years of the Women's Institute. This experience and a lifetime of conversation and correspondence within the family about local, national and imperial politics gave these women extraordinary influence as confidantes to their brothers.

Joseph towered imperiously over the lives of his children long after his death at the beginning of the First World War: his outlook permeated their approach to public service. As a young metal manufacturer in Birmingham, he caught a glimpse of how the wealth he acquired could and should be shared with the workers to preserve and enhance the wellbeing of the town. That hope led him into public service, first in education, then in local government, and up into national politics and the aggrandisement of the Empire. Joseph's dream was refracted among his children, and its underlying values shaped both their accomplishments and their failures.

The family were fiercely loyal to each other and the paternal inheritance. What bound them still more closely to each other was the mother most of them never knew. Their story began, as it was to end, in tragedy. There were in fact two mothers. Beatrice and Austen were the children of Harriet Kenrick, who died in 1863 giving birth to Austen. Neville, Ida, Hilda and Ethel were the children of Harriet's first cousin Florence, who died in 1875 giving birth to a child who died a few hours later. Florence was the only mother Beatrice and Austen really knew. Beatrice was twelve and Austen eleven when Florence died. She had surrounded them with the same love that she gave her own children. Austen remembered seeing her after her marriage to his father 'running from the rockery where she was planting the ferns they had gathered on their honeymoon in the Lakes, pulling off her gauntlet gloves, with the trowel still in her hand and a loving welcome for her new children which', he added, 'never failed in her short life.'[3] Beatrice treasured the letter that Florence wrote to her a few months before her death, in which she described a visit by the Prince and Princess of Wales to Birmingham and the banquet over which Joseph as mayor had presided. Revealing her radical predilections, Florence told Beatrice she was not impressed by the grandees: 'the people were the real sight – I never saw such crowds.'[4]

In terms of political impact on her husband, Florence was the most influential

---

3 Austen Chamberlain, *Politics from Inside* (London: Cassell, 1936), 16
4 Florence to Beatrice, 6 Nov. 1874, Southbourne, BC3/1/29

of Joseph's wives. Though physically fragile, she shared her husband's toughness of purpose, and she sharpened his radicalism. She was committed to the advancement of women and improved her own education through night classes. She encouraged Joe's entry into local and national politics. He discussed every step of his advancing path with her. She edited the articles he wrote in the *Fortnightly Review* to proclaim the new Radicalism. In the letter he wrote for her children after her death, Joseph described how 'the result of this complete similarity of task & identity of interests has naturally been to knit us together so that I can now say that there is no thought or action of my later years which my wife has not shared with me, & no plan or ambition or desire formed for the future which has not been shattered by her death.'[5]

He was devastated. Unable, after making the burial arrangements, to cope with his loss, he simply fled. Without waiting even for the funeral service, he moved his young family into the nearby home of his first wife's father, left the town of which he had been re-elected mayor, and ran from the country without quite knowing where he was going. He passed through France to Algiers. He returned eventually to Birmingham, but stayed just long enough to write some essential letters. Then he took his brother Arthur and brother-in-law William Kenrick north to lose himself fishing in Scotland.

When he finally came back to Birmingham, he threw himself into a whirlwind of political activity. 'Drive on,' he wrote to the friend who had accompanied him to Algiers, '– we shall come to the journey's end in time & perhaps then we shall know where we have been going and whose business we have been doing all the time.'[6] Working at a frantic pace, he transformed the government of Birmingham, creating in doing so the prototype for what became known as 'gas and water socialism'. A year later he gained election to Parliament as a Member for Birmingham and transferred his energies to the national arena. He transformed the national organisation of the Liberal party, creating yet another political model, one which the Conservative party adapted to its own purposes. Within five years of Florence's death, he pushed his way into the Cabinet of a new Liberal government which the party organisation he set up had helped to elect. Ceaselessly he accelerated the pace of British politics for another quarter of a century, until a stroke pushed him off the central stage.

Absorption in public activities pulled him further from his young family. His time away from home increased with his election to Parliament, which necessitated

---

5  Letter by Joseph 'For Florence's children', 5 Apr.1875, BC5/2a/1a
6  Joseph Chamberlain to Jesse Collings, 12 Sept.1875, copy, JC5/16/47

living in London, though he returned to Birmingham most weekends. He also spent a good deal of his holiday time away from home, whether travelling on the Continent or fishing in Scotland. Though he loved his children, they reminded him of his renewed loss. He could not forget that his first wife Harriet died giving birth to Austen. And his youngest child, 'the little gipsy Ethel',[7] bore a haunting resemblance to Florence. Though, like a lightning rod, Joe Chamberlain attracted the fiercest emotions of devotion and hatred throughout his public life, he found it difficult to handle strong emotions in his family life. He could not cope with bereavement. He had also fled from home after the death of Harriet, leaving their two babies in the care of her father; and it was there again that he left his younger children after the death of Florence.

Joseph did not help them deal with Florence's death. Preoccupied by his own loss, he did not tell the children of theirs. Ida, Florence's eldest daughter, could not recall even being told of her death; and she remained distressed by her inability to remember anything about her mother other than the rustle of her skirts when Neville and she knelt beside her to say their bedtime prayers. Neville remembered vividly being told of his mother's death, not however by his father but by Aunt Louie (Louisa), Florence's identical twin sister who had married Joe's brother Arthur and lived nearby. Joseph told the children that they were 'all I have to live for now'[8]. But he recoiled from any allusion to the wife he had lost. He wrote a long letter of remembrance for her children, ending with an account of her final hours. But he could not speak to them about her, nor could he bear any mention of her. So they could not speak of the mother they never knew. Their only help came from their aunts and uncles. The tragedies that devastated the inner family drew the broader family to the rescue. Joseph asked one of his younger sisters, Caroline, known as Lina, to move into his home and look after his family; and when Lina married, he asked his youngest sister, Clara, to take over.

&

Bereft of a mother and in the absence of their father, the children turned to each other for support. The threat they most feared was separation. They found a way to deal with it. Their father pointed the way, seconded by Beatrice. Though unable to reach out to his children face to face, he did so by letter. He began during his flight from home, writing to Beatrice from Algiers. That particular letter has not

---

7 Joseph to Beatrice, #4, 7 Sept.[1877], BC3/1/9
8 Austen Chamberlain to Mr Sayle, 27 Oct. [no year], AC.L.Add.68

survived, though from then on she treasured his letters. He wrote the next one during his stop in Birmingham en route to Scotland. We do not know whether he saw the younger children, but Beatrice was away at school. She had sent a reply to his first letter, and he found it waiting for him at home. So he replied, giving her a lively account of his travels on the way back from Algiers through France. This letter revealed the remarkable education the girl of twelve had already received by listening to the conversation of her parents. 'I went,' he reported, 'to the Assembly – that is the French House of Commons, – & heard a debate which lasted some hours. Mr. Gambetta, of whom you may have heard during the great French war with Germany, was one of the speakers ... Paris was besieged by the Germans & taken after many months –& some of the houses & streets still show marks of the cannon shot & rifle balls.'[9]

His capacity for description of the passing scene grew with each letter. 'Along the route' to Scotland, he told Beatrice, 'we found the country in many places covered with snow & all the mountains were like the Alps in Switzerland gleaming white & brilliant in the sun light.'[10] He closed with instructions about local postal times for her reply, and asked her to pass the letter on to Austen. Joseph insisted that this family correspondence be reciprocal. He wrote to Austen with instructions to 'forward the letter to Beatrice when read ... each of you is to forward my letters to the other.' Rationing the time he would devote to his children, he added, 'I can only write one every week.'[11] There was more command than compassion even in this form of communication with his children. Joseph nonetheless initiated the practice of letter-writing within the family. His children developed the practice far beyond the example he set; and he left them to it, often relying on them to transmit his wishes to one another. They used their correspondence to give each other the familial approval which neither mother nor father was on hand to provide. But there was an element of tragedy here too in this correspondence, particularly for the younger set, the children of Florence, for they came to rely almost exclusively on each other.

The dependence of the children on each other began before all of them could write. Lack of parenting left them leaderless. Beatrice, the eldest, strode into the breach. She had a strong personality, too strong for Austen who at the age of six was sent away to school at Rugby to release him from the 'absolute sway' she had established over her 'delicate little brother'. Bea or Bee, as her siblings sometimes called her, had models of strong women to follow. The one who affected her most

9 Joseph to Beatrice, 21 Mar.1875, Southbourne, BC3/1/1
10 Joseph to Beatrice, 16 Apr.[1875], from Rossshire, BC3/1/2
11 Joseph to Austen, 15 May 1875, Southbourne, AC1/4/4a/5

deeply was her mother's elder sister, known eventually to all the children as 'Auntie'. Unmarried after 'an unfortunate love affair',[12] Auntie took charge of Harriet's children after her death. Hilda later remembered her as 'a striking but, to most people, rather formidable personality. Tall, dignified, very upright, with almost black hair, she did not easily make friends, either with adults or children, but from her earliest days, Beatrice was absolutely devoted to her ... Auntie reciprocated her affection and her influence gave a direction to Beatrice's whole life'.[13] Bea's other strong model, in spite of fragile health, was Florence, who took over the charge of Joseph's household from Auntie when Bea was six.

Both Auntie and Florence were staunch radicals. Florence gave voice to her radicalism through her husband. Auntie expressed hers directly in the field of education. Though she hated campaigning, she stood for election to the School Board set up in Birmingham under the 1870 Education Act; and she continued to serve in that capacity for more than twenty years. She took a hard line on religious instruction, insisting in the interests of neutrality that it be excluded entirely from the curriculum. Her primary concerns in education, however, were for the teachers, 'especially those in the poorest "ragged schools" as they were called. For them, she organised treats, established flower shows ... and above all gave sympathy and encouragement to the teachers individually: – often very lonely, being isolated by their education and work from their own class.' Beatrice eventually followed Auntie into the same line of work.

Florence too was concerned with education, for herself through night school, and for her children in the expanding nursery. When Florence died, Beatrice took over this concern for the education of the younger children. She was receiving a good education herself at the newly established High School for Girls in Birmingham; 'and her quick intelligence and enthusiastic response made her early top of the class.' She wanted the same for her siblings.

But she was not oppressive about it. Hilda thought of Bea 'as the perfect playmate.' Bea transformed the garden behind their first family house, Southbourne in Edgbaston, 'into a marvellous world. She was full of imagination ... Pirates and Roman and Pagan heroes, explorers and adventurers.' Bea included in these adventures the cousins who lived nearby in Birmingham and holidayed with them in Wales or Scotland. The Chamberlains were a much intermarried family. Joe's sister Mary married Harriet's brother, William, and Joe's brother Arthur married

---

12 Cecily Debenham's Recollections, 1947/8, with notes by John Kenrick, 1996, in the possession of Martin Kenrick
13 Recollections of Beatrice drafted after World War II by Hilda, BC5/10/2

Florence's twin sister Louise. They proceeded to build great houses close to each other, Joe at Highbury, Arthur at Moor Green, and William at The Grove. So the children referred to each other by the names of their houses, the Highburies, the Moor Greens and the Groves. After the death of Florence, Joe and Arthur appointed a governess to teach their younger children all together. But the governess was overshadowed by Beatrice, especially when the families holidayed together.

The children remembered these holidays for the rest of their lives. Hilda's happiest memories were 'of the month's holiday at the seaside or in the mountains where we went every summer.' Beatrice was the invariable leader. 'Long walks for the elder children over mountains and moor were under her charge ... Beatrice launched out with her map, with each child carrying a small packet of sandwiches and a wrap of some sort strapped round their waist. ... Bathing at the sea, shell collecting, walking and flower collecting, with some geology or inspection of old ruins all added to our good times.' Bea's cousin Cecily, who had a good sense of dress style which Bea lacked, winced at the memory of their 'get up'. It was 'practical & hideous, blue serge skirt & jersey, longish skirts as we grew older, plaid shawl & macintosh on a strap round the waist ... black button boots & a tam-o-shanter. Thus attired we tramped the countryside as much off the road as possible with long swinging strides & arms in unison – we covered the ground but were certainly not elegant.'[14]

The primacy of Beatrice among her siblings was accentuated by the remoteness of their father. Hilda had only fleeting memories of him from her early years when she was 'generally rather in awe of him'.[15] She could not 'remember his coming up to our bedrooms to say "good night"'. He 'did not often find time to take us for excursions himself but sometimes he drove with us ... in the carriage & pair to get daffodils at Northfield or primroses at Weatheroak Hill'. She recalled visits to the Horticultural Gardens in London after his election to Parliament, '& once' – only once – 'he took us to the House of Commons'. She did not see much of her father on week days: 'but as we grew older, we used to come down at his dinnertime & sit beside him.' Sundays were better: 'after lunch we used to get one on each knee & one hanging over his shoulder' to look at the *Illustrated London News*. Papa 'always went through it with us, telling us stories about the pictures, – except when the Zulu war took place, when he used to pass hastily over what, I think, were probably highly imaginative drawings of horrors, which he considered unsuitable for us, & which consequently I always wished particularly to see.'

The other children had similar impressions of their father. Neville, as Florence's

---

14 Cecily Debenham's Recollections
15 Hilda's notes February 1916, BC5/10/5

eldest child, was the one most aware of her death. Though he did not immediately understand how 'this dreadful blow' had 'hardened' his father, Neville was well aware that 'for a good many years I respected and feared him more than I loved him.'[16] Both sons felt that they were disappointments to their father. Austen, the least assertive of the children, did not 'feel that I was good for something' until his final years at Rugby.[17] Joseph towered god-like above them. 'He never used many words to enforce his displeasure,' Hilda recalled, but 'once he looked coldly on you, it was more than a long sermon from anyone else. ... On the other hand when he smiled his whole face changed & lighted up with an extraordinary sweetness & tenderness, which rewarded one for anything.' He was 'always the arbiter in the last resort' to whom the younger children made their final appeal against the aunts in charge of the household. 'With what gratitude we regarded him when he represented to Aunt Clara that the bread & butter pudding had not half enough currants, or when he decreed that the tapioca, which we all loathed, should never be forced on us again.'

Joseph found in gardening the activity that absorbed his restless soul at weekends. And it was in the garden that his children found him most expansive. Hilda's 'liveliest recollections of Papa' at Southbourne were 'connected with the garden or the visiting of the green houses. He used to take us to see ... the conservatory which was given up to gloxinias which he grew remarkably well, & of which he was very proud; & we generally had a flower given us to take away. I recall too one ever-memorable Summer's day going out with him in the morning, & having our pinafores filled with the roses he was cutting, after which he gave us each a rose bush for our very own.'[18] Joseph also tried to engage his children in competitive board games, backgammon, draughts or chess. But the only one who rose to this challenge was little Ethel. She 'played rather well, & could hold her own,' Hilda enviously recalled. Ethel was feisty, though always frail in health. When Neville came upon her during a holiday in the Highlands blue with cold, he called her a 'miserable object'. Refusing to take offence, she embraced the description and thereafter signed her letters 'the Ob'.

The girls showed no resentment at the frequent absence of their father and his preoccupation with politics. Even at a young age they found his political involvements exciting. Ida was seven when Gladstone came to Southbourne en route to

---

16 Neville to his children Dorothy and Frank, written at his Birmingham home on 6 July 1914 within days of his father's death, NC1/6/11
17 Austen to Ida, 7 Nov.1925, Twitts Ghyll, AC5/1/368
18 Hilda's notes February 1906, BC5/10/5

the town centre where he was to inaugurate the National Liberal Federation which her father was setting up: 'we children were able to look out of the nursery window & see the procession arrive with Mr. Gladstone in an open carriage with four horses & mounted police men in attendance.' But she 'felt a little injured that Mr. G. should be coming in for most of the glory & Papa took only a second place.'[19]

Away from the garden and aside from the occasional game, Joseph found only indirect and distant ways of expressing his affection for his children, mainly through letters. He did not write about his family sentiments. But he could write about his travels and the things that captured his interest, about how ordinary people earned their daily bread, and above all politics. He used his letters to educate his children. He wrote to Beatrice about a rough voyage across the North Sea to Lapland, about the cramped sleeping conditions on board ship and the indented coastline in which 'it is impossible to say 10 minutes beforehand whether the next turn will be to the right or to the left.'[20] He told her of the local economy based on timber and fish. He wrote about the difficulty communicating where only Swedish was spoken, no English, German or French, in all of which he could get along and wanted his children to become fluent.

The next summer he headed for Austria. This time he numbered the accounts he sent home, and they cast historical shadows that lingered long after his death. En route from Munich to Salzburg, he found himself in the same train as Bismarck. 'The Prince,' he reported to the aunt who looked after his children, 'is like his portraits, a big, burly, coarse looking man with signs of power in his big head, bushy eyebrows & firm mouth. He looked the presentment of the blood & iron theory – with a good deal of Champagne hinted in his nose. ... we ... are now going in a carriage to Berchtesgarden [sic] a small village three hours off said to be very beautifully situated'[21] – as Neville would later confirm when he visited Hitler there. Joseph turned his attention to the economy of Austria, so different from Birmingham. What fascinated him was the method of salt production he found. Large chambers in the mines were filled 'with water which is left to soak up the salt for months till it becomes thoroughly impregnated & is then conducted in wooden pipes to the Salt works where the water is evaporated & the salt refined.'[22]

Joseph aimed his early letters at his older children, trusting them to transmit

19 Ida's Reminiscences, BC5/9/3
20 Joseph to Beatrice, 24 Aug.187[6], Luleä, BC3/1/7
21 Joseph to Lina, #2, 25 Aug.1877, Salzburg, NC1/6/5/4
22 Joseph to Beatrice, #4, 7 Sept.[1877], Ischl, B C3/1/9

his messages to the young. There was a clear line of division between Harriet's children, who were at least six years older and often away at school, and the children of Florence who remained at home. 'Upstairs in the attic Beatrice & Austen had their play rooms'; and Ida recalled how, 'on rare & solemn occasions we were invited up there. ... sometimes Austen showed us slides on his microscope & there was a general sense of uplift about the proceedings.' Going away to school made all the difference. The 'first great sorrow' in Ida's life occurred when Neville left home at the age of eight for preparatory school in Rugby. She was shocked to hear that 'Papa had asked him how he would like to go to school, & he had replied "very much". Another shock awaited me when he returned home at the end of the first holidays; & when I proposed that he & I should go off together into the garden as usual he expressed a desire that Hilda & Ethel should come too ... the idea of sharing him with the younger ones had never entered my mind.'

The children of each mother forged their strongest bonds with each other. Writing to Austen after Bea's death, one of her classmates at school recalled how Austen was 'the person nearest to her heart ... In those early days the others were still children & she felt as if you & she belonged to another generation.'[23] Similarly Neville and his sisters forged their strongest relationships with each other. Ida trotted after Neville as he hunted bugs and butterflies. 'I am sure,' she later confessed, 'that naturally I had no taste whatever for entomology. What I enjoyed was the opportunity of being with Neville & sharing his favourite occupation.' He was the animating centre in her childhood, an 'excellent mimic ... with a keen sense of humour' and 'a first class story teller'. In face of this bond between Ida and Neville, Hilda and Ethel formed their own special companionship.

&

Joseph furthered the education of the elder pair of children in ways that reflected his widening political vision. He took Beatrice to Fontainebleau to finish her education at Les Ruches, a school for girls which attracted progressively-minded families among the governing elite in the United States and Germany as well as Britain. Eleanor Roosevelt went later to its successor school, Allenswood, and adored it. Les Ruches was led by a pair of teachers, one of whom, Marie Souvestre, made an even greater impact on Beatrice than Auntie had. A rich woman well connected among the intellectual and political leadership of the French Republic, Marie Souvestre intensified Bea's already lively imagination and love of language. Some

---

23  Marian P. Whitney to Austen, 1 Jan.1919, 227 Church Street, New Haven, AC5/1/116

students found the impact of Marie Souvestre emotionally overwhelming. Bea's cousin Cecily attended Allenswood, established in Wimbledon by Souvestre after the break-up of Les Ruches; and she found Souvestre 'shattering ... She certainly went to the head like Champagne ... The light seemed to go out of my world when she died.'[24] Les Ruches and Allenswood were emotional hothouses.

But Beatrice was a calmer person than Cecily. Bea's talent lay in drawing other people out rather than in mesmerizing them. Ida recalled that 'unlike the rest of us she made friends wherever she went, perhaps because she would always see only the best in everybody.' One odd consequence of this talent was that letters from Bea were in themselves uninteresting. She was animating in conversation. But when, after her death, Ida and Hilda looked for 'some permanent memorial of her vivid personality,' they found to their dismay that her letters were 'singularly colourless'.[25] Hilda filled the gap by writing a sensitive memoir of Beatrice. In spite or because of their conspicuous differences, Beatrice and Marie Souvestre drew each other out. Marie Souvestre was strikingly beautiful, Beatrice 'had distinction if not actual good looks'. Marie Souvestre dressed with elegance, Bea 'dressed unbecomingly, probably from indifference.'[26] Bea was enlivening, Marie Souvestre dazzling. She was also more than thirty years older than Bea. Yet they took to each other instinctively. Austen treasured the report of an American student at Les Ruches in Bea's time, Marion Whitney, later President of Vassar College: 'All the professors who came from Paris to lecture ... extolled [Bea's] intellectual power. One said she wrote French like a Sévigné.' Yet 'her kindness to the smaller fry was as striking.' In some ways Marie Souvestre had less in common with Bea than with her father. One day Joseph dined at the school, a 'slim dapper gentleman with a monocle. There he stood by the door talking to Mademoiselle Souvestre as if he enjoyed it. She looked radiant in a perfect toilette of dark blue silk with the unfailing frilled elbow sleeves showing that she was fully aware of a beautiful arm and hand ... there was a touch of romance in the obvious friendship of these kindred spirits.'

Joseph enhanced his public stature and transformed the life of the family with the construction of a grand house, the greatest in Birmingham. He called Highbury after the part of London where he had spent his youth. Designed by the leading local architect, J.H. Chamberlain (no relation), and perched on the south-west edge of the town looking out over the hills of Worcestershire, with enough land for extensive gardens and a home farm, Highbury marked Joseph as the most

---

24 Cecily Debenham's Recollections
25 Recollections of Beatrice drafted after World War II by Hilda, BC5/10/2
26 News clipping entitled 'Beatrice Chamberlain at School', AC6/1/791

ambitious of the industrial princes of Birmingham, indeed of Britain. Beatrice was groomed to take eventual charge as chatelaine at Highbury.

It was not, however, quite ready for occupancy when Joseph's place in the political world soared upwards. There was no sign of the impending ascent at the beginning of the parliamentary year in 1880. He reported from London to Beatrice that, 'Public affairs are dull here & I do not expect a very lively session.' Within weeks, however, the political scene was transformed in a general election that swept the Liberals into office and enabled Joseph to push his way into the Cabinet as President of the Board of Trade. Five months elapsed before he next found time to write to Bea. He wrote at midnight, still at the House of Commons, 'worked to death & bothered beyond endurance by Committees & Deputations & Irishmen & Scotchmen & all sorts of other importunate bipeds.' Clearly he loved his busy life. Nor could he suppress his enjoyment of the touches of glamour that went along with his position, though a favourite phrase of Ethel's reminded him of his former republicanism and guiding purpose. 'I am getting very intimate with Royalty & am to dine with the Queen at Windsor next Saturday ... I wish I cared more about this sort of thing ... but as Ethel used to say – "it doesn't interest me" & rather adds to the nuisances of official life. However, all this is nothing, if we can succeed in giving practical effect to our principles.' He proposed that once Bea and Austen came home from their schools for the summer holidays, they 'should come to London & take care of your Rt. Hon. Papa ... and then you can go to the theatre & the pictures & perhaps to the House of Commons & have larks!'[27]

Austen left school at Rugby two years later, heading for Cambridge. Before going, he accompanied Joseph on his first official trip abroad as a member of the Cabinet. They passed through Denmark en route to Russia. Accompanying his father was part of Austen's apprenticeship for a career in government. Joseph asked him to describe the passing scene to Beatrice for reading to the younger children. Taking Bea's political education seriously, Joseph also explained the purpose of the trip to her: he was to make himself available for discussions with the crowned heads and chief ministers of the countries he visited. The King of Denmark used this opportunity to explain the constitutional struggle in which he was engaged with Norway. Joe looked closely as always at the society, economy and culture of the countries through which he travelled. He was impressed with the Finns, 'who looked more like hard featured Yorkshire men than anything else. They seem a more capable race than the Russian people & are said to be honest in affairs & in office & to be making great progress in commerce & manufactures. Society in

---

27 Joseph to Beatrice, 9 July 1880, House of Commons Library, BC3/1/17

Russia,' he went on, 'has been going through a terrible time since the assassination of the late Emperor, but they are beginning to hope that the worst has passed.'[28]

After Bea's final departure from Les Ruches at the age of twenty-two, Joseph deemed her ready to take charge of his arrangements at Highbury, including local political as well as social engagements. There was no thought of Bea going, like some of her fellow students at the School for Girls in Edgbaston, to one of the new colleges for women in Cambridge or Oxford. Like Austen and Neville, she was groomed to serve the needs and ambitions of her father and family. Her first political assignment in 1884 was to arrange for Joseph's participation in the local campaign to extend the parliamentary franchise to all adult male householders in the kingdom.

Bea's responsibilities were extended by Joe's purchase of a house for the family in London just below Hyde Park on Prince's Gardens. That residence placed a double strain on the family. The financial costs exceeded the salary Joseph received as a Cabinet minister. To make matters worse, Britain was in the throes of what would long be remembered as 'the Great Depression'. Joe began to feel the limitations of the fortune he had reaped upon his retirement from business ten years earlier. He looked forward to the day when Neville would replicate his career in industry and build up the family's wealth. At the moment, after discussing with Beatrice the supply of horses needed at Prince's Gardens as well as Highbury, he shook his head: 'the demands of the family ... are very large. ... We will go on as long as we can but if things continue as bad as they are now, you will all have to take cabs.' His need as a leading statesman to spend the first seven or eight months of the year in London also disrupted the lives of all his children except Austen, who was being groomed to sit alongside his father in the House of Commons. Joe's other children were wrenched away from their home, friends and favoured activities in Birmingham for long stretches of time not of their choosing. Ida complained bitterly about having to spend each summer in London: 'How we hated it, – all the more because it was very hot ... it was a joy to get back to Highbury at the end of the Summer & rush to visit our gardens & sniff the sweet peas which were always out then.'[29]

The mid-1880s were years of political crisis that twisted the trajectory of Joseph's career, with enduring consequences for his family. He expected that the widened franchise enacted in 1884 would place his radical wing of the Liberal party in charge of Britain's future. But the radical rhetoric that he deployed during the general election of 1885 alienated moderates and led to a hung Parliament in which Irish Nationalists held the balance of power. Gladstone returned to office

28  Joseph to Beatrice, 1 Oct.1882, Moscow, BC3/1/20
29  Recollections of their father's & my Childhood, BC5/11/1

determined to give Ireland a generous measure of self-government or Home Rule. Gladstone's proposals were too generous for Chamberlain, who wanted strong central government to bring about social reform; and he resigned from Gladstone's ministry. His resignation split the Liberal party, driving it from power for the next twenty years. Joe interpreted his resignation as a principled action taken regardless of the personal cost, for it dashed his hopes of becoming leader of the Liberal party. He had to build his political position anew, now as a crusader against Home Rule rather than a potential Prime Minister. His children were deeply impressed by this self-sacrifice. They placed him at the pinnacle of the political pantheon as a man who placed principle above the highest office.

Bea was in charge of her father's household during these critical years, and they turned her natural enthusiasm into a protective vehemence on all issues that touched the political fortunes of her father and brother. Even so, Joseph's absorption in his fight for political survival left her lonely, far from her beloved mentor and friends at Les Ruches. She found solace among her siblings and in the riches of literature that Marie Souvestre had opened up to her.

Austen moved away from home but never from her heart. After graduating from Cambridge in the summer of 1885, he embarked upon the next stage of his political apprenticeship. Austen's instinct was to stay in England and fight to support his father in the general election. Looking far ahead, however, Joseph sent him to France to gain fluency in the language of international diplomacy. Austen reported to Bea on his progress, and she asked Marie Souvestre to assist him. He was housed with a Parisian family where he had to converse in French. Once his French was good enough, he was to attend classes at the institutions of advanced education in the city. Almost before he was ready, he was caught up in the social life of Paris, thanks to introductions furnished by Marie Souvestre to her glittering circle of friends. 'I shall be in an awful fix,' he confessed to Bea, 'if her friends begin to make themselves agreeable as soon as I get to Paris, for I am absolutely incapable of conducting an intelligent conversation.'[30] But his French improved quickly; and he soon bemoaned 'that there are but 7 days in the week & you can't dine in two separate places on the same evening.'[31] After Christmas the pace grew still dizzier. Austen had at least three engagements every evening, with 'the not unnatural result that [he was] hardly ready' for his classes next morning.[32]

This social whirl never blinded him to the political turmoil back in Britain.

---

30  Austen to Beatrice, 23 Sept.1885, AC1/8/6/4

31  Austen to Beatrice, 1 Dec.1885, AC1/8/6/13

32  Austen to Beatrice, 23 Feb.1886, AC1/8/6/21

Austen did what he could to keep his father abreast of the parallel campaign of the radicals in France led by Clemenceau. Upon arrival in Paris, Austen asked his father for a letter of introduction to Clemenceau. Austen thus met the leaders of the Third Republic including the President, Jules Grévy. But he still yearned to stand by his father, especially when the terms of Gladstone's Irish Home Rule bill drove Joseph to resign. 'I keep thinking,' Austen told Beatrice, 'how cruel must be Father's position, & what a terribly anxious time he must be having. Sometimes it seems almost impossible to stay here; I fret over my separation from all that is going on & lose all patience.'[33]

Austen nonetheless fell in love with France, a love with long-lasting consequences. It turned him against Germany even before he went there, as his father intended that he should. Less than two months after arriving in France, he confessed that he did not 'at all want to go to Germany. I hate the Germans & I hate German.'[34] He delayed his departure for Berlin and 'suspended German lessons to be more free'.[35] When he finally dragged himself to Berlin, he found to his disgust that the place where he was to stay was a boarding house. And he went to bed as soon as he could, 'wishing Germany & the Germans at the bottom of the sea ... but things have turned out better since.' The house was splendidly located at the heart of the city, close to the Tiergarten and within ten minutes walk of Unter den Linden.[36] Austen's stay in Berlin was to form as important a part in his political education as did Paris. Berlin also increased his self-reliance.

The slower pace of his social life in Berlin developed his powers of observation and his understanding of the international situation. Standing beside a lake where Berliners came to skate, he saw Moltke, the veteran Prussian general, 'walking there alone, as I believe he not unfrequently [sic] does, saluted with every mark of respect by all who saw him. And glad they are to see him out too; for if he has time to take a walk, they say, all the preparations for war must be complete & they may go home with their minds at rest. At rest however they are not, for the rumours of a war with Russia in the near future are very disquieting.'[37]

Austen's connections in the German capital increased markedly once letters of introduction arrived from his father. Joseph Chamberlain was the central enigma in British politics at this time. In uneasy alliance with Lord Salisbury's Conservatives

---

33  Austen to Beatrice, 16 Apr.1886, AC1/8/6/27
34  Austen to Beatrice, 1 Dec.1885, *loc.cit.*
35  Austen to Beatrice, 2 May 1886, AC1/8/6/29
36  Austen to Beatrice, 4 Feb.1887, AC3/2/1
37  Austen to Neville, 1 Mar.1887, AC3/2/5

and conservatively-inclined Liberals led by Lord Hartington, he brought about the defeat of Gladstone's Home Rule bill in the House of Commons and of the Gladstonian Liberals in the ensuing general election. But Salisbury's Conservatives did not win enough seats to form a government on their own. They had to depend for a majority in the Commons on the followers of Hartington and Chamberlain, now known as Liberal Unionists. There were international ramifications to the change of government in Britain because of the tensions in Europe after the defeat of France in the Franco-Prussian War and Britain's occupation of Egypt a decade later, again to the discomfiture of France. The German government sought to cultivate good relations with Britain. Joseph Chamberlain could be pivotal towards this end, given his influence with Lord Salisbury. The arrival in Berlin of Austen, who looked so like his father, soon attracted attention.

The first significant German to pick up the trace was Bismarck's banker, Bleichroder, who invited Austen to dinner. Talking in French, Bleichroder 'pleaded for Britain to take a stronger line on Egypt, not annexation but declaring a protectorate ... with the support (moral, of course) of Germany'.[38] Austen knew that Bleichroder was treating him as a conduit to his father. Even so, this was a heady moment in his education, and more was in store. Less than three weeks later, Austen wrote to Beatrice in excitement at his dinner with the great man of Germany. 'At present I am almost too stuck up to write to anyone. And why? Because I dined the day before yesterday with the Chancellor. I got a note from Count Herbert saying "Prince Bismarck having heard a great deal about your Father & knowing that he is one of our foremost statesmen" had charged him to ask me to dinner. It was almost a family party – Bismarck, Count Herbert, B's daughter & her husband, his secretaries & his doctor ... I took his daughter in to dinner & sat between her & the great man, or one of the great man's dogs I should say, whom he kept one on each side of him & stuffed with everything. Bismarck was jolly, talked no politics either German or foreign, but told stories of his student days ...Count Herbert send kind messages to Father'.[39] This dinner marked a turning point for Austen. Engagements now succeeded 'each other as fast as I can want & faster. ... I have just been interrupted by a fifth invitation for tonight! ... All the Secretaries etc of the Embassy here are madly jealous of me for having dined with Bismarck. Such a thing has never been known: not one of them has ever exchanged so much as a "good day" with him, & even the ambassadors only dine with him once a year on the Emperor's birthday'.[40]

---

38  Austen to Beatrice, nd but before 2 Mar.1887, AC3/2/8
39  Austen to Beatrice, 20 Mar.1887, AC3/2/9
40  Austen to Beatrice, 17 May 1887, AC3/2/15

Bea was disappointed to learn that the conversation with Bismarck had been conducted in English, which he spoke 'wonderfully well'.[41] But as soon as Austen's German allowed him to follow debate, he spent a morning in what he called the Prussian House of Commons. The House was 'discussing a new government bill for repealing more of the May Laws against the Catholics ... the door from the ministers' private room into their box slowly opened & Bismarck appeared, dressed in his dark blue general's uniform with orange collar. All his colleagues got up to greet him, & there was what the reporters call a sensation in the galleries. ... Richter, leader of the ... Liberal party ... spoke for about three quarters of an hour, fiercely attacking Bismarck ... Meanwhile the Chancellor, having run through his notes ... was fidgeting uneasily. He is said to be very sensitive to attack, & though he says sharp things of others, cannot bear them himself. ... At last Richter finished & he got up. His speeches read well, but the words do not flow easily as delivered. He always uses the right word, but sometimes it takes him a long time to find it. And his sentences are broken by a short disagreeable cough ... But everybody listens with intense interest, for his speeches are full of matter, illustrated from history or contemporary facts in other countries, & some argument, lit up by jokes at the expense of his opponents, apt quotations – more often from Shakespeare than any other writer – or now & again an amusing story. Finally, as the last touch to the speech, there comes – if the situation is critical & a majority for the Gov. uncertain, as is the case in these Church laws – a threat of resignation ... the majority is secured & the end attained in spite of the jeers of the opposition who remember to have heard all this before ... To make the picture complete I need only add Bismarck sustains himself during his oratorical exertions by drinking copiously strong brandy & water, a tumbler to every quarter of an hour I counted!'[42]

Austen thus had a ringside seat at the central arena of European politics which he observed with rapidly growing understanding. Germany held the balance among the rival powers; and for the moment Germany meant Bismarck. Austen was both fascinated and repelled by what he witnessed. His only impediment was his still shaky command of German. His report on the debate in the Reichstag owed much to briefing from staff at the British embassy. So he resolved to spend the summer in Switzerland to improve his German. He explained to Beatrice from Berlin that, 'There are too many English here.'[43] When he returned to Berlin in the autumn, he could hold his own in German conversation; and he established

41  Austen to Beatrice, 2 Apr.1887, AC3/2/11
42  Austen to Neville, 22 Apr.1887, AC3/2/13
43  Austen to Beatrice, 23 May 1887, AC3/2/16

relaxed relationships with the politically powerful. 'I dined last night at Herbert Bismarck's,' he reported; 'H.B. was in great spirits, talking about father with great admiration & said I must bring him over here.'

Able now to take notes in German, he looked for 'some lectures at the University which I hope will be interesting'[44]. He chose Heinrich von Treitschke's lectures on the history of Prussia. The lectures shocked him. Treitschke 'opened to me a new side of the German character – a narrow-minded, proud, intolerant Prussian chauvinism. And the worst of it is that he is forming a school. If you continuously preach to the youth of a country that they stand on a higher step of the creation to all other nations, they are only too ready to believe it ... I fear my generation of Germans & those a little younger will be far more high handed, will presume far more on the victories [in the Austro- and Franco-Prussian wars] than those who won them.' He noted also that, 'They are likely to find a friend in Prince William, who is said to be thirsting for warlike distinction & is the idol of the military party & the youth.'[45]

So strongly impressed was Austen by the significance of what he heard that, for the first time in his life, he resisted a proposal from his father. Joseph won the respect of Lord Salisbury by fighting off Gladstonian efforts to drive him into the political wilderness. As an honourable though temporary escape from these difficulties, Salisbury offered him the leadership of a diplomatic mission to Washington to seek a solution to a dispute between the United States and Canada on fishing rights in the Gulf of the St Lawrence. Joseph enquired through Beatrice whether Austen would like to accompany him on this mission to the new world. But Austen's attention was riveted on the old. He was 'working hard' on his German, he explained to Bea, '& don't see that I can "put on a spurt" – especially as after all what is particularly useful for me is knowledge of men & of the ways of thinking of the Germans so that I may be able to judge news from Germany & understand German views of England. This takes time; but now that I can talk freely, I am learning much more. As far as I am concerned' – and the emphasis on I was his – 'in spite of the great temptations of a trip to America with Father, I think I should gain more by staying here.'[46] Sticking to his guns, he wrote directly to his father: 'the last part of my stay is likely to be much more useful than the first, owing to the greater ease I have in conversation.'[47]

44  Austen to Beatrice, 7 Oct.1887, AC3/2/23
45  Austen to Beatrice, 31 Oct.1887, AC3/2/26
46  Austen to Beatrice, 31 Oct.1887, AC3/2/26
47  Austen to Joseph, 16 Nov.1887, AC3/2/28

The gravity of what Austen discovered from von Treitschke's lectures deepened into alarm with news that the Crown Prince, heir to the German throne and a man of liberal sympathies, was dying. A leader of the Liberal party, Dr Bamberger, spelled out the significance of the tragedy to Austen, which he duly transmitted to Beatrice. The Crown Prince 'was their last hope ... now they must look forward to Prince William's accession, a high tory prussian officer, caring for nothing but soldiering & anxious above all to win his spurs. Again as Dr. B. said "We must pray that Bismarck may be spared." Fancy this from a member of the party on whom the Chancellor has so trampelled [sic]. What irony of fate! But he feels that Bismarck can keep Prince W. in order, & perhaps no-one else could.'[48] When his father left for Washington to be away over Christmas and the New Year, Austen resolved to spend the holidays in the German capital. In his final letter to Bea before returning home, he relayed a lot of the political gossip in Berlin. He had received an extraordinary education in international politics, and never forgot his introduction to the hardening militarisation of German nationalism.

Neville's experience of school and apprenticeship was very different from Austen's. Ida, Hilda and Ethel followed Bea's footsteps to Allenswood, the successor school to Les Ruches. Neville also followed Austen to Rugby: but there the similarity stopped. Away from the chilly parenting he experienced at home, Austen at Rugby felt at last that he 'was good for something'. But Neville was disconcerted by Rugby: he found the teachers unsympathetic, and he was bullied by the other boys. He took to solitary pleasures, hunting bugs and butterflies. Joseph destined his younger son for a career in business to free the rest of the family for public service and politics. So when Neville advanced toward the upper years at Rugby, Joseph transferred him to the newly-formed 'Modern Side'. There, as Ida recalled, Neville 'found himself alone of his age amongst much younger boys.' Disheartened, he received a succession of bad reports which 'gave Papa a good deal of anxiety ... it seemed that it was the will to work that was lacking.' Disappointed in Neville and also less interested these days in business than in politics, Joseph did not give Neville's further training the same thought that he gave to Austen's.

After Rugby, Joseph sent Neville to Mason College in Birmingham. Though Mason College had none of the prestige of Austen's Cambridge, Neville found much to interest him in the classes on science and engineering that the college provided. But here again his formal education only extended his loneliness. He did not find congenial company at Mason College. He lived at home in Highbury. But by now, for much of the year, the rest of the family were away, his younger

---

48  Austen to Beatrice, 18 Nov.1887, AC3/2/29

sisters at school in Wimbledon, his father at Westminster. Nevertheless it was at Mason College that, as Ida later recalled, Neville's mind 'began to develop rapidly ... thinking for himself & reaching out in all sorts of directions, beginning to take an interest in art & literature & above all in science. ... he started reading Darwin, & became an ardent & enthusiastic Darwinist.' Neville became something of an autodidact, immersing himself in music more than anyone in the family but Hilda, and in Shakespeare more than most of his eventual peers in Parliament.

Joseph continued to underestimate his younger son, and also failed to take note when Neville developed a steely temperament more like that of his father than was Austen's. Neville's interest in evolutionary science and natural selection did not appeal to Joseph. 'Science & heredity were entirely new subjects in our family', Ida explained; '... politics had always had pride of place & [Neville] got little sympathy from Papa, who always took the line that it was [a] waste of time discussing questions as to which we did not & could not know the answers' – as if answers to political questions were clear. But Neville's burgeoning interests strengthened his relations to his sisters. His love of music drew Hilda to him. His fascination with the world of nature 'infected [Ida] with his own enthusiasm & therewith started a new interest in which later on Hilda & Ethel shared'. Ida also found in Neville 'a remarkable memory & an astounding power of describing the contents of any book he had read ... He retained this power all his life,' she remembered admiringly after he died, '& it was one of the things that made his conversation so interesting.'

Neville served his apprenticeship in far lowlier places than Austen. After two years at Mason College, Joseph apprenticed him to a leading accountant in Birmingham. Neville did so well that the accountant placed him on salary without waiting for the usual term of an articled clerk to expire. Neville 'rather enjoyed the responsibility when he was sent about the country to audit accounts for various business firms.' He came back with 'most amusing accounts of the ways & customs of the commercial travellers whose haunts he invaded.' But these stories were for his family alone. By nature 'intensely reserved', Neville 'had, especially when young, a disconcerting habit of maintaining complete silence when some remark or observation was made to him about which it took time for him to make up his mind. This put off people who did not know him ... &,' Ida added, 'I think it remained rather a handicap to him all his life.' While Austen's natural geniality had flourished among the glitterati of Paris, Neville's natural reserve stiffened among the commercial travellers of English county towns.

The liveliness of the family was increased and the relationship between Joseph and his children was much warmed by his remarriage in 1888, nearly fourteen years after the death of Florence. He had felt drawn to attractive women for some time but kept these feelings, like those for his children, sternly subordinate to his political ambitions. Amid the less inhibited surroundings of the New World, however, he found an American beauty, Mary Endicott, who brought happiness to him and his entire family. Mary also transformed the internal dynamics of the family and brought Austen to the fore.

Austen's entry on to the political stage was fast approaching when his father left for Washington. Before departure, Joseph and Austen discussed the next step, a parliamentary constituency for which Joe hoped Austen would be selected as the Unionist candidate. Known as the Border Burghs, the constituency lay in the Scottish lowlands. Joe had been cultivating support for Liberal Unionism there since the last general election. Soon after Austen returned from Berlin he took the train north to meet the local party organisation. He carried an encouraging letter from his father; his sisters got up early to wave him goodbye; and Neville accompanied him to the station. Austen won quick endorsement at the Border Burghs. 'I do believe these people w'd have been pleased with anything from father's son,' he reported modestly to Bea. Austen's apprenticeship in Paris and Berlin made no impression on the lowland Scots. The chairman of the local Liberal association 'didn't see what good my German & French w'd do the Burghs & ... as far as dining with Bismarck went, that was rather a disqualification than otherwise!'[49]

The pleasure of the family at Austen's first step on the political ladder was, as always, overshadowed by what his father achieved. Joe returned from Washington with two prizes. His diplomatic mission was crowned with success of a sort. He hammered out a treaty that satisfied the three parties to the negotiations. Britain, Canada and the Democratic administration of President Grover Cleveland. The treaty was doomed to rejection by the Republican majority in the Senate. But Joseph and the US Secretary of State also devised a *modus vivendi* that gave effect to the terms of the treaty without ratification by the Senate. Lord Salisbury showered Joe with praise on his return. 'Would you like me to become Sir Joseph & be a Grand Cross of the Bath?' he asked Ida. 'I hope not as you are never likely to have this satisfaction. Plain Mr. Chamberlain sounds well enough for me.'[50]

Gratified as the family were by Joe's diplomatic achievement, they were preoccupied with his other prize, an American fiancée. His engagement might well have

49 Austen to Beatrice, 8 Apr.1888, Woodburn, Selkirk, AC3/2/39
50 Joseph to Ida, [March 1888], Highbury, BC4/1/4

been problematic for his children; stepmothers conventionally drive families apart rather than draw them together. Joseph was so radiantly happy upon his return to Highbury, however, that his children welcomed what dispelled the sadness which had hung over them since the death of Florence. All they knew about their prospective stepmother to begin with was what he told them. News of the engagement was strictly confined on both sides of the Atlantic to the immediate families and intimate friends. Mary's father insisted that the engagement be kept secret until after the presidential and congressional elections in the United States, not due for another eight months.

William Endicott was, as Joe reported to Beatrice, the Secretary of War in Grover Cleveland's administration. 'He is of the bluest New England blood, descendant of the first Governor of Massachusetts and still residing at the house occupied by his ancestor who must have been a pretty grim old Puritan since he is said to have hanged 20 Quakers in one day for Nonconformity.' There was some of that grimness in Secretary Endicott too. But Joe's attention was diverted from the Secretary to his daughter, 'one of the brightest and most intelligent girls I have yet met.'[51] Mary was not the first girl in Washington to catch his eye. 'I am compelled to admit that as far as I have seen the average of American female beauty is higher than ours,' he told Bea tactlessly. 'You see a very large number of nice looking girls in the streets and the proportion of good figures and of well dressed women is very large.'[52] He threw himself into the social life that swirled around his diplomatic mission with an abandon that astonished the staff at the British Legation. One of them called him 'an accomplished flirt'.[53] The reputation Joe acquired was such that, when he arrived in Toronto during the Canadian leg of his journey, he 'found a large dinner party "of the prettiest women in Toronto" waiting for me. This I am informed in the Papers was because I am well known as a connoisseur in female beauty.'[54] At a Leap Year's party back in Washington, he was heralded by one of the ladies as the 'belle' of the ball.

The flurry of dances and dinner parties obscured his intense courtship of Mary. No one in Washington sensed what was afoot. Her family had no difficulty suppressing the news of her engagement on the eve of Joe's departure from the city, barely three months after his arrival. The Chamberlain family might have been

51 Joseph to Beatrice, 9 Dec.1887, The Arlington Hotel, Washington, DC., copy, JC1/2/6
52 Joseph to Beatrice, 2 Dec.1887, The Arlington, copy, JC1/2/5
53 Cecil Spring Rice quoted in Stephen Gynn, *The Letters and Friendships of Sir Cecil Spring Rice* (London: Constable, 1930), I, 79
54 Joseph to Beatrice, 3 Jan.1888, Washington, copy, JC1/2/9

disconcerted by Mary's age. At twenty-three, she was two years younger than Beatrice and a year younger than Austen. Concern at first focused on how Bea would react. She was her father's chatelaine and closest confidante among his children. He reported to her on his diplomatic mission. He relied on her to keep him in touch with the splinter party he led in Birmingham. He valued the news she conveyed to him. But it was information that they conveyed to each other, not advice. Joe gave Bea permission to show his Washington letters to his closest political associate, Jesse Collings, once the family had read them; 'but please get it back & keep all for future reference.'[55] He meant his letters to serve as an aide memoire on his return.

Bea was not reluctant to relinquish the role of personal private secretary. Like her beloved Auntie, she was a woman of strong opinions but did not challenge the basic policies set down by her father, something her friend Beatrice Webb (née Potter) discovered that he would not tolerate. Mary was like Beatrice Chamberlain in this regard, but without strong political convictions of her own. In Washington Mary mirrored the convictions of her father, a very conservative Democrat; and she imbibed Joseph's quite different convictions as he wooed her. Joseph found in Mary, as he later told her, 'an immense & hitherto untried capacity of love & devotion. The deeps have hardly been stirred at present, but there lie hidden in them courage, resolution, intensity of purpose & a great power of self-sacrifice.'[56] He found self-sacrifice alluring.

That sort of self-sacrifice was not in Bea's nature. Instead she retreated from her duties as chatelaine to her books whenever she could. Hilda later recalled that, 'The nicest thing [about her room at Highbury] was the bookshelf running all along the side opposite the fireplace, with all her beautifully bound books, with the bookplate ... of which she chose the motto herself – "The Desire of Wisdom bringeth to a Kingdom".'[57] Bea sought wisdom rather than a kingdom. Joe's demands upon her also impinged on her friendships. As chatelaine she had to focus on the men in public life with whom her father wished to consort. She fared well in that company. But the range of people to whom she felt drawn was wider and more varied. She attracted friends 'of all ages and classes, of very different powers of mind and of disposition', and of women more than of men. She formed her closest friendships through her educational work in the poorer parts of London. The arrival of Mary freed Beatrice to spend more time there.

The two women reached out to each other with endearing grace. Mary

55  Joseph to Beatrice, 12 Nov.1887, #2, Brevoort House, NY, AC1/4/5/37
56  Joseph to Mary, 8 June 1888, JC28/A1/28
57  Hilda's memoir of 'Beatrice Mary Chamberlain, 1862–1918', copy, BC5/10/2

responded sensitively to Bea's letter of welcome: 'One could not but have a lurking fear that one might be regarded as an interloper, & you have dispelled it entirely.'[58] The understanding between them deepened quickly. Mary approached the rest of the family through Bea, asking her to offer Austen her congratulations on his first appearance in the Border Burghs, and to thank Neville for his letter of welcome. 'Thank you,' she went on, 'for what you tell me of Ida. It was very lovely of her to receive the news so kindly. Indeed I don't know that I have made you feel how truly & sincerely I am touched by the absolute readiness with which you all accepted the change which is to come into your lives ... my first feeling was that it would only be natural that it would be a blow to you ... Your father's confidence that I took an exaggerated view, reassured me ... but the realization of his hopes was far beyond my fairest dreams.'[59] Even so, happily though Beatrice stepped aside, she forfeited the primacy she had hitherto possessed among Joe's children.

Almost imperceptibly, Austen replaced his older sister as the pivotal child in the family, a primacy he retained for more than twenty years. He owed that position partly to his commission to follow his father into politics, but also to Mary. Austen found in Mary a soul mate. He was more closely akin to her than to anyone in his family, in particular his father, a fact that Joseph never glimpsed till near the end of his life. Austen had a propensity to self-sacrifice that was quite alien to his father. Joseph did not understand Austen any better than he did Neville. Both Austen and Mary were conservative by nature, with tastes associated in Britain with the landed classes. Mary came by her conservatism more naturally than Austen. After all, she belonged to one of the most patrician families in New England. Her brother did not at first take kindly to her engagement to an industrialist, feeling that she was marrying beneath her. But there was nothing of the industrialist in Austen. What he loved most about Highbury was the farm that formed part of the estate. Of all Joe's children, Austen felt the least attachment to industrial Birmingham; and he ceased to make his home there as soon as he married. Mary also abandoned Highbury as soon as Joseph died.

The only serious difference in values between Austen and Mary regarded religion, for which Austen, like his father, had little time, while Mary was a devoted Episcopalian. The friendship between Austen and Mary took some time to develop. But they understood each other instinctively; jointly they replaced Beatrice as the channel through which Joseph transmitted his wishes to the rest of the family. Neville and Ida also shouldered some of Bea's responsibility for keeping the

58  Mary to Austen, 26 Mar.1888, 1313 Sixteenth Street, Washington, AC1/8/7/1a
59  Mary to Beatrice, 26 Apr.1888, 1313 Sixteenth St., Washington, AC4/9/5

members of the family in touch with each other. But Austen's presence began to be felt among them as never before. Ida felt that she scarcely knew Austen until Mary arrived. His position was further strengthened by his ability to keep his father in touch with the lower echelons of the Liberal Unionist party.

The special relationship between Austen and Mary was obscured by Mary's speedy conquest of the entire family. During the summer of 1888, between engagement and marriage, Mary learned all she could from Bea about the younger ones yet she never lost sight of Bea. Joseph and Mary expected to reach England by the beginning of December. That, said Mary, would give Beatrice and her 'several weeks before Christmas ... These we must make the most of, & before Ida comes home [from school] you & I must be as if we had known each other all our lives.'[60] She encouraged Bea to tell the youngest two, Hilda and Ethel, news of the impending marriage sooner rather than later, and was delighted at their response. 'Indeed dear Beatrice I must repeat to you, what a difference it has made to me in having you all so ready to welcome me. ... Will you thank the children for their letters? & please tell them with my love that I too am looking to the time when I shall see them.'[61]

For the rest of his life, Austen remembered that, shortly after telling him of his engagement, Joseph spoke of his mother: 'as the conversation drew to its close, I said to him, "Do you know, Sir, that this is the first time that you have ever spoken to me about my mother?" "Yes," he said, "I know. Until happiness came again into my life, I did not dare to – and even now I can't do it without the tears coming into my eyes."'[62] Once Mary reached Highbury, the rest of the family recognised what Austen had been the first to see: her ability to overcome the remoteness of their father. His 'nature softened', Neville said of his father, and he became 'the most delightful and helpful of companions'.[63]

Mary brought Joe home and made him a lively presence among his children. The dining table at Highbury became the centre of family life during his weekends in Birmingham, and the halls rang loudly with their conversation. The younger children joined in enthusiastically during the school holidays. One by one, the girls settled back at Highbury once they left Allenswood. Mary added sparkle to their social life by introducing the American fashion for dancing cotillions, to the delight of the Groves and the Moor Greens as well as the Highburies. The only problem was the surfeit of girls.

60  Mary to Beatrice, 27 July 1888, White Sulphur Springs, West Virginia, AC4/9/9
61  Mary to Beatrice, 2 Sept.1888, Nahant, AC4/9/10
62  Austen Chamberlain, *Politics from Inside* (London: Cassell, 1936), 17
63  Neville to his children, 6 July 1914 after the death of Joseph, NC1/6/11

The family also began to take holidays together. Hitherto Joe had taken his vacations with a close colleague or two while the children went on holiday under the care of their aunts or Beatrice. The newly married couple in their first year together sometimes went away alone. But in this first year they also established what became their more common pattern for holidays, when a party of ten was put together, including four of the Groves and Joseph's long-time travelling companion Jesse Collings. Hilda and Ethel remained at school in Wimbledon while Austen nursed his prospective parliamentary constituency. These three spent their Christmas together at Highbury, envying the larger contingent who travelled through Italy to Egypt. The destination alone made the trip momentous. Britain had seized control of Egypt from the French who had built the Suez Canal, the artery that linked Britain to the heart of its empire in India. Joseph, who was emerging as the voice of a more assertive imperialism, wanted to examine this lifeline for himself. For Neville and Ida this trip had a further significance. It marked their entry into a world beyond the familiar confines of home and homeland.

Italy was different. Writing to Hilda and Ethel from Milan, Ida expressed amazement at what she and Neville saw: 'At one of the stations Neville was much amused at seeing a fat little man leaning out of a window. Another man suddenly rushed up the steps, seized him by the hand & kissed him on the face affectionately. It is the custom of this country, but it looked queer.'[64] Later in Venice they attended a service at St Mark's. Ida was captivated but Neville scornful: 'The priests came in from behind dressed in white with great red copes, & there were five others, one of whom I believe was the Patriarch ... who stood before the altar & were dressed in gold vestments. Neville irreverently called them Mikados, & they did look rather like. ...but ... it was certainly very impressive.' Responding to Ethel's more earthy interests, Ida confirmed 'that the Canals <u>are</u> full of orange peel, & old papers, & cabbage stalks, & that the smells are poisonous but one overlooks these minor details in such a lovely place as Venice.'[65] Wherever they went, the Chamberlains, the young following the old, trawled their way through the art galleries, becoming discriminating observers. Austen could be carried away by the art he saw; but not Neville. Looking at one depiction of St George and the dragon, he scoffed at the commentator's description of the 'glorious head with his hair breaking on his shoulders in tendrils of living life.'[66]

Neville nonetheless had a keen sense of the impression which the sights and

64  Ida to Hilda and Ethel, 16 Nov.1889, BC4/4/2
65  Ida to Ethel & Hilda, 18 Nov.1889, BC4/4/3
66  Neville to Aunt Lina, 21 Nov.1889, Venice, NC1/11/1

travel reports would make on his correspondents back home. Once they reached Egypt, he wrote to Ethel that, while Italy might have its oddities, 'in Egypt you feel that you are really in a foreign country. The people, the houses, the trees & the flowers are all strange.' What always captured his imagination was the natural world, the flowers, birds and butterflies, which he observed with knowledgeable affection: 'even here one finds some familiar things. A large grey backed crow caws just like our rooks, the sparrow with very little change chirps under the eaves.'[67] His examination of insects was a touch macabre. Ida reported that 'Neville ... slaughters all the skeeters he meets, & makes little hecatombs of them, which he counts at the end of the evening.'[68]

The Chamberlains were no ordinary visitors to Egypt; and they did not have an ordinary reception. Joseph's influence with the Salisbury ministry made him of crucial importance to the Egyptian government, controlled as it was by British officials. Ida reported with evident delight that, 'Mr Baring, the agent general offered Papa his carriage, so Mary, Beatrice, Aunt Mary & Mr Collings had that. It was a most gorgeous turn out with a Nubian coachman, & two runners dressed ... with embroidered coats to be before, & a magnificent gentleman on the box, to act as Dragoman.' That put the remainder of the party in secondary position: 'we were obliged to content ourselves with the Hotel vehicles, & no runners, & looked quite poor & mean in comparison.'[69]

Sometimes Ida preferred her less exalted position. As they proceeded up the Nile she reported that, 'This evening Papa & Mary, Uncle William & Aunt Mary, Mr. Collings & Neville ... are going to an Oriental dinner at the British consuls. They have been hearing the most gruesome accounts of what they will have to do ... How not only they will have to eat out of their own fingers, but how their host will present them with choice morsels with him; how they drink unfiltered Nile water, all out of the same tumbler, & how you must eat of every dish that is offered you etc. etc. The Consul has just sent in an invitation for the rest of us, but Papa refused for us to our great relief.' Next day she was able to report that, 'they have returned, & they are still alive! ... Suffice it to say that when they came home they were obliged, most of them to resort to brandy, before they could at all recover themselves.'[70] Travelling together brought out differences in character within the group. Ida singled out the women including Joseph's sister Aunt Mary as 'the young

---

67 Neville to Ethel, 11 Dec.1889, along the Nile, NC1/14/1
68 Ida to Hilda and Ethel, 29 Nov.1889, Cairo, BC4/4/5
69 *Ibid.*
70 Ida to Hilda and Ethel, 14, 15 and 16 Dec.1889, Denderah, BC4/4/8

& enthusiastic members of the party,[71] including herself of course. The men in the family displayed distaste for religious things which the women did not share. 'Papa persistently declares that he doesn't care a rap for all the Temples of Egypt,'[72] attracted more by the irrigation works that brought prosperity to the Nile valley.

The party broke up as they headed back to England. The Groves were the first to leave. Joseph stopped off in Paris. But his children made straight for home, eager to catch up with the rest of the family. The trip consolidated Mary's achievement in bringing the family together. Neville was still a little stiff with her on their return, but by the end of the summer he too relaxed. The next trip was to draw the family still closer together, though in an eventually harsh way.

---

71 *Ibid.*
72 Ida to Aunt Louie, Xmas Day, Abou Simbel in Nubia, BC4/4/5

*Neville and Ida inseparable before his exile*

# 2

# Exile

In the autumn of 1890 Joseph plunged into an imperial investment that shook the family's financial foundations. The opportunity seemed promising for a politician interested in developing the economic resources of the British Empire. But the venture lay far outside the experience of the Chamberlain clan in metal manufacturing. The industrialists of Birmingham thought of the Empire as a market, but they knew little about production there, and nothing of agriculture. Joseph's brothers, who were still in business, counselled caution; but it was the Empire, not business investment, that quickened Joe's imagination in those days. When this imperial venture ran into difficulties, he deepened his investment in it.

He left the task of making it pay to Neville, who was both seared and steeled by its ultimate failure. Neville insisted that he alone was to blame for the failure, and Joseph did not attempt to share the responsibility. The financial consequences were eased, if not removed, by Joseph's return to salaried high office. But Neville's mettle was hardened by the ordeal which he underwent for six long years in his mid-twenties. He was forced to work on his own far from home and family, but he turned that necessity into a prized virtue, refusing help from any partner. At the same time, the isolation deepened his dependence on his correspondence, especially with his sisters.

When the family came back from the trip to Egypt, Neville resumed work with the accountant to whom he had been assigned by his father; and he remained in Birmingham when the older half of the family, Joseph, Mary, Bea and Austen, left for their next voyage. This time they headed for the New World, to Mary's home in Massachusetts. Her family there, as Austen commented, hung 'together very closely'[1] and, like the Chamberlains, formed part of a federation of families. Rich as well as blue-blooded, the Endicott clan extended through the Peabodys into the banking world of J.P. Morgan and spread from the New England states into upstate New York. Overcoming the reserve of Mary's father and the hauteur of her brother, the Endicotts 'put a world of warmth into their welcome' of the Chamberlains.

They moved from one branch of Mary's family to another, travelling from Massachusetts through the Adirondack Mountains toward the Eastern Provinces of Quebec. Joe seized the opportunity to visit Montreal, a pivotal city in the commerce of the British Empire. There he met Sir Ambrose Shea, British governor of the Bahamas who, like Joe, was an advocate of cultivating the undeveloped estates of the Empire. Shea dangled in front of Joseph's already rose-coloured eyeglass the prospect of lucrative investment in sisal in the Bahamas to make hemp. Joe was worried about the erosion of the capital he had acquired upon the sale of his share in the monopoly that the Chamberlains and their Nettlefold cousins had built up for the mass manufacture of screws. He had received £600,000 for the Chamberlains' half of the business, which seemed enough to maintain his family in affluence for the rest of his life. But marriage to Mary made his expensive lifestyle more costly: she had expensive tastes, tastes that Austen learned to share. The profit Joseph acquired in industry was the result of a strategic investment his father had made in metal manufacturing in the Midlands. Joe hoped to improve upon that achievement by investing in a still more promising field across the Atlantic.

Accordingly he cabled Neville 'to come out by the next steamer'. Neville later recalled that, 'I was at the time a very shy youth and had never done anything except by the instructions and under the guidance of my elders.'[2] After barely two years in accountancy, still little more than an articled clerk, he was summoned to develop a business upon which the ability of the rest of the family to devote itself to public service might depend. He knew from the start that the ultimate purpose of the enterprise was political funding, that building up the business was not at end in itself. Politics was at the back of his mind as it was to the fore for the family. He was twenty-one, younger than Austen at the beginning of his apprenticeship in politics. Wide-eyed with excitement as he set sail, Neville met Austen in New York. Together they boarded a train, picked Beatrice up at New Haven, and headed to the Endicott family home in Massachusetts, where his father and Mary were

---

1  Austen to Ethel, 24 Sept.1890, West Point, AC1/8/6/33
2  Neville to his children, 6 July 1914, NC1/6/11

waiting. Almost immediately, still accompanied by Austen, Neville found himself again at sea, this time crossing to Nassau. 'The sea is of the same wonderful blue that we admired so much in the Mediterranean,' he wrote to Hilda, 'and at night the water round our sides sparkles & flashes with phosphorescence as it did there.' Austen found the passing scene even more dazzling than 'the unpoetical Neville': 'last night,' Austen told Mary, 'the sky was a colour I have never seen it before, pale mauve & lilac shading away into more brilliant tints at the horizon.'[3]

A week later the two brothers found themselves on a piazza in Nassau outside Government House where they were guests of the Governor. They stood on the commercial edge of the British Empire where economic and political interests intertwined. It was virtually impossible for the two young men in their exotic sur-roundings to arrive at a sober assessment of the investment which the governor wished their father to make. The Governor talked of the vast fortune to be made, but he could not substantiate his calculations. Austen and Neville recognised the marketing hyperbole, but the numbers they came up with were equally impres-sionistic. There were in fact no hard figures to be found. Joseph had placed Austen as the elder brother in charge of the mission; Austen reported in close consultation with Neville. But Austen was an innocent in business, and neither brother had any of the local knowledge that Joseph had been able to call upon at the outset of his career in Birmingham industry.

The beautiful surroundings mesmerised Neville with his love of nature. 'I have eaten oranges off the trees,' he told Ida, 'I have watched the humming birds sucking the honey from strange and brilliantly coloured flowers, I have bathed before sunrise & not felt cold, I have seen the sea bottom through 20 ft. of clear blue water & the octopus swimming about in his native pools, &, had not the night we had chosen been unpropitious, I should have fished for sharks by moonlight.'[4] When Austen read the part about oranges, he informed Ida tartly that he had 'eaten them too! I prefer mine in future plucked for me & ripened by a sea voyage. When I reproached him with conveying false impressions, he replied that he had nowhere said they were ripe oranges which he plucked.'[5] But the young men were dyspeptic about the society that greeted them in Nassau. Few of its members had been outside the Bahamas, and those few were pretentious. The governor's wife dropped French phrases into her conversation that she did not understand. Austen also missed the political excitements back in Britain, where Joseph's enemies, the

3  Austen to Mary, 9 Nov.1890, S.S. Cienfuegos, copy, NC1/19/2
4  Neville to Ida, 23 Nov.1890, Nassau, copy, NC1/19/4
5  Austen to Ida, 26 Nov.1890, Nassau, copy, NC1/19/5

Irish Home Rulers, were tearing themselves apart over the adultery of their leader, Charles Stewart Parnell: '... your political news,' Austen wrote his father, 'reads like the most exciting of romances.'[6] A sharp deterioration in Joseph's existing investments intensified his need for a lucrative investment in the Bahamas.

Under distant direction from their father, the brothers tried to size up the prospect Sir Ambrose Shea dangled before them. Joseph told them to turn their attention first 'to the questions of capital expenditure & cost per ton of the finished product landed in London.'[7] They interviewed the few people in the Bahamas with experience or interests pertinent to the production of hemp; but they learned little, for there was virtually no local expertise to call upon. One merchant told them 'that he had made no exact calculations, that he could not say what capital would be required, that he did not know how much the fibre would cost to produce, but that the margin seemed so large that he thought it was a good thing.' Recognising the uselessness of such a response, Austen and Neville undertook 'to investigate the cultivation of the hemp plant for ourselves ... cost of the buildings, labour, machinery, etc.' They estimated that a capital investment of £6,620 would be required in the first year, £1,500 in the second, £3,700 in the third; and in the fourth, when the plants would reach fruition, they predicted a profit. But through basic operational ignorance they missed many items that turned out to be required, and underestimated the cost of items which they had included. They also minimised the difficulties of production: 'the cultivation of the hemp plant appears extremely simple,' Austen told his father: 'It is not known to suffer from any disease, it requires no protection by fences or otherwise. Neither drought nor excessive rains seriously injure it, though the former somewhat delays its growth.' They did, however, appreciate that the railway needed to transport the sisal to fibre-extracting machinery would prove expensive.

Only one consideration led Austen to question whether the game was worth the candle: the demands the enterprise might make on Neville. The conditions of life on the remote Bahamian islands worried Austen. Away from Nassau, the islands were sparsely populated with illiterate blacks and a few uneducated whites. 'If you decide to go in to the hemp business,' Austen told his father, 'it would I think be very desirable for Neville to be here for six months or a year to set the thing going & give your manager our ideas. But I should be very sorry to think of his staying here for five years, as life is very rough in the out islands & quite unfit for the girls, & there is no society of any kind.' Otherwise, the more the brothers looked into the investment, the better it seemed. 'Although we have been three

---

6 Austen to Joseph, 22 Dec.1890, #5, Nassau, NC1/6/10/7
7 Austen to Joseph, 23 Nov.1890, #2, Government House, Nassau, NC1/6/10/2

weeks at work,' Austen reported, 'Neville & I have failed to find the weak point of this business.'[8] The initial costs of cultivating sisal could, so it seemed, be offset by planting earlier maturing cotton alongside the sisal. Calling upon his interest in botany, Neville reported that the sisal plants they intended to use were prolific, had a life span of fifteen to twenty years, and produced superior fibre. He also identified a potential resident manager, Michael Knowles, a man with 'much experience in the cultivation of the hemp plant,' some knowledge of machinery, familiar with the local population, and 'thoroughly honest'.[9]

Joseph was not immediately carried away by these reports. 'When I talked it over with you,' he reminded Austen, 'I spoke of it as a Gold Mine with possibilities of enormous profits: now it seems to be an ordinary Commercial enterprise with perhaps more than ordinary probabilities of a <u>fair</u> return.' Moreover, the 'Capital is likely to be much larger than I expected.' Joseph also learned from botanists at Kew Gardens and merchants familiar with the hemp trade that the 'value of the article in London is much less than we were led to expect.'[10] This report shocked Shea and enabled the young Chamberlains to stiffen their demands upon him. But they remained dazzled by the dividends they foresaw: 'Even allowing a considerable margin for unforeseen contingencies ... we should still have a net profit of over 50% on the capital employed. These results are so fabulously good that they appear almost impossible, but we have worked them out ourselves, as far as possible verifying all the statements by actual observation &, where that was not possible, testing to the best of our ability the sufficiency & trustworthiness of the accounts given us.' Taking the personal price for Neville into consideration but underestimating it along with all the other costs, the brothers sent their father a cordial recommendation: 'do we, & especially Neville, think the sacrifices entailed worth making? If you think it necessary that Neville should live out here for any length of time – no, we do not. ... But it seems to me', wrote Austen, 'that if Neville were here for the first year & again for a year when the putting up of machinery & the process of manufacture began, that would be sufficient. All that would be required in after years would be that one of us should make an annual visit or perhaps in time a biennial one. If you think this would be sufficient, why then our answer would be: yes, we will gladly undertake this.'[11]

These glittering prospects overcame Joe's doubts and deterred him from giving

8  Austen to Joseph, 28 Nov.1890, #3, Nassau, NC1/6/10/4
9  Neville to Joseph, 29 Nov.1890, with #3, NC1/16/10/5
10  Joseph to Austen, 4 Dec.1890, #1, 40 Prince's Gardens, AC1/4/3/2
11  Austen to Joseph, 22 Dec.1890, Nassau, NC1/6/10/8

further thought to the personal cost for Neville. Instead Joseph redoubled the pace of the enterprise, fearful that if he did not do so, other investors would come in, increasing the supply of sisal and reducing the price it could command. He now wanted 'to get as large an area under cultivation as possible in the shortest possible time and thus get the benefit of the good prices after which it would be easy to sell out & retire with a handsome fortune.'[12] He calculated that at this pace the business ought to yield 'a profit of £10,000 a year & allow us to indulge afterwards in reasonable extravagance.'[13] Once this decision was made, Austen and Neville headed home, Austen impatient to throw himself back into the political fray, Neville to prepare for his return to the Bahamas.

8a

Neville's subsequent departure from Highbury to take up his assignment opened a new chapter in the life of the family. The change was felt least by Joseph and Austen, who remained immersed in politics. Joe's centrality in British politics was accentuated by his election to lead the Liberal Unionists in the House of Commons and by the setback to the cause of Home Rule over Parnell's adultery. In these circumstances he found it hard to give his mind to the Bahamian business and relied upon Austen to transmit his instructions to Neville. For the rest of the family, Neville's departure was a severe blow. He was sent into 'exile', as even his father put it.[14] Once again the family was sundered, not by death this time but by a vast geographical separation. Ida was the hardest hit. 'I have been to say good night to Ida in her room,' Bea wrote to Neville on the night he left, numbering her letter in what she knew would be a long sequence: 'She was crying, poor thing. She has been splendid all day & did not break down even after you left till now. It is not easy to say how low we all feel at losing you, but we shall try to keep ourselves busy ... your first letter, though only a note from New York, will be a great event. Good night dear boy. All good go with you.'[15] Physical separation drew Neville and his sisters closer than ever, living from letter to letter, Neville craving understanding and approval. The cost of the Bahamian venture to him personally proved higher than Austen had feared.

All awaited the first letters. 'Nassau at last!', wrote Neville on arrival; 'And such

---

12  Neville to his children, 6 July 1914, *loc.cit.*
13  Joseph to Austen, 18 Dec.1890, AC1/4/3/3
14  Joseph to Neville, 19 Nov.1891, #4, Highbury, NC1/6/9/4
15  Beatrice to Neville, #1, 24 Apr.1891, Highbury, BC2/1/1

an accumulated pile of wealth in the way of letters ... Beatrice Nos 1–2, Austen Nos 1–3, Ida Nos 1–4, Hilda Nos 1–3 ... the first words I have had from home.'[16] The letter he sent on docking in New York had already reached Highbury. But his first words from the West Indies took another month to reach the family, now in London. Beatrice captured the excitement: 'I was down to breakfast this morning punctually, in fact at 2 minutes before 9.0; I sauntered to my correspondence picked up a big circular envelope without looking at the address & opened it with feeble interest. Behold! A Bahama letter! ... Arrival of Austen, Hilda & Ida in quick succession B. tearing through ahead, family fighting for stray sheets, A. reading aloud, B. interposing select bits, breathless comments, map flying round, no breakfast, horses at door, train to be caught, snorts, shrieks, rejoicings, general satisfaction. How large! How beautiful! How nice!' They seized on every suggestion Neville made to recreate in the Bahamas something like home: 'we will come & stay in your house, but we won't wait for the lawn, lest it should not grow. Ida however builds much on the pony, & I on the cow & the pig. Mary is going down to Highbury on Saturday, when the linen will be despatched ... We are particularly rejoiced that you have got so well through your first hardships & that you seem so tough.'[17] 'You should have seen the effect on Ida [of your letters]', Austen added. 'She came down to breakfast with a bad cold, & an hour later she was enjoying a capital ride in the Park with me, & her cold had disappeared as if by enchantment.'[18]

Neville swiftly finalised the basic arrangements for the enterprise. He secured better terms from the Governor for the purchase of land than any other would-be planter had obtained. He selected the island for his plantation: Andros, by far the largest in the Bahamas. Andros had its drawbacks. The terrain was rough and broken up by knots of bad land. But the coppiced land was the finest Neville had seen anywhere in the Bahamas, and there was some fine hardwood. He estimated that there were at least 10,000 and probably more like 20,000 acres of good land on the island. There was a potential harbour at Mastic Point, offering anchorage protected from the winds. Neville's imagination raced ahead: 'At Mastic Point the ground rises gently to a height of about 30 ft above the sea level and this will, I think, be an excellent site for a house. There are plenty of shady trees round it, it is breezy, healthy, out of the way of insects of which there are fewer at Andros than at most of the islands, and it commands a beautiful view of the sea.'[19]

---

16  Neville to Mary, 25 May 1891, Government House, Nassau, NC1/20/1/5
17  Beatrice to Neville, 22 June 1891, Eastbourne, #9, BC2/1/9
18  Austen to Neville, 23 June 1891, 40 Princes Gardens, #6, AC5/3/9
19  Neville to Joseph, 6 June 1891, #2, Nassau, NC1/6/10/16

Surveying Andros nevertheless subjected Neville to 'the toughest day's work I ever had in my life. The ground was of the very roughest and most crumbly description ... I had to lead and force my way through dense thickets of bush and lofty fern, at this season all matted together with various vines and creepers. The sun poured down with merciless heat ... When we emerged we were in a sorry plight. Our feet were black and blue, our shins were scarred and bruised from knee to ankle our hands were covered with scratches and mosquito bites, our boots were in shreds and our clothes were as black as an engine driver's.'[20] After a brief trip to Nassau to sign the purchase agreement, he returned to Andros to 'live in a negro's house which I shall hire until I can get my own put up which will not be for 2 months at least.'

A house of my own: here was the stuff of dreams. The house was to be 'about a hundred yards from the shore on a little hill ... At present it is covered with coppice containing some very fair trees ... if I can get some grass to grow under them they will be very shady & pleasant in summer. I mean to get some ornamental trees & shrubs from Nassau to make a garden with, and I shall also plant fruit trees. Oranges I think I shall import from Florida ... I also have a mind to try grapes. Cocoa nuts already are on the spot ... The water in front of my place is very smooth, of beautiful colours and full of fish, and a sail along the shore in the cool of the evening is perfectly delightful. ... I kept one eye open for excursions to take you when you come to see me.' But the brutal realities soon struck him; and when they did, he longed to be back at Highbury. 'The weather has been fearfully oppressive,' he told Austen: 'The natives all say to me with a shake of the head, Ah! Wait till next year, then you'll find you'll have quite lost all this energy, but next year I hope I shall be elsewhere.'[21] The demands of the work kept Neville on edge, eager to prove equal to the challenge but stunned by a sun as hot as a Black Country furnace. The problems stemmed mainly, but not solely, from the alien environment. The black population of Andros foresaw a bright future for themselves from the plantation, with good wages for their labour. They knew nothing of the work discipline with which Neville was familiar from the industrial Midlands. The hours Neville demanded on Andros and the low wages he paid soon led to a strike. Revealing a tough streak not previously displayed, Neville broke the strike by bringing in workers from Nassau who were willing to work on his terms.

By mid-July the strike was waning, and Knowles was working well as foreman. These successes cushioned the blow from the higher than anticipated costs of

---

20 Neville to Beatrice, 7 June 1891, Government House, Nassau, NC1/13/3/2
21 Neville to Austen, 17 June 1891, Andros, copy, NC1/19/29

clearing the land. 'I am afraid,' Neville told Austen, 'that our estimate of expenses in the first year will by no means cover those actually incurred on account of the many items we did not take into account,' though he remained hopeful that 'we shall be able to keep within the mark afterwards.'[22] To his sisters Neville confessed that the brutal climate and rough work were taking their toll. The heat and strain made him sick, and the poor quality of the food repelled him when hungry. After admitting this, he tried to pull himself together. 'I am all right again today after a long night's sleep. ... After all there are no worse effects than temporary sickness or exhaustion ... How glad I shall be when my house is done! ... Almost every night I dream that I come home and in company with you all make the round of [Highbury] the garden the stables the farm and the greenhouses. But I am not homesick; there is too much to interest & occupy me; only I look forward to mail time!'[23]

Overwrought by mid-September, he reacted angrily to a letter that Austen wrote on behalf of Joseph urging Neville to clear the land as quickly as possible. 'I can assure Austen,' Neville wrote directly to his father, 'that I am fully aware of the importance of getting as large an early production as possible and I have spared no effort to get on as fast as possible ... I cannot tell you how glad I shall be to leave my present accommodation where I live under every circumstance of discomfort. Merely to walk the mile to and from the plantation is terribly fatiguing after tramping all day over newly felled ground, stumbling over sharp stakes and falling into holes, always in an exhausting heat and often without food.'[24]

Neville desired sympathy, but he did not want help. He was determined to prove that he could handle his assignment without any assistant other than Knowles, able even to shoulder Knowles' burden as well. When Austen suggested finding a full partner in the enterprise, Neville rejected the idea. 'My business keeps me from being homesick,' he explained with conflicting emotions to Beatrice, 'as it absorbs nearly all my thoughts and it gives me a good deal of pleasure of a somewhat anxious kind ... If only Austen was here it would be delightful but I do not want him – at least not yet – for two reasons. Firstly I think it is good for me to have to manage the thing myself ... and secondly the life would be much too rough for him ... but I do consider that I have made a real sacrifice in coming here & one which I would not have made if it had been a question of myself only. Even if I only give 5 years to it I do not think that is a negligible quantity especially at my age when perhaps a man has most capacity for enjoying

22  Neville to Austen, 21 Aug.1891, Andros, #4, AC5/3/111
23  Neville to Beatrice, 1 Sept.1891, Mastic Point, NC1/13/3/5
24  Neville to Joseph, 12 Sept.1891, #9, Mastic Point, NC1/6/10/24

social life. But I would not withdraw now and if the thing turns out the success I believe it will I hope I shall not regret having lost anything.'[25] Still he ached for the music he loved in Birmingham: 'every night my ears are tortured with hideous sounds from various tuneless flutes & horns with which these devout scoundrels try to accompany hymns.'[26]

His father never quite grasped the price that he was asking Neville to pay. Though Joseph recognised that the work was hard, he hoped 'that as things get into order there will be more routine & less call for excessive exertion than at first. ... I feel,' he went on, 'that this experience, whatever its ultimate result on our fortunes, will have had a beneficial & formative effect on your character.'[27] He still harboured doubts from Neville's performance at Rugby that he was entirely willing to throw himself into a task. Joseph was nevertheless quick to explain to Neville that 'any suggestions we may make from time to time are to be taken as proof of interest in all you do & not as criticisms.' Neville's reaction made Joseph fearful of pressing him too hard. 'Do not overdo yourself', he counselled: '– no success in the undertaking will repay us for any injury to your health.'[28] These assurances gave Neville, so he said, 'unbounded gratification ... so long as I can get such letters ... I have courage and, what is harder, patience for anything.'

Yet he retained a keen sense of his unsatisfactory position: In addition to his responsibilities as the man in charge, he was doing pick-and-shovel work at a level that Joseph never experienced in his career as a metal manufacturer. 'Reviewing my present life, it is undoubtedly very hard and moreover it is not the kind of work which is worthy of me ... I am doing second man's work as well as first. Nevertheless someone must do it and on all considerations it seems to me right and proper than I should do it.' He welcomed Sir Ambrose Shea's recommendation to spend the next summer in England. And he cherished a hope that Joseph and Mary would visit him in Andros the following winter. 'Every day I make plans to be carried out when you arrive and every day I give them up to make new ones.'[29]

Paradoxically, to prove his worth to his father, Neville prized the need to do the work at every level all alone. His insistence on this surprised his family. Though the most imperious of men, Joseph had learned in business to work with partners; and in politics, though he always wanted to get his own way, he could work well in

25  Neville to Beatrice, marked private, 20 Sept.1891, Mastic Point, BC2/2/1
26  Neville to Austen, 6 Nov.1891, #6, Andros, AC5/3/113
27  Joseph to Neville, 17 Sept.1891, #2, Highbury, NC1/6/9/2
28  Joseph to Neville, 27 Sept.1891, #3, Highbury, NC1/6/9/3
29  Neville to Joseph, 12 Oct.1891, Nassau, NC1/6/10/27

cabinet harness. Bea liked 'to work, if possible, with an equal, but different person, who supplies my shortcomings & owes something to my qualities.'[30] But she saw how Andros brought out Neville's 'powers of self-reliance, organisation, ingenuity, forbearance & industry'. And he confirmed how the opportunity gratified him: 'the chief advantage I derive from my position is the fact that I am "boss," that everything not initiated by myself must be submitted to my judgement and that I thus am obliged to foster those qualities of self reliance &c which you are good enough to say I am showing. But suppose another man comes out. He must in experience, judgement & force of will be either my inferior, my equal or my superior. In the first case, he might just as well stop at home as he would be a mere cipher. In the second, I should no longer be free to use my undivided judgement and the responsibility which I prize would have to be shared and in the last case I should naturally lean on him and destroy the only good which this life can do me.'[31] The roughness of the challenge which Neville confronted alone on Andros enabled him to prove himself at a distance from his father but also hardened his self-reliance and aversion to working in partnership with consequences that marked him for the rest of his life.

While his sisters seized every spare moment to write to their absent brother, they moved on with their own lives, as he with sadness knew they should. The world opened up most for Beatrice as she approached her thirtieth birthday. The probability of spinsterhood held no terrors for her. Mary's takeover of the household management released Bea to develop her educational activities in London. She managed two groups of elementary schools under local governmental control, one in Fulham, the other in Hammersmith. Like Auntie, she paid close attention to the recruitment, needs and performance of the teachers. On occasion she taught classes herself. But the closest bonds that she forged – in this so different from Neville – were with her fellow managers. She worked with some of them for many years, above all with Rose Paul, a woman from a less affluent part of London who became Bea's best friend. The institution to which Beatrice and Rose were most attracted was the Children's Country Holidays Fund (CCHF), set up to provide a taste of rural life to those who knew nothing but urban deprivation. Beatrice chaired the branch that looked after the then poor western stretches of London along the Thames in Fulham. The demands on her kept rising. She made her debut as a public speaker at the prize-giving of an evening school. Ever her father's daughter, Beatrice proved effective because she knew whereof she spoke. 'I

---

30  Beatrice to Neville, 13 Oct. & 19 Nov.1891, Highbury, BC2/1/27 & 33
31  Neville to Beatrice, private, 2 Nov.1891, Andros, BC2/2/2

had an audience of over two hundred, consisting of the girls, their friends & their mothers,' she told Neville; '... I was not frightened, when I once began, as I know I had something to say to them, which I wanted them to know.'[32]

'Mastic House!!!!' Neville heralded the construction of his house at Mastic Point jubilantly. 'Here I am, actually in the south west room of my house all snug & comfortable. ... I could dilate for hours on the airiness, the coolness, the cleanliness, the absolute luxury of the place. Perhaps you would not consider it luxury with no doors or windows no wardrobes or chests and a frightful scantiness of water but if you had lived in a pigstye [sic] for nearly 5 months you would appreciate the difference.'[33] His euphoria did not last long. He was depressed at his inability to secure enough sisal plants to maintain the pace of planting which his father thought necessary. His cot was 'so uncomfortable that I cannot sleep at night,' he told Mary, and went on to confess that he had resorted 'to sleeping draughts: a vicious habit at best. I think I have been through enough roughing to last a life-time and I am heartily sick of it & long for civilisation & comfort. But I suppose everyone is subject to fits of depression at times & perhaps next week I shall be more cheerful.'[34]

At that Joseph took alarm. 'Please be careful about taking sleeping draughts,' he urged: '– they are very dangerous & should only be used in the last extremity & for a very short time. ... If you get depressed – or overworked or in any way out of sorts I should be glad for you to throw up everything & take a short holyday [sic].'[35] He was, he assured Neville, very pleased with his work: 'you have done splendidly & exceeded my anticipations. I am sorry that you are bothered about plants but this will all come right in time & you may be sure that I shall never blame you for such contretemps which must be encountered in such an undertaking as ours.'[36] At last Joe appreciated the determination of his younger son, though he still failed to recognise the extent to which Neville had imbibed the family commitment to political service and public life.

The New Year opened with another death in the family that hit Neville hard. Aunt Louie, his mother's twin, died suddenly of heart failure. Neville's sisters knew how the news would affect him. 'It is impossible,' wrote Bea, 'to say how much we have suffered for you, thinking of your bearing so heavy a blow alone. I think Aunt

32  Beatrice to Neville, 27 Oct.1891, #27, Highbury, BC2/1/29
33  Neville to Ida, 8 Nov.1891, NC1/16/2/9
34  Neville to Mary, 26 Nov.1891, Andros, NC1/20/1/7
35  Joseph to Neville, 21 Dec.1891, #5, Highbury, NC1/6/9/5
36  Joseph to Neville, 23 Dec.1891, #5a, Highbury, NC1/6/9/6

Louie felt you to be almost her son.'[37] Neville reeled at the death of this surrogate mother, the one who had told him of his own mother's death, and it shattered his emotional reserve. 'It is very hard to be away at such a time and have no one to talk to about her. I can't bear to think of coming home and finding her place empty.' 'I remember almost as if it were yesterday how she came nearly 17 years ago and told us ... of Mamma's death. I remember even her very words and the questions I asked.'[38] For months he found it hard to come to terms with this second death: 'I think about Aunt Louie every day.'[39]

Though none affected Neville so deeply, there were other important developments in the life of the Chamberlains in the opening months of 1892. Austen was adopted as Liberal Unionist candidate for East Worcestershire, on Highbury's doorstep. When this opportunity opened up, Austen dropped the Border Burghs, where success was uncertain. His acquisition of East Worcestershire would extend his father's sway over the West Midlands. But the Chamberlains' brand of Liberal Unionism did not go down readily among the countrified Conservatives of Worcestershire. The national leadership of the Conservative party had to force the rank and file in East Worcestershire to do as they were bidden. Austen entered Parliament without a contest two months before the general election expected that summer.

The only worrying implications of Austen's election were financial. The Liberal Unionists of the Border Burghs had been willing to shoulder the electoral costs that he would incur standing there. In East Worcestershire the Chamberlains, who were supposed to be rich, would have to bear those costs themselves. At the beginning of the year, Joseph divided the capital of the Andros venture into tenths, one each for Mary, Austen and Neville, and one jointly for the four girls, Joseph retaining the remaining six tenths. But he was worried about the mounting costs of cutting and clearing on Andros. And the returns from his other investments were falling. Though he did not share these worries with Neville, they could not be kept from him indefinitely. Bea confided that 'Papa gets anxious about the money question & our future. ... Stocks & shares have gone down very much, sisal of course must tie up a great deal of money for some years to come. In the long run no doubt everything will right itself, but Papa thinks to himself' – and obviously not just to himself – 'that if he were to die suddenly, the situation would be very difficult to liquidate, & we should not be left as well off as he intended. ... Of course the situation is not

37 Beatrice to Neville, 22 Jan.1892, #41, Highbury, BC2/1/43
38 Neville to Beatrice, 4 & 5 Feb.1892, Andros, NC1/13/3/9
39 Neville to Beatrice, 8 Apr.1891, Andros, NC1/13/3/11

very serious, as Papa does not propose to cut down our establishment in any way ... Nevertheless when it comes to his curtailing the garden expenses ... as he has done very strictly this year – one feels that he must be really disturbed.'[40]

The pressure that had been put on Neville was increased with this message. His most urgent task at the moment was to ransack the surrounding islands for plants. The work involved perilous voyages, slogging over rough terrain to reach the plants, and execrable, if any, food. Joseph continued to coerce Neville, telling him that the dearth of plants would 'delay seriously the time when we may hope for an adequate return' and 'very largely increase the proportion of capital outlay on the land actually planted.'[41] Neville took heart from the growth of the crop already planted. 'I have no doubt,' he assured his father, 'of their coming into bearing in 4 years and indeed I think we may get something in 3 years.'[42] In June he sailed happily for home, spared the worst of the summer heat.

&.

He returned to a political maelstrom. The general election of 1892 pitted the two alliances formed by the most divisive issue in late-Victorian politics, Home Rule for Ireland, against each other. The prospects for the alliance of Conservatives and Liberal Unionists depended on how well the latter would do against the main body of the Liberal party under Gladstone. Joe Chamberlain spearheaded the Liberal Unionists' electoral fight in the pivotal West Midlands, where Austen stood beside him. This time Austen faced Gladstonian opposition. Unlike his father who 'smashed' his opponents, Austen disarmed his with 'his good humour'.[43] The Unionist alliance expected their Gladstonian and Irish opponents to win but managed to make their margin of victory thin. Gladstone replaced Salisbury as Prime Minister; but a slim majority in the Commons was difficult to present as a popular mandate for the granting of Home Rule.

The Chamberlains focused their attention on the election and change of government. Neville shared the family preoccupation but took no part in the election. He did not enjoy his inactivity. Like his father but unlike Austen, Neville enjoyed the strenuous life: 'when everyone else is busy, it is very dull to be idle.'[44] He was

---

40  Beatrice to Neville, 15 Mar.1892, #49, 40 Prince's Gardens, BC2/1/51
41  Joseph to Neville, 6 May 1892, #10, 40 Prince's Gardens, NC1/6/9/11
42  Neville to Joseph, 15 Apr.1892, #21, Andros, NC1/6/10/42
43  Ida to Mary, 1 July 1892, Highbury, BC4/2/8
44  Neville to Beatrice, 13 Oct.1892, Nassau, NC1/13/3/14

happy to return to Andros in September, and still happier that Austen was able to accompany him during the autumn recess of the new Parliament. The brothers got along well, whatever their differences in temperament and occupation. A lot of good-natured ribbing went on between them on the voyage, but they preferred each other's company to any other. Once they reached the Bahamas, Austen accepted subordination to his younger brother. 'I trot about at his heels & from time to time get lit up a little by a ray of his glory.'[45] The family at Highbury were relieved by Austen's account of Neville's house: 'The drawing room is a splendid large bright airy room, very pleasant to sit in either during the day or at night. His bedroom also looks extremely comfortable. ... From the outside both [Neville's and Knowles's] houses are charming & their colours very good, whilst they have splendid piazzas the whole way round. I do not know of any better houses in Nassau ... You will be glad to hear too, that he has now an abundant supply of good water both for drinking & washing purposes.'[46] Neville himself was delighted at what he found on his return: 'the growth of the sisal is simply astounding ... the plants have put on such growth during the rainy season that our most sanguine hopes of early cutting seem likely to be realised.'[47] Joseph beamed.

Austen returned to Highbury for Christmas. In the New Year, attention focused on the opening of the new Parliament. The Chamberlain women scrambled for seats in the galleries and reported at length to Neville on the debates. Inside the Commons, all eyes focused on Joe and his son. Where would they sit in the House? With their Conservative allies on the Opposition benches? Or alongside the Gladstonian Liberals on the other side? The Liberal Unionists wanted to sit on the government side to reaffirm their credentials as Liberals. But the Irish Nationalists wanted the same seats in order to fight alongside their Gladstonian allies. Austen arrived at the House of Commons early on the first day of debate to secure the corner seat below the gangway on the government side for his father. Austen himself became the focus of attention later in the session when he delivered his maiden speech. He was 'very miserable' with anxiety beforehand, but scored a great success. Gladstone declared his speech to be one of the best made against the Home Rule bill. Neville was delighted at the report, 'which pleasantly tickles my family pride.'[48]

While politics was at the heart of family conversation, the other members

45  Austen to Ethel, 13 Oct.1892, Nassau, copy, NC1/19/77
46  Austen to Beatrice, 16 Oct.1892, Mastic Point, copy, NC1/19/79
47  Neville to Ida, 16 oct.1892, Andros, copy, NC1/19/78, and Neville to Joseph, 22 Oct.1892, #31, Andros, NC1/6/10/47
48  Neville to Beatrice, 8 May 1893, Andros, NC1/13/3/19

pursued their independent interests in other places. Beatrice accompanied Marie Souvestre in a dazzling return to Paris where they were fêted by the cream of society and hosted by the Prime Minister. Ethel was invited by a German girl who had a 'flame' for her at Allenswood, Lili Siemens of the great industrial family, to accompany her family to their villa at Lake Garda. 'We are to go first to Switzerland,' Ethel reported, '& stop about two days there & then go on to Italy where I think we shall mess about for a few days before settling down at the "beside the lake lying villa Margherita" as Mrs Siemans calls it.'[49] Like Neville, she was unimpressed in Venice by Mass at St Mark's which she found 'more like Hyde Park on Sunday morning than a church service', what with all 'the people walking about and talking & looking & carrying their chairs about from one part to another of the church'.[50]

Letters from Ethel gave Neville comic relief from his mounting concerns on Andros. He sent his father 'unpleasant rumours ... that our plant polls in 7 years from time of setting out.' Early polling cut the leaf-bearing period of growth to three years. More planting would be required to maintain leaf production at profitable levels. That necessity locked Neville into an endless search for more plants, whether from surrounding islands or suckers from the sisal already planted on Andros. But 'in order to allow suckers to grow up ... one would have to plant at least 11 ft apart. If this proves true, I fear it will knock off a very large percentage of our profits'. Neville therefore recommended abandoning his father's push for rapid expansion: 'it would be wise to stop cutting at 3000 acres till we see how things are going to turn out.'[51] Joseph had yet another set of concerns. They involved transport, first of new plants by sea to Andros and by rail across its rough terrain, then of the grown leaves to the extractive machinery, and finally of the fibre to harbour.

Dismissing Neville's warning, however, he consoled himself that 'the prospect as regards quality & quantity of production & also as to price are favourable & if we should be able to cut a year earlier than we supposed this will go far to cover the extra capital required for roads & plant.'[52] Relying on the botanical knowledge he acquired cultivating orchids, he thought, so Austen reported, that their sisal plants would probably last 'long enough to give good profits. ... Even if it naturally polls at 7 years & then dies he thinks it very probable that cutting the leaves will postpone polling, & that cutting off the poll when it first shows will secure a longer life to the plant, as is the case with so many other plants.' He insisted that Neville plant 5000

49  Ethel to Neville, 22 Mar.1893, NC1/14/57
50  Ethel to Neville, 26 Apr.1893, Gardone Riviera, NC1/14/60
51  Neville to Joseph, 5 Jan.1893, #3, Andros, NC1/1/10/52
52  Joseph to Neville, 4 Jan.1893, Highbury, NC1/6/9/12

acres 'as fast as possible'.[53] Neville countered that the early polling was not his only concern. He was worried about the costs of rapid expansion. 'If we go on clearing at our present rate ... it will take us two years to get the 5000 acres cleared. Before that time we shall have to get a good deal of our plant laid down and in working order and at the same time the clearing work will be at a great distance from the houses. I think we should have to double our staff. It would also I think necessitate steam tractors instead of mules on the tramways ... Of course,' he conceded, 'the question is simply a matter of how much capital Father intends to put in.'[54]

Joe was too wrapped up in parliamentary debate to give his investment the attention it needed. When he 'at last found a few minutes to look at last year's accounts which till now has been impossible owing to my political occupations', he noted that there were 'a lot of new items which we did not take into account & which will increase the capital before there is any return ... Still', he concluded, 'we shall do all right if prices keep up' – and he went on to talk about orchids, for which Neville shared his father's love.[55] Anxiety about the outlook on Andros did little to curb Joseph's extravagance at home. He gave Bea on her return from Paris a dark topaz 'set in diamonds, with a figure carrying a wreath & a palm cut in it'.[56]

He hoped to see Andros for himself that autumn. In October 1893, after Neville's summertime sojourn in England, he brought Joseph along with Austen to the Bahamas for this tour of inspection. It was hurricane season; and they ran into the consequences off Cape Hatteras. Once on Andros, Joe was plagued by a succession of ailments from headache to toothache. He lapsed into inactivity and 'rather hung round the house'.[57] When he ventured out, he was impressed with the extent of the plantation, but disappointed with the size of the plants. Rather than scale his investment back, however, he increased it. He asked Neville and Knowles to look into the experience of planters on Cuba and Yucatan with tramways and processing machinery. Neville came back from Cuba with an estimate of the costs of railway construction that was far higher than Joseph had anticipated. Neville insisted on 40 lb. rails: 'everyone strongly advised me not to make the mistake of getting them too light.'[58] Correspondingly large locomotives, 'a competent engineer' to look after them, and housing for the processing machinery would also be necessary. And

53  Austen to Neville, 24 Jan.1893, #4, Highbury, AC5/3/52
54  Neville to Austen, 16 Feb.1893, Andros, AC5/3/120
55  Joseph to Neville, 31 Mar.1893, #3, Highbury, NC1/6/9/14
56  Beatrice to Neville, 23 Jan.1893, #17, Highbury, BC2/1/76
57  Neville to Beatrice, 28 Oct.1893, Andros, NC1/13/3/2
58  Neville to Joseph, 12 Nov.1893, S.S. Cienfuegos, NC1/6/10/64

he recommended the purchase of 'a large barge' which his schooner could tow to bring the rails and machinery to land. For a moment Joseph reacted nervously: 'If we are to employ Engineers at £500 a year & to buy Locomotives for £1100 ... we must reconsider how far we can employ animal carriage & ordinary roads.'[59] Yet when Knowles reported from Yucatan that no locomotives and only portable rails were used there, Joseph dismissed that experience as too lackadaisical and unscientific for application on Andros. What worried him was Knowles's report that much more sisal was being grown in Yucatan than they had expected, and that the fibre was sold at a price the Chamberlains could not easily match.

The year ahead threatened to be even more challenging for Neville than the year past, and in new ways: not so much the physical work as the technological and financial demands of railways and extractive machinery. His family were little help on the technological side. 'What is a countershaft?' Austen asked.[60] The New Year opened on a note of financial alarm from Joseph: 'Every investment seems to be declining in value while it is impossible to reduce expenditure in proportion to diminished income. Meanwhile I have to find capital for the Fibre business – & all sales are made at great disadvantage.' He transferred the pressure to Neville: 'I hope that the result of your exertions will restore the balance.' At the same time Joe frantically raised the stakes by increasing his investment on Andros. In order to pay for the railway and extractive machinery, he turned the family business into a limited company by selling debentures to raise £20,000. Meanwhile, though he ordered the rest of the family to curb household expenses, familial pride demanded that he extend the Highbury estate to keep the neighbouring mansion of the Cadburys and the urban sprawl of Kings Heath out of sight. The political outlook in Britain did nothing to clarify his sense of direction. At long last Gladstone retired from office. Joe doubted that his replacement as Prime Minister by Lord Rosebery would do the Unionist Opposition much good. As he explained to Neville, 'we have the same fight before us without the personal influence of Mr. G's age & character.'[61]

The year had a more encouraging start for Austen. He was cultivating his constituency to good effect: 'we are gaining ground there,' he told Neville, '& ... our men are no longer afraid to declare themselves openly.' He also accepted 'the directorate of ... the "Union Marine Insurance" of L'pool ... I think the work will be interesting & not very hard, & it will bring me in £200 a year which will be very

59　Joseph to Neville, 5 Dec.1893, No.1 of New Series, 40 Prince's Gardens, NC1/6/9/17
60　Austen to Neville, 8 Apr.1894, #12, 40 Prince's Gardens, AC5/3/80
61　Joseph to Neville, 11 Mar.1894, #4, 40 Prince's Gardens, NC1/6/8/20

acceptable for Parliament & E. Worcester add very largely to my expenses.'[62] His interest in maritime matters was deepened through an encounter with the writings of the American naval authority A.T. Mahan on the influence of sea power on history. Austen found what Mahan had to say 'most interesting and suggestive,'[63] and it added a new dimension to his understanding of international relations.

Meanwhile Neville pressed ahead with the enterprise upon which the financial well-being of the family depended more than ever. Though disheartened by the 'way new expenses keep turning up,' he crushed his uneasiness by insisting that 'we are going to make money out of this thing'.[64] He ordered 40 lb rails as advised in Cuba because lighter ones would not be much cheaper and mules would in one way or another cost even more. So deep and personal did his commitment to the railway become that he resisted his father's command to come home that summer: 'I cannot & will not leave while the railway is being laid.'[65] When Joseph insisted that he leave Andros by the end of June, Neville cried out that to do so would 'leave the railway unfinished perhaps scarcely begun. ... This railway has especially been my own work. I went to Cuba, & studied up the specifications and decided on the loco the rolling stock & the rails ... I have laid out the course, directed the levelling & prepared the road bed and if now I am to be taken away and the completion of the work given to [Knowles] it will be a great disappointment to me.'[66] Neville's plea only stiffened his father's command: 'You will understand that this is not a matter of argument but a final decision which, I am sure, you will carry out.'[67] The young man complied 'with the more equanimity'[68] because the rails were slow to arrive, and he hoped to get back to Andros in time to lay them.

※

The skies darkened relentlessly for Neville once he returned to Andros that autumn. Knowles had to leave for Nassau to recover from his summer's responsibilities. Then tragedy struck. 'I am in very great trouble,' Neville wrote home in shock: 'Mrs Knowles died two days after reaching Nassau giving birth to a child prematurely.

62  Austen to Neville, 25 Jan.1894, #3, Highbury, AC5/3/72
63  Austen to Neville, 2 Mar.1894, #5, Highbury, AC5/3/74
64  Neville to Joseph, 16 Feb.1894, unnumbered, Andros, NC1/6/10/70
65  Neville to Austen, 25 Mar.1894, Andros, copy, NC1/19/132
66  Neville to Joseph, 6 Apr.1894, Andros, NC1/6/10/76
67  Joseph to Neville, 21 Apr.1894, #5, 40 Prince's Gardens, NC1/6/9/21
68  Neville to Austen, 24 May 1894, Andros, copy, NC1/19/139

... Knowles ... was very ill when he left here, completely run down, but this on top of it is enough to unhinge his mind.'[69] Neville told him to take a long voyage and not return until he was physically strong again. The loss of Knowles and his wife, whose company, cooking and house cleaning Neville had much appreciated, pushed Neville himself to the verge of breakdown. The Governor of the colony sent an experienced assistant to help him. For the first time Neville was grateful, not so much for the assistance as for the company. 'I have stood the mental & physical strain this week very well,' he reported, '& no doubt could last out some time longer but not till Knowles came back.' Meanwhile he reduced the work load and stopped the mechanical leaf processing. He poured out his sense of loss to Beatrice: 'I miss Mrs Knowles very much indeed; she was a most unselfish & warm hearted woman ... Constantly I think of something to tell her that will amuse her & then remember. ... what little social life I had is gone absolutely, & I see myself condemned for an indefinite period to a life of total solitude, mentally if not physically.'[70]

No sooner had Neville returned to Andros than another blow struck. A distant hurricane generated enough wind and wave to prevent the railway-building components and coal from docking in Mastic harbour; and the work of planting as well as leaf-processing had to stop. Neville took the stoppage to heart: 'several hundred people are now dependent on me for their daily bread,' he told Ida: 'I can't tell you how much I feel this failure.'[71]

Neville's days were further darkened by worries about the sisal. The plants 'certainly are not doing what they ought in many places,' he reported in mid-January; 'Anxiety about this weighs on me day & night and takes much of the pleasure out of the work.'[72] Joseph was simultaneously worrying about the falling price of sisal on the London market while production costs continued to rise. At last he decided to suspend further clearing on Andros and 'reduce expenditure as much as possible'.[73] But it was now too late. At the end of March Neville despatched a truly alarming report. 'Infertile spots appear all over our land,' he wrote; and even the sisal planted on the better quality of land would not produce fibre of marketable length for five to six years. The problem was not limited to Andros. All the plantations in the Bahamas were 'in a bad way'.[74] The accumulating news took a

---

69 Neville to Joseph, 24 Nov.1894, unnumbered, Andros, NC1/6/10/86
70 Neville to Beatrice, 26 Nov.1894, Andros, NC1/13/3/27
71 Neville to Ida, 7 Dec.1894, Andros, copy, NC1/19/150
72 Neville to Joseph, 17 Jan.1895, #66, Andros, NC1/6/10/30
73 Austen to Neville, 21 Mar.1895, #7, 40 Princes Gardens, AC5/3/103
74 Neville to Joseph, 26 Mar.1895, #70, Andros, NC1/6/10/95

personal toll on Neville, who was stricken with neuralgia and 'passed some of the most miserable hours I have known out here.'[75]

He was grateful for his father's insistence that he come home for the summer. He confessed that he found life on Andros 'much harder ... than it used to be, especially since Mrs. Knowles' death. You have no idea of the barren, weary monotony of the evenings without society or any change whatsoever.'[76] Meanwhile he pressed on with the work almost frantically, like his father after the death of Florence. There was still hope of profit if he could fertilise the land with guano and accelerate planting on the land already cleared. He brought the railway quickly to completion to carry plants all day every day to the waiting fields. His main concern now was with the cleaning machines, 'a constant trouble ever requiring adjustment & alteration causing loss of time & waste of fibre'. Without waiting for approval from his father, he purchased automated machinery and constructed a shed to protect it and the precious fibre from the elements. It was, he admitted, 'a large expenditure'; but only in this way could he reduce the costs of cleaning, drying and baling the sisal to levels at which the Chamberlains could make a profit, maybe even 'a fortune'.[77] He was heartened by Knowles' return to work. Chastened by the mounting difficulties of the enterprise, Neville was ready now to treat Knowles almost as a partner and felt no uneasiness about leaving the business in his hands when he returned to England in June.

Nevertheless, on the eve of his departure from Andros, Neville sent Austen a grim assessment of the prospects there. 'I should some time ago have set everything before Father, but we are so deep in now that we cannot withdraw.' The early polling of the sisal sharply reduced its productivity, invalidating Joseph's orchid-based expectations. Still worse was the slow growth of the plants. 'In some places the plants seem absolutely to be standing still in others they grow but very slowly. ... the constant sight of so many plants not much better than when they were put in brings on long fits of depression.' Neville took it personally. 'What is to become of me in the future if this thing fails I don't know, the mere sense of failure after so much hard work & sacrifice in other ways is enough to crush a man by destroying self confidence. ... Sometimes when I think of what failure means for Father & Mary I can hardly hold up my head.'[78]

While he sailed for home, the world he was returning to was transformed for his family by the change of government. The Liberal ministry of Lord Rosebery

---

75 Neville to Mary, 30 Apr.1895, Andros, copy, NC1/19/163
76 Neville to Austen, 24 Mar.1895, Andros, private, AC5/3/132
77 Neville to Joseph, 24 Apr.1895, #72, Andros, NC1/6/10/97
78 Neville to Austen, 29 May 1895, Andros, Private & Confidential, AC5/3/131

was defeated in a snap vote in the House of Commons and resigned. Thereupon Lord Salisbury formed a government in coalition with the Liberal Unionists. Offered his choice of position, Joseph opted to become Secretary of State for the Colonies, till then deemed a secondary office but through which Joe aimed to invigorate the British Empire. The new government precipitated a general election and won a massive majority in the Commons, more than enough to keep it in power for the rest of the century. These events changed the position of everyone in the Chamberlain family, including Neville. All eyes were now riveted on his father. At the same time Neville's burden of financial responsibility was reduced by the salaries for ministerial office that not only his father but also Austen received: for Austen took junior office as Civil Lord of the Admiralty, gratifying his interest in naval matters. Still, Joseph's elevation in power and wealth led him once again to overestimate the prospects for his investment in the Bahamas and blind him to its deterioration. Once he found time to discuss the situation with Neville, Joseph encouraged him to proceed 'in good hope of recovering the capital invested & making a respectable, if not a very large profit'.[79]

With the demands of the general election behind him and after an introductory run through the concerns of the Colonial Office, Joseph took the whole family on holiday through France to Spain. Neville accompanied them as far as the Pyrenees and then sailed for New York and Nassau. Andros looked fruitful on his return. He found that his sisal plants had 'grown more this summer than they had for 3 years'.[80] Things did not look so promising, however, when he toured the rest of the plantation. On some 200 or 250 acres of the best coppiced land, he found that the plants would be ready for cutting within a few months. But this good land was interspersed with patches of bad coppice and pine land where the sisal was much further behind. He questioned whether the plants would 'ever be big enough to cut in such places, & if so how many crops they will give us'. Yet he did not challenge the optimistic approach to the business which his father had encouraged him to adopt during the summer. And two weeks later, after an exhaustive survey of the property, he sent home a more encouraging report. He was sleepless with excitement when the fibre-extracting machinery finally arrived.

A succession of blows over the next four months bankrupted the business. Just before Christmas the baling shed beside the engine house caught fire, 'the roof fell in, the walls soon followed & all the fruits of 6 weeks ... were reduced to a small

---

79 Joseph to Neville, 30 Mar.1896, #3, House of Commons, NC1/6/9/29
80 Neville to Austen, 5 Nov.1895, Andros, copy, NC1/19/170

heap of white ashes.'[81] Ten days later, Knowles's mind gave way. Unbeknownst to Neville, he had been sleeping badly. Neville found him one morning with 'bloodshot eyes, muttering & chattering & laughing to himself or entreating me not to shoot him'.[82] Neville sent him to Nassau to recover, and thus lost the man upon whom he had become increasingly dependent. Two weeks later Plymouth Cordage, the company he hoped would buy the plantation produce, sent word that the sample fibre they had received was too short and stiff for its purposes. Still undaunted, Neville resolved 'to spare no efforts to get our produce as good as possible even if it costs more money'.[83] The blow that finally crushed him fell after another month when he discovered that his sisal plants simply 'don't grow'. The discovery left him 'despondent about the whole concern'. The supply of plants mature enough for harvesting could not 'possibly last longer than the end of March & then we must wait till the plants are ready to cut again'. A few might have been ready within a couple of months, but it would be perhaps two years before there would be anything more substantial. 'Meanwhile everything will be disorganised. All the order & discipline that I have worked up will be lost, all the people will go away, for I shall have nothing for them to do & I myself shall be at a loose end.' He closed his report with a cry: 'this is my failure'.[84]

Despair did not make him rash. He continued to do what he could to improve the fibre already on hand, washing it before drying in an attempt to meet Plymouth Cordage standards. He still identified the basic difficulty with the plantation as the land rather than the plants: 'for the most part the failure of our plants is due to absolute lack of soil.' They did well on good coppice: but the good coppice came only in patches, broken up with bad coppice and pine land for which the outlook was very doubtful, and rocky stretches which were useless. Without rushing but also without blinking, he pointed his father toward the probable conclusion. He proposed, 'with the help of a new map of the estate [to] go carefully into the question of growth'. But 'if I cannot feel sure of a much better result in the further part of the plantation than in the nearer, it will be my duty to advise that we face the loss & get out of this business as fast as we can.' Unless they 'really have cause to hope that an immense difference will make itself felt in a few years it is folly for me to go on wasting your money & my own time here.'[85] Having thus stared failure in the face, Neville went

---

81  Neville to Mary, 23 Dec.1895, Andros, copy, NC1/19/175
82  Neville to Beatrice, 3 Jan.1896, Andros, copy, NC1/19/176
83  Neville to Joseph, 17 Jan.1896, #81, Andros, NC1/6/10/107
84  Neville to Joseph, 27 Feb.1896, #84, Andros, NC1/6/10/110
85  Neville to Joseph, 14 Mar.1896, #85, Andros, NC1/6/10/111

bird-watching on the nearby islands while he waited for his father's response.

Joseph replied from the House of Commons, where he was fighting for his political life during an inquiry as to who was responsible for the Jameson Raid in South Africa. He found it hard in these circumstances to accept what Neville told him, and implicitly shifted the blame for the debacle from his own decisions on finance to Neville's on planting: 'you seem to contemplate as a possibility the entire abandonment of the undertaking in which I shall have invested altogether (with the liabilities I have accepted) about £50,000. ... if we are really in this position that we have planted 7000 acres with a plant that cannot & will not grow in the situation we have chosen we must of course take the consequences ... In this case, we shall lose I suppose every penny of our money. There is no value in land, machinery, buildings or plant apart from the undertaking &, whatever others might do, we cannot pass over to others at any price, a speculation which we know is doomed to failure. ... no final decision can be arrived at till you next visit home as it is too serious a matter to be decided by correspondence.'[86] Joseph still hoped that something could be done to produce enough profit from the business to make it saleable. But that hope soon died. This letter proved to be his last to Neville on Andros.

Preoccupied with the political excitements in Britain, Neville's sisters paid little attention to his demoralising situation, of which Joseph may not have fully informed them. Beatrice was the only one to mention it; and for once her counsel was woefully inadequate: 'Don't dwell on it more than you can help,' she advised; 'Slack times seem to try you more than they did & solitary occupations to be less satisfying. Would it be a good plan ... to organise a plan of study for yourself?'[87] As Neville promised his father, he undertook a close examination of all the land on their estate. It turned out to be 'worse even than [he] anticipated,'[88] and forced him to admit that 'there is only one conclusion to be drawn', which he did 'with the greatest reluctance & with the most bitter disappointment.' He could 'no longer see any chance of making the investment pay'. He placed the blame squarely on his own 'want of judgement. You & Austen have had to rely solely on my reports but I have been here all the time & no doubt a sharper man would have seen long ago what the ultimate result was likely to be.'[89] He never could bring himself to question Joseph's handling of the capital for the investment, nor did he care to think of Joseph's rejection of his advice to slow down the expansion of the plantation.

---

86  Joseph to Neville, 30 Mar.1896, #3, House of Commons, NC1/6/9/29

87  Beatrice to Neville, 2 Apr.1896, #26, Highbury, NC1/13/2/95

88  Neville to Joseph, 24 Apr.1896, #87, Andros, NC1/6/10/113

89  Neville to Joseph, 28 Apr.1896, #88, Andros, NC1/6/10/114

Neville found it terribly hard to give up. His survey dashed his father's hope of eking enough profit from the estate to make it saleable. But what about buying some better land? He conveyed his mixed emotions candidly to Beatrice: 'I can't bear to give up & yet I don't see how we can go on without getting deeper into the mire.' Unable to criticise his father, he exaggerated his own responsibility for the failure. 'Father is very good in absolving me from blame but I cannot conscientiously acquit myself. I feel that I have shown a most deplorable want of judgement if nothing worse & I have lost a good deal of the self-confidence that I was building up. I don't know what the end of it all will be. To come home & begin again with the consciousness of this gigantic failure behind I feel will be hard ... I have suggested to Father that we might start over again on a smaller scale if I could find better land in a suitable position & I should like this best.'[90] Still Neville recognised that no final decision could be reached until he returned home.

Neville spent the entire summer at Highbury and did not head back to Andros until October. His final voyage to the Bahamas was the worst he ever experienced. The bulwarks of the ship stove in during a gale, flooding the saloon and some of the cabins. Resolving that, if he were going to drown, he would rather it happened quickly, he shut himself up in his cabin and did not leave until the danger passed. Having survived, he had to kill off the enterprise in Andros; and that death was painfully slow. The very fact that the Chamberlains were leaving slashed the prices Neville could obtain for what he salvaged. No one was on hand to cheer up his last Christmas on Mastic Point. Knowles had been drinking heavily and was sent away, 'a degraded looking spectacle, dirty, his face bloated & unshaven, tottering, & half out of his mind'.[91]. The final three months were even more depressing. Because Neville did not anticipate that terminating the business would take so long, he had not planted any vegetables for the New Year; so he was left with nothing 'but fish & rice for dinner'.[92] By the end of February his house was stripped of all his books. Yet 'the nearer the time for departure comes the harder it seems to go', and he felt 'desperately reluctant to leave'.[93] The day of his departure was tragic, not so much for Neville as for the black residents of the island who looked to him for their livelihood. 'People came & sat in my office,' he reported to the ever understanding Beatrice, '& sobbed while they watched me packing up ... about 70 came to see me off and wept. It was awful.'[94]

90  Neville to Beatrice, private, 3 May 1896, Andros, BC2/2/4
91  Neville to Austen, 18 Dec.1896, Andros, AC5/3/139
92  Neville to Beatrice, 14 Jan.1897, Andros, BC2/2/7
93  Neville to Hilda, 23 Jan.1897, Andros, NC1/15/2/28b
94  Neville to Beatrice, 9 Mar.1897, Nassau, BC2/2/8

*Ethel and Hilda Mary*

## 3

# An Imperial Family

Neville's cry of failure passed unnoticed across the Atlantic except by his family. It was drowned out by the imperialist chorus which his father roused by everything he said and did to invigorate the British Empire. 'As for Papa his name is never out of the papers,' Hilda exclaimed.[1] Even financially, the home to which Neville returned was not depressed by the loss on Andros. Mary had to rein in her wish for improvements to Highbury; but otherwise the salaries Joseph and Austen received as ministers of state made serious economies unnecessary so long as they remained in office. Joseph also drew substantial income from the remainder of his industrial fortune, and the income Austen derived from a few directorships was not insignificant. Nor did the failure of Joseph's investment in the Bahamas affect his determination as Colonial Secretary to cultivate the undeveloped estates of the Empire. Joe and the Empire rose to their peak of popularity in the closing years of the century. And no audience was more enthralled by his performance than the family gathered round his dinner table.

But the mood darkened in 1899 when war erupted in South Africa, a war which it took Britain nearly three years to win. In its wake, Joseph's hitherto wide-ranging agenda narrowed to concentrate on what came to be called tariff reform: economic consolidation of the Empire through the establishment of a network of preferential tariffs to foster trade between the mother country and the colonies. His devotion to tariff reform heightened the impression that his children first gained of him in the crisis over Irish Home Rule as a statesman who placed principle and patriotism above self-interest, for this crusade damaged his political prospects

---

1 Hilda to Neville, 20 Nov.1895, Highbury, NC1/15/3/53

and shattered his health. There were other deleterious consequences. It curbed the freedom of conversation which the family had hitherto enjoyed at dinnertime and imprisoned Austen as his father's political heir apparent, though conversely it gave Neville an opportunity to prove his political worth. Tariff reform was an intensely divisive gospel, attacking as it did the basic British belief in free trade, that genera-tion's form of globalisation. Joe's proposals split the alliance of Conservatives and Liberal Unionists as badly as Gladstone's proposals for Irish Home Rule had split the Liberals. The resulting feud among Unionists – as the allies were collectively known – only hardened Joseph's insistence on an imperial tariff. But his refusal to compromise doomed his crusade to defeat.

❧

The excitement Joe could generate reached new heights early in 1896 as Neville drank the dregs of failure on Andros. The House of Commons began to debate on the recent incursion which an armed posse of imperialists led by Dr Jameson had launched into the gold-rich South African Republic, commonly known as the Transvaal. Historians still argue about Joseph's responsibility for the Jameson Raid. He had positioned Jameson's men on the base in Bechuanaland from which they launched their raid. Had it succeeded, he would have basked in reflected glory. But it was an ignominious failure, and the invaders found themselves languishing in a Johannesburg jail. Cecil Rhodes, premier of the British Cape Colony to the south, had certainly connived with the raiders, and he was forced to give up his political position though not his economic base in the royally chartered British South Africa Company. But did Chamberlain have any prior intimation that the incursion might take place? His condemnation of the invasion as soon as it was launched, and before it failed, suggested otherwise.

Day after day, Beatrice, Ida, Hilda and Ethel took turns securing seats in the Ladies Gallery of the House of Commons 'in the expectation of hearing Papa's speech on the Transvaal'. When they received a note 'half way through dinner ... to say Papa was going to speak', they 'scurried off' and made it just in time for 'the great speech. It was a splendid & most successful effort.' Hilda had never 'seen the House so intent & so unanimous before. ... the most extraordinary thing is, that Papa's speech really satisfied everyone.'[2] Joe indeed managed to hold the wolves of the Opposition at bay and at the same time to put his Unionist supporters in good heart. The Opposition focused its fury on Rhodes.

---

2  Hilda to Neville, 12 Feb.1896, 40 Prince's Gardens, NC1/15/3/71

Apart from these excitements, most of Joseph's children threw themselves into public service at the local level – all but Austen, who was absorbed at the national level, and Ethel, who had no taste for it. Ida and Hilda shared Bea's interest in education. 'Yesterday morning Beatrice & I tramped all over Fulham paying about 16 visits on the parents of various C.C.H.F. children', Hilda reported to Neville. Neville too was drawn to this level of local service, which brought out in him and his sisters the practical social concern and close attention to costs that had drawn their father originally into local government. Hilda confessed that 'at first one does feel rather a brute, when asking people with 5 or 6 children, & paying a rent of 7/6 to contribute 6/- for each child out of a weekly wage of about 25/-. It is astonishing tho' how much some of them manage to pay, particularly the widows.'[3] Hilda welcomed every opportunity to help with the schools in Fulham. 'Tuesday was a great day,' she wrote with a glow to Neville: '... I was really enabled to send an invalid small child away to a convalescent Home. One is always trying to do some thing for some wretched creature but it so seldom comes off, that I really feel I have done a great work this Spring. Positively I have provided two children with very defective eyesight with glasses which ought to enable them to learn something at school & may possibly permanently improve their sight, & I have sent one child away to a Convalescent Home. Wonderful! wonderful!'[4]

Ethel – and also Mary – found this work for school children rather tedious and uninteresting. Ethel loved the drama of political life, and Mary was completely engrossed in her husband's career. Ethel found her delight in dances and house parties, the more uproarious the better. The glamour of the society to which she was introduced in London after her father became Colonial Secretary made her disdainful of provincial Birmingham. 'Why is it,' she asked, 'that B'ham men are not more interesting to talk to. They are most worthy & painstaking and some of them anyway have got a good deal in them but certainly they do not seem able to get it out at any rate at a dance.'[5] Her family took her to task for unabashed flirting, making eyes over her best pink feather fan.

While Ethel toyed with ideas of marriage, her sisters faced the prospect of spinsterhood. They were not much older than Ethel, Hilda one year, Ida two. Ida was just twenty-four when she gave up dancing. She was the least extroverted member of the family, though she enjoyed the court functions that daughters as well as wives of ministers of state were expected to attend. Otherwise she gave no sign

---

3  Hilda to Neville, 4 Mar.1896, 40 Prince's Gardens, NC1/15/3/74
4  Hilda to Neville, 8 May 1896, Great House Farm, Witley, Surrey, NC1/15/3/80
5  Ethel to Neville, 3 Dec.1896, Highbury, NC1/14/147

of wanting a wider social life or close relationships outside the immediate family. Hilda hoped for more. She had a warm heart, especially toward children, and looked forward to having children of her own. Like any girl of twenty-three who did not have a partner in sight, she recognised that she might remain single. But unlike Bea and Ida, she shuddered at the thought.

Neville had a more immediate concern than marriage on his mind. He needed to find a place in business to restore some of the wealth that his family had lost in the Bahamas. Everyone insisted that Neville was not to blame for the failure: some of his uncles privately accused Joseph of rashness. Still Neville could not but be deeply shaken by it. He tried in later years to persuade himself that the venture on Andros had forced him 'to put out my best and to my astonishment I found myself capable of much more than I had supposed possible. The experience taught me much, it gave me self reliance and readiness to take responsibility in a way that perhaps nothing else could.'[6] But he was never quite convinced by this interpretation and remained hypersensitive to any suggestion of failure, anxious to justify himself and secure appreciation for whatever he accomplished. All of his uncles were involved in Birmingham business, two of them prominently so; Arthur Kenrick in hollowware manufacturing and Arthur Chamberlain in the manufacture of explosives at Kynoch's. Joseph asked them all about business prospects for Neville.

His return to Highbury brought the family fully together once again. Neville added to the liveliness of mealtime conversation. The political concerns of the country continued to revolve around Joseph; and whenever he dined at home, he sparked the conversation. But in his absence, it was ignited by Neville and equally by Beatrice. For a decade after Neville's return from Andros, the Chamberlain dinner table was a cauldron of conversation. Hilda savoured ever afterwards the memory of these conversations: 'four sisters, Mary & Papa, Austen occasionally, & Neville, whenever we were at Highbury. How exciting, how stimulating, how laughter provoking ... Dinner time almost any day, but the remembered lunches were those [at Highbury] on Sunday, when we all adjourned for coffee to the big conservatory where Papa & the boys smoked large cigars, & talk ranged over the doings of the week both in the family & in the world.'[7] The men set the political agenda; but the women participated vigorously in the discussion; and the subjects ranged far beyond politics, at least until Joseph launched his campaign for tariff reform. Then, to Hilda's disappointment, everything else was driven from

6  Neville to his children, 6 July 1914, Westbourne, NC1/6/11
7  Hilda, Recollections 'For Dorothy & Frank' (Neville's children), BC5/10/6

his mind. Even then, 'Papa made no difference in his conversation between girls & boys, & we were as likely to hear political secrets or ideas talked of when only we were present, as if Austen & Neville were there too.' Hilda also noted Neville's penchant for acting alone, an inclination she welcomed: 'Neville also never seemed to need a "man" to talk to in place of his sisters.'

Bea's conversational talents carried her to the heights of American political society when she visited Mary's family in Massachusetts. She was welcomed by leading figures in American public life as the daughter of Britain's most famous statesman. But she made her own mark among women of independent mind and upon men of her own age, who admired her boldness of spirit. In Boston she was introduced to the head of Radcliffe, the women's college, whom Bea admired because she spoke about college education for women without 'overlooking the drawbacks' or 'making a universal panacea' of her work.[8] Bea was no feminist. She endorsed her father's opposition to votes for women. But she had benefited too much from the tutelage of Marie Souvestre to disparage advanced education for women. Her closest friendships were with women, but she attracted strong-minded conversationalists of both sexes. In Washington she dined with the leading Massachusetts senator Henry Cabot Lodge, under whose roof she met Theodore Roosevelt. Roosevelt 'had the lion's share of the conversation', Bea reported to her father, who was in many ways the British prototype of the future American President. 'We did not get on foreign politics, where I understand he breathes fire & slaughter, or rather battleships & annexation.' Later she noted, 'The people here say that … he lacks judgement, but he has plenty of ability & courage & acts up to his convictions.'[9] She saw him often with great pleasure – 'and he me, so he says.'[10] Another frequent guest at these dinner parties, the future Supreme Court Justice Oliver Wendell Holmes, sent her 'a beautiful valentine' and 'a bunch of roses, pink & white'.[11]

Shortly after Bea left for Massachusetts, Neville secured the sort of position in business that his father had wanted for him. Neville had already acquired a directorship with Elliott's, manufacturers of copper tubing, but it gave him only part-time employment. One of his uncles finally located a going concern that Joseph could buy and place Neville in charge: Hoskins, a manufacturer of ships berths. This branch of metal manufacturing did not appeal to Neville as much as

8  Beatrice to Ida, 24 Dec.1897, 211 Commonwealth Avenue, Boston, BC1/1/10
9  Beatrice to Joseph, 16 Jan.1898, 1600 I Street NW, Washington, DC, 16 & 18 Jan.1898
10  Beatrice to Hilda, 20 Jan.1898, 1600 I Street NW, Washington, DC, BC1/1/15
11  Beatrice to Ida, 13 Feb.1898, 458 Beacon Street, BC1/1/19

the work at Elliott's. But Austen, from his experience at the Admiralty, assured Neville that his interest in the work would grow. Hoskins had the further advantage of being twenty minutes by bicycle from Highbury. As Neville put it to Ida, 'he had begun to strike root again at home & did not at all want to pull himself up & transplant himself again'.[12] Joseph found half the purchase price of Hoskins from family resources, and borrowed the rest. Overcoming Neville's aversion to assistance, he and Joseph kept the 'very energetic & pushing' manager of the firm, Hall, in position and made him a director. 'He is said to be irritable & suspicious', Neville reported with some anxiety, but was 'strictly honourable and a persona grata to the great shipbuilders'. Neville threw himself into the business. To Ida's dismay, he left for work right after breakfast and 'hardly ever returns before 6:30 when he bolts a cup of tea & retires to write letters or study patents'.[13] He retained his directorship at Elliott's but reduced his time there to one day a week. His first test at Hoskins came with a strike by the engineering workers. Along with other employers, Neville stood firm; and though it cost them dearly, they brought the strike to an end without concessions.

Living at home brought Neville closer to his father and the primary family business of politics. Though Joe had little interest in science, he found his greatest relaxation of a weekend breeding orchids in the greenhouses of Highbury. Neville was the better botanist and would accompany his father 'down the houses on Sunday morning, spending an hour or two there before going round the garden' with the rest of the family.[14] Neville had felt badly, even resentfully, out of touch on Andros with the all important political concerns of his family. Now he again sat at the dinner table enthralled by his father. Neville hated missing anything Joseph had to say, and indeed resented the need to talk to guests. Joe's capacity for initiative in public life seemed boundless in the late 1890s. Not content in the autumn of 1897 with expanding the British Empire in West Africa, he proposed to turn Mason College, the institute for advanced technological education that Neville had attended in Birmingham, into a fully-fledged university. Joseph astonished his family by revealing that he intended the university to enhance the reputation of the city, and that he planned accordingly to secure funding from its principal industries for distinguished professorships.

Education in one form or other was central to the family's public service. Ida taught at night school for working-class girls in Birmingham's Jewellery Quarter.

---

12  Ida to Beatrice, 3 Nov.1897, Highbury, BC1/2/9
13  Ida to Beatrice, 7 Dec.1897, Highbury, BC1/2/16
14  Hilda's Recollections for Dorothy & Frank, BC5/10/6

When in London, she monitored the costs that the Children's Country Holidays Fund incurred and the charges it levied. Bea and Hilda took charge of the central management of the CCHF. The sisters supervised teaching as closely as finance and were concerned for the physical as well as the intellectual development of the children. Drills for exercise formed part of the curriculum. Eyes needed to be tested and corrective glasses secured. Hilda loved this part of the work: 'Angel child,' Bea called her.

There were light-hearted as well as earnest sides to the sisters' activity. They held a weekend house party in Highbury at the end of the holiday season in 1898 complete with dancing, and thought it 'a great success'. But there was a shadow over these festivities: 'Poor Ethel was not able to dance' and had to look on while others did what she so loved. Next day, when the rest of the party headed off for lunch and some bicycling, Ethel remained at Highbury. 'Mr Bernard Holland who,' according to Ida, was 'a trifle mousey preferred to stay behind & go in to B'ham to see the Art Gallery, so he & Ethel enjoyed a tête à tête lunch at home (Imagine Ethel's feeling.).'[15] Though 'awfully thin,'[16] Ethel rallied occasionally for a brisk ride or 'some capital jumping'. She was well enough that summer to visit the Siemens' fifteenth-century fortress in Germany. When she encountered signs of militarism there she told her adoring father that her 'free-born British soul swelled with indignation, but it looked very picturesque'.[17]

All of these activities touched upon Joseph's political concerns and served his purposes. Trips abroad were informative interludes; service in education reflected his social vision; Austen reinforced his father's purposes at Westminster; and Neville's business funded the primary family enterprise in public life. And control of Neville's business activities remained in Joseph's hands. He decided how profits were distributed. He set Neville's salary. Joseph rediscovered the merits of caution after his rashness in the Bahamas. When Hoskins began to make money, he advised Neville against an increase in the family dividend and called instead for the creation of 'a large reserve fund to meet the bad times when they come'.[18] Neville in turn drew upon his experience in the Bahamas to help his father find ways to assist West Indian sugar planters in the face of foreign competition. Neville was also happy to enter upon another kind of apprenticeship, helping his father to control the

15  Ida to Beatrice, 2 Feb.1898, Highbury, BC1/2/29
16  Ida to Beatrice, 8 Nov.1897, Eastbourne, BC1/2/10, & Hilda to Beatrice, 11 Feb.1898, 40 Prince's Gardens, BC1/2/32
17  Ethel to Joseph, 28 July 1898, Ahlsdorf bei Schönewalde, Halle, BC6/4/1
18  Joseph to Neville, 27 Feb.1900, 40 Prince's Gardens, NC1/6/9/32

Unionist party in Birmingham. Besides politics and orchids, Joseph and Neville shared a less welcome concern. Both suffered from gout. But they differed in their approach to it. While Joseph immersed it in port and champagne, Neville sternly soldiered on.

&

However widely Joseph's political vision ranged, it remained rooted in Britain's industrial economy. He was an industrialist in politics. Despite the aggressiveness of his imperialism, he was not by nature a man of war. Though the Prime Minister Lord Salisbury called the armed conflict that erupted in South Africa 'Joe's war', Joe was drawn into it somewhat reluctantly by the British High Commissioner in South Africa, Sir Alfred Milner. That war probed the weakest joints, both military and financial, of the imperialism which Joe Chamberlain embodied. He declined to take charge of Britain's military response, but he threw everything he had into his final effort to uphold the economic strength of Britain and the British Empire. The Boer War thus hardened Joseph's imperialism and gave it an economic twist. In doing so he sharpened and intensified, even warped, the political purpose of everyone in his family.

The twist came in the prescription Joseph devised to strengthen the imperial economy. He called it imperial preference; the construction of a wall of tariffs to protect British industry against foreign competition while favouring Britain's colonies. The war in South Africa dragged on until the spring of 1902. Upon its conclusion, over the next three and half years, Joseph hammered out his tariff proposals and strove to impose them upon the Unionist alliance and the country. His crusade for tariff reform became not only his consuming mission but the cause to which his family would devote itself long after he died.

Ethel's failing health cast a shadow over the family for the next three years. Austen reported anxiously to Mary on his holiday with Ethel near Salisbury: 'The country was lovely & the riding magnificent. I hope you thought her looking better when she got back. The wind & sun put some colour into her cheeks. She was _not_ communicative & I asked no questions & dropped no hints, so I hope you will consider that I was discreet.'[19] That summer, at the age of twenty-six, Ethel married Lionel Richards, a friend of Neville's from his Rugby days, who had been captivated by Ethel for years and was now a barrister. Lio, as he was called, knew that Ethel's health was precarious. They enjoyed 'a pretty and a brilliant wedding, but

---

19 Austen to Mary, 19 Apr.1900, Barry Docks nr Cardiff, AC4/1/34

not altogether what the society papers would call a fashionable one'.[20] It took place in a Unitarian chapel in Birmingham rather than in one of the grand churches of London. Lili Siemens was among the bridesmaids. When the bride and groom returned from their honeymoon to Highbury, Ethel admitted that she had not been feeling well 'but said she was ever so much better for the few days change here'. She was 'in excellent spirits' but 'of course very prudent until she knows what she is in for'.[21]

Thereafter, though insistently independent as she and Lio set up their own home, she never lived far from her family until she died. What she was in for was both obscured and brightened by childbirth. Ethel named her baby Hilda Mary after her closest sister and her stepmother. But she always called the baby 'Cherub'. And a cherub she was to her adoring grandparents and aunts and uncles as well as to her mother and father. Still, the responsibilities of motherhood did not improve Ethel's resilience: 'after Hilda Mary's birth she was always an invalid'.[22] Joseph tried to ease the pressures on her and get her out of doors by offering her a carriage. But Ethel declined the offer, insisting that Lio and she could afford 'whatever is a necessity ... & even if it were a little strain we feel we ought, at any rate to some extent, to be dependent on ourselves & bear our own burdens.'[23]

Nothing, not even anxiety about Ethel, lessened the family's preoccupation with politics. Neville joined his father and brother in campaigning around Birmingham in the general election that Joseph precipitated in the autumn of 1900. Always formidable at election time, Joe marshalled the Unionist forces to repeat their massive victory of 1895. In electoral terms, things could not have turned out better: but not militarily. The Boers responded to their defeat in the conventional clash of massed forces in 1900 by resorting to guerrilla warfare. All Joe could counsel was 'Patience! Patience! Patience!'[24]

In the run up to the general election and in its wake, the war touched one of the most sensitive nerves of his family. The Welsh Liberal David Lloyd George, facing failure at the polls, attacked the war-related industrial concerns of the Chamberlains. Joe's brother Arthur manufactured explosives for the military market. Some of the ships' berths made by Hoskins under Neville's direction went to the navy, while Austen was a Civil Lord of the Admiralty which awarded the contracts.

20 *Birmingham Daily Post*, 23 Aug.1900
21 Ida to Mary, 24 Oct.1900, BC4/2/40
22 Hilda's Recollections for Dorothy & Frank, BC5/10/6
23 Ethel to Joseph, 30 May 1902, 13 Addison Crescent, BC6/4/6
24 Joseph to Neville, 10 Nov.1900, 40 Prince's Gardens, NC1/6/9/32

Joseph had distributed shares in Hoskins to his immediate family, including Austen. Lloyd George twisted it, 'As the Empire expands, the Chamberlains contract,' an attack on the honour of the family which cut Joseph to the quick. He watched grimly as the House of Commons divided on Lloyd George's motion of censure; he never forgave those who voted for it. The accusations ended up inconclusively in the courts. The charges centred upon Arthur but extended to Neville. Beatrice and Austen sought to numb the pain by concentrating on other things. But Hilda, travelling with Bea in Italy, could not endure such stoicism. 'Send me some papers, do!' she pleaded to Ida; 'Bee is no satisfaction on the subject as she ... won't have the subject mentioned & would rather I would not buy the paper. That is all very well, but it does not really console me.'[25]

After the eventual Boer surrender, Joseph embarked on a mission to pacify South Africa. He went in the unfamiliar role of peacemaker, intent on reconciling Boer and Briton. He met with remarkable success in the northern Transvaal where the Boers followed him 'in a cavalcade ... the first thing we knew the horses were taken out & we were being drawn by them – under a triumphal arch of flags & Welkom, into a crowd of women & children who all gave us the warmest of greetings'.[26] Praise was heaped on Joseph back in Britain from every part of the political spectrum. For a moment he ceased 'to be a party man. The general tone is more & more, "of course Mr. Chamberlain is doing the right thing in the right way ...." In fact,' Ida added with a laugh, 'I think soon the Liberal party will claim all the credit & speak of "Our Joe".'[27]

But he was detached from the political infighting in the Cabinet. He had left London in high hopes of Cabinet agreement to a first small step toward imperial preference, reducing a recently introduced registration duty on imported corn in order to favour the export to Britain of wheat from Canada. During his absence in South Africa, however, the Chancellor of the Exchequer, Lord Ritchie, dug in his heels against any breach in Britain's strict adherence to free trade. Joe returned to Britain shortly before the Budget was to be presented to Parliament, but he was too late to change its total repeal of the registration duty on corn.

Denied the opportunity to take a small step toward his desired goal, he took a giant one, and delivered the most momentous speech of his entire career. He challenged the country to break with its free-trading past and construct a preferential tariff to protect Britain against foreign competition while strengthening the

25  Hilda to Ida, 23 Mar.1901, Florence, BC4/4/18
26  Mary to Hilda, 30 Jan.1903, #9, Kimberley, BC4/3/2
27  Ida to Mary, 2 Feb.1903, Highbury, BC4/2/52

Empire. He reinforced his challenge with a question: 'whether the people of this country really have it in their hearts to do all that is necessary, even if it occasionally goes against their own prejudices, to consolidate an Empire which can only be maintained by relations of interest as well as by relations of sentiment.'[28] His challenge hit the political world with explosive force. It united the Liberals against any departure from free trade, it split the Unionist alliance into not just two but three fragments, and it turned his supporters into zealots. Within the family, the effect was to bind his sons to a cause that determined their course for the next thirty years.

The bonds within the family were tightened by another message received while Joseph was en route to South Africa. Tests in London to find out what was wrong with Ethel proved fruitless. With the approach of winter, she was sent to convalesce in the gentler climate of Eastbourne, taking the Cherub with her. Ethel had lost a lot of weight and had little stamina. The baby devised games to rouse her mother. Her brothers and sisters took turns to visit and report to Joseph. At last a test in Birmingham identified the root of the problem: a tubercular bacillus. How would Ethel respond to the news? Ida was 'afraid she might feel as if it was just no use struggling on, but she says it is far better to know there is a definite disease which may be cured than to be told you are all right when you are not.' Ethel was 'determined to get well & <u>soon</u> & if courage & pluck give her any better chance she certainly has them'.[29] By the beginning of February Ethel was able to write 'at some length' to her father, 'longing to go back to London where I hear the bulbs are all coming up & looking most promising'.[30]

The identified threat to Ethel's health intensified the anxieties of the family at the same time that they rallied to support Joseph's challenge to free trade. Fear of violating this ingrained national commitment gripped the least adventurous members of the Cabinet, led by the Whig Duke of Devonshire. Joseph's inability to bring the Duke round during the summer of 1903 led to a dramatic breakup of the Cabinet in September, when both Joe and the diehard opponents of imperial preference resigned, followed by the waffling Duke. Joe used his freedom from the trammels of office to carry his appeal directly to the public, believing that the Unionist government would adopt his policy once it was assured of popular support. As an apparent pledge of that understanding, Austen not only remained

---

28  Speech in Birmingham, 15 May 1903, in Joseph Chamberlain, *Imperial Union and Tariff Reform: Speeches delivered from May 15 to Nov.4, 1903* (London, 2nd ed., 1910), 13
29  Ida to Mary, 12 Jan.1903, Highbury, BC4/2/50
30  Ethel to Joseph, 5 Feb.1903, Eastbourne, BC6/4/8

in the Cabinet to which he had recently been appointed, but was elevated to the Chancellorship of the Exchequer. That appointment tightened the bonds between father and son in a way that did not work out as either of them hoped. Austen found his bondage sometimes painful, while Joe drove ahead with frustrated urgency.

There was no ambivalence in the rest of the family. Their commitment to Joseph's cause grew only stronger as his difficulties mounted. They thought of him as a crusader for the greater good of Britain and the Empire. Hilda regretted the way imperial preference drove all other subjects out of the family's dinner-time conversation. But Joseph's departure from the Cabinet also meant that he spent more time in Birmingham, to the delight of Ida, as well as Hilda, and above all Neville – Beatrice and Ethel were now London-based.

But Joseph's shift towards Birmingham was unfortunate for Austen. He lost the ready access to his father that he had enjoyed in London during the parliamentary year and raised the possibility of division between father and son, with Austen bound by collective responsibility to his Cabinet colleagues while Joseph sought to force their pace through a national agitation. When Austen took up residence as Chancellor at 11 Downing Street, he wrote to his father in some bewilderment: 'I cannot close my first evening away from your roof ... without writing a line to you. It is so great a change in my life & all about me is so strange that as yet I hardly realise it. But what I do realise is how much I owe to you & how very dear to me is the close friendship which you have encouraged between us ... my prayer tonight is that the perfect confidence which I have enjoyed for so long may continue unimpaired by our separation and that I may do something to help you in the great work which you have undertaken.'[31] Joseph was 'touched & pleased' by Austen's letter. 'I have sometimes feared in these later years,' he replied, 'that I might be standing in your way & I have been glad that, without any dereliction of duty on my part, the time has come when you have the opportunity of showing that you can do without the possibility of your worst enemy – if you have any – saying that you are shining with a reflected light'.[32] But Joe still set the direction in which he meant his elder son to move, and his light continued to outshine Austen's.

Neville, meanwhile, was in torment of a different sort. His manufacturing interests, though never enormously profitable, were faring well, and he extended them into Wales and Scotland. It was not the fluctuating fortunes of business that tormented Neville, but the ups and downs of love. Rosalind Craig Sellar was the object of his devotion, a professional singer who performed at the Triennial Festivals in

---

31 Austen to Joseph, 11 Jan.1904, AC1/4/5/31
32 Joseph to Austen, 12 Jan.1904, Highbury, AC1/4/5/17

Birmingham. She was not, he assured Mary, associated with the fast set, but was entirely 'our sort'.[33] Rosalind was a friend of Hilda, who met her at the festival in 1900. Neville did not meet her until the festival of 1903. He fell for her in a matter of days, just before he was to accompany Ida and Hilda on a trip across Italy. Rosalind gave him enough encouragement to keep him on tenterhooks throughout the trip. He took Mary into his confidence before he left Birmingham, but did not tell his sisters until they set off. They were taken aback by the speed of his attachment. Still Hilda showed him 'much sympathy in little ways that I appreciate'.[34] He was easily overwrought, 'got into a very depressed condition, & tormented myself with every kind of imaginary obstacle, but I had a long talk with Hilda at Amalfi which seemed to put things in a different light,' and since then was in 'very good spirits'. He feared that rival suitors would take advantage of his absence to advance their case. He was stunned to learn that Rosalind had 'said jokingly to Hilda "Take me with you to Italy". ... by Jove, wouldn't it have been a gorgeous opportunity!'[35]

Once back in England, he seized every opportunity to woo the young woman, whose family did not live far in London from the Chamberlains' place on Prince's Gardens. His hopes rose and fell repeatedly as winter turned to spring. Everyone in his family did what they could to help. After a dinner party at Prince's Gardens, 'Hilda manoeuvred so well (assisted by Lio who executed a masterly movement & carried off an obstructive [sic] at the right moment) that I had her to myself for a good half hour, and I am only now slowly descending to earth again.'[36] When Rosalind recoiled at Neville's impetuosity, Ida counselled him to pursue 'a more cautious policy ... it won't do to hurry matters'.[37] Rosalind too could be overwrought, and her doctor ordered her to convalesce on the Continent. But when she returned, she brought Neville's courtship to an abrupt halt. He poured out his dismay to Mary: 'Just for a little while she came into my life & made it very bright & now she is gone again & has left me nothing but the memory of her strength & sweetness, her earnestness & simplicity & her beautiful womanliness. I chose the best & highest ... I have been taken up to the top of the mountain & had my glimpse of the Promised Land, and now I must descend again into the wilderness ... grinding through the weary round with all the spur & hope taken out of it.'[38]

---

33  Neville to Mary, 15 Nov.1903, Perugia, NC1/20/1/39
34  Neville to Mary, 28 Oct.1903, Rome, NC1/20/1/38
35  Neville to Mary, 15 Nov.1903, Perugia, NC1/20/1/39
36  Neville to Mary, 3 Mar.1904, Highbury, NC1/30/1/41
37  Ida to Mary, 23 Feb.1904, 40 Prince's Gardens, BC4/2/58
38  Neville to Mary, 1 May 1904, Highbury, NC1/20/1/43

Though his family responded sympathetically, they had more pressing setbacks to deal with. Ethel was well enough to rejoin Lio in London and even do a little skating. But Joseph's health was a concern. He had suffered a nasty gash to the head in a cab accident soon after the Boer War. He seemed to have recovered before he left for South Africa; and his endurance there through the summer heat won amazed admiration. But soon after his resignation from the Cabinet, his health showed unmistakeable signs of the toll that his advancing age, now sixty-seven, and his eight years in office had exacted. He was dogged by gout and headaches during the nevertheless astonishing campaign of speeches that he delivered through the autumn of 1903 advocating imperial preference. His family looked on with admiring anxiety. Following the news as they travelled through Italy, Neville and his sisters could not help but be 'amazed at your proceedings. Gout & headache & cold only seem to bring out your speeches in greater number & with greater vigour than ever. ... your reception every where, along the line and in the streets, reminds one of the accounts of S. Africa.'[39] Once Joseph completed this campaign, Mary took him away to recover on a voyage across the Mediterranean to Egypt. She reported that 'the sea air has smoothed some of the tired look out of your Father's face, & he has much improved in regaining his natural vigour of movement.' Still he remained 'headachy at times'.[40]

In Joseph's absence, his children sought to fill the political gaps he left. Neville provided leadership in Birmingham, speaking on behalf of the tariff reforming Unionist candidate in a by-election in Birmingham South. The Unionists had fared badly in by-elections since the end of the Boer War, but Birmingham reversed the trend. Neville reported jubilantly that 'all Unionists are proud of Birmingham & old Brum is very pleased with itself'. Birmingham was the exception, however. The Unionist alliance deteriorated everywhere else, most seriously in the House of Commons. Ida sent Mary and Joseph a lively account of the infighting between tariff reformers, free traders and those who followed Lord Salisbury's successor as Prime Minister, Arthur Balfour, in insisting that the unity of the party was more important than differences on fiscal policy. The infighting extended from the floor of the Commons to the Ladies Gallery where Ida and Hilda stood guard. 'The Ladies Gallery was full of Liberals and Free Fooders,' Ida reported; 'but Hilda & I rejoiced to find that our people yelled even louder than the other side. Mrs. Asquith [wife of the front bench Liberal Herbert Asquith] was dancing round in a frantic state & was more intolerable than usual ... Austen vows that he knows it as

39 Neville to Joseph, 3 Nov.1903, Rome, NC1/6/10/123
40 Mary to Hilda, 15 Feb.1904, S.S. Mongolia, BC4/3/5

a fact that she asked to go over to 10 Downing Street, & having done so expressed herself satisfied except that more bedrooms would be needed for the children!!'[41]

Austen was of course the primary representative of his father in his absence. As Chancellor he had to be in the House frequently to respond to the endless questions. Helped by his sisters, he also sought to put the party in good heart socially with dinners at Prince's Gardens. All, including Ethel, turned up for Austen's major addresses in the Commons. But the tension between his duty as spokesman for a government anxious to maintain stability, and his duty to his father who wanted the government to change course, placed him in a hopeless position. As Chancellor he was responsible for the very area of policy over which Unionists were most bitterly divided. 'I try to forget the Budget,' he lamented to Mary, 'but it haunts me. There is no credit to be got out of it. With such a party I can do nothing but tread the beaten track. I don't think the plan to which I am driven will displease my father, but it will give him no pleasure & gives me none.'[42]

Joseph cut his holiday short, to Ida's dismay: 'a month is not a long enough holiday after 8 years of strain', she argued, to no avail.[43] She was nevertheless right. Joe tried but failed during his holiday to find some resolution to the political predicament in which he and Austen found themselves. On leaving Cairo for home, he sent markedly different messages to his two sons. To Austen he emphasized, indeed exaggerated, his own detachment from the frustrations of parliamentary politics. Yet he could not disguise his anger at the manner in which free-traders threw away the benefits they could reap from their enormous investment in the Empire. Egypt was in effect a British colony; and Joe observed the benefits that British investment of more than £10,000,000 on Egyptian agriculture brought everyone but 'the stupid philanthropic, benevolent & unbusinesslike British nation.'[44] His tariff proposals were designed to turn this situation around. But much of the Unionist alliance refused to embrace his programme. Some Unionists like Winston Churchill insisted on the maintenance of free trade. Others led by the Prime Minister, Arthur Balfour, struggled to secure some neutral position. 'In these circumstances,' Joe concluded, 'the best thing that can happen is that we should be beaten' at the next general election. Afterwards he would drive free traders like Churchill out of the party and persuade the rest to embrace the full programme of tariff reform and imperial preference. Still he hesitated to force the pace. 'In no case am I going to

---

41 Ida to Mary, 10 Mar.1904, 40 Prince's Gardens, BC4/2/59
42 Austen to Mary, 3 Apr.1904, Highbury, AC4/1/47
43 Ida to Mary, 18 Mar.1904, 40 Prince's Gardens, BC4/2/60
44 Joseph to Austen, 11 Mar.1904, Cairo, AC1/4/5/32

fight against Balfour's Government', he assured his apprehensive elder son: 'I would much rather go out of politics.'

From Sicily two weeks later, Joe struck a more aggressive note in writing to his younger son. It was the longest letter Neville had ever received from his father, and turned out to be the last. It was momentous for both men. Pleased by the South Birmingham by-election, Joseph sought to turn the city into the base from which he could push the Unionists nationally to embrace his policy. He had, however, lost his chief political organiser, Powell Williams, whose death had precipitated the by-election. Joseph asked Neville to assume many of Powell Williams' local responsibilities. To begin with, Neville was to orchestrate a meeting of the Grand Committee of all Liberal Unionist associations in and around Birmingham. At that meeting Joe would introduce the next steps by which tariff reformers could advance their cause without undermining the Balfour government. 'Qui m'aime, me suivra' was the motto Joseph chose. It typified his demand for unswerving loyalty: 'one of the most important things to be done now is to see who are the stalwarts.'[45]

Neville felt honoured by the request. It gave him what he longed for, to be asked by his father to contribute to the primary business of the family, governing Britain. Neville's commission did not extend to London; Joseph took responsibility himself for the national organisation and for leading the tariff reformers in the House of Commons. Neville was nonetheless delighted by the confidence placed in him. He had already postponed a business trip for Hoskins in order to deal with the civic responsibilities he was taking over from his father for the hospital and university in Birmingham. After receiving his father's commission to take over management of the Unionist party in the city, he never again treated business interests as of overriding concern. Indeed he turned down the most golden of business opportunities, a pressing invitation from his uncle Arthur Kenrick to join the board of Lloyds Bank with the 'likelihood that in due course [he] would have been elected chairman'.[46] Neville was now his father's heir at one end of the Birmingham-Westminster axis around which Joe sought to push the Unionist party toward tariff reform.

Joseph asked Neville to send his letter on to Austen, and Austen found it uncomfortable reading. It sharpened the conflict he sought to blunt between his father and Arthur Balfour. Balfour's refusal to contemplate anything more than retaliatory duties against foreign dumping was 'worse than nothing' in Joseph's estimation. 'Are we to work for the success of the Unionist Party,' he asked, '& then find the Balfourites in command of the ship feebly steering her on the rocks

45 Joseph to Neville, 25 Mar.1904, Palermo, NC1/6/9/36
46 J. Arthur Kenrick to Neville, 15 May 1904, Berrow Court, NC1/24/24

of a partial & half-hearted retaliation?' Austen strove to keep the conflict between the two men from open rupture, but he could not hide his unhappiness at their antagonism. Writing after dinner with his father, Austen tried to assure Mary that, 'though he would talk of nothing but the political situation ... there was not a whiff of difference between us. I should like to have got his mind on other subjects but that was evidently not possible & I did not try.'[47]

❧

Everyone in the family felt pulled down that autumn. All but Ida and Hilda, who stayed behind to take charge at home, sought revival through travel. Joseph and Mary were the first to head away, accompanied initially by Austen and Beatrice, to Italy and Austria. Neville went next to India, trying to obliterate the memory of Rosalind farther afield, in company with his cousin Byng Kenrick who had business there. Ethel did not leave till November. She agreed with Lio to spend the winter alone, without the demands of husband or child, in the mountain air of Switzerland, considered the best place for recovery from tuberculosis. Her father insisted that no expense be spared to save her from 'the least risk or even any discomfort' and give her every pleasant diversion in her 'exile'.[48] Ida and Lio made the arrangements, selecting Adelboden because it was higher in the Alps than most resorts. Ida visited Ethel in her London home shortly before she left, and found her looking 'very cheerful, considering. ... I went out with her on Friday morning to get her a cap to skate in & some books.'[49]

The cures sought by the various members of the family had mixed results. Joseph wrote grumpily from Siena about the one sphere of activity at home that he could still control: the garden. Neville threw himself into his exotic adventures with abandon. In Ceylon he acted 'on Austen's principle of eating everything new', without dire consequences. Unable to hire a servant, he followed local practice and bought himself a slave. He went panther shooting in West Bengal. He sent his family enthralling accounts of all he saw and did. 'Love to you all,' he wrote from a boat on the Rangoon River; 'I hope you are not having a very bad winter & that Ethel is comfortable in Switzerland.'[50] Enchanted by his outlandish experiences, Ethel replied brightly from Adelboden: 'your letter made me feel wildly excited & the flying foxes seemed the last touch that really brought the place home to me. ...

47 Austen to Mary, 4 July 1904, House of Commons, AC4/1/51
48 Joseph to Ethel, 7 Oct.1904, 40 Prince's Gardens, BC6/2/1
49 Ida to Mary, 20 Nov.1904, Highbury, BC4/2/68
50 Neville to Beatrice, 8 Dec.1904, #4, S.S. Palitana, NC1/22/3

What a lot of questions I shall have to ask you when we both return!'[51]

Neville wrote on her letter: 'I received this on the 23rd January 1905 at Patiala. Ethel died on the 15th Jan & the news was telegraphed to me the same day.'

No one expected Ethel's death to come so swiftly. They all recognised that her chances of ultimate recovery were slim. But she was 'full of courage & made so good a fight' that periodically she convinced her family that she might win it.[52] Her doctor saw no cause for immediate alarm, and when Lio proposed to join her for Christmas, advised him strongly against it. Lio spent the holiday at Highbury, where Ethel's sisters looked after little Hilda Mary. Without any sense of urgency, the family decided that Hilda should leave for Switzerland in the New Year to give Ethel quiet company for a few weeks. When Hilda arrived, Ethel's condition was being treated as serious but, as Hilda put it, 'there was no idea of any immediate danger. I went in twice that evening & she seemed just like herself, & not nearly so ill as I have often seen her.' Hilda retired for the night, 'feeling more hopeful'. But 'in the middle of the night I was called up & after that she sank very rapidly on account of her great weakness. ... the end was so peaceful I hardly knew when it came.'[53]

Hilda sent word by telegram to Lio in London and to Mary in Highbury, who relayed it to Neville. Lio dashed to Switzerland, tormented by his absence from his wife's deathbed – until he saw her looking beautifully at peace, a true reflection, Hilda assured him, of the way in which she died. She 'passed away without suffering & without feeling the pang of parting. That was what we all feared so terribly, that she might have felt herself dying & have asked for Lio in vain.'[54] 'Now that I am satisfied,' he wrote, 'that my own darling did not know, did not ask for me, and that the end came swiftly, some of the bitterness is taken away.' He buried her in the churchyard at Adelboden: 'There seemed no spot on earth so pure and beautiful as the place we stood by and while the last words were being said a light snow came gently over her and there was peace and calm intensified.'[55]

For the family at Highbury, the news brought back memories of the death of Florence, to whom Ethel bore so close a resemblance. They responded with an outpouring of letters to each other which faced up to their grief and thus prevented their unmistakeable pain from turning bitter. Mary played the central part in this process. She was free, as the one Florence had never touched, to help the others

---

51  Ethel to Neville, 18 Dec.1904, Adelboden, NC1/24/35
52  Beatrice to Neville, 19 Jan.1905, Highbury, NC1/13/2/120
53  Hilda to Neville, 17 Jan.1905, Adelboden, NC1/15/3/84
54  Ida to Neville, 19 Jan.1905, Highbury, NC1/16/3
55  Lio to someone not named, 20 Jan.1905, 13 Addison Crescent, Kensington, BC6/2/7

deal with what she saw as 'the first break in a family circle which has been one of unusual intimacy & mourning'.[56] All eyes turned to Joseph, whose reaction to the death of Florence had so scarred them. With assistance from Mary, he met this new grief in ways that helped rather than hurt. He gathered the family together to read the burial service while it was being performed in Adelboden. Then, breaking the pattern of the past thirty years, 'he spoke to us a little about her'. Beatrice told Neville, 'He has fought the reserve that makes it so difficult for him to speak of those who are gone. Just now it must mean a breakdown very often, but we have all felt what it was to lose the beloved names from amongst us'.[57] Deeply thankful for the example Joseph thus set, the family resolved to reminisce frequently about Ethel, above all to Hilda Mary to keep her memory of her mother alive.

Hilda 'felt as if all my youth died' with Ethel. Yet her death deepened the bond between Hilda and Neville. Hitherto Hilda had thought that feelings were more womanly than manly. She changed her mind when Neville returned from India. It was springtime and Hilda was at Folkestone looking after Joseph and Mary who had come down with flu: '... all that Spring afternoon we sat on the beach, just Neville & I first telling him of the last days ... & talking my heart out, but what helped me most was the way he shared my loss, telling me how much he felt being away at the time & showing such a deep & understanding sympathy with what I had gone through, that for the first time I felt as if I could pour out all I felt, & the comfort of his presence enabled me to start again.'[58] Neville also felt able to share with Hilda his disappointment over his unhappy love affair. 'I miss you terribly,' he wrote to Hilda when she was away the following Christmas, '... especially in these holiday times when there is time to think and get disgruntled with the world in general.'[59]

No matter how well they dealt with it, the death of Ethel provided a sombre background to the deteriorating political situation. The health of everyone in the family crumbled. Austen fared worst because the political difficulties that oppressed the family stemmed from the impasse between the two men he most admired in public life, his father and Arthur Balfour. Joseph feared that the longer a general election was put off, the worse the fallout would be. He therefore did everything he could, short of all-out opposition, to shorten the life of the government that Balfour wished to prolong. When Balfour finally tendered his resignation at the beginning of December 1905, he did so in hope that divisions among

---

56  Mary to Lio, 16 Jan.1905, Highbury, BC6/2/2
57  Beatrice to Neville, 19 Jan.1905, Highbury, NC1/13/2/120
58  Hilda's Recollections for Dorothy & Frank, BC5/10/6
59  Neville to Hilda, 26 Dec.1905, Highbury, NC1/5/2/29

the Liberal leaders would prevent them from replacing him. His gamble failed. The Liberals formed a government and promptly called the general election Joseph desired. It was set for January, a year since Ethel's death.

❧

Hilda was out of the country when the election was called, on her way to Egypt to rid herself of lumbago which had reduced her to 'an ash-heap'.[60] Egypt worked its magic, though she found the anniversary of Ethel's death 'a sad & trying time'.[61] The rest of the family gathered at Highbury. Beatrice was down with a headache. Austen was in worse shape. Returning from a speaking engagement, he collapsed, 'a total wreck & suffering from the most excruciating sciatica'. He was forced to lie flat on his back, and 'every time he moved a fresh paroxysm came on'. There was considerable doubt over his ability to participate in the election campaign. His only chance was 'to keep absolutely quiet' in the meantime.[62]

Earlier in the autumn Joseph's health had also caused the family 'the gravest anxiety';[63] and Neville had accompanied him and Mary on holiday to recuperate in the south of France. But the cry of electoral battle that sent Austen to bed summoned the old warhorse to the colours. After visiting the party agent in charge of all the Birmingham constituencies, Joseph informed the family that he would make two speeches a day. They were appalled, and Neville intervened to slow him down. He went on his own to the party agent and reduced his father's engagements sharply, 'never ... two nights running or twice the same night except once in his own constituency.' When Joseph insisted on keeping engagements he had made Neville 'had a serious talk with him representing that he owed it to his family to observe some moderation in the strain he put upon himself'. Joseph agreed to a compromise on his own terms, speaking no more than in the last election. 'I cannot go half speed,' he told Neville, 'I must either do my utmost or stop altogether and though I know the risks I prefer to take them.' The risk was a stroke, of which the family lived 'in constant dread ... from this time onward.'

Austen's ability to take part in the campaign remained in doubt until the last moment. Beatrice was drawn in to mobilise support among his female constituents who, though unable to vote, had powers of persuasion over their men-folk. She found

---

60 As Ida told Hilda, 5 Jan.1906, #7, Highbury, BC4/4/30
61 Alice Beale to Ida, 19 Jan.1906, Luxor, BC4/6
62 Ida to Hilda, 16 Dec.1905, #2, Highbury, BC4/4/24
63 Neville to his children, 6 July 1914, Westbourne, NC1/6/11

that she had considerable talent for this work and, to her surprise, quite enjoyed it. Neville took to the platform, speaking first in Birmingham and then farther afield. He began uneasily: 'His matter was very good but he spoke a little too fast & ... his voice [was] rather thin & even slightly nasal.'[64] But he improved. After he spoke to a packed hall in Northampton, 'the whole meeting rose to its feet shouted & cheered'. Austen was the last to join the fray. But once he got through his first speech he felt 'better mentally for finding he could do it'.[65] Always out in front, Joseph campaigned in 'rollicking' style, '& keeps throwing us into states of alarm by the cheerfulness of the reports which he receives from all over the country. From time to time some one utters the horrid thought – "Suppose we were to get in", & a shudder runs through the company' – for Joseph wanted the chastening of defeat to draw the party together in opposition. Ida predicted a Liberal victory with 'a very small majority'.[66]

If only that had been the case! Voting in those days stretched over ten days. Reporting to Hilda, Ida was aghast at the first results, which indicated that the Unionists were 'in for the most complete smash that has been seen for a long time.' They lost eight seats in Manchester and Salford, 'including Mr. Balfour's, who is out by 2,000!! – There is a pleasing catastrophe to begin with!'[67] 'Calamity has overtaken us,' she reported as she waited for the results from Birmingham to come in: 'the Unionist party has been mostly swept from the face of the earth ... the Midlands are being submerged as completely as elsewhere.' What did it mean for the cause Joseph had at heart, for tariff reform and imperial preference? The Chamberlains searched the results for evidence that tariff reform was not to blame: 'the odd thing in so many cases,' Ida observed, 'is how small a factor Tariff Reform seems to be in the fight. Mr. Balfour does not think it had anything to do with his defeat, but on the other hand it does not seem able to save many of the stalwarts. The few, very few people who have slightly increased their majorities have been Tariff Reformers & that is all one can say.' She found little comfort as the voting continued close to home. 'I think I may be sure of Papa's return, but Austen I know I shall feel very nervous about.'[68]

She despaired too soon – and ended her letter to Hilda with an exultant cry: 'Joy! Joy! Hurra! Hurra! Good old Birmingham. It has remained true in the midst of adversity. We have won all seven seats & Papa's majority is 5079!! – an increase of 801 votes on last time! ... B'ham was almost beside itself last night. ... New Street

---

64  Ida to Hilda, 5 Jan.1906, #7, Highbury, BC4/4/30
65  Ida to Hilda, 9 Jan.1906, #8, Highbury, BC4/4/31
66  Ida to Hilda, 31 Dec.1905, #5, Highbury, BC4/2/28
67  Ida to Hilda, 14 Jan.1906, #9, Highbury, BC4/4/32
68  Ida to Hilda, 17 Jan.1906, #10, Highbury, BC4/4/33

was a packed mass of people shouting & yelling. Little groups caught each other's
arms & danced round in circles shouting "Good Old Joe" & cheering like mad,
while continually there came cries of "Are we downhearted?" followed by stento-
rian shouts of "No!!!" ... Papa sent for the port & we drank the health of Birmingham & shook hands & nearly wept in each other's arms with joy & relief. – Now we
don't care what happens. We know we are beaten, badly beaten, but the top of Mt.
Ararat still appears above the waves & though small it is uncommon lofty.' When
Austen's result in East Worcestershire came in, giving him a majority of 4,366, it was
clear that the Unionists in and around Birmingham had run against the national
tide. They retained their monopoly of the parliamentary seats for the city, and by
increased majorities. But Birmingham remained the great exception. Everywhere
else the Unionists went down to a defeat of staggering proportions. Highbury was
inundated by congratulatory letters. But Ida admitted that 'the magnitude of the
correspondence may be taken as a sign of the magnitude of the defeat'.[69]

Austen and Joseph reacted to the outcome in different ways, reflected in their
physical health. As soon as Austen completed his speaking commitments, his sciatica returned and he sank back into a 'deep depression'.[70] But Joe was invigorated by
the campaign. Even before it came to an end, he plunged into discussion of future
policy '& adumbrated future programmes with a vigour like that of a man of thirty'.
As Joe explained to Mary's mother: 'My special interest – that of Tariff Reform &
Imperial preference – , has not suffered I think so much as my opponents would
like to make out.' While admitting that 'its success is postponed indefinitely', he
rose as always to the challenge: 'there is still a big fight before me.'[71] His burst of
energy made his family anxious about the toll it might take, not so much on him as
on Austen. Austen was in no fit state to respond to a bombardment of ideas from
his father which were bound to reactivate the quarrel with Balfour – as they did.
Balfour came to see Joseph, who was staying in Torquay 'out of reach of the people
who want to come in & pour their grievances into his ear'.[72] They talked for four
hours. Mary sat silently. But at Balfour's first words, her 'heart sank. It was evident
that his view of the lessons of the Election & ours was wholly different ... Birmingham left him unimpressed – & having considered the situation he was prepared to
go on as before – minimising so far as possible the differences & concentrating on
the agreements – setting aside fiscal problems, & attacking the Government. And

69  Ida to Hilda, 21 Jan.1906, #11, Highbury, BC4/4/35
70  Quoted by Ida to Hilda, 11 Feb.1906, 40 Princes Gardens, BC4/4/41
71  Joseph to Mrs Endicott, 30 Jan.1906, Highbury, AC1/8/8/30
72  Ida to Hilda, 11 Feb.1906, 40 Princes Gardens, BC4/4/41

that is all! ... I am afraid we must expect a set back such as even the triumph of the Liberals has not given to the Cause.'[73] Austen's health deteriorated further at the news, so much so that his siblings questioned whether a short holiday would be enough to put him back in shape. 'He is becoming a chronic invalid,' said Neville. He felt none of Austen's ambivalence about the stand-off between his father and Balfour. Quite the contrary, Neville found Balfour 'enough to drive one frantic. What a misfortune to have that sort of man in that particular place where even his good qualities do harm because they prevent some people from realising the mischief he works by perpetually putting on the drag.'[74]

At last, with considerable assistance from Austen, Balfour agreed to an exchange of letters with Joseph, issued on February 14, the so-called Valentine compact. Staunch tariff reformers trumpeted the compact as a climb-down by Balfour. Austen knew better: 'the letters do not indeed contain anything which Balfour had not said before, but by bringing together in half a dozen lines what was scattered over ten times that number of columns in the newspapers, they give to his position that clearness & precision which was so terribly lacking in his previous utterances.' Crucially for Austen, now that Balfour and his father stood 'shoulder to shoulder, all will be well'.[75]

Joseph was not so sure. He responded to uncertainty as Austen had done to ambivalence: Joseph's health gave way, and he 'touched the lowest depths' with influenza, biliousness and accompanying depression.[76] The agreement with Balfour would amount to little more than words if Balfour did not stop the men in charge of the Conservative party organisation from resisting the inroads of the tariff reformers. Reluctantly Joseph agreed to accompany Mary for a recuperative holiday on the Riviera, while Austen headed for Algiers. Austen was plagued by sciatica all the way south. When he reached Marseille, he 'was seized with such cramps & pains that I could go no further & had to be wheeled off in an invalid's chair'. He delayed his departure for Algiers until he could walk at least a hundred yards. 'It is provoking to have such a relapse & be absolutely unable to do anything,' he moaned.[77] Mary replied from the Riviera that 'the change of air & scene must do something ... I am feeling much refreshed by the change ... & though he would not admit it, it is good for your Father too.'[78]

---

73  Mary to Neville, 4 Feb.1906, Torquay, NC1/20/2/1
74  Neville to Mary, 10 Feb.1906, Highbury, NC1/20/1/53
75  Austen to Mrs Endicott, 20 Feb.1906, 40 Prince's Gardens, AC1/8/6/39
76  Hilda to Neville, 17 Mar.1906, 40 Prince's Gardens,, NC1/15/3/85
77  Austen to Mary, 5 Apr.1906, Algiers, AC4/1/63
78  Mary to Austen, 8 Apr.1906, Beaulieu-sur-mer, AC1/8/7/3

*Part II*

# THE CHILDREN'S ASCENT

*Ivy and Annie on the eve of marriage*

*4*

# Until Death Do Us Part

The sequel to the springtime searches by father and son for renewed health differed dramatically. By the end of July Joseph lay paralysed while Austen was married. The stroke that Joseph suffered shook everyone in the family. But it did not fundamentally overturn the relationship between father and children. His paralysis stiffened his control over the women in the family, upon whom he was now dependent. His attempt to control the direction of the Unionist party was similarly rigidified, though he relied on Austen to carry out his wishes. Even in these straitened circumstances, his children managed to develop their individual interests and careers – all but Austen. Unlike anyone else in the family in temperament and talent, Austen was pressed into a political mould that did not fit him and in which he did not succeed, to the acute disappointment of his father.

૪

For Austen the outcome of his springtime convalescence could not have been happier. Within two weeks of his arrival in Algiers, he was able to 'walk fairly well & sleep again well without drugs'.[1] That was enough to account for his decision to extend his stay. But the news two weeks later that he was not only 'on the high road to what seems complete recovery'[2], but had taken to dancing, led the family to suspect that more was going on. 'Sweet are the uses of sciatica!' Ida exclaimed when she learned that Austen had fallen in love. Everyone in the family was delighted at

---

1 Austen to Mary, 19 Apr.1906, Hotel St. George, Musapha-Algiers, AC4/2/65
2 Mary to Austen, 1 May 1906, 40 Prince's Gardens, AC1/1/7/6

Austen's engagement, none more so than Mary, whose world had been transformed by marriage. 'Is it not delightful Austen, & is not the whole world a new place? & does not life open out before you in such a light as you have never seen before? And,' she went on in a great tribute to her marriage, 'the best of it is that as the years go on the love which has transformed everything for you will broaden & deepen & strengthen & you will wonder as you look back at the small restricted existence you left behind, which in its time seemed to be something – if incomplete, & marvel at the difference.'[3] Her only concern was that a wife might impinge on the friendship Austen and she had developed since her marriage to Joseph. 'Have you told her how close you & I have been to one another? I am sure you have – & that her love for you will make some place for me in her heart.'[4]

Neville's response to the news was less predictable. 'What a relief,' he exclaimed, 'I feel as if a great load had been lifted off my mind and I had grown years younger!' Austen's descent into disability and depression over the past six months had frustrated Neville's attempts to shake off his own 'glooms' over his disappointed hope of marriage. He was relieved rather than envious of Austen's success, though he still longed for it himself: 'now he has found the one solution which will cure everything.'[5] Austen responded with a testament to the happiness both brothers had seen marriage give their father: 'You know how poor I have always felt that life alone was, even in the closest family circle, compared to what it might be in the fullness of the great love of man & wife ... God bless you, my dear Neville & grant you the same great wealth of love & happiness in your life.'[6]

The way the whole family welcomed Austen's fiancée gratified him deeply. They expressed 'in different words the same great & touching message – the woman you have chosen is sure to be the woman we should wish to welcome to our circle.' 'How few families could feel such perfect confidence one in another!' Ivy Dundas belonged to a family of Church of England clergy and military officers, very different from the Unitarian Chamberlains. She knew 'nothing of politics' and, incredible though it seemed to the Chamberlains, came from 'a world where they were not spoken of, but,' Austen assured them, 'she is very interested & will delight in the largeness of this new life. I tested her interest in the early days, for I deliberately talked politics at her ... all one evening. I was satisfied with what I saw of interest in her face out of the tail of my eye.' He was not deceived. On the way upstairs that

3  Mary to Austen, 7 May 1906, 40 Prince's Gardens, AC1/8/7/7
4  Mary to Austen, 10 May 1906, 40 Prince's Gardens, AC1/8/8/9
5  Neville to Mary, 9 May 1906, Highbury, NC1/20/1/55
6  Austen to Neville, 15 May 1906, NC1/27/1

evening, Ivy told her companion 'half seriously, half in earnest but as yet with no suspicion of what was in my mind ... "Take me away from here. If that man goes on talking like that, I shall fall in love with him."'[7] The other great difference between the families was in wealth. By Chamberlain standards, the Dundases were poor. Austen delayed his return to England in order to buy dresses for Ivy from Mary's Parisian couturier, Worth, and he asked Mary how to manage the purchase of the wedding gown from Worth, 'for I think it is impossible for her people to do it for her.'[8] He found the differences between his world and Ivy's refreshing. She diverted him from the political tensions that depressed him. As Neville sensed, she reached the roots of Austen's malaise.

The fruits of Joseph's holiday were much less substantial, and he handled them badly. Reluctant to recognise that he needed a holiday in the first place, he used the energy it gave him to press ever harder towards his goal of imperial preference. He knew he was pushing himself to the limit. For three days before a big party meeting in March, headache disabled him from preparing his address. Yet he refused to give the meeting up. Neville later recalled how his father succeeded that night, 'by an extraordinary effort of will in delivering his speech. ... it was painfully evident to everyone that he was on the verge of a collapse and every moment I expected to see him fall to the ground.'[9] Joseph sensed with foreboding that imperial preference was unlikely to be secured in his lifetime.

But Moses-like, he could at least outline the goal in unforgettable terms. He was to turn seventy in July, the same month that would mark the thirtieth anniversary of his election as Member of Parliament for Birmingham. He threw himself into the planning for a three-day celebration of the double anniversary. It would begin with festivities at the elementary schools through which he had made his debut in local and national politics. It would move to the Council House to celebrate his transformation of Birmingham into a model of local government for the industrial world. The celebrations would reach their grand finale in the largest hall in the city, where the crowded thousands would pay tribute to their greatest fellow citizen and listen to his climactic address. This schedule set a gruelling pace for a man of seventy, though not much harder than he maintained in general elections.

---

7 Austen to Mary, 14 May 1906, AC4/1/70
8 Austen to Mary, 23 May 1906, Paris, AC4/1/75
9 Neville to his children, 6 July 1914, Westbourne, NC1/6/11

To wave upon wave of applause, he concluded his speech at the close of these celebrations with a string of premonitions, ending with a couplet:

Others I doubt not, if not we,
The issue of our toil shall see.

Keeping up the pace, he took the train to London the next day for a meeting of the commission he had set up to hammer out the details of the tariff reform he desired. Dressing for dinner that evening, he fell to the ground, conscious but paralysed all down his right side.

Mary reacted to Joseph's stroke with a form of denial. She kept the extent of the stroke even from Austen. He reported to Ivy next morning that his father 'had a fairly good night, but he had a slight heart attack early this morning' and 'is better now'. 'He has talked a good deal to Mary. The rest of us have not been allowed to see him.' Austen asked Ivy to continue with the arrangements for their wedding two weeks later, and it went ahead on schedule. Joseph's absence gave the public its first indication that his illness was serious. But even the family did not yet know how serious. Austen remained in happy oblivion on honeymoon until the summer's end. Neville at Highbury remained equally ignorant until he visited their London home toward the middle of August. By the end of the month Mary had to admit to Austen that the recovery was slow. Still she clung to the hope that Joseph would recover, if not all his former forces, at least enough to provide the campaign for tariff reform with the gifts of leadership that he uniquely possessed.

For more than a year the family did their best to keep the news of Joseph's paralysis from the outside world. Sight, speech, ability to write and to walk: all were badly damaged. Recovery, if possible, would be extremely protracted. A return to active participation in public life was unlikely. But rather than allow any sense of this outlook to reach the public, the family adjusted themselves to the demands of Joseph's disability. In October he was moved back to Highbury, while Austen and Ivy fitted out the London house they found for themselves on Egerton Place. Beatrice settled into her educational work in London. The responsibility of tending Joe fell mainly upon Mary, but full-time assistance was required from Ida and Hilda. Austen became surrogate for his father as leader of the tariff reformers in Parliament and the country.

❦

Austen was the one member of the family whose standing was enhanced by his father's illness. His marriage buoyed him up to meet his responsibilities. 'I have now the something that was lacking in my life,' he wrote to Mary, '– the something that in its way is everything, though it seems ungrateful to all of you at home who have done so much for me to say so. But you and Father know the world of difference there is between my present political missions, with Ivy to help and sympathise and encourage, and my old solitary excursions, with nothing but my own fancies to brood on.'[10] Marriage meant even more for Austen than it had for his father, whose ambition had driven him to the heights of political prominence before he found Mary. The joys Austen found in marriage dulled for a little while his appreciation of the terrible difference between his father's situation and his own. But the political tensions that undermined Austen before he met Ivy surfaced again at the opening of Parliament in the New Year. Balfour and those Unionists who regarded party unity as supremely important struggled to avoid commitment to a fiscal policy which a minority in the party regarded as death and damnation. But the general election had left tariff reformers the strongest faction within the shrunken Opposition. Austen's assignment, imposed upon him by his father, was to impose the will of that faction upon the leaders of the party, many of whom he liked and admired, as he did Balfour above all. By nature a congenial man, Austen had to become gang leader. The gang stood behind him, uncertain that he was tough enough for that role. His stricken father waited apprehensively for Austen's 'news from the Front'.[11]

Austen reported to him through Mary. Joe left no doubt about his own reflexes; and since he could no longer hold a pen, Mary conveyed them to Austen. Driving straight to the point which caused Austen most pain, she told Austen that his father 'had an instinctive feeling that the time has come to go on with or <u>without</u> Mr. Balfour. Of course you want to carry him with you, but if this is not possible, & it does not look as if it were, he believes that you will gain by independent action, & it is your surest hope of victory in the end.' A combative organiser, Joseph told Austen that 'success depends on complete support of all [Tariff Reformers] in the House. I have a strong feeling that if you can really organize them you will put such encouragement into them, that you will get the best that every man can do out of him.'[12] Austen did as he was bid. But his heart was not in it. He spoke of the tariff reformers as 'my friends'; but they were often not the men he found most congenial.

---

10 Austen to Mary, 10 December 1906, Hans Crescent Hotel, London, in Austen Chamberlain, *Politics from Inside: An epistolary chronicle, 1906–1914* (London 1936), hereafter *Politics from Inside*, 42

11 Austen to Mary, 20 Feb.1907, House of Commons, in *Politics from Inside*, 53

12 Mary to Austen, 13 Feb.1907, Highbury, AC4/2/1

'All morning I fought with beasts,' he reported, '*very* nice beasts, I confess ... It is not pleasant to sit doggedly saying "My friends will &, what is more, I will do my best to urge them on" when all your colleagues say, "don't!" & paint alarmist pictures of the consequences. Still, it has to be done; & I will say for my colleagues that they recognise my position & tho' they are grieved they are not angry.'[13]

While Austen fought the beasts he so liked in London, Neville took Mary and his sisters with his father to the Riviera. Mary prayed for the Riviera to display its restorative powers. She described Joseph 'sitting in the "Maquis" (the scrub of Pines & heather) with a beautiful view & Hilda is reading to him. The sun brings out the scent of the pines, & the air is full of life & must I think bring him health & strength. Ah me! I hope so – for much as he has gained he still has a long long road to travel, & sometimes I find it difficult to keep up my hope & courage. ... it rends my heart when I stop to think of how hard it is for him.'[14]

The entourage who accompanied Joseph and Mary to the Riviera might have found their assignment similarly disheartening. But Ida and Hilda were made of resilient stuff. Writing to Neville on his birthday a year earlier, Hilda remarked that although birthdays 'become more sad than joyful ... as we get older ... it is wonderful, & satisfactory how much more interesting life gets even if less brilliant.'[15] Still the duty of tending their stricken father could not be but sad work. His removal from active politics cut Ida and Hilda off from the world they enjoyed in London. Their freedom to travel was also curtailed. Neville's heart ached for them. After Joseph died Neville commented that, while Mary 'had behind her 20 years of complete married happiness', Ida and Hilda 'had still their lives to make. Yet they gave up all their leisure, so much so that they never had more than 2 hours to spend together as they liked free of calls upon them, they gave up all opportunities of meeting those who might be friends or something more in the future and they gave up their youth.' The eight years that elapsed between Joseph's stroke and his death made both Ida and Hilda look '20 years older than when he was struck down.'[16] But Neville underestimated their resilience. Hilda inherited 'Papa's capacity for "coming up" quickly' when things looked black.[17] She and Ida seized every opportunity to escape from their duties on the Riviera into the surrounding countryside.

---

13  Austen to Mary, 12 Feb.1907, in *Politics from Inside*, 50, & Austen to Mary, 17 Feb.1907, 9 Egerton Place, AC4/1/139

14  Mary to Austen, 8 Mar.1907, Suveret, AC4/2/5

15  Hilda to Neville, 17 Mar.1906, 40 Prince's Gardens, NC1/15/3/85

16  Neville to his children, 6 July 1914, Westbourne, NC1/6/11

17  Hilda to Neville, late March 1906, 40 Prince's Gardens, NC1/15/3/83

Like Neville, they were keen botanists; and there was nothing Ida enjoyed more than to paint the unfamiliar flowers they came upon.

Nothing stirred Joseph like politics. Providentially, imperial politics were particularly stirring that spring when the premiers of the self-governing colonies arrived in London for the Colonial Conference. The last one, over which Joseph had presided, had fuelled his hopes for an empire-wide network of preferential tariffs. Austen joined the colonial premiers at a great gathering at the Albert Hall. The assembly was permeated with a desire for imperial preference, though the British government under the Liberals would have none of it. The Prime Minister presided over the formal discussions of the premiers. But the man they all had in mind sat far away in the south of France in an invalid chair. Through Bea, Joseph gave Austen detailed instructions on how to censure the government's handling of the conference. Austen did his best to speak for his father at the Albert Hall. Joseph had Hilda read the press report to him, and then dictated to Ida what proved to be his last letter to Austen. 'It is evident that you have during the last twelve months made great advances in platform speaking, both in the matter, which is free from platitude & clear & definite, & in the manner which is free from monotony, & as I am told by Hilda & others who have been present at recent speeches, is excellent in style. There is no one as far as I can see that can hold a candle to you now, in the front rank.'[18] Still Joseph couched his praise in terms that criticised Austen's previous performance and accentuated how far short it was of Joe's erstwhile attainment.

The Colonial Conference made it almost impossible for Austen to hide the seriousness of his father's stroke from those who most admired him; and when Joseph returned to England from the Riviera, Austen and Mary at last permitted his most devoted disciples to see him. The first to come was Frederick Lugard, who had carved out the colony of Nigeria while Joe was Colonial Secretary and was about to leave on his next assignment. 'Mr. C. is my deity,' he told Austen, '& to go away for five years without seeing him seems such a long separation.'[19] Thereafter Mary 'made preliminary arrangements with whole rows of them to come & see' him,[20] whether in London or back on the Riviera when he returned there.

Neville was meanwhile acquiring additional significance for his father, though not yet the place or rank occupied by Austen. The family depended increasingly upon income from Neville's business at Hoskins, now that Austen as well as Joseph lacked a ministerial salary, while the costs of care for Joseph mounted. Joseph was

---

18 Joseph to Austen, 29 Apr.1907, Suveret, AC1/4/5/35
19 Austen to Mary, 13 June 1907, London, AC4/1/199
20 Ida to Austen, 29 Jan.1908, 40 Prince's Gardens, AC1/8/8/1

delighted by Neville's account of how the flood of British emigrants to the colonies filled the family coffers. Hoskins manufactured ships' berths at every price level. 'The emigrant season has now set in with great virulence & we are getting large orders for steerage,' he reported.[21] Neville also assumed increasing political importance as his father's representative among the supporters of tariff reform in Birmingham and as his father's heir in the service of the city. He joined the governing council of the university. But the sphere of civic concern that most interested Neville was health rather than education. He joined the House Committee of the General Hospital and in 1908 became its chairman. He did battle with the doctors over a dispensary scheme he hoped to establish, disregarding a caution from Joseph about the magnitude of the difficulties.

Austen and Ivy spent the second half of the year at Highbury awaiting the birth of their first child. The Chamberlains were all too aware of the dangers of childbirth, and it proved difficult for Ivy. But the birth of a son, promptly named after his grandfather, delighted them. Joseph found in his namesake a joy which he relished for the rest of his life. The grandparents were delighted that the baby remained in their keeping in the New Year when Austen and Ivy returned to London. Ida and Hilda also adored looking after the baby, and they were sorry when they had to leave for the Riviera.

The baby was not the only one Hilda was sorry to leave. The person she most missed was Ethel's 'cherub', now six. After Ethel's death, Hilda became a surrogate mother to her namesake, Hilda Mary. She treated the cherub as the child she always wanted. Neville had been afraid that Hilda would marry someone unsuitable simply in order to have a child. But when that prospect came to naught, things took another unhappy turn. Lio grew uneasy about the intensity of the bonds Hilda formed with his daughter, and when he found another woman to be his wife and hence stepmother to Hilda Mary, he tried to sever her connection with Hilda. Hilda was terribly hurt. Neville reached out to her by letter. 'It is always a pleasure to receive your letters because they are so personal,' he wrote. 'I mean they aren't merely a diary of your doings ... but contain comments on various members of the family which I find most interesting. The one only you leave out is yourself.' He directed his sharpest comment at his father. Joseph had been dictating short letters, soon published in the press, to tariff reformers, encouraging them to believe that he might return to active political life. 'Does he really believe that,' Neville asked, 'or is it only part of the old game of keeping up appearances?'[22]

His letter released a flow of reflections from Hilda: 'I admit I have had some

---

21 Neville to Mary, 21 Apr.1907, Highbury, #10, NC1/20/1/60
22 Neville to Hilda, 27 Apr.1908, Highbury, NC1/15/2/30

black moments. I have always been one of those people who, sort of unconsciously, live with the idea of a delightful future, to which one looks forward, when you will have all you care most about, but as time goes on, it is harder & harder to do so, for you can not see anything cheerful in the future to plan for, & yet I can not make up my mind to dwell contentedly in the present without looking forward. I suppose in time harmony will come of confusion'. She continued: 'the fact is Hilda Mary has of late been growing more & more to seem like my own child, & consequently it gets worse every day as she grows older to bear the long separations. ... I want her daily & hourly, & I can't bear the thought of her being in any one else's hands.' Turning to Neville's comment on their father, Hilda suggested that he wrote as he did 'in order to keep his own spirits up. ... he is generally pretty low, though with that indomitable optimism (which happily he has transferred in some measure to several of us) he sometimes almost persuades himself that he is going to get well.'

Then Hilda literally opened a window in her exile onto the countryside of the Riviera. 'It is pure joy,' she wrote, 'to open the window & put your head out in the morning into that clear air & drink up the sweet scents from the flowers. Insects hum along the walls, frogs croak, butterflies flutter & birds sing from all the bushes, & before one thinks, one's heart sings too, for the glory & beauty of the world. That, at least, is one of the best gifts to man, the appreciation of the outside world, (& we both possess it) because you can carry it with you all your life.' Turning finally to the plans for civic improvement that Neville was introducing, she concluded: 'It is so nice to see B'ham once more leading the way in schemes of reform, & a Chamberlain there to do it in a practical way.'[23]

Little wonder that Neville was magnetised by his correspondence with Hilda for the rest of his life. 'I would sooner have one letter like that,' he replied, '... than fifty ordinary ones, and it does seem too stupid that you and I should ... say so little of the things that really matter when we think so much alike and can ... help each other by talking of them. Of course I have been aware how much you have been troubled over Hilda Mary ... I don't see the way out. Of course the natural & proper way out is for you to have a home of your own and it does seem hard that neither you or I who want that so much have been able to find it yet. Fortunately we have one another and that is a great deal but my greatest would be to see you happily married & I guess you feel the same about me.'[24] The bond between Neville and his younger sister was consolidated during these 'hard years'. 'It seems rather a mockery to wish you many happy returns of the day,' Hilda wrote on his birthday,

---

23 Hilda to Neville, 1 May 1908, Villa Victoria, Cannes, NC1/15/3/93
24 Neville to Hilda, 4 May 1908, Highbury, NC1/15/2/31

'when you are entering on your fortieth year'. But she remained a woman of irre-pressible hopes. 'You have got a fine position in the town by the work ... which you have put into it, & it is a wonderful tribute to the way in which character & ability tell. Besides, in spite of your forty years, you impress everyone with your promise, as well as your performance.' Looking back and prophetically forward, she contin-ued: 'You will be like Papa in that, you will go on growing & developing every year, instead of standing still or sinking back into the ruck of the middle aged as so many men do. You are the prop of the family financially, but you are a great deal more than that to all of us, & you are life & spirit itself to me.'[25]

❧

Only to Hilda was Neville 'life & spirit itself' these days. Austen was rising well to the challenges of political leadership. He remedied weaknesses in his father's record, devising, for example, a way to apply tariff reform to India, the star in the imperial crown which Joseph had always, inexplicably, neglected. Austen also deepened his understanding of the relationships among the great European powers which Joseph had handled clumsily. Unionists were recovering from the electoral disaster of 1906. Though Austen still had to fight in the highest councils of the party to keep tariff reform at the forefront of its demands, he succeeded these days more often than he failed. The Liberal government, meanwhile, lost its momen-tum and sense of direction. Austen, rarely an optimist, scented victory at the next general election. His prominence in parliamentary debate and improvement as a public speaker enhanced his standing as spokesman for tariff reform. When he did well, however, staunch tariff reformers praised him for speaking 'more like your father than like you'[26] – and he took it as a compliment.

The pace quickened, but the outlook for the Unionists turned cloudy in the spring of 1909 when the Chancellor of the Exchequer and bête noire of the Cham-berlains, Lloyd George, introduced his budget. In order to meet the demand for more battleships as well as the cost of old age pensions and further social reform, Lloyd George introduced a range of proposals to tax the rich, including a super-tax, higher death duties, and taxes on wealth derived from land. Austen recog-nised the electoral appeal of these proposals. Lloyd George presented his budget in a lacklustre speech which suggested that he did not entirely understand what he proposed. But his budget offered an attractive alternative to tariff reform as a

---

25  Hilda to Neville, 16 Mar.1909, Villa Beatrice, Cannes, NC1/15/3/101
26  Leverton quoted by Austen to Mary, 21 Mar.1909, *Politics from Inside*, 163

way to pay for the desired services at home and abroad. He thus took some of the wind out of the sails of tariff reform and restored a sense of direction to the Liberal government. The great question was: budget or tariff reform?

That was how the Chamberlains hoped to present it, but the issue soon took on a still more disturbing shape. The battle between budget and tariff raised constitutional questions that propelled the entire Unionist party, tariff reformers and free traders alike, into extremist rhetoric. Though Joseph and Austen sensed the danger, they were caught up in the riptide the controversy generated. Lloyd George's proposals so infuriated the Unionists that they turned to the citadel they controlled, the House of Lords, trusting the Lords to reject the budget. But to do so would violate the age-old convention that money bills were the business of the Commons. The Unionist appeal to the upper house enabled Lloyd George to turn the question of budget or tariff into a more emotive cry: the peers versus the people.

Joe returned from the Riviera to be close to Austen. Though Mary ensconced him in Highbury, Joseph was elevated in the public eye by another tariff-reforming celebration of his birthday, this time in London, while a thousand letters and telegrams rained down upon him in Birmingham. Mary wondered 'if any other Statesman has ever had such a demonstration once in his active life, & repeated after 3 years of retirement.'[27] Austen meanwhile led the parliamentary opposition to the budget through six months of clause-by-clause debate until it left the Commons for the Lords. In November, when the House of Lords threw the budget out, the government called a general election for January. Joseph threw his remaining strength into the campaign. Though unable to speak in public, he dictated statements for his daughters to dispatch. He stood for re-election in West Birmingham, and peppered the national and regional press with letters applying the principles of tariff reform to the particular circumstances of every constituency where tariff-reforming Unionists stood for election. Liberals feared the effect of these letters enough to spread the rumour that they could not possibly be the work of the old invalid. They helped the Unionists to slash the Liberal majority of 1906, bringing the two major parties to a virtual tie. But victory still eluded the Unionists. The support that the Liberals received in the new House of Commons from the fledgling Labour party and Irish Home Rulers prevented a change of government.

This composite majority in the Commons was inevitably fractious. It kept the Liberal government and the Unionist opposition on tenterhooks while the agenda oscillated between the budget and the future of the House of Lords. The fluctuating outlook in the Commons riveted Austen to his seat there. But Joseph fell into

---

27  Mary to Austen, 13 July 1909, Highbury, AC4/2/58

depression. His hopes of electoral victory had been dashed, and he saw little likelihood of improvement. He left for the Riviera, detached from a state of affairs now 'so complicated & change[able]' that he could offer only the most general counsel on how to respond. When he gave advice, it was turned down, as Austen scarcely needed to explain: 'The situation changes from day to day and from moment to moment.'[28] Exhausted and discouraged, Joseph's health gave way. His speech deteriorated 'so much that it is a great trouble to him & does make it difficult for our visitors.'[29] Hilda reported after a month that his 'speech is better again, & can be quite good when he takes the trouble. Alas the chief difficulty is that he won't try ... last year he was pleased & anxious to discuss the political situation with anyone, whilst now he is decidedly down & ... does not wish to talk politics. He is tremendously interested in all Austen's letters, but gloomy at the outlook.'[30]

Mary refused to accept the change in Joe's mood. She was shocked when 'he threw out the suggestion that he didn't think he should stand again' for Parliament when the next general election took place. She laughed the idea off and 'did not pursue the subject'. But knowing that 'it may arise at any moment', she asked Austen to write 'him a letter, for me to keep & use only if required, putting the political considerations before him, & the claim they have on his co-operation.' It was not so much these political considerations, however, as Joseph's personal need that concerned her: 'I feel that the best thing for him is to keep him in touch with what has been the mainspring of his life. Remove this link & I think the consequences would be very serious ... there would be danger of his relapsing into a hopeless invalid with all incentive gone.'[31] Austen agreed.

Three weeks later Mary received a second shock with which Austen was less able to help her. Neville, tending the family finances, had 'finished Father's accounts' and was alarmed at what he saw. He asked for leave to make some immediate changes in his father's investments, abandoning consideration of their financial position generally until he could talk it over with Mary. 'It is not,' he explained, 'the expenses which have gone up so much as the income which has gone down ... I don't think any very heroic measures are necessary yet'. Less reassuringly he added, 'it is all a question of how long we can go on on our present scale.'[32]

28 Mary to Austen, 25 Mar.1910, Villa Victoria, Cannes, AC4/2/72; Austen to Mary, 26 Feb.1910, in *Politics from Inside*, 207

29 Mary to Austen, 8 Mar.1910, Villa Victoria, AC4/2/66

30 Hilda to Neville, 8 Apr.1910, Villa Victoria, NC1/15/3/111

31 Mary to Austen, 23 Mar.1910, Villa Victoria, AC4/2/71

32 Neville to Mary, 17 & 23 Apr.1910, Highbury, NC1/20/1/72–3

Mary responded with a torrent of anxiety. She had no experience of financial limitations and did not know how to deal with them. The disaster on Andros had left Joseph financially anxious, and he told Mary repeatedly of his concern. Whatever Neville said, Mary knew that 'our expenses ... have increased in some directions, thus counterbalancing any advantage we might have gained from the quiet life we have led.' But her overriding concern was to keep Joe close to his political world and friends. 'I feel sure,' she told Neville, 'that if we could not have given him all the things which contribute to this ... he would not be where he is. Unfortunately the general scale on which we live – the power of entertaining family & friends – Highbury ... & last but not least Cannes & the proper situation etc. etc. of our villa, are the things which ... [have] eased the great trouble which has come upon us.' She had no idea how to economise, short 'of altering the whole style of living & curtailing in every direction'; and to 'do this ... would be the beginning of the end.'[33] She turned to Austen for understanding. They shared a taste for beautiful objects, the cost of which shocked Neville. Nothing delighted Austen and Ivy more than to walk 'about the drawing-room admiring all our things – our cabinets, our china, our pictures'.[34] Neville was disturbed to learn that Austen and Ivy had been buying 'more china. ... I also heard ... that he paid too much for it.'[35] Mary meanwhile told Austen that she had 'invested in a new Cabinet – Chippendale period ... It just fits into the corner of the breakfast room.'[36]

Joseph and Mary were not the only members of the family to be depressed by the January general election. Beatrice fully shared her father's dream of the greatness and prosperity that imperial preference could bring to Britain and its Empire; and hence she shared his dismay at the unwillingness of the electorate to seize that promise. She had done her best during the election to mobilise support for the cause among the women of East Worcestershire, Austen's constituency. But afterwards, worn out and dismayed at the results nationally, her never sturdy physical health crumbled; she required minor surgery and succumbed to disabling headaches. So her family encouraged her to head away for a prolonged holiday with the friends she had made on the other side of the Atlantic. Hilda begged her, 'Immerse yourself ... in American politics & be refreshed inside & out by a new atmosphere, where you can forget our stupid old woes, & odious politics & knavish tricks, &,' she added, mimicking Chamberlain rhetoric, 'may you return to find us

33  Mary to Neville, 20 Apr.1910, Villa Victoria, NC1/20/2/3
34  Austen to Mary, 21 Apr.1910, in *Politics from Inside*, 260
35  Neville to Mary, 13 Mar.1910, Highbury, NC1/20/1/71
36  Mary to Austen, 20 Aug.1910, Highbury, AC4/2/87

flourishing under the mild & beneficent rule of a Unionist government, whilst the magic words Tariff Reform bring work to the workless!!'[37]

Bea was soon caught up in American politics at the highest level. At first she found 'American politics vastly more confusing, considered from close at hand, than they were afar off.' The Republican party, with whose domestic and expanding imperial ambitions she sympathised, was divided between the radical inclinations of her friend the immediate past President, Theodore Roosevelt, and the conservative incumbent, President Howard Taft, whom she now found more attractive. 'I am rapidly coming to the conclusion,' she told her family, 'that Roosevelt was 'doing more harm than good in these days.'[38] After turning down a couple of invitations to meet Taft, she was placed beside him at a dinner in New Hampshire. He struck her as 'very pleasant, unaffected straightforward & attractive', regardless of his enormous weight. 'He eats very little,' she observed, 'but that doesn't seem to save him.' Taft talked to her 'interestingly of Cuba'. Turning to domestic politics, he spoke 'very freely on various points, defending Mr. Roosevelt from adverse criticism'. Like Austen, Taft lacked the killer instinct in politics. He would much rather have distinguished himself in the judiciary. 'Is it not hard,' he said, 'that it should fall to me to appoint another man to the office that I have longed for all my life? i.e. Chief Justice of the United States.'[39]

Back in Britain, the stalemate created by the general election was further complicated by the death of King Edward VII. The new king, George V, asked the leaders of the two major parties to see if they could work out some compromise to provide the country with stable government. In view of his inexperience, the party leaders could not in honour turn the request down. Austen nonetheless feared that in conference he would be pressed to give up some vital principle and be 'damned irretrievably'. Joseph took 'a more cheerful view'. If the inter-party conference succeeded, 'all will be well – if not there may be a bad time to go through, but,' Mary assured Austen, 'he does not think you need fear utter annihilation'. Joe was relieved that Austen would be among the conferees 'to hold the flag aloft. He fears always that Mr. B. [Balfour] may ... yield what need not be yielded.' The conference lifted Joseph's spirits, renewing some of the radical interests that led him originally into politics, and his health improved. Back in England after the death of Edward VII, he kept regular contact with Austen for the rest of the year. The conference nevertheless put a strain on the family. The leaders of the two parties insisted on a high level of secrecy in their discussions. Austen was not permitted to keep his

---

37  Hilda to Beatrice, 29 Sept.1910, Ardtornish, Morven, Argyll, BC3/3/8
38  Beatrice to Hilda, #3, 12 Oct.1910, BC3/2/2
39  Beatrice to Ida, 17 Oct.1910, #4, Walpole, New Hampshire, BC3/2/4

father fully abreast of what went on; nor was he himself fully informed of the most secret talks between Balfour and the Prime Minister, Herbert Asquith. The conference dragged on into the autumn, forcing Austen to travel daily from Highbury to London to take part in its proceedings. Eventually disenchanted with the conference, Joseph grew 'anxious it should be broken off'.[40]

Hitherto little involved in public life, Ida opened a new chapter for herself and the life of the family that autumn when she accepted an invitation from Neville to assist at the General Hospital in Birmingham. Like Neville, ill at ease outside the family, Ida shied away from face-to-face service of people in need such as Bea and Hilda enjoyed at their schools. But again like Neville, Ida was a natural administrator, good with statistics and adept at the solution of practical problems. Neville and his sisters remained rooted in the social economy of Birmingham, the world that gave rise to their father's political vision, unlike Austen and Bea whose efforts were concentrated in London. Neville made his home in Birmingham for the rest of his life. And though his sisters eventually made their homes elsewhere, they carried with them the concerns that they developed in the city of their birth.

Neville asked Ida for help in establishing an almoner service at the hospital. She questioned her ability to handle the assignment. 'I feel deeply oppressed by my ignorance, & only hope ... that it will keep me from talking when I had better be silent.'[41] But she made her mark immediately. At her first meeting with the responsible committee, she resisted the attempt of the chairman to appoint an undistinguished applicant – one of whom Neville had approved. Thereupon the rest of the committee authorised her to interview other candidates. 'At any rate I am glad to know that they are prepared to look favourably on my proceedings & not to regard me as a useless piece of intrusive pretence,' she told Beatrice with satisfaction. 'You will also perceive ... that I find the work interesting.'[42] She foresaw one problem, which all Joseph's daughters had to surmount. The need to accompany his annual migration to London at the beginning of the parliamentary season and then to the Riviera interrupted their social service. It had taken Bea years to gain permission to stay in London when her educational responsibilities required her presence there. Ida struggled to stay in Birmingham until Joseph and his entourage left for the Riviera. But by then she had proved herself 'peculiarly capable as an organizer. That is clearly the work she is born to, & not for visiting or case work.'[43]

---

40  Hilda to Beatrice, 15 Oct.1910, & Ida to Beatrice, 25 Oct.1910, Highbury, BC3/3/13 & 16

41  Ida to Beatrice, 3 Oct.1910, Highbury, BC3/3/10

42  Ida to Beatrice, 18 Oct.1910, Highbury, BC3/3/14

43  Hilda to Beatrice, 30 Dec.1910, Highbury, BC3/3/34

❧

Late one November night Ida was in the midst of a letter to Bea when she broke off: 'The deed is done! – a telegram from Neville says "All fixed up this afternoon" & I can drop this foolish silence & come at once to the only real matter of importance in the world at present.' Though cryptic, Neville's message gave the family the news they were waiting for: his engagement to marry Anne Cole, Annie as she was known. Neville's failure to win the hand of Rosalind Craig Sellar had etched hard lines in his face, already hardened by Andros. He unburdened himself these days only to Hilda. 'I suppose,' he wrote at her birthday, 'in most families as time goes on brothers & sisters get less dependent on each other for their happiness. With ours I think it is just the reverse and that is the compensation for other wants. You especially have made yourself the principal source of my enjoyment of life and I think you know that I am grateful for it.'[44]

Yet even from Hilda he tried to hide his new courtship. Everyone in the family was aware of it. They had in fact done their best to bring it about. And Neville dimly knew it. At Mary's prompting, Beatrice had introduced him to Annie. Neville and Annie thereupon contrived to be at the house party of his aunt Lilian Cole whom Annie also called Aunt Lilian. Five months elapsed before Hilda could report impatiently that Neville was again 'away with the Coles ... He said he had a pleasant time, & we learnt that <u>she</u> was there, but nothing else. ... we have done our best, & perhaps ... "something will come of this!"'[45] That something came within ten days. Acting at last with speed, Neville swept Annie's hesitations away. The first word to reach Highbury came in a telegram: 'Send frock coat two shirts ... to Euston Hotel by first passenger train. Anxious time but hope for decision tonight.'[46]

His sisters responded to the news with delight mixed with dismay at their impending loss. Highbury had been a sombre home since Joseph's stroke, deserted for nearly half the year with the furniture under dust covers while he convalesced in France (Neville was then its only occupant). His uncles criticised Joseph for leaving Neville alone to maintain the home and family finances in good order. When Joseph and his entourage returned to Birmingham, they looked to Neville to brighten their days with accounts of his work and the city. It will, Mary confessed, 'be a wrench to let him go'.[47] 'How are we to come home to a Highbury

---

44  Neville to Hilda, 15 May 1910, West Woodhay House, Newbury, Berks., NC1/15/2/33
45  Hilda to Beatrice, 28 Oct.1910, Highbury, BC3/3/17
46  Ida to Beatrice, 8 Nov.1910, Highbury, BC3/3/19
47  Mary to Beatrice, 11 Nov.1910, Highbury, BC3/4/1

with no Neville in it?' Beatrice cried.[48] Ida and Hilda refused to 'be dismal over the future, when we have been longing for years to have this happen'; and they reached out to Annie warmly. But Hilda could not disguise her anxiety. 'He has been all to me that a brother could possibly be,' she told Annie, '& during these last years the tie has grown so close, that there could be only one closer.'[49] Even little Hilda Mary, Ethel's cherub, was 'shocked at the news' of the engagement, afraid that 'once married Uncle Neville will cease to be funny!'

Though they had contrived to bring Neville and Annie together, the family took longer to embrace her than they had Ivy. Ivy had become part of the family during the birth of little Joseph, and she returned to Highbury during the political stalemate after the death of the king. Upon learning of Neville's engagement, Joseph hurried 'to inform Ivy... that though no doubt we should assimilate Annie into the family as was our way, yet never, never under any circumstances could she take the place Ivy had taken'. Hilda added, 'we all feel the same... it seems impossible any one else should suit us each & all quite so well'. Ivy and Annie both came from military families. Both at marriage were in their twenties, Ivy a slightly younger wife to Austen than Annie to Neville. Yet Annie came across as much younger, attractively so to Neville who found Annie 'the most piquant mixture of child and woman'.[50] Hilda was disconcerted by Annie's seeming youth, even immaturity; and Annie spoke of Neville's sisters as 'the aunts'. Neville was aware of her many differences from the Chamberlains. He told Beatrice that even Annie's relatives considered her 'to be erratic & undecided... but,' he added, 'that is because they don't understand her. She doesn't change her mind at all about big things; about the little things she does but not more than all of us only she always says what is in her mind whereas most of us are more cautious & don't let on what we think till we have reached a final conclusion. But though she is the most outspoken person I know she never says anything that hurts anyone because she is naturally so sympathetic that she has the best sort of tact.'

There was something charismatic about Annie, a quality no one else in the family possessed except old Joe. His charisma was electrifying and divisive; Annie's charisma drew other people out. Neville loved that talent because he lacked it himself: 'she is a very responsive person and can always take interest in other people's interests which makes her easy to get on with among shy people like ourselves.'[51] She was quite unlike Neville in other ways. Happy sunbathing, Annie

---

48  Beatrice to Ida & Hilda, 'Private', 10 Nov.1910, New Haven, BC3/2/11
49  Hilda to Annie, 9 Nov.1910, Highbury, NC1/21/17
50  Neville to Mary, 14 Jan.1911, Tunis, NC1/20/1/76
51  Neville to Beatrice, 12 Dec.1910, Highbury, BC2/2/17

recoiled from the strenuous Highland sports Neville loved. And after a recital of music by Bach, Schumann, Mozart, Chopin and Neville's favourite Beethoven, he learned that Annie 'liked the Beethoven but was under the impression she was listening to Mozart!'[52]

Neville and Annie wanted to marry as soon as possible, and settled on the beginning of January. The pace of events within the family was also accelerated politically. Ten days after Neville announced his engagement, the conference among the leaders of the Liberal and Unionist parties broke up without agreement: Parliament was dissolved, and another general election called for December. Apart from the absent Beatrice, the Chamberlains dutifully threw themselves into the campaign. Neville took time to deliver six speeches around Birmingham. Austen, freed from a contest in his own constituency, campaigned around the country. Joseph responded to 'shoals of letters & telegrams'.[53] But their hopes were tempered by the attraction many Unionists felt for the idea of a referendum on the least-liked feature of tariff reform, a tariff on foodstuffs, essential though it was to imperial preference. Austen's hopes for the election were dashed on its eve when Balfour committed the party to such a referendum in the event of a Unionist victory. Though Austen protested as strongly as he could, Balfour's pledge renewed the tension between Austen and his father over Balfour's leadership. As Ida explained to Bea, 'Papa is furious & as he has no Balfourite present to smash he vents some of his indignation on Austen, – that is to say he is inclined to argue that A. should give no further assistance to Mr. B. Of course this is not really a feasible line & Papa knows it. If Austen were to chuck it now he would only break up the party & do no mortal good to the cause.'[54]

Though the first results gave Annie 'the most exciting day of her life',[55] the outcome of the general election did not cheer up anyone in the family. Many seats changed hands, but the position of parties in the new Parliament remained virtually unchanged. Balfour's referendum pledge made no apparent difference, though Joe continued to grumble about the spineless folly of it. 'I won't speak of the elections,' Bea wrote home; 'They don't bear talking about. I feel it bitterly for Papa & Austen, & though I will not despair of my country, while it's possible to hope, I do not feel that "it stands where it did."'[56]

52  Neville to Hilda, 37 Eaton Square, in Robert Self, ed., *The Neville Chamberlain Diary Letters*, IV, 164

53  Ida to Beatrice, 26 Nov.1910, 40 Prince's Gardens, BC3/3/25

54  Ida to Beatrice, 6 Dec.1910, Highbury, BC3/3/27

55  Hilda to Beatrice, 1 Dec.1910, Highbury,BC3/3/26

56  Beatrice to Hilda, #19, 8 Dec.1910, Vassar College, BC3/2/19

Neville and Annie's wedding did not raise the family's spirits. The day itself was 'about as unattractive as they make 'em in London in early January rain at intervals, raw, cold & damp, but at any rate there was no fog'.[57] The couple hurried away, travelling via Paris and Marseilles to Tunisia and Algeria. Their honeymoon further complicated the relationship between Neville's bride and his sisters. He could not conceive of separation from them without keeping in touch by letter; and that was something for which Annie had no inclination. 'She is a very bad correspondent,' he told Beatrice; and he proposed to show Annie the way by undertaking 'that her mother shall have a letter every week whilst we are on our honeymoon.' In any case he was determined to write often to his sisters. 'It seems very difficult to find time to write letters on one's honeymoon,' he explained apologetically; but he 'got a short note off to Ida' from Marseilles. Sailing across the Mediterranean that night, 'now that Annie has gone to bed,' he 'seize[d] the opportunity to begin one' to Hilda, blissfully unaware that Annie might resent this behaviour. Hilda was never far from his thoughts: 'Sometimes I feel a little guilty at being so happy when I know that my absence will not make things easier for you, and of course my marriage is bound to make more of a gap in your life and Ida's than Austen's did because we have been so much more together especially these last few years.'[58]

He sustained the flow of letters with his sisters throughout the honeymoon. Hoping to involve Annie in the exchange, he showed her the letters he received from Ida and Hilda. Annie did not welcome the contrast with her own attempts: 'the more she reads your and Hilda's letters the more she sees why I thought her letters short and lacking in details, but she declares that she will never be able to satisfy me if I am going to demand that she shall write as you do.'[59] He gave up. Once back in Birmingham, Annie's talent for drawing people out worked its magic on the family, not least on his sisters. Eventually they drew closer to Annie than to Ivy. Annie remained, however, jealous of the special bonds that the letters forged between Neville and his sisters.

Joseph's health deteriorated after the wedding and the two general elections within one year. He became more dependent on his children for his interest in life, and more irritable with Mary and his carers. He grew more demanding of Austen's presence on the Riviera, and asked every day for letters from Bea. As the time for his return to England approached, concern about his ability to travel grew acute. Mary sent painstaking instructions to Beatrice: 'you can expect us ... at Charing

57  Hilda to Beatrice, 5 Jan.1911, 40 Prince's Gardens, BC3/3/37
58  Neville to Hilda, 9 Jan.1911, S.S. Carthage, NC1/15/2/34
59  Neville to Ida, 3 Feb.1911, Mustapha-Algiers, NC1/16/2/39

Cross at 5.12 please, with ... the steps for the train ... In addition to the orders I gave you about your Father's bed – please to have a hot water bottle warming the foot of it.'[60] Neville, who was to meet the returning party in France and accompany them across the Channel, was alarmed by a warning from Hilda: 'I can see that she thinks the end has come perceptibly nearer ... Thinking it over quietly I cannot really wish that Father's life should be prolonged for his own sake; he has so little to live for.' What Neville feared was the 'very heavy blow' that his father's death would deal to Mary and, surprisingly, to his sisters. 'I don't know what will become of them all.' He looked to Annie for help in meeting their needs: 'by taking them into our life as it were we can do more for them than in any other way'.[61] However much he loved them, it never occurred to him that his unmarried sisters might make a good life for themselves.

But no sooner had Ida returned to Highbury than, now chairman of the Almoners' committee, she held her own against Neville as chairman of the General Hospital about the training of almoners. A fairly new profession envisioned for women, almoners were not yet well established in Birmingham. They were caught between the social needs of the patients they wished to serve and the medical claims of the doctors with whom Neville sympathised. Ida had secured the appointment of an able woman to establish the service at the General Hospital. She wanted to give the woman at least three, but preferably six months training at the hospital with the most experience in this field, St Thomas's in London. Doctors questioned the need, but after a struggle Ida won the six months she desired. In doing so, she foreshadowed the work she would do for public health elsewhere after her father's death; and Neville, by then Minister of Health, would be grateful for her advice.

All of Neville's perceptions at the moment were coloured by the happiness he found in his marriage. He crowned that happiness with the springtime announcement that Annie was expecting. Neville wished for a boy, the first of 'the troop' of children he hoped would fill the nursery. Annie had mixed feelings about her pregnancy, for it cut short the social life that she enjoyed as wife of the rising star in the civic life of Birmingham. She found 'politics great fun', Neville reported, 'and can't have too much of them. ... she fully shares my desire to be hospitable & is continually having people to tea pending more substantial meals to be provided when we have a cook.'[62] Neville had difficulty holding her back when they discovered that she was

---

60  Mary to Beatrice, 10 May 1911, Villa Victoria, BC3/4/8
61  Neville to Annie, 15 May 1911, Westbourne, NC1/26/7
62  Neville to Mary, 26 Mar.1911, 19 Highfield Road, Edgbaston, NC1/20/1/78

pregnant: 'she keeps forgetting to be careful although she knows how important it is.'[63]

When Bea returned from New England, she found Neville 'enjoying the discovery of his own unsuspected popularity in B'ham ... & Annie finds the welcome she gets everywhere very pleasant'. She was also 'wisely refraining from all criticism & only saying the pleasant things she feels about the place'.[64] Like many newcomers to the city, Annie was not initially taken with Birmingham; and she hoped that Neville would enter a broader arena. An opportunity soon arose with the death of the Unionist Member of Parliament for South Birmingham. Neville seemed the obvious replacement; and Annie was thrown into 'a great state of excitement at seeing [his] name in all the papers'.[65] But he rejected the overture, preferring to make his mark on the City Council as Birmingham was enlarged to embrace its suburbs. Keeping lesser local worthies at bay, he secured the nomination in South Birmingham for Leo Amery, a national luminary in the tariff reforming movement who, decades later, would play Brutus to Neville's Caesar.

Joseph endorsed his son's decision. Hilda explained the family's thinking to Annie, beginning with financial considerations. Neville could not 'be spared from his business when he has just become a married man & is to undertake the responsibilities of a family!' Turning to political concerns and the impending enlargement of Birmingham, she described Neville's particular orientation. The Unionists were not, she argued, ready to be lifted out of their current difficulties 'by a Radical (such as Neville really is.) There are quite too many of the old conservatives, making up the mass of the party, to follow an advanced leader, & they don't want to be saved by bold measures ... At the present time I believe there is real & important work to be done for B'ham & Greater B'ham, & that he will help them to put things on the right lines.'[66] Like Ida, Hilda fully sympathised with Neville's priorities.

❦

Austen, however, was held in the national arena more relentlessly than he liked. He too was tired after two general elections and the intervening manoeuvres. He was also depressed by Balfour's weakening of the Unionist commitment to a tariff

63  With Annie to Hilda, 21 Apr.1911, NC1/15/2/43
64  Beatrice to Ida, 4 Apr.1911, BC3/2/47
65  Neville to Beatrice, 19 Apr.1911, 19 Highfield Road, BC2/2/21, & Annie to Hilda, 21 Apr.1911, NC1/15/2/43
66  Hilda to Annie, 27 Apr.1911, Villa Victoria, NC1/15/4/17

on foodstuffs. Depression left him prone to illness. 'Every day I seem to get some new little warning ... a most irritating rash all over my body being the last symptom ... But my real illness is known only to Ivy and myself,' he told Mary for Joseph's benefit: 'Balfour's Albert Hall speech knocked the heart out of me ... the bottom has fallen out of the world ... and the stimulus to work and fight has gone.'[67]

No matter how hard he tried, Austen could not ease the discomfort he suffered from his father's uncompromising rigidity on tariff reform. The tensions between them were renewed in 1911 when Canada and the United States reached a Reciprocity Agreement, an early form of North American free trade. The Liberals in Britain were 'jubilant over the whole affair', which they saw as 'the death once more of Tariff Reform & Preference'. Austen trod a fine line in opposing the Agreement, for he had to appeal to imperial sentiment without offending Canadian national feeling. He did so skilfully, arguing 'that even apart from Imperial considerations, Canada as an independent <u>nation</u> runs much risk of being controlled by the huge corporations & capitalists of the U.S., if there should once be free trade in natural products'.[68] But his attempt to adapt the case for tariff reform to changing circumstances reignited his differences with his father. 'Papa says we should change nothing & go on just as before,' Hilda reported, criticising her father: '...He says "do nothing" because he cannot himself originate a new policy, & feels ... that his own old policy must be best.' Hilda's sympathy gave Austen only cold comfort, because his assigned purpose in politics, as he saw it, was to make his father's dream come true. Dressing himself to look like the mirror image of his father, Austen saw himself as Joseph's creation. 'He has *made* me in every sense of the word,' Austen told Mary, 'and, if I accomplish anything in my career, it will be due to his teaching and his example.'[69]

A change in the subject of debate drew the old man and his elder son back together. The Liberals introduced a so-called Parliament bill to curb the powers of the House of Lords. Austen took little part in the debate on the bill in the Commons, partly because of the government's insistent closure of debate there, but also because the crucial debate from his point of view would take place in the House of Lords with its huge Unionist majority. He had begun to appreciate that the Lords had made a mistake in rejecting Lloyd George's budget. But that was no reason, as Austen saw it, for the House of Lords to accept a bill that would severely curb all its powers. He was infuriated when the Prime Minister wrested a promise

---

67  Austen to Mary, 23 Mar.1911, in *Politics from Inside*, 332
68  Hilda to Beatrice, 5 & 10 Feb.1911, 40 Prince's Gardens, BC3/3/45 & 47
69  Austen to Mary, 7 May 1911, in *Politics from Inside*, 337–8

from the King to create enough peers if need be to force the bill through the upper house. 'Our men howled Asquith down this afternoon,' the usually mild-mannered Austen told Ivy, '& frankly I am glad of it. The more I think of how he has tricked & deceived a young King, the more angry I feel. It was a very excited House & I am almost surprised that there was nothing more than shouting. Any spark might have caused a violent explosion.'[70] No compromise could be found once the government indicated that it would treat significant amendment of the bill as equivalent to rejection. At last together, Austen and his father insisted that, 'having entered into the struggle we were bound to see it through.'[71]

Alongside his father, Austen championed intransigence, a change in temper for which he paid a high price. The Unionist party, already fractured by tariff reform, split along further and different lines over the Parliament bill once it reached the upper house. The new lines of division aligned some tariff reformers including Austen with some Unionist free traders, pitting them against a similarly anomalous mixture of tariff reformers and free traders – and thus exacerbated Unionist internecine feuding. The Diehards, including Austen, insisted that the Unionists use their majority in the Lords to maintain the principle of parity between the two Houses of Parliament regardless of the threatened consequences. But the leaders of the party, including Lansdowne in the Lords and Balfour in the Commons, favoured letting the bill through rather than see the upper house swamped with new Liberal peers.

Balfour's stance intensified doubts about his capacity as leader. He had always been a disappointment to ardent tariff reformers. He did not stir any hearts in public life aside, oddly, from Austen's. But Balfour's referendum pledge had broken Austen's heart: and though Austen struggled to separate the question of the leadership from the Unionist argument about the Parliament bill, he stood no chance of success. His hard-line stance on the Lords damaged his own chances of becoming party leader if Balfour chose to resign. Austen now looked all too much like his father; and country gentlemen backed away from both. The deepening argument soured the relationship between Austen and Balfour; and they issued letters which wounded each other. 'I cannot say how bitterly I feel such treatment from a leader for whom I have made great sacrifices of opinion & some of reputation,' Austen told Ivy: '… it is not easy to forgive an injury which is as deep as it is undeserved.'[72] Austen's behaviour grated against the Conservative instinct of loyalty to the leader.

---

70 Austen to Ivy, 24 July 1911, 9 Egerton Place, AC6/1/86
71 *Politics from Inside*, 320
72 Austen to Ivy, 26 July 1911, 9 Egerton Place, AC6/1/88

But he insisted, 'I cannot & will not steer my course only to avoid opposition to my personal advancement.'[73] Bitterness in the party reached a height when a score of Unionist peers provided the votes that allowed the Parliament bill to pass. 'Well, we are beaten but certainly not disgraced,' Austen reported to Highbury; '... Balfour and Lansdowne between them have produced the one result which Balfour least desired ... the victory of the Government by Unionist votes. ... it is a misfortune, but it seems to me that [the fight the Diehards put up] has averted the calamity which a total surrender would have been.'[74] Austen and Ivy headed away to Italy to distance themselves from the scene.

They enjoyed their holiday undisturbed until an obscurely worded telegram arrived from Neville: 'return as soon as possible join movement feeling in country real and widespread.' Austen saw no need for haste. But he found when he reached London that Diehard anger had intensified since the passage of the Parliament Act, deepening Unionist divisions and undermining Balfour. The Diehards were united in feeling rather than in policy, demanding intransigence on ever more issues without agreeing on all of them. Though Austen agreed to maintain his association with the Diehards, he struggled to keep them up to the mark on tariff reform. But what worried him most was the impact of all this ferment on Balfour's leadership. Unionist factional fighting over the Parliament bill damaged all the leaders, present and potential, including Austen. The Chamberlains hoped that Austen would sooner or later succeed to Balfour's place. But as the eventual victor put it, 'A man who may be leader of the Party mustn't get identified with a section or take the lead in sectional fighting.'[75] Austen's alignment with the Diehards over the Parliament bill enabled his chief rival, Walter Long, to mount a campaign against him among the Tory squirearchy. Austen could only hope that Balfour would delay his departure until the feelings generated by the Parliament bill subsided.

But Balfour resolved to resign the leadership without further delay; and he notified his foremost colleagues, including Austen, to this effect. Balfour harboured little if any bitter feeling toward the Chamberlains, less than he felt toward Long, whose trumpeted defence of Balfour during the summer had only accentuated the challenge to his leadership. Austen was devastated by Balfour's decision. 'The blow has fallen,' Austen told Mary, 'and I am sick as a man can be. ... I love the man, and though as you know he has once or twice nearly broken my heart politically, I now can think of nothing but the pleasure of intimate association with

---

73 Austen to Ivy, 27 July 1911, House of Commons, AC6/1/89
74 Austen to Mary, 12 Aug.1911, in *Politics from Inside*, 344
75 Bonar Law in August to F.E. Smith, quoted in *Politics from Inside*, 374

him, the constant personal kindness he has shown to me and the great qualities of mind and character he has brought to the discharge of the tremendous duties of his post.'[76] He was daunted at the thought of assuming those duties himself. As for ambition, Austen never 'had more of it than is necessary to make a man stick to his work,'[77] until Balfour issued his pledge of a referendum on food taxes. But then, 'colleagues & the course of events suggested the possibility – & indeed it seemed at the time the probability of my succeeding him. Then my ambition was fired, for that seemed to open great possibilities & I dreamed like others of being head of a ministry that should make some history, domestic & imperial.'

Never were the issues for which the leader of the Unionist party would have to fight greater than in the autumn of 1911. Over the next three years, under the terms of the Parliament Act, Home Rule for Ireland could be forced on to the statute books regardless of the House of Lords. The Parliament Act had also, in Austen's opinion, wiped the slate clean of previous commitments, including Balfour's pledge on food taxes. As leader of the party Austen would be able to plant the flags of tariff reform and preservation of the Union together in front of his forces.

The imperial cause was everything to him. It was consecrated by what he saw as the self-sacrificial price his father had paid, first in abandoning his hopes of becoming Prime Minister in order to keep the Kingdom united, and then in devoting his life's energies to crusade for the economic consolidation of the Empire. But Austen never regarded himself as synonymous with the cause he fought for. The decisive consideration in allowing his name to go forward for the leadership was the knowledge that his father longed for that outcome to fulfil his own dream. Austen could not fight for himself. Once the news of Balfour's departure was made public, Austen stayed away from the House of Commons, repelled by even the faintest suggestion of canvassing for support.

But he could not prevent the contest from becoming personal. Walter Long insulted him to his face by impugning his conduct as a gentleman. Long appealed to Tory backbenchers who found Austen's Nonconformity in religion and Liberal rather than Conservative brand of Unionism distasteful. Long dwelt also on Austen's disloyalty to Balfour in supporting the Diehard campaign against the Parliament bill. Austen was supported by the party whips and almost everyone who had served with him and Long in Balfour's Cabinet. Yet Austen recognised that backbenchers had no experience of Long at close quarters. He saw too that Long would

---

76 Austen to Mary, 4 Nov.1911, in *Politics from Inside*, 377–8
77 Austen to Ida, 4 Nov.1917, 9 Egerton Place, in Robert Self, ed., *The Austen Chamberlain Diary Letters*, 60–1

be a sore loser, sure to undermine him in the challenging months ahead if he became leader. Even so Austen hoped to win the leadership, more than he liked to admit.

He never forgave the man who shattered that hope. Andrew Bonar Law had been a Member of Parliament for a much shorter time than either Austen or Long and had never held cabinet office. Still he commanded respect as a firm tariff reformer: he had not played a prominent part in the Unionists' summertime quarrels; and though admittedly none of them was known for oratory, he was the best speaker of the three. Law may have put his name forward to mark himself out for future rather than for immediate leadership. But his entry made the outcome of the contest problematic and would necessitate a second ballot. More to the point, he refused to withdraw his name from consideration, regardless of the fact that he was few people's first choice.

That determination made him the winner. Law possessed what the others lacked: the will to seize the leadership, a will essential in a would-be Prime Minister. Austen did not have it; and Long's main motive was to keep Austen out. Law's determination blackened the prospect for Austen. To win on a second ballot would deny him the clear mandate that he wanted to overcome the carping criticism that Long (though not Law) was sure to put up and to uphold tariff reform. There was another way for Austen to reach the top. He could withdraw in favour of Long, whom insiders expected would not last a year as leader, given his spitefulness and frequent changes of mind. Then the party would welcome Austen as his replacement. The chief wire-puller in the party proposed that course to Austen. So did Bonar Law. But Austen dismissed the idea as 'Satan's suggestion'.[78] The coming year could be of crucial importance for the causes Austen had at heart. Conscientious to a fault, he refused to consign the party to inept leadership at such a time.

Once Bonar Law's determination to stay in the race became clear, Austen took an initiative extraordinary by the standards of most aspiring politicians but quite in character for him. He proposed to Walter Long that they both withdraw, leaving Bonar Law as the unanimous, because least divisive, choice of the party. Long, having achieved his objective, agreed. After pushing the leading contenders out of the race, Law squirmed in embarrassment at his obvious self-seeking. He asked to see Austen, saying that he was 'undecided about accepting' the leadership. Austen described their encounter to his father: "'Well, Austen,' [Law] began, "this is a very serious thing for me. I am not sure that I can accept." "My dear Law," I said, "you must. You have no choice now. You allowed your name to go forward. ... you altered the situation by doing so; you cannot now shrink from the consequences."

---

78  Austen to Mary, 9 Nov.1911, in *Politics from Inside*, 388

... We talked on about his qualifications and disqualifications a little longer and then he left, his last words being, "Well, I suppose that I shall have to accept, but it will make no difference to our personal friendship, will it?" "No," I said, "none." And that promise I must keep. I confess I feel a little grieved. I don't think that if our positions had been reversed I could have acted as he did, but I must just get that feeling out of my mind and keep it out.'[79]

But Austen could not rid himself of 'that feeling'. Years later, at another low point in his fortunes, he reflected on the difference it would have made if he, rather than Bonar Law, had become leader. 'He is a weak man & I thought him strong. He has little experience, but I thought he would learn. He does not learn & he will remain an amateur to the end of his days. He is a curious mixture – at one and the same time over-confident & over-modest, over-daring & over-timid, ambitious & fearful, satisfied with his own judgement in theory & utterly dependent on his surroundings in practice. And with it all, his two or three intimates are ... born intriguers, utterly incompetent to advise him, without knowledge or sagacity... Bah! I am working myself into a temper, but by Jove! If I had been made leader some things in our Party record & I think some things in our National history would have been different.'[80]

Old Joe was not so philosophical. During the contest he sent Austen assurances of approval. But afterwards, as he thought it over, his disappointment deepened. At the outset he dismissed Bonar Law as not 'equal to the situation'.[81] But Law's insistence on staying in the race impressed Joseph as 'an indication that with the rise of his ambition he has developed strength which we did not suspect of him'.[82] Implicit was Joseph's sense that Austen had not displayed that strength. Would Bonar Law continue to do so? The eventual answer only deepened Joe's disappointment at his son's abandonment of the contest for the leadership. Though a firm tariff reformer, Bonar Law waffled in the face of Unionist uneasiness about tariffs on foodstuffs, particularly on wheat, which the Canadians regarded as indispensable to imperial preference. Walter Long identified himself with this uneasiness; and 'anxious not to quarrel with' Long, Bonar Law found it 'very difficult to reject his advice',[83] as Austen reported to his father. Joseph stiffened his son's resistance: 'After all,

79  Austen to Mary, 8 to 11 Nov.1911, in *Politics from Inside*, 382–393, p.390–1

80  Austen to Ida, 4 Nov.1917, in Self, ed., *The Austen Chamberlain Diary Letters*, 61

81  Mary to Austen, 6 Nov.1911, Highbury, AC4/2/121

82  Mary to Austen, 12 Nov.1911, Highbury, AC4/2/124 – words which Austen interestingly did not include in his publication of much of this letter in *Politics from Inside*, 394–5

83  Austen to Mary, 19 Feb.1912, in *Politics from Inside*, 416

who made the greater sacrifice, you or Walter Long, & why should he dictate the policy?' Bonar Law now seemed to Joe 'too much impressed by his correspondence, & not to realize enough that more letters always come from the people who want to persuade you to take a line they think you will not take than from those who agree with you & consider a question beyond dispute.'[84] Prompted by his father, Austen told Bonar Law 'that there were some general questions on which it was useless to try and gather the general opinion of the Party or to be finally guided by it; that ... I thought [a tariff on foodstuffs] was one of them and that the leaders must decide for the Party and convey their decision clearly to the Party.'[85] Though never personally assertive like his father, Austen had imbibed his father's authoritarian approach to party leadership. For the moment Austen's advice was endorsed by most men in the inner councils of the party, and Bonar Law fell into line with this consensus. Not for long.

After the storms of the past few years, a saddened tranquillity settled over the Chamberlains in the spring of 1912. Joseph found delight in the attentions of his grandchildren. Neville's daughter Dorothy was 'very partial to Grandpa's eyeglass & watch chain & sits on someone else's lap close to him & leans forward & grabs at them & tries to tear them off their respective fastenings.'[86] But these moments were touched with pathos. Joseph 'could not even talk to [his grandchildren] he could only make uncouth noises which often frightened them & it was most touching to watch his efforts to attract them.' He was also depressed by 'the gradual failure of his eyesight; he lost the power of focusing and could not read or distinguish any object clearly. ... His physical condition,' Neville later recalled, 'brought out ... his great tenderness to his own family.'[87] It was obvious that his health was deteriorating. He had pain in leg and back, and was sometimes suffused with gout. Ida reported that 'he spends most of his time when alone with Mary in wishing he was dead, which is trying for her' – and for them all.

Rather than despair, Ida and Hilda forged ahead with their own interests. They collaborated on a little book about the scrubland or maquis that surrounded the Villa Victoria where the family stayed each year. Hilda wrote the text while Ida, an

---

84  Mary to Austen, 21 Feb.1912, Villa Victoria, AC4/2/130
85  Austen to Mary, 1 Mar.1912, in *Politics from Inside*, 435
86  Ida to Neville, 10 Aug.1912, Highbury, NC18/2/0b
87  Neville to Dorothy & Frank, 6 July 1914, Westbourne, NC1/6/11

accomplished miniature painter, did the illustrations. They dedicated their book 'To J.C. whose never-failing interest in their expeditions and discoveries has been a constant source of pleasure and encouragement to the authors.'[88] On returning to England, they canvassed the prospects for publication. At the end of August Ida 'heard from Routledge. He thinks if their book were produced in a neat style, it would have a small, but continuous sale. Much would depend on the illustrations ... But if he approves them, & Ida & Hilda will produce £30, he will bring out the book & allow them 25% on the sales of the first 1000 & 20% afterwards & do any reprinting, if called for, himself.' With help from their brothers, Ida and Hilda raised the necessary £30. 'We are quite prepared to pay that for the pleasure of having our fling,'[89] said Hilda.

Politically, however, the year ended with a rumble of thunder. Bonar Law remained uneasy about his decision to maintain the party's commitment to a tariff on foodstuffs. Lansdowne, as party leader in the Lords, reaffirmed the commitment toward the end of the year; and it was reinforced by Austen and then Bonar Law. But their action only whipped up the dismay lower in the party at what was regarded as a millstone around its electoral neck. The dismay spread like a cancer among hitherto stalwart supporters of tariff reform; and they joined the chorus demanding release from the commitment. Austen pleaded with Bonar Law to stick to his guns and embark on a campaign such as old Joe had conducted in 1904 to convert a free-trading country to imperial preference. Bonar Law too was a man of conviction. But he was also, like Austen in this regard, a consensus-seeker by instinct: and he quailed before a storm that spread to every corner of the party. Rather than abandon his convictions, he offered to resign as leader and allow someone more in tune with current opinion to take over. But the offer turned the tide against food taxes into an all but universal plea among Unionists for Law to stay. The plea expressed itself in a letter which, when modified by prominent tariff reformers, every Unionist MP agreed to sign, apart from Henry Chaplin and Austen. Even Austen 'told friends that I could not <u>urge</u> them to sign if they felt they ought not to do so and that I was in no way responsible for the terms, but that on the whole I should be glad if they could sign,'[90] a recommendation his father could not have made.

---

88  I. & H. Chamberlain, *Common Objects of the Riviera* (London: George Routledge and Sons, Limited, 1913), v

89  Beatrice to Neville, 28 Aug.1912, Highbury, NC1/13/2/144, & Hilda to Neville, 1 Sept.1912, in Wales, NC18/2/0c

90  Austen to Mary, 8 Jan.1913, in *Politics from Inside*, 509

There was no way to minimise the blow to his father's hopes and dreams. 'I have prepared you and Father for what this letter has to tell,' Austen began his report to Mary, 'yet I find it a very difficult one to write. I have done my best, but the game is up. We are beaten and the cause for which Father sacrificed more than life itself is abandoned!'[91] Mary recognised that the defeat hurt Austen as much as his father; but she said so in terms that only deepened the blow: 'my heart is just aching for you,' she wrote. 'I know how bitter is this blow to you, both because of the deep conviction & strong faith in the cause for which you have worked with unswerving devotion.' But '... now when, as we believe, it could have been brought to fulfilment, to see it dashed to the ground through sheer weakness & hesitancy is a high trial ... Your Father will meet this as he has met the other great sacrifices of his life. Ah me, that he should be called upon for yet another! ... I had come to believe that if God in his mercy spared his dear life a little longer he would see his great ideal come into being, & know that he had laid the foundation truly & well, & his work would go down to generations yet unborn, who would look upon it as the turning point in the development & union of a group of nations welded into one great Empire.'[92]

Bonar Law's surrender to the critics of food taxes did not amount to their rejection. In his search for consensus, Law clouded his wording of the stance that the party now took: 'if, when a Unionist Government has been returned to power, it proves desirable after consultation with the Dominions to impose new duties on articles of food in order to secure the most effective system of Preference, such duties should not be imposed until they have been submitted to the people of this country at a General Election.'[93] Austen scoffed at this double-speak: 'Food taxes will not be imposed or defended, but they are not abandoned. They may never be revived, but the Party still carries the load ... we shall have all the disadvantages without the advantages of either clear course. In short it is the half-way house policy which never saved anyone or anything.' Still he found some consolation: 'I am rather glad, since they would not fight boldly on my line, that they have yet not wholly abandoned the policy and keep the flag still flying somehow.'[94]

Even so, it induced the man who first raised the flag to leave the battlefield. When Joseph reached the Riviera for his annual convalescence, he resolved to abandon his seat in the Commons at the next election. The decision was 'not an

---

91  Austen to Mary, 7 Jan.1913, in *Politics from Inside*, 508
92  Mary to Austen, 8 Jan.1913, Highbury, AC4/2/156
93  Bonar Law to Lord Balcarres, 13 Jan.1913, in *Politics from Inside*, 504
94  Austen to Mary, 25 Jan.1913, in *Politics from Inside*, 518–9

easy one for him,' Mary told Austen: 'though he is cool & calm about it ... It marks an era ... He feels it deeply – though I doubt if he will ever show you how much.'[95] Mary admitted that she felt it no less, perhaps even more. Hilda doubted that the decision would 'permanently depress Papa'.[96] But Mary knew better; she feared that he would never recover from the loss of his driving purpose in life. What made the decision bearable was Austen's willingness to stand in his father's place as Unionist candidate for West Birmingham when Parliament was dissolved. There was one advantage for Austen in agreeing to give up his current constituency of East Worcestershire. A great urban constituency like West Birmingham would strengthen him more than his county seat could do. Yet he could not disguise his regret at abandoning a constituency that had stood by him loyally and was closer to his heart. He found the country lanes of Worcestershire more congenial than the back-to-backs of Birmingham. Yet once again Austen subordinated his predilections to his father's imperious desires.

Joseph was now nearly blind, and deeply depressed. 'He refuses to do anything or see anyone if he can help it, always giving the same answer, "I can't see".'[97] Mary found an oculist who brought about some improvement in his vision and raised his spirits. But ceaselessly vigilant care took its toll on his carers. Mary fell dangerously ill with ptomaine poisoning followed by emergency surgery for appendicitis. The operation was successful, but recovery slow. Austen, Bea and Neville came in turns to the Riviera to help Ida and Hilda look after the two convalescents. But the task proved almost too much for them. Beatrice readied Prince's Gardens for Joseph and Mary's return from the Riviera while the family homes in Birmingham, Highbury and Westbourne were alerted to receive the exhausted younger sisters.

That autumn Austen was preoccupied with the prospective enactment in the coming year of the Irish Home Rule bill. Once again a subject other than tariff reform brought father and elder son together. Austen was privy to negotiations between party leaders in Britain in search of a compromise to avert civil war in Ulster; but they broke down at the turn of the year. He looked for a solution along the lines of his father's ideas in the 1880s to counteract Home Rule for Ireland by setting up provincial councils throughout the United Kingdom. But Austen's appetite for compromise was destroyed by Bonar Law's behaviour over food taxes. All the Chamberlains reacted to the Home Rule crisis in the same way. It was articulated best by Beatrice speaking to the Women's Auxiliary Unionist Tariff Reform

95  Mary to Austen, 2 Mar.1913, Villa Victoria, AC4/2/166
96  Hilda to Neville, 15 Mar.[1913], Villa Victoria, NC2/15/3/131
97  Hilda to Austen, 28 Feb.1913, Villa Victoria, AC5/2/11

Association: 'we are a Unionist party;' she declared, 'all that makes for union, whether amongst citizens of different classes, or of different parts of the United Kingdom, or of different regions of the Empire, is our province. ... At the present moment it is natural to concentrate our main effort on the defence of the Union. Home Rule is the pressing danger, the calamity which threatens our national existence. ... But I have always referred to Tariff Reform as an integral part of the same great policy.' She concluded in the ringing accents of her father: 'The Whole Policy then and with All our Might!'[98]

Austen's change of constituency was intended to mark him out as his father's successor not only in West Birmingham but as leader of the Unionists in the city as a whole. Neville from his vantage point on the City Council upheld Austen's local leadership. Bea urged Neville on: 'there is much to be done before [Austen's] position is established as I want to see it ... West Birmingham first ... & then I hope meetings of the [citywide organisation] & a group of B'ham members, speaking with one voice & recognizing Austen as their leader.'[99] But Austen had mixed feelings about his rising responsibilities. He found the shouting out of speeches at big rallies 'a subtly degrading occupation. It is well to go into the country to recapture one's soul after such an orgy. I will pick primroses and forget politics for a week.' After breaking away from this letter to Mary for a little gardening, he continued: 'that last sentence sums up the difference between Father and me in our outlook on politics. Did he ever <u>want</u> to forget politics? I doubt it; but I constantly do. ... For which reason, as well as for many other and bigger ones, I shall never be in politics what he was.'[100]

Dutiful nonetheless to a fault, Austen kept his father in touch with the escalating crisis on Ireland, writing 'almost hour by hour each scrap of information as it came to me – true or false, confirmed or subsequently amended or discredited.'[101] Northern Ireland reached the brink of civil war when British army officers resigned their commissions rather than use force against Protestant Ulstermen. 'Papa is stirred to all the old joy of the fighter, when there is a great battle on,' Hilda reported.[102] Mary was grateful for the flow of information from Austen. 'Even you can hardly realize all the difference that it means to your Father & us all to be kept in

98 Speech delivered ... 17 Nov.1913, printed by Jas. Truscott & Son, Ltd., London, under the title, 'The Principles of a Patriot', BC5/7/1
99 Beatrice to Neville, 11 Feb.1914, Villa Victoria, NC1/13/2/147
100 Austen to Mary, 6 Apr.1914, in *Politics from Inside*, 637
101 Austen to Mary, 24 Mar.1914, in *Politics from Inside*, 631
102 Hilda to Austen, 26 Mar.1914, Villa Victoria, AC5/2/25

touch with such stirring events.' Joseph's health stabilized for a while, though his speech grew 'rather telegraphic'.[103] They returned to London earlier than planned. Austen welcomed their return with an anxious account of the political situation: 'We jump from dangerous concession to still more dangerous strife and back again from talk of civil war to talk of patched-up peace, that would be only one whit less bad than war.'[104]

A month later old Joe travelled up to Birmingham to bid farewell to his West Birmingham constituents. Flanked by Mary and Austen on a sunny afternoon, he was wheeled back and forth over the terrace at Highbury to acknowledge the cheers of the people for the last time. The family then returned quietly to their London home. There, on July 2nd, he died, surrounded by everyone in the family except Annie, who remained in Birmingham to look after her newborn son. At midnight Austen wrote to assure her: 'The end was very peaceful. The heart just failed & there was no suffering. Father was interested in politics this morning & early this afternoon spoke of you as he did of us all. Then he slept & passed away.'[105]

103  Mary to Austen, 5 Apr.1914, Villa Victoria, AC4/2/196
104  Austen to Mary, 2 May 1914, in *Politics from Inside*, 642
105  Austen to Annie, 2 July 1914, 40 Princes Gardens, NC1/27/142

*Beatrice in her wartime ascendancy*

# 5

# War

With the death of Joseph Chamberlain, his children lost the centre around which their lives revolved. Highbury ceased to be the family home, and Birmingham ceased to be the base of operations for any but Neville. Joseph's death also removed the light that guided his children. But the brightness of his light had denied them lights of their own. His legacy continued to guide them politically, though the world in which that legacy had been shaped was shattered by the war that broke out a month after he died. His children, now middle-aged, gradually made their own mark. But the war slowed the advance of Joe's sons much longer than that of his daughters. Austen was shunted to the political sidelines throughout the war, and Neville was led into a failure more humiliating that anything he endured on Andros.

The lessons Joseph instilled in his family had little to do with war. He approached every level of political life, whether local, national, imperial or international, in economic terms readily appreciated in an industrial city. Neville worked well in the same environment. But his understanding of Birmingham proved misleading at the national level in wartime. Austen alone among the Chamberlains had some appreciation of the role that armed forces played in conflict between nations. But he lacked the will and skill to push his way forward in the infighting which the war intensified in cabinet circles. Ida and Hilda, on the other hand, found in their new home new ways of serving community and country at the local level where, like Neville, they fared best. Meanwhile the imperial fervour of Beatrice was intensified by the war. It was into her hands that her father's fiery torch fell, and it burned her out.

۽

The most pressing issues for the family after reading Joseph's will regarded Highbury. They had no choice but to sell. His estate was valued at just over £125,000,
upwards of £8 million today. This was more than Neville expected and more than
Joseph took from the metal-manufacturing partnership of Nettlefold and Chamberlain when he retired from the business. His disastrous investment in Bahamian sisal had not permanently diminished his wealth. The division of his estate
under the will provided well for his widow and daughters, but left his sons to fend
for themselves. They were left with a residue of £12,000, of which Austen was to
receive three quarters and Neville one quarter. That was satisfactory for Neville as
the businessman of the family. But it left Austen in precarious circumstances. He
had no official income apart from the small salary that Parliament had recently
instituted for its members. He supplemented it with earnings from a few directorships. But he was already living beyond his means, and the income from £9,000
would not make a great difference.

The family made no attempt to hang on to Highbury. It was too big and expensive for them, and in any case they had little wish to stay. They vaguely hoped that
Highbury might remain a shrine to Joseph's memory. But they all wished to live
elsewhere. Neville already did so, in nearby Edgbaston. Austen lived in a fashionable part of London, but without much garden; and he longed for a place in the
country. Mary hoped to retain Prince's Gardens, the family house in London. Bea's
work and friendships had long kept her largely in London, and she welcomed the
prospect of a place of her own there 'with as much satisfaction as any young bride'.[1]
She bought a small house on Egerton Crescent around the corner from Austen.
Ida and Hilda pooled their resources to acquire a home in a country village within
ready reach of the capital.

The task of dismantling the Highbury estate fell largely upon Mary. Austen
gave her what help he could, but his political duties held him in London. He kept
track of the independent income she received under her marriage settlement, a
considerable but diminishing sum which rarely matched her expectations. Neville
was still trying to convey some basic points of financial management to her before
her final return from the Villa Victoria: 'I don't quite understand your point about
not deducting the excess of expenditure over income from the capital,' he wrote in
some exasperation.[2] Austen strove patiently to keep her in line over the retention

---

1  Hilda's memoir of Beatrice, BC5/10/2
2  Neville to Mary, 20 Apr.1914, Westbourne, NC1/20/1/88

of Prince's Gardens. 'I think ... you can afford Princes Gardens,' he counselled; 'But I still hope that you will undertake the least possible <u>capital</u> expenditure at the outset ... it would be most aggravating to find that it had been thrown away if a change was forced upon you.'[3] Quite aside from these financial considerations, the break-up of Highbury bore heavily upon Mary. She had to dismiss its staff and dispose of its contents. Neville's Westbourne and Austen's Egerton Place were fully furnished, though Austen welcomed a substantial addition to his collection of pictures, and Neville responded gratefully to Mary's Christmas gift of the Highbury dinner service. There was some room in Bea's place in London, and still more where Ida and Hilda settled in Hampshire. But Prince's Gardens was lumbered with Highbury furniture for a long time.

Mary remained based at Highbury through the autumn. But at the same time she found refuge in London at the home of the Reverend William Carnegie. He had been Rector of St Philip's Church, Birmingham, when it was turned into a cathedral. He was then appointed Rector of St. Margaret's, Westminster and a Canon of the Abbey. 'Canon Carnegie is to be "in residence" at the Abbey again,' Mary told Austen, '& I shall therefore have another Sunday of the Abbey services, which I love.' She infused her surroundings there with marital memories. 'I shall always feel your Father's presence in the Abbey, for we have so often been there together.'[4] She did not think of returning permanently to the United States. Austen welcomed her decision to settle in Prince's Gardens, close to Egerton Place: 'I have felt for a long time that your home must always be in England & I am glad to know that it will soon be so close to us that we may see as much of one-another as in the past & keep ever fresh the friendship & loving memories that 26 years have woven between us.'[5] Mary echoed his sentiments: 'My home could not be anywhere but in England – & it will make it all the easier for me to begin my solitary life that you & Ivy & your children are close at hand. There will always be a welcome for you at Prince's Gardens which I hope will still be the centre of the family life.'[6]

That hope could not be fulfilled, now that Joseph had gone and the family was scattered. Yet the family drew closer together than ever through their correspondence. The flow of letters accelerated after they left Highbury. And it was greatest among those who made their homes outside London rather than within easy walking distance of each other. The epicentre of the correspondence shifted from

3 Austen to Mary, 28 July 1914, 9 Egerton Place, AC4/1/1137
4 Mary to Austen, 29 Oct.1914, AC4/2/211
5 Austen to Mary, 15 Nov.1914, 9 Egerton Place, AC4/1/1149
6 Mary to Austen, 16 Nov.1914, Highbury, AC4/2/213

Birmingham to the Hampshire village of Odiham. There, within two months of Joe's death, Ida and Hilda found the home they wanted. It was a spacious Queen Anne and Regency house with ample room for a garden. Called 'The Bury House', it stood beside the church and churchyard of a village not far from Basingstoke, which had good rail connection to London.

For the first time they had a home of their own; and it gave them a new lease on life. They almost exploded with delight as they moved in. 'All our furniture has arrived & unpacked, & somehow or another insinuated into the various rooms,' Ida reported: '... our drawing room looks lovely even with a pile of covered up chairs filling up its centre. ... You would have laffed [sic] to see Hilda & me visiting the butcher & baker & candlestick maker this afternoon & ordering in supplies for our servants, the middle price of a neck of mutton, & gallon of potatoes (weird measure) & pounds & half pounds of tea & sugar & currants & such like trying to look as if we knew what we were about. ... We are both very well & simply <u>thrilled</u> over our house. It gets nicer & nicer every hour & between whiles we rush out & visit our pots in the conservatory, & we <u>would</u> sit in the verandah if it were not being painted.'[7] They could not wait to leave the village hotel where they stayed during the move. 'We are quite determined to go in to the house tomorrow ... How thrilling it will be to sleep, – or at any rate pass the night – at the Bury House tomorrow.'[8]

Christmas found Neville almost as happy as his sisters. Annie and Westbourne warmed him up: Hilda recognised that 'he needed the sunshine of his own home to bring out all his sides'.[9] And now they had the baby boy, they desired to join Dorothy in their nursery. Neville's businesses prospered almost embarrassingly from wartime demand, and after four years on the City Council, he was spoken of as the next Lord Mayor. The death of his father made less difference to Neville than to any of his siblings. In his approach to business and civic politics, Neville was a truer reincarnation of his father than was Austen. Shortly before Joe's death, Neville took the entire workforce at Hoskins on a day's outing to Merseyside. He used the occasion to announce 'an innovation that I am rather keen on', one that reflected his father's desire to share the benefits of industrial capitalism with labour. 'I have told them that by way of experiment we are going this year ... to declare a bonus to them which will be in proportion to their own earnings during the year and our profits.' He was candid about the self-interest in this gesture towards

7  Ida to Mary, 15 Dec.1914, The George Hotel, Odiham, BC4/2/90
8  Ida to Mary, 18 Dec.1914, The George Hotel, Odiham, BC4/2/91
9  Hilda to Annie, 31 May 1915, The Bury House, NC1/15/4/1

socio-economic harmony: '...if it saves us from a strike or even from having our men drawn into a Union it may save us many thousands in a single year.'[10] Neville had another passion that his father did not share, for music, though here too he focused his attention on Birmingham. Neville was pleased that the Promenade concerts at the city's Theatre Royal attracted 'very good attendances ... so I hope they will go on again next year. ... they have undoubtedly achieved their object in raising the popular taste in orchestral music and giving people opportunities of hearing many works that are not often played.'

੶

The outbreak of war at the beginning of August pushed this interest temporarily aside, as it did so many things. The war began to reshape the Chamberlains' world almost immediately, though the terrible toll that it would take did not become apparent for another couple of years. Its initial impact for Neville was to increase demand for ambulance beds from Hoskins to provide for the wounded from the western front. That demand soon confronted him with one of the central dilemmas of industrialised states at war: how to reconcile the manpower needs of the battlefield with the demands of industries essential to the war effort.

First Neville had to address a related personal question. His young cousin Norman, Aunt Lilian's son, asked him about enlisting in the army. Norman did outstandingly good work among boys in the poorest parts of Birmingham, getting them off the streets and prepared for employment at home or in Canada. 'He feels he is more useful where he is,' Neville told Annie, 'but he doesn't see how he can avoid enlisting when he is the right age & unmarried and pressure is so strong.' Neville knew that Norman would 'suffer a good deal, if he doesn't enlist', and when Norman asked for guidance Neville 'refused to give any but I guess what I said rather confirmed him in the decision to which he is rapidly coming, viz. to enlist. I don't really see how he can avoid it.' Neville added sombrely, '... it probably means the front in the end.'[11]

It took another year for the seriousness of the war to register with most of the women in the Chamberlain family. The sinking of the *Lusitania* and the first Zeppelin raid on London brought it home. Ida and Hilda provided meals and eventually accommodation for officers awaiting orders to the front: 'it would all be very pleasant & very good fun,' Ida remarked, 'if it were not for the ever present thought

---

10 Neville to Hilda, 28 June 1914, Westbourne, NC1/15/2/44
11 Neville to Annie, 3 & 4 Sept.1914, Westbourne, NC1/26/56 & 57

that the men with whom you are laughing & joking today will probably be killed or wounded a few months hence.'[12] By now Neville was attracting national attention in his search for ways to meet the manpower needs of war-related industry, and he was tracked down by *The Times*. His civic as well as business commitments made him attentive to the concerns of labour which he knew locally. But he also recognised that the needs of industries essential to the war effort would have to be addressed at the national level, a level at which as yet he had no experience. Here lay a tangle of contradictory interests whose complexity he underestimated. He tackled it boldly, but had a much better grasp of the economic issues than of political repercussions. 'The more I think over it and the more I hear and see of the attitude of men in the factories the more certain I feel that National service is the only solution of the present situation ... It must however be accompanied by either a surtax on or a limitation of profits for all, because workmen will never consent to restrictions which would have the effect of putting money into their employers' pockets. Personally,' he added patriotically, 'I hate the idea of making profits out of the war when so many are giving their lives and limbs.' He was not afraid of governmental compulsion, though he was thinking less of military conscription than of the economy. 'Give us compulsion and each man will be doing what he can do best. In this way we shall get more munitions & more exports and the whole life of the country will be less disturbed than it has been during the last 13 months.'[13]

Austen had just been brought into the coalition government which the Liberal Prime Minister Asquith formed with the Unionists to deal with the wartime emergency. Asquith kept his Liberal colleagues in key posts and assigned the Unionists to positions peripheral to the war effort. Rather than push himself forward, Austen, to the horror of his family, offered to take a subordinate post if that would facilitate the creation of a more effective government. Treated with honour rather than respect, he was made Secretary of State for India with a seat in the Cabinet. But Bea recognised that, while 'nothing can be said against it in point of dignity', the India Office was 'at this moment a backwater'. She consoled herself that it would give Austen 'administrative work of a very important although not of a showy kind. ... At least now your voice must be heard in council & must have weight ... it is only by thinking of one's country first that one can arrive at being glad that you are in office at this time.'[14] Austen was soon disheartened by Asquith's lack of drive. 'This Cabinet is the worst managed of any of which I have ever heard,' he cried.

---

12  Ida to Mary, 2 June 1915, The Bury House, BC4/2/99
13  Neville to Annie, 3 June & 29 Aug. 1915, Westbourne, NC1/26/66 & 79
14  Beatrice to Austen, 29 May 1915, The Bury House, AC5/2/28

'Asquith has many virtues & he is the only man the Liberal Party will follow, but he is incurably haphazard in his ways & is content to preside without directing.'[15] Austen told only Ivy of his concerns, fearful of violating his oath as a privy councillor not to divulge Cabinet secrets. But the result was that he seemed to the family to be contributing less to the war effort than his younger brother or even his sisters.

Neville agreed to become Lord Mayor of Birmingham. The mayoralty still provided the executive leadership of the city and was not yet the ceremonial position it later became. Nor were the powers of city government gutted as they would be later in the century. Neville was therefore able, as leader of England's second city, to make a significant contribution to the national war effort. Hilda was delighted by Neville's acceptance of the post: 'in all the increasing gravity of these times, with new trials, new struggles & new conditions arising every day, it is impossible to exaggerate the importance of having strong men, – & by that I mean men able to take a big decision & adhere to it'.[16] Austen offered Neville only tardy congratulations, as Neville noticed. Being Lord Mayor had its costs. The one Neville most regretted was the time that it would prevent Annie and him spending with their children. There were also financial drawbacks. The salary that accompanied the office did not cover the costs of official entertaining, to say nothing of income lost from inattention to private business. Neville's uncle Sir George Kenrick offered to give him immediately the £4,000 legacy – upwards of £220,000 nowadays – that he would otherwise leave Neville in his will. Sir George, a wealthy man who chaired his family's hollowware business, was childless; and as the younger brother of Neville's mother Florence, he was devoted to her children, particularly to Neville, who shared his passion for fishing and shooting in the Scottish highlands where Sir George owned a large estate. Neville accepted the gift gratefully.

The member of the family who provided the most outstanding service throughout the war was, however, neither Austen nor Neville but Beatrice. At the outbreak of the war, she threw herself into the establishment of the French Wounded Emergency Fund, making use of her fluent French and leadership skills to send supplies to French hospitals. Ida brought the managerial experience she acquired with the almoners' service in Birmingham to Bea's aid. She stayed with Bea in London three days a week, and a room was set aside at the Bury House for Bea's weekend recovery from her labours. But Bea was driven by a punishing sense of duty; she came to the Bury House much less frequently than her sisters would have liked: 'Beatrice is not coming today,' Hilda reported sadly, '& she telegraphs she has one of her headaches.

---

15  Austen to Ivy, 26 Apr.1916, 9 Egerton Place, AC6/1/201
16  Hilda to Neville, 31 July 1915, The Bury House, NC1/15/3/149

Not the result of the Zeppelin raid I expect, but overwork.' When Beatrice eventually reached the station closest to the Bury House, she insisted on carrying her luggage rather than using the car her sisters put at her service. Accordingly she came to them 'thoroughly tired out & without any mental spring'.[17] When infighting among the volunteers disrupted the French Wounded Emergency Fund, Bea and Ida found other ways to assist the war effort. Ida straightened out the 'fearful muddle' in the Belgravia Workroom set up to send surgical dressings and clothing to the front. Bea also took up what Hilda described as 'the least spectacular and most unattractive war work: – leading a band of workers to press the necessity of "savings" on the general public,' a campaign the government eventually asked her to extend to 'all the big towns of the country'.[18]

Hilda meanwhile concentrated her energies at home in Odiham. She took charge of a local effort to make parcels for prisoners. But her main concern was to keep the family in touch with each other by fostering their correspondence. She gave Neville encouragement in his work, which he appreciated: 'it is very nice that you should be so much interested in our doings and it encourages me to go on writing you my egotistical letters in reply.'[19] She and Ida thereupon crystallised a pattern of letter writing which they followed with Neville for the rest of their lives. The two sisters alternated in writing to Neville each week on Thursday or Friday in time to reach him for reply on Sunday. Beatrice joined this conversation on paper less frequently, while Austen remained largely out of it for another year.

The bonds between Florence's and Harriet's children were never as strong as they were within each group. Yet it may have been Beatrice who prompted Neville to turn his attention at the beginning of his mayoralty to the encouragement of wartime savings by the working men of Birmingham. War did not stimulate his political imagination as it did hers. But drawing upon his knowledge of the civic and economic instincts of his city, Neville turned Bea's suggestion into an enduring institution. Wages were rising conspicuously in response to the demand for ever more munitions. Neville outlined his scheme to Hilda: 'My idea generally is to start a municipal savings association. The town would guarantee the interest at say 4½% but the object of bringing in the municipality is really to lend the scheme the prestige & weight of the local authority. The men are to be persuaded (probably [by] the Lord Mayor aided by the local labour leaders) to *ask their employers*

17  Hilda to Neville, 29 Oct.1915, 35 Egerton Crescent, NC1/15/3/155
18  Hilda's memoir of Beatrice, BC5/10/2
19  Neville to Hilda, 12 Dec.1915, Westbourne, in Robert Self, ed., *The Neville Chamberlain Diary Letters*, I, 103

*to deduct* from their weekly wages the amount they desire to save ... and hand it over to the Association ... the idea being that you will never do any good unless you save at the source. ... Moreover no one until the end of the war or some other fixed period is to draw out any money except with the sanction of the local committee.' As in old Joe's day, Neville wanted Birmingham to set the model for the country: 'If it caught on here and we published weekly statistics other towns might follow suit.'[20] When he tried his ideas out on his elder brother, Austen poured cold water on them, 'saying that I was wasting my time as he thought the Govt "must have a compulsory scheme in view on somewhat similar lines".'[21] But Neville dismissed the Asquith government as timorous, and pushed on.

Hilda welcomed his decision and amplified his thinking from a woman's standpoint. 'I am very glad to hear you are going ahead,' she wrote, 'for one cannot but feel that any Govt. scheme, if we are to judge by past experience, will take at least six months of talking before anything is done & even then they will probably back down the moment opposition shows itself. ... I feel so absolutely with you that ... any real saving must be made by taking the money at the source & then the men will not feel it. I very much doubt whether the sum given to the wife regularly by the man has increased in anything like the proportion of his rise.'[22] Hilda brought Austen round to their way of thinking. 'I don't know what you said to Austen about my savings scheme,' Neville responded, 'but the result was that he wrote to say that perhaps I had better go on with it.'[23]

This municipal savings scheme was only the most prominent of a range of locally-based, war-related initiatives that Neville and his sisters took in the opening months of 1916. Neville generated most of them, making him, in a small way, a model of the enterprising leadership which the national government clearly lacked. He peppered the Treasury, Home Office, War Office, Local Government Board and Board of Agriculture with his proposals. He spoke from platforms in London as well as Birmingham. Bea was delighted at the attention he attracted: 'It is becoming quite monotonous to be greeted everywhere with "Your brother Neville is stirring up the Midlands, is taking a strong line about air raids, is –" this and that & the other.'[24]

Neville's proposal in the unlikely field of agriculture gave a lasting direction to the work Hilda and Ida took up in Odiham and surrounding Hampshire.

20  Neville to Hilda, 28 Nov.1915, in Self, ed., *The Neville Chamberlain Diary Letters*, I, 101–2

21  Neville to Ida, 5 De.1915, in Self, ed., *The Neville Chamberlain Diary Letters*, I, 102–3

22  Hilda to Neville, 10 Dec.1915, The Bury House, NC1/15/3/156

23  Neville to Hilda, 12 Dec.1915, in Self, ed., *The Neville Chamberlain Diary Letters*, I, 104

24  Beatrice to Neville, 27 Feb.1916, 35 Egerton Crescent, NC1/13/2/150

Enlistment for the army depleted the supply of labour for farming as well as industry, and hence threatened the country's food supply, already jeopardised by German
torpedoing of supplies from abroad. Women were being trained to take the place
of men in munitions manufacturing. Why not for farming? Neville called for the
formation of a land corps of women. Hilda leapt into action: 'we ought to get to
work at once.'[25] She talked to one local farmer who thought women capable only
'of the most unskilled work such as weeding & hoeing turnips'. Hilda knew from
gardening that women could do much more: 'if they can't get men's labour they will
have to turn to the women, & then we shall come in.' Another farmer told Hilda
and Ida that 'it would not be difficult for people like ourselves to learn enough very
quickly to superintend others. So,' Ida gleefully warned her brother, 'perhaps Hilda
& I shall find ourselves hoeing turnips or digging ... I am sure I should prefer hoeing
turnips (or watching others hoeing them) in June to stuffing it in London'.[26]

Most but not all Neville's initiatives as Lord Mayor had to do with the war. He
still wanted to cultivate interest in orchestral music. At the interval in a concert at
the Town Hall, he 'addressed the multitude on the Future of Orchestral Music in
Birmingham,' and 'dropped a little bombshell by suggesting that we should have a
first class local orchestra and contribute to its support out of the rates! I have been
told since that "only a Chamberlain would have had the audacity to propose such a
thing" but really it has long been in my mind and I don't see why music should not
be subsidised ... Of course nothing can be done now but I thought I might as well
start to get people used to the idea.'[27] He underestimated the impact of his speech:
it 'made a deep impression upon local musical people and under its influence ...
they have all banded themselves into a new organisation of which I am to be President.' He persuaded the best-known conductors of the day, Sir Thomas Beecham
and Sir Henry Wood, to come up from London in support of a luncheon he was
to give to 'clinch the thing' with the 'Press present'.[28]

Responding to good wishes from Mary on his forty-seventh birthday, he
observed contentedly that, 'if the good things came to me rather later in life than
they do to some I am making up now for lost time.'[29] Refusing to be daunted when

25  Hilda to Neville, 25 Feb.1916, The Bury House, NC18/2/5
26  Hilda to Neville, 10 Mar., The Bury House, & Ida to Neville, 16 Mar.1916, 35 Egerton
Crescent, NC18/2/6–7
27  Neville to Beatrice, 24 Mar.1916, Westbourne, typed copy, NC1/13/3/38
28  Neville to Hilda, 2 Sept., & to Ida, 1 Oct.1916, Westbourne, in Self, ed., *The Neville
Chamberlain Diary Letters*, I, 153 & 159
29  Neville to Mary, 19 Mar.1916, Westbourne, NC1/20/1/102

the Treasury obstructed the legislation needed to make his municipal savings bank a reality, he committed himself to the scheme only more deeply and publicly. In doing so, he accentuated the inertia of the national government. Proud of her birth in Birmingham, Bea declared: 'Salvation once more must come, if at all, out of Nazareth. It is not to be found in Jerusalem.'[30] Austen eventually used his stature as a former Chancellor to pull his brother's municipal banking scheme out of limbo. Austen continued to find the coalition ministry disheartening; and he felt acutely uncomfortable on the Treasury bench with his fellow Unionists massed on the benches opposite: 'there is no use pretending that the coalition is popular with our people either inside the House or out of it.'[31]

Meanwhile the demands of war played havoc with the political and social order. Neville spoke sympathetically of 'State Socialism, the sinking of the old party divisions, the new position of women and the altered relations between employers and employed.'[32] Bea was equally alive to the upheaval, and opened her house to Unionists unhappy with the listless Asquith ministry. Dining together one evening, Beatrice and Ida 'had a good big swear ... over party leaders & party organisations, all & sundry.' They were particularly fed up with Bonar Law, whose participation in the coalition deprived the Unionist party of its distinctive commitments and purpose. Bea steamed on: 'we shall all be swept away at the first opportunity & ... the Unionist party will disappear the most completely, because it seems to be at present the only one entirely precluded from advocating Unionist principles! The principles were right, & are right, & will be carried through – but I doubt if any of us will survive politically to carry them through. Well, I don't care! ... for I believe the nation & the Empire will survive & flourish, & will enjoy Union & Tariff Reform & all the good things we ought to have secured for them – & didn't, from want of courage mostly. I shouldn't wonder if a reorganised Labour party were the agent to bring the new era. Who cares if it be but a patriotic one? I don't! – All [of] which doesn't prevent me from having accepted the chairmanship of Gen[era]l Purposes of the Women's Unionist & Tariff Reform Association ... No, I'll stick to the ship & go down with her, but it shall be with colours flying & no attempt to look like a Liberal tramp or a neutral Coalition steamer, laden up with German goods & friends of Germany!'[33]

---

30  Beatrice to Neville, 17 Mar.1916, 35 Egerton Crescent, NC1/13/2/151

31  Austen to Mary, 21 May 1916, 9 Egerton Place, AC4/1/1176

32  Neville to Hilda, 26 Feb.1916, Westbourne, in Self, ed., *The Neville Chamberlain Diary Letters*, I, 118

33  Beatrice to Neville, 17 Mar.1916, 35 Egerton Crescent, *loc.cit.*

While the rest of the family responded to the demands of the war, Mary dealt expeditiously with her bereavement. Within seven months of Joseph's death, Canon Carnegie had become her regular companion. The family hesitated to put their early impressions of the Canon on paper. But Austen found his conversation provoking. He put it tactfully to Mary after a dinner *à trois*: 'The Canon – & your champagne – made me very talkative & argumentative. The Canon always does!'[34] In the spring of 1916, braving the German torpedoes, Mary sailed for Massachusetts to tell her family of her engagement to the Canon. The Chamberlains accepted her choice without enthusiasm. In Ida's words, 'as long as she is happy we are satisfied. I wish he was a little more sympathetic to me personally but that is a matter of temperament & can't be helped.'[35] Hilda 'never did find his conversation very stimulating, but ... we need not have too much of him. ... one felt that one must necessarily get further & further apart as our lives got fuller, but now it will be merely a natural & painless growth.'[36] Austen and Neville found the marriage service a trial. Austen tried 'to think only of what it means to you,' he told Mary. 'But you have asked of me more than you know. Count it for righteousness!'[37] Neville 'had never been present at a communion service before', and was 'scandalised to see the priest go & drink up the remains of the wine when he thought no one was looking just like the waiters after a party. But Ivy explained to me that ... those remains are part of the priest's "perks". She didn't use that word but that is what I understood.'[38] Thereafter Austen's long correspondence with Mary dwindled away, and she moved to the periphery of the family, though as wife to the chaplain of the House of Commons she continued to witness its triumphs and tragedies.

Mary was not the only loosening link in the Chamberlain family. Austen was no longer in close touch with his siblings, and they did not like it. 'It seems absurd with them living in London,' Ida told Neville, 'that it should be more difficult to keep in touch with Austen & Ivy than with you or Annie, & yet it really is so. We don't correspond & they are so busy I hardly ever see them ... & when I do Austen is always either dog tired or speechless with a chill or a toothache or something.'[39] This sense of distance had something to do with Austen's political position. Ida

---

34  Austen to Mary, 11 Aug.1915, 9 Egerton Place, AC4/1/1167
35  Ida to Neville, 30 June 1916, The Bury House, NC18/2/22
36  Hilda to Neville, 22 July 1916, The Bury House, NC18/2/26
37  Austen to Mary, 22 June 1916, 9 Egerton Place, AC4/1/1180
38  Neville to Hilda, 6 Aug.1916, Westbourne, in Self, ed., *The Neville Chamberlain Diary Letters*, I, 149
39  Ida to Neville, 25 Aug.1916, The Bury House, NC1/16/1/58

and Hilda shared Neville's disgust when Austen declined to resign in protest at the Irish Home Rule settlement that Lloyd George worked out for the duration of the war. Austen even offered to exchange the India Office for a subordinate post if that would assist the coalition ministry: 'he is impossibly generous,' Hilda sighed.[40] But Austen internalised the political stresses he felt – he had objected to the Irish settlement but refused to resign over it – and they pulled him down physically. Hilda found him 'looking horribly white & thin ... I took him a short walk of about a mile or very little longer & he returned perfectly exhausted.'[41]

She refused to let him drift away. During the political upheaval that led to Lloyd George's replacement of Asquith as Prime Minister, Hilda brought Austen into the regime of letter-writing that she and Ida had developed with Neville. 'I am afraid this letter will arrive at a most inopportune time,' she wrote; '... but ... I feel dreadfully that I am getting so cut off from your & Ivy's life, & you from mine.' So she proposed 'to write to you more or less regularly to give you our news, hoping when you have time & inclination you will answer ... I hate to feel I know nothing of how matters are going with you, – of your health & Ivy's & the children's & of your private & public plans.' Hilda also dared to hope that Austen's position might be raised in the reconstruction of the government. 'Whether you will continue to be a Minister I conclude is still unsettled, but naturally I hope so though,' she noted perceptively, 'I admit there is only one position in which I really very much wish to see you, – that of Foreign Minister, for which I believe you are pre-eminently well suited,' before adding tartly, '& which I therefore suppose will never be offered to you.' Then she told him a bit about herself: 'It is astonishing what a lot of things there are to be done in a small village like this! I feel as if one might start a number of things like poultry clubs & goat clubs & I know we ought to start an infant Welfare centre if only one had twice as much time.'[42] Austen responded by rejoining the family letter-writing circle, though never so fully as Neville.

❧

The Cabinet crisis at the end of 1916 drew the family together. Austen, who remained at the India Office, scarcely knew what to make of the new order under Lloyd George. 'I take no pleasure,' he told Hilda, 'in a change which gives me a chief whom I profoundly distrust – no doubt a man of great energy but quite

40  Hilda to Neville, 6 July 1916, The Bury House, NC18/2/24
41  Hilda to Neville, 20 Oct.1916, The Bury House, NC18/2/38
42  Hilda to Austen, 6 Dec.1916, The Bury House, AC5/2/35

untrustworthy; who doesn't run crooked because he wants to but because he doesn't know how to run straight.'[43] As chairman of a Manpower Distribution Board, Austen had worked with Lloyd George when he was Minister of Munitions, and was worn out by their arguments. 'How I wish,' he told Neville, 'that our lines were so cast that I could dine with you every Saturday ... What wouldn't I give to talk myself out to you & get your advice & help?'[44]

The reconstruction of the government suddenly gave Austen an opportunity to make his wish come true. From his place on the Manpower Distribution Board, he took part in the search for someone to fill the newly created post of Director of National Service. He immediately thought of Neville with his experience of manpower issues in Birmingham. The post was offered first to Edwin Montagu, who had served alongside Austen on the Manpower Board. When Montagu turned it down, Austen sent Neville's name to the inner War Cabinet. It agreed with alacrity, and sent Austen to the telephone to summon Neville to London. Learning that Neville was already in London, Austen tracked him down and hurried him to an interview with the Prime Minister. Lloyd George told Neville that the leaders of the Labour party were particularly enthusiastic about him. Neville demurred and spoke of the responsibilities of the Lord Mayoralty to which he had just been re-elected. Lloyd George interjected, 'But the Empire', making an appeal he knew no Chamberlain could resist, and hurried Neville away before he could regain his footing: 'Think it over for ten minutes & send word by Austen. It would make all the difference if I could announce it now.' Knowing his brother, Austen 'did not offer to talk but sat silent & waited for his decision. He sat looking very unhappy & thinking hard for some five or ten minutes & then said, "Well, if is it put like that I suppose there is only one answer that one can give – Yes. But I don't like it. I know I can do my present work. I don't know about this. It will all be new to me, but I suppose I have no right to refuse." And so [Austen] rushed into the House [of Commons], caught Ll. George almost on the hop, [and] said "he accepts".'[45]

Mary happened to be in the Speaker's Gallery that afternoon. She was, as she told Neville, 'suddenly electrified when I heard you were to be Director of National Service. Dear Neville I can only tell you from my heart that I am proud

43  Austen to Hilda, 14 Dec.1916, 9 Egerton Place, in Robert Self, ed., *The Austen Chamberlain Diary Letters*, 37

44  Austen to Neville, 17 Nov.1916, 9 Egerton Place, NC1/27/5

45  Austen to Neville, 21 Dec.1916, 9 Egerton Place, AC5/1/4 & Neville to Ida, 24 Dec.1916, Westbourne, in Self, ed., *The Neville Chamberlain Diary Letters*, I, 178

& thankful!'[46] But his sisters responded to the news uneasily. 'I hardly know what to say to you,' Ida confessed, 'whether to congratulate or condole with you first. ... it is another good mark to the new Government ... that it should go outside & use the brains that are in the country without thinking of politics.' But 'when I think of B'ham, then I could weep salt tears! Poor B'ham. Just when it was humming with life & energy & beginning to feel itself once more the hub of the universe.' Hilda added perceptively, 'your title, magnificent & comprehensive as it sounds, is yet a trifle vague.'[47] Austen, with little appreciation of what Neville accomplished in Birmingham, had fewer doubts about his appointment: 'if this gigantic task can be discharged by any one, I believe that Neville is the man ... everyone who has spoken to me since has said the same thing: "What a task! but if anyone can do it, it is your brother!" What a tribute to the position which N has made for himself!'

Neville reeled at the 'appalling responsibility' he had accepted. 'If it was only my own career that was at stake I wouldn't care a rap,' he told Ida, 'but the outcome of the war may depend on what I do.' Like Hilda, he was also disturbed by the indeterminacy of his position and responsibilities. 'I have never had even a scrap of paper appointing me or giving me any idea of where my duties begin and end. I don't know whether I have Ireland or Scotland as well as England I don't know whether I have Munition volunteers. I believe I am to have a salary but I don't know what. I suppose I can be dismissed by some one but I don't know who.' He spent a day 'visiting various offices, 2 interviews with the P.M. unable to get anything settled about staff, faced with a demand for a scheme to be produced instantaneously'. 'I do wish I had you to cheer me up & tell me I am not so utterly incapable of grappling with this job as I feel at present,' he moaned from London that night to Annie, who felt equally at a loss in Birmingham where she was recovering from a miscarriage.

Meanwhile Ida and Hilda also found new tasks in the public service. Lady Mildmay, wife of their local grandee in Hampshire, came to call, saying that 'the War Office want to get the camps at Aldershot & Bordon supplied with vegetables etc from the neighbourhood & if Cooperative Unions can be formed they will undertake to buy all the produce at market prices'. Ida leapt at the suggestion: 'just the thing I have been looking for ... it would be congenial work & ... would go on after the war & it would make me known & if I subsequently wanted to become a Guardian or go on the County Council, both things I have sometimes thought of, it would make it much easier for me.' Ida had some experience of farm management from her custody of the family farm at Highbury. Hilda was delighted that Ida

---

46 Mary to Neville, 19 Dec.1916, 17 Dean's Yard, Westminster, NC1/20/2/12
47 Hilda to Austen, 22 Dec.1916, The Bury House, AC5/2/38

would spend the working week as well as the weekend with her at the Bury House. And Austen shared her delight: 'We shall miss Ida's visits to London,' he wrote; but 'I have never been satisfied that her present work was equal to her capacity.'[48] Ida duly became secretary of the branch of the Grower's Cooperative Association for Odiham and the surrounding parishes. She strode 'out in one direction or another every day to interview possible Growers or to try & get orders for her seeds.'[49] Hilda meanwhile started an infant welfare centre. Together they also organised a war savings society. That initiative involved yet 'another house to house canvass of the parish; – I think for the fifth time since I have been here! They must hate the sight of us coming to their doors.'[50]

By springtime Ida's Grower's Cooperative was producing so much that they had to rent storage space in the village. Hilda's Infant Welfare Centre led her into still more forms of public service. She made her first public speech to a mothers meeting, and discovered that she shared some of Bea's talent. Work with the Infant Welfare Centre also raised 'the question of feeding the school children'. Hilda felt 'that it could be a very good thing particularly in winter to provide meals for the school children ... with the fearful rise in price of food stuffs these children cannot be sufficiently fed ... the next move must be to propose it to [the school] Managers & if they agree to form a small committee of ladies to go into the questions & see what can be done.' She turned to the question of costs: 'success depends on its being more or less self supporting. ... I don't see that we could charge less than 2d a meal & I don't know if the parents would pay that, but where there were several children we should have to reduce the price or we should not get the very ones we need.'[51]

While Ida and Hilda adapted to the wartime needs of Hampshire, with the approach to public service they had learned in Birmingham, Beatrice emerged as an oratorical echo of her father. The exhortations she delivered in her various wartime campaigns attracted national attention. She was asked by the Headmaster of Bradfield to speak at the distribution of the college prizes. Inspired by the address her father had delivered many years ago at the University of Glasgow on 'Patriotism', Bea applied his message to a country at war. 'Those who are but a few years your elders are giving themselves, and will give themselves for their country,' she told the schoolboys gravely; 'and therefore a harder task than usually falls to

48  Hilda and Ida to Neville, 22 & 29 Dec.1916, The Bury House, NC18/2/49, & Austen to Hilda, 24 Dec.1916, The India Office, AC5/1/5
49  Hilda to Austen, 16 Feb.1917, The Bury House, AC5/2/48
50  Ida to Austen, 2 Feb.1917, The Bury House, AC5/2/46
51  Hilda to Neville, 30 Mar.& 25 May 1917, NC18/2/58 & 67

those of your age will be left to you. There will be less playtime in your lives than is usual in the lives of grown men. You will have to take their places as well as your own.' The work the boys would have to shoulder at the end of the war would be 'the work of peace'. That work might seem less glamorous than the battlefield. But 'each one of you must remember that what is worth doing at all is worth doing well. It does not matter whether you are going to take up life at home, to plan the defence of the country against any future foe, whether you are going to maintain her outposts, whether to work in her offices, whether to cure her sick bodies or to tend her sick souls, it is all worth doing well'. She assured them that glorious achievements awaited them because the British had been 'stirred to our depths. You will find ears unstopped, hands that are willing, minds open as never before. ... you will be able to make a new earth'.

In closing, she attempted to broaden the social horizons of the privileged youth in front of her. She began with the working man, whose demands his social superiors often dismissed as unreasonable. 'I want you to try to understand his difficulties. Remember he has gone into the trenches and has fought side by side with the best you had to send of your brothers and your fellows. ... Never let your minds be shut to your fellow Britons in any class of life. Let us get rid of that. Let us build up a better England.' Then she turned to 'the men from Overseas. ... They are fighting the battle of each of us, their own as well as yours and mine. Let us remember to make a place for them. Let us remember, too the native races ... And then the boys ... cheered the daughter of the great Imperial statesman and went up, a little shyly, to receive their prizes.' The boys of Bradfield were not the only ones to cheer. *The Observer*, Britain's leading weekly, published an extensive account of her speech.[52] Austen sent Ida and Hilda a copy: 'Just read this report ... & tell me if you are not proud of her! ... how Father would have rejoiced in such a message delivered by his daughter. ... his spirit lives in her.'[53]

Joe's sons had a much harder time than his daughters that year, especially Neville. The year began for him with 'a restless and nightmary night' in London when he 'kept dreaming about the Lord Mayoralty ... I thought how I had been for a little while the "first citizen" of Birmingham and how I should never again be first anything anywhere, and it all seemed a bitter pill to swallow.' He was encouraged next day by encounters with officials familiar with the task he faced. His spirits then swang to the other extreme. He toyed with 'vast and revolutionary notions of turning the whole war industry of the country into a State owned concern in

52  25 Mar.1917
53  Austen to Hilda, 25 May 1917, 9 Egerton Place, AC5/1/20

which every one should be only an officer or a private and all the surplus should go to the State!!!'[54] He was slow to recognise that the pledges Lloyd George gave to organised labour not to impose any form of industrial conscription ruled out Neville's reliance upon state control of Britain's manpower. Similarly, though Neville knew his way around the Council House in Birmingham, he knew next to nothing of Whitehall and Westminster. At the close of his first week on the job, he was warned by a prospective chief of staff that the civil service 'had perceived that I had really no powers' and that 'accordingly I must put up a memorandum to the War Cabinet asking to be made a Minister, which would involve my going into Parlt.' Neville checked with Austen, who blissfully reassured him that the War Cabinet, of which he was not a member, 'would give me any powers I wanted as soon as I was in a position to define them.'[55]

Ida, on the other hand, already discerned the possibility of failure. She consoled Neville 'with the belief ... that if there is any way out you will find it, & that if you don't find it, it will be because it doesn't exist. In that case I should be sorry indeed that you should be connected with the failure but I should feel sure no one else could have done better.' Neville now 'wasn't quite certain whether I should be "sacked" or resign'. And his fortunes fluctuated sharply. One week the newspapers praised his speeches, and Lloyd George smiled upon him 'most benevolently'. Next week the press turned on Neville, and his credit with the Prime Minister fell. Austen supported Neville in meetings of the full Cabinet: 'but we have not got our way – yet!'[56]

Neville never got his way because his approach to the work of government was fundamentally incompatible with that of Lloyd George. Neville's approach was to go 'personally into all the details and satisfied myself that the scheme was workable before I launched it. ... it is extraordinary how loose many people are in drafting out the outlines of a plan.'[57] That very looseness in drafting epitomised Lloyd George. He possessed an intuitive talent for unconventional initiatives – like his appointment of Neville as Director of National Service. But these initiatives were not accompanied by a detailed grasp of the underlying issues. Neville also faced an

---

54  Neville to Annie, 3 Jan.1917, 35 Egerton Crescent, NC1/26/96

55  Neville to Annie, 8 Jan.1917, 35 Egerton Crescent, NC1/26/99

56  Ida to Neville, 18 Jan.1917, The Bury House, NC18/2/51, Neville to Ida, 21 Jan.1917, Westbourne, & to Hilda, 10 Feb.1917, 35 Egerton Crescent, in Self, ed., *The Neville Chamberlain Diary Letters*, I, 182 & 186, & Austen to Ida, 10 & 25 Feb. & to Hilda, 17 Feb.1917, AC5/1/10, 12 & 14

57  Neville to Hilda, 10 Feb.1917, 35 Egerton Crescent, in Self, ed., *The Neville Chamberlain Diary Letters*, I, 187

enormous bureaucratic challenge. The office to which he was appointed did not exist; he had to put it together. And he had to do so in face of competing claims for the staff and services from established departments of state, particularly the War Office and the Ministry of Labour. The Ministers in charge of these departments defended their turf more fiercely, Neville remarked, than the Germans did their trenches in Belgium and France. And he lacked a position in Parliament on which to stand his ground against them. Austen lent Neville his aid. But since Austen was not a member of the inner War Cabinet, his aid proved ineffective, and his assurances actually misleading.

Neville became aware of the precariousness of his position within weeks of his appointment. But it took half a year to become obviously untenable. Toward the end of June Neville tried to force the War Cabinet to a clear decision on the future of his department. Lloyd George put him off, always able to claim that there were more pressing demands of the war to deal with. Neville vented his frustration to his sisters, who shared his depression at 'the unsatisfactory state of your job. It is sickening ... to be given a new job with "plenary" powers only to find that everything is taken out of your hands first by one dept. & then by another.'[58] The deepening impasse reminded Neville again and again of Andros. 'I am in a position that reminds me of the Bahamas when the plants didn't grow. With all the Departments against me and a chief who won't help I see no chance of success.'[59] Ida and Austen encouraged him to resign: 'although like you I hate the idea of your giving up & admitting failure,' Ida wrote grimly, '...I am sure you are right to resign rather than remain in a situation in which it is impossible to accomplish anything.'[60] Yet Lloyd George contrived to deny Neville a clear issue for resignation. His predicament was worsened by 'vicious attacks' by the press. They threatened to realize his worst fear: that after 'having threatened resignation & being kept waiting for a month I should be dismissed in an atmosphere already prepared for my decease.'[61]

At last he gave his resignation to a Prime Minister who was only too ready to accept it. Lloyd George thus earned Neville's lifelong loathing. He poured out his anguish to Hilda, praying that the implications of his resignation would prove harder for Lloyd George than for himself. 'I hate giving up an unfinished job

---

58 Hilda to Neville, 28 June 1917, The Bury House, NC18/2/70

59 Neville to Hilda, 1 July 1917, Rowfant, Crawley, Sussex, in Self, ed., *The Neville Chamberlain Diary Letters*, I, 208

60 Ida to Neville, 7 July 1917, The Bury House, NC18/2/71

61 Neville to Hilda, 22 July 1917, Rowfant, in Self, ed., *The Neville Chamberlain Diary Letters*, I, 213

especially in an atmosphere of failure but ... under a man like Ll.G. it was impossible to go on. He really is quite impossible to work with & I am convinced that sooner or later he will come to grief. No one can carry on his work if he does not command the confidence of those about him & one after another his friends and supporters are becoming estranged. ... the poison of mistrust is spreading though the House [of Commons] & is bound presently to extend to the man in the street.'[62] His sisters shared his sentiments: 'we both feel like congratulating you on being free again, though it is difficult to prevent one's blood boiling at the thought of the way you have been treated. That mean little skunk takes all without the slightest hesitation, & feels neither gratitude nor any sense of obligation or decency. ... If he comes to grief, – well you are better outside than inside ... & I don't think he can stand long.'[63]

Mary placed a more positive gloss on Neville's resignation. 'I have felt for some time that sooner or later the breaking point would come,' she wrote, '– and I am glad it has come. It is intolerable to be placed in such a position as you have been, & the longer you stayed in it the more involved you would have become. ... lately various people who look on from the outside have spoken of you & said "he has been most unfairly treated" ... I was proud to have you take up the call – & now I am proud to have you refuse to go on against your judgement. ... I do not feel in the least that you have failed, I feel you have bought experience which will one day repay you, for properly dealt with there is a great opportunity before you. ... you have tried to give of your best, & have given all that you were permitted to do, but not all that it is in you to give if you can get a hearing. Surely the House of Commons is the place for this – & I hope you will now try to see whether you can enter it, & enter it quickly. ... your Father's sons stand apart & have shown that they "will do right".'[64]

Mary applied reassurance to Austen as well as Neville. The year had proved little kinder to the one than to the other. In January Ivy gave birth prematurely to a boy, Laurence, who at 3¾ pounds was 'the wee est of wee things'.[65] He was subject to what Austen called blue-cold fits, and his survival remained in doubt for weeks. The precarious health of the baby added to Austen's financial concerns, for he felt obliged to hire two nurses. Ivy's health also deteriorated; she spent much of the

62  Neville to Hilda, 12 Aug. 1917, Rowfant, in Self, ed., *The Neville Chamberlain Diary Letters*, I, 214
63  Hilda to Neville, 10 Aug.1917, The Bury House, NC18/2/73
64  Mary to Neville, 10 Aug.1917, Newquay, NC1/20/2/13
65  Austen to Hilda, 12 & 20 Jan.1917, 9 Egerton Place, AC5/1/6 & 8

rest of her life abroad in costly searches of recovery for her premature child and herself. Austen spoke to his siblings fully about Laurence's condition. But he said next to nothing to them about his concerns as Secretary of State for India. The war, which stretched into the Middle East, was bound to affect the western approaches to India, including what was then called Mesopotamia, now Iraq. Austen tried to keep 'within the narrowest possible limits'[66] the attempt by the British commander of the Indian army in the area to seize Baghdad. Austen urged caution also on the Viceroy, who nevertheless encouraged the venture. Austen voiced alarm at the conditions in the hospitals for casualties of the campaign; but again to no effect. When the attempt to capture Baghdad collapsed, the Mesopotamian campaign drew criticism in Parliament and necessitated an enquiry. Little criticism was levelled at Austen. Yet he was formally responsible for the maintenance of British interests around India.

The Mesopotamian Commission issued its report at the height of Neville's troubles, and it broke through Austen's reserve with his sisters and brother. The report, he told Hilda, was 'the most appalling document that I have ever read. The worst features are that not only was the expedition ill-found from the first but that high placed & responsible officers deliberately concealed the truth & reported falsely in reply to my enquiries.' Even so, Austen did 'not altogether escape blame ... I am blamed ... for saying in "private" telegrams or letters what I ought to have said in public'.[67] The report hence touched Austen's sense of honour. Behind his façade of reserve lay the most vulnerable of Chamberlain hearts. He unburdened himself to Ida and Hilda during a day-long visit to the Bury House: 'there is no one that I would rather be with when anxious & in sorrow than my sisters,' he wrote on his return to London. 'I know you feel <u>with</u> me as well as <u>for</u> me & that you understand; & you say just what is necessary & no more & you let me talk & follow my thoughts, & I can be just what I feel & am at the moment. ... I have been blessed more than most people – in my wife, in my home from childhood till now, in my brother & sisters – & in my own way I thank God & I thank & love you all. ... Papa would be very pleased with his children. ... My dear sisters, the tears come to me as I write & they are a relief after the strain of those hours of anxiety.'[68]

After this visit to the Bury House, Austen opened up with Neville. Both brothers were now contemplating resignation. Austen was offered the Paris embassy as a way out of his difficulties, but Neville warned him that to accept would bring

---

66  Austen to Ivy, 4 June 1915, 9 Egerton Place, AC6/1/176
67  Austen to Hilda, 7 June 1917, House of Commons, AC5/1/29
68  Austen to Ida, 24 June 1917, 9 Egerton Place, AC5/1/30

his political career at home to a close. Austen declined. None of Austen's siblings, however, endorsed his inclination to resign as Secretary of State for India. 'Of course dogs will always bark,' said Ida, 'but I don't see that anyone can make anything of a case against him, & if he is attacked he will find it easy to vindicate himself. But he always carries other people's burdens & he hates to have his subordinates attacked.'[69] What tipped Austen over the edge was the Cabinet's decision to hold another enquiry. He despised procrastination of this sort. Though it was out of character for Lloyd George to act indecisively, he was willing to procrastinate whenever it suited him.

The resignations of the two brothers had quite different impacts. Austen's resignation enhanced his reputation: 'what has specially pleased me has been the inducement of feeling that "you have an instinct for the right courses"; "we always knew you would do the right thing" & so forth, which are all testimonies to character.'[70] But Neville had clearly been let go, and his reputation for competence in the public service was badly damaged. He felt 'the intense bitterness of a failure which is not my fault but with which I must inevitably be associated. I feel I ought to have a gold stripe as one wounded in the war, but seriously it is only by thinking of those who have had their careers broken by wounds that I can reduce my own misfortunes to their proper proportions. Between ourselves,' he told Mary, 'I don't feel that Austen quite realises the difference between his resignation and mine. ... My whole life has been thrown into the melting pot. He ... has so much improved his personal position that many are asking why he should not prove the alternative to Ll.G.'[71]

Neville did not know what to do next. He could hardly re-establish himself in municipal politics after his precipitate resignation as Lord Mayor. He could always concentrate on his business interests, but that had never been his primary ambition. His family would not leave him to lick his wounds, and with one accord they agreed that he should go into Parliament at once, 'for a B'ham seat of course'. They recognised 'that all politics now are peculiarly distasteful to him, – but after all his future is in public life'. Hilda felt that 'after the war the country would be in great danger simply through its disgust & dislike of "politicians" & politics',[72] and would look for a different, untainted kind of leadership. 'You are a natural born leader of others,' she insisted; '... I don't mean that you will be P.M. for many

69  Ida to Neville, 6 July 1917, The Bury House, NC18/2/71
70  Austen to Ida, 25 July 1917, Rowfant, in Self, ed., *The Austen Chamberlain Diary Letters*, 49
71  Neville to Mary, 14 Aug.1917, Rowfant, NC1/20/1/111
72  Hilda to Annie, 18 Aug.1917, Newquay, NC1/15/4/25

things may open or bar the way to such a post, but that you will be a leader with a devoted following before long, I am very sure.' She knew that, like all the men in the family, Neville 'could never be content to sit down to make a fortune for yourself & the children ... No, public service claims you, & you recognize its claims.'[73] She hit the mark. 'Your letter was abominable clear sighted & brutal in pulling off all the clothes under which I had crawled,' he replied. 'I suppose I have had a sort of uncomfortable feeling all along as to how things would turn out but I have tried to avoid coming to a decision even in my own mind. ... I couldn't back out of public work of some kind ... I have what you may call made up my mind to go into the House.'[74]

Beatrice endorsed Neville's decision in words reminiscent of her speech to the boys of Bradfield. At forty-eight, Neville would normally have been deemed too old to embark upon a parliamentary career. But Bea felt confident that 'his age will not be the bar to getting into the swing of it or to making himself felt, that it would have been in normal times. ... I suppose no statesman ever achieved for his country the half – nay, perhaps the quarter – of what he planned, – but yet I cannot believe that anyone of them regretted giving himself to his work, – especially if it was permitted him to add – not the whole story he planned, but – some new hall, or library, or watch tower to the noble building of our national inheritance. ... One must be prepared for the taste of ashes & for constantly recurring trials, but then one may hope for not infrequent compensations & when they come, they are grand.'[75]

Austen gave Bea's words a doleful echo. 'You know enough of this life,' he told Neville, 'to know what you are undertaking, how much drudgery & waste of time there is in it & how great would be the change required in your domestic arrangements. You know also whether you can afford it. On these questions, only you & Annie can decide; but if you decide them in the affirmative, I believe there is a real opportunity open to you to secure a position of influence & to do really good & useful work. I should not say so to every man of 48 nor even to you at every time, but this is a formative & creative time, old ties are loosened, new ideas & policies are forming & I believe you have both the special ability & special experience which would make you a career in the House. You know how I should welcome

73  Hilda to Neville, 24 Aug.1917, Newquay, NC18/2/75
74  Neville to Hilda, 27 Aug.1917, Rowfant, in Self, ed., *The Neville Chamberlain Diary Letters*, I, 218
75  Beatrice to Annie, 25 Aug.1917, Victoria Hotel, Newquay, NC1/13/5/11

you there', he added. 'Your aid & council [sic] would be very valuable to me.'[76] Neville was also moved by the response of the staff at the National Service department to his departure. They were in tears when they presented him with parting gifts. Like Austen, what gratified Neville most was their tribute to his character: 'so many of them laid stress on the fact that they had had to deal with a "straight" man' – in obvious contrast to Lloyd George. As one put it, 'He's a <u>clean</u> man – an <u>honourable</u> man & a perfect English gentleman.'[77]

Finding a constituency in Birmingham proved more difficult than anyone in the family had anticipated. Neville was forced to wait for the general election expected at the end of the war. The wait grew increasingly painful as the national press renewed its attack on his performance with the National Service. Austen eased Neville's sense of helplessness by asking for his ideas 'as to the basis or principles on which we should seek to rally people' after the war. Austen thought of himself as 'on the whole' a man 'of conservative tendencies',[78] and assumed Neville to be of like mind. But Hilda recognised Neville's Radical tendencies and encouraged them. His experience as Lord Mayor and Director of National Service had increased his interest in collaboration with moderate spokesmen for labour. He wanted to explore the possibilities for electoral cooperation between the Unionist party and 'the best labour men'. In business too he looked for various forms of cooperation between the owners and the work force. His ideas on post-war reconstruction accordingly gave Austen 'much food for reflection',[79] but he did not pursue the discussion.

To the consternation of everyone in the family, Austen was drifting in another direction. Little more than two months after his resignation, Lloyd George and Bonar Law approached him with 'nice words & more than hints, that in a very short time he will have offers of a seat in the Govt again, that his brains & capabilities must not be lost to the country'. Ida and Hilda shook their 'cold blooded heads & [said] Oh yes – the P.M. is beginning to get uneasy. Here is a man who might become the nucleus of an opposition, a possible alternative to <u>me</u>. – Let us secure him. Let us get him back into the fold, – since then we need pay no more attention

76  Austen to Neville, 26 Aug.1917, Headland Hotel, Newquay, NC1/27/8
77  As Annie reported to Beatrice, 20 Aug.1917, Rowfant, NC1/13/3/41
78  Austen to Neville, 12 & 24 Sept.1917, Rowfant, NC1/27/10 & 12
79  Neville to Ida, 7 & 14 Oct.1917, Westbourne, in Self, ed., *The Neville Chamberlain Diary Letters*, I, 224–5

to his advice than we have done hitherto. We will find him a nice place which has as little bearing as possible on the conduct of the war & once there he is so loyal he will always stick to us through thick & thin, no matter how we treat him.'[80] Hilda thought Austen was 'so afraid of stickling for his own position or being supposed to look for his own advancement, that the more he hates an office the more he feels as if he ought to take it if offered to him.'[81] The position under consideration was the Home Office, which would take Austen even farther from wartime concerns than the India Office. Ivy and Mary joined Ida and Hilda in urging Austen to settle for nothing less than a position in the War Cabinet. But Austen was coming to think that 'our present P.M. is still the best man for the place & our present Govt as good as & stronger than any by which it could be replaced.' Finding 'the whole family opposed to his going back,' he reconsidered his stance but refused to 'exclude from [his] mind the possibility of entering [the government] again if asked.'[82]

All such concerns were subordinated, however, by the report that Norman Chamberlain was missing after a frontline engagement at Cambrai. The family had followed his fortunes from his days at Eton to Oxford, where he introduced his illustrious uncle Joseph to the Oxford Union. The London-centred members of the family were disconcerted by the attention Norman lavished afterwards on the unemployed boys of Birmingham who lounged around New Street station. As Austen saw it, Norman was 'attempting to reclaim the gutter-snipes of the streets. He is getting very socialistic, very wild.'[83] But like Joseph and Neville, Norman saw in Birmingham a microcosm of industrial England. He preferred service in Birmingham to a seat in Parliament, and served on the City Council for two years before Neville was elected to it. The young councillor and his older cousin grew steadily closer until Norman became Neville's 'most intimate friend.'[84] Though temperamentally poles apart, both were 'above all things practical in [their] ideas.'[85]

Norman's experience of the army after his enlistment shook up the assumptions of both men. Norman enlisted in a local regiment, where he was welcomed and respected. But his regiment did not leave England for over a year. Frustrated by the inaction, he secured a commission in the Grenadier Guards and headed for

---

80 Ida to Neville, 26 Oct.1917, The Bury House, NC18/2/81
81 Hilda to Neville, 2 Nov.1917, The Bury House, NC18/2/82
82 Austen to Hilda, 29 Oct.1917, 9 Egerton Place, in Self, ed., *The Austen Chamberlain Diary Letters*, 59, & Hilda to Beatrice, 11 Nov.1917, The Bury House, BC3/3/66
83 Austen to Mary, 18 Mar.1908, #5, 9 Egerton Place, AC4/1/232
84 Neville to Hilda, 23 Feb.1918, Westbourne, in Self, ed., *The Neville Chamberlain Diary Letters*, I, 256
85 Neville on Norman after his death, in a press cutting, NC1/18/3/95

France. Neville hoped he would 'come through all right' because he would 'be so useful in civil life afterwards if he gets the chance'.[86] The death on the frontline of another cousin, John Chamberlain, sobered but also inspired the family. Neville thought that John 'played the game with all his might' and left 'a splendid example behind him'.[87] Bea knew that John had hated soldiering: but that only heightened her praise. 'I think,' she wrote to Norman in her customary hyperbole, that 'the men who are fighting our battles now are more heroic than the soldiers of any previous war ever waged, because a large proportion of them <u>hate</u> it, hate everything about it, & do it because they know it's right.'[88]

But Norman was repelled by the social assumptions of his elite Guards regiment. 'My frame of mind must be the result of muzzling a City Councillor with military discipline!' he admitted; 'when I am given a silly order, or come across some ineptitude,' he longed 'to argue with those who give the order, or take steps to abolish the ineptitude.' He was also infuriated by the inflated rhetoric of political leaders and the press back in England: 'at the end of the war, those of us who survive & return to civil life must hold a sort of Inquisition on all & sundry – & just let them have the pent up truths – and punishments'. He had a little list: 'politicians, red tabs, newspaper men & all – including, I feel sure, Bishops "lately returned from the front"', but never Austen and Neville. 'You're like a breath of fresh air & hope,' he told Neville, 'after all the sloppy inefficiency one sees on all sides out here.'[89]

Suddenly he was struck by a 'very disagreeable – & humiliating' blow, one that Neville suppressed in his eventual biography of Norman. It was to Austen as head of the family that Norman told his story:

> You know how I have chafed at the irresponsibility & loss of initiative – & waste of time of a subaltern's life in this Regt. – & at some of the traditional attitudes towards people & things which grate on one ... & always felt ... I should be more happy & more successful when I got a company. Well I've had my company since ... my Co[mpan]y Commander got wounded – & was delighted at the increase in work & responsibility & the new opportunities for initiative.

86  Neville to Ida, 19 Mar.1916, Westbourne, in Self, ed., *The Neville Chamberlain Diary Letters*, I, 121

87  Neville to Ida, 20 May 1917, Rowfant, in Self, ed., *The Neville Chamberlain Diary Letters*, I, 201

88  Beatrice to Norman, 2 June 1917, The Bury House, BC3/7/1

89  Norman to Neville, 26 Apr.1916, 'Same address', NC1/18/2/3

Now – yesterday – the Commanding officer has told me he's not satisfied with my work – in any respect, apparently, except that I try: he won't let me keep the Co[mpan]y, but is sending me to our Reinforcement Camp ... he's ... followed out his principles by "strafing" or "chasing" me ever since I took the Company – as if I was an idle private school boy. And of course the result has been the opposite to what he's intended – it's made me worse & not better. ... I still feel I've <u>not</u> done so badly – others say I haven't ... so many of the things over which I lost my name were notoriously not my fault. ...

Anyhow – here I am much humiliated – a failure – a wash out – & very disappointed because I was so keen on the job & so full of ideas to work out – & (especially) keen on getting rid of some of the eyewash & camouflage which is the curse of the division – probably common to the army!

And I feel I've disgraced the family too – it's too bitter, & no chance of justifying oneself or thrashing the thing out.'[90]

The family did not know what to make of Norman's demotion. Ida recognised that 'soldiering [was] <u>not</u> a congenial profession' for him, and deeply regretted 'that he should be taken away from what he can do so well, to do something else that try as he may he only does badly.'[91] Neville took the blow to Norman personally. Ida and Hilda received a letter from Norman after he returned to the front that made them uneasy about his frame of mind. He certainly proved himself a hero when back in charge of a company. Ordered to attack a German position, 'he led his men unswervingly to their objective under extremely heavy fire keeping them perfectly controlled & without a trace of disorder'. Once they gained their objective, the Company Commander on Norman's right ordered the whole line to retire. Norman either did not hear or did not heed the order. He was last seen slightly ahead of his men, still advancing.[92] His body, when discovered in No Man's Land, was surrounded with 'about 18 Grenadiers and 20 Germans. ... it [looked] very much as though Chamberlain & his men caught the Germans in the open with the bayonet, and then unfortunately got caught by a Machine Gun.'[93]

'I am sick at heart,' Neville cried.[94] Though still determined to enter Parliament

90  Norman to Austen, 2 Oct.1917, same address, AC1/8/8/37
91  Ida to Neville, 26 Oct.1917, The Bury House, NC18/2/81
92  Captain Heywood Lawford, Norman's fellow officer, to Lilian Cole, Norman's mother, 6 Dec.1917, NC1/183/11
93  Lt. Col. Crichton Maitland to Lilian Cole, 5 Feb.1918, NC1/18/3/34
94  Neville to Ida, 9 Feb.1918, Westbourne, in Self, ed., The Neville Chamberlain Diary Letters, I, 254

at the next election, he doubted, as he approached fifty, that he would distinguish himself there. 'Wasn't it Mr. G[ladstone]. who said that a man could no more become a member of Parlt. at 40 than a woman could become a ballet girl at the same age?'[95] Austen said nothing to his siblings about Norman's death. He was travelling in his own orbit, on the edge but not in the centre of power, supportive but sometimes critical of the government. He admired the defence that Neville offered to the Birmingham Unionists of his performance as Director of National Service. Austen thought the speech 'extraordinarily powerful and the severest criticism which Lloyd George and his Government have yet received. ... Such a speech delivered in the House of Commons would have put the Government on their trial and I think they would have found it hard to answer it.'[96] Lloyd George's subsequent offer to Neville of the G.C.B.E. in belated recognition of his services made Austen think better of the Prime Minister. Everyone in the family endorsed Neville's refusal to accept the honour. But Ida and Hilda scorned the very idea of gratitude to Lloyd George. In Ida's eyes, Lloyd George was 'just throwing a bone to a dog to stop it growling.'[97]

Despite the low spirits of their brothers, the Chamberlain sisters began the New Year eager to embrace every opportunity to address the wartime needs of their community. Ida and Hilda were buoyed up by papers from their uncle Sir George Kenrick 'to say that we had received in lieu of the legacy in his will the sum of

**Four thousand pounds,**
**each!!!!**

There's a staggerer for you!' Ida exclaimed: 'we suddenly find ourselves rich beyond the dreams of avarice!'[98] They used the opportunity to buy a car to help them meet their widening responsibilities in Hampshire.

The wartime shortage of food prompted a string of requests from the ascending levels of local government to Ida for her help. She seized each request as a step towards more responsible office. First came an invitation from the Parish Council to serve on a Food Economy committee. She took over as secretary and widened the provision of school meals to embrace eleven of the seventeen parishes in the

95  Neville to Beatrice, 28 Mar.1918, Westbourne, BC2/2/26
96  Austen to Hilda, 19 Dec.1917, 9 Egerton Place, AC5/1/51
97  Ida to Neville, 4 Jan.1918, The Bury House, NC18/2/92
98  Ida to Mary, 30 Dec.1917, The Bury House, BC4/2/120

district. A month later she agreed to serve on the District Council. 'I think in local politics I should be a radical,' she warned Austen: 'I can't stand the frame of mind that considers that the poor should be kept in their places & live in a perpetual state of gratitude towards those above them who so kindly look after their creature comforts.'[99] She regarded the District Council as 'a stepping stone to higher things in the future.'[100] 'Yesterday I attended my first meeting,' she reported, 'Board of Guardians at 11 o'clock, District Council at 1.15 ... Everyone very polite & kind, appeared to think I might find it formidable, & be nervous – Didn't – wasn't.'[101] She concentrated on housing and Poor Law administration, issues in which Neville was interested because of their bearing on post-war reconstruction. Brother and sister exchanged detailed notes on the housing they hoped to develop. Ida was dismayed by 'the viciousness of a system where the wages are insufficient to allow the labourer to pay an economic rent'; and she found Neville's ideas on a minimum wage 'a great step in the right direction.'[102]

It was far from clear in the early months of 1918 that this was to be the final year of the war. Bombs fell, and Zeppelins conducted raids over London. As German submarines intensified their attack on the sea lanes, food had to be rationed. Revolution had knocked Russia out of the war, freeing Germany to mount an all-out assault in the west before the military might of the United States was brought to bear. Ida groaned that, 'with Huns you feel sure that once they had established themselves in Russia & had her resources at their back they would return to their old ambitions & once more set out to dominate the whole of Europe. The idea that another generation might see a repetition of the horrors of this one is not a cheerful one, & the only remedy one sees, the military defeat of Germany, seems as far off as ever.'

The intensifying assault only accentuated Beatrice's defiance. Hilda thought she took it too far over the Zeppelin raids in London. 'I realise that you don't want to appear to fly from them,' she conceded, 'but I think it is ridiculous to say you won't go away at Xmas because conceivably one might take place.'[103]

Bea threw all, indeed more than all, her strength into the struggle to mobilise the country's resources for the war and post-war reconstruction. She carried her campaign for war savings around the country. She dedicated still more of her

---

99  Ida to Austen, 23 Jan.1918, The Bury House, AC5/2/84
100  Ida to Beatrice, 12 Feb.1918, The Bury House, BC3/3/77
101  Ida to Neville, 29 Mar.1918, The Bury House, NC18/2/105
102  Ida to Annie, 14 Apr.1918, The Bury House, NC1/16/4/13
103  Hilda to Beatrice, 11 Nov.1917, The Bury House, BC3/3/66

energies to extend Unionist women's organisations. She chuckled over her own 'vehemence', but could not help exaggerating the importance of her objectives: 'if we don't organise the party, which cares first of all for national freedom, honour & strength to guard the right, we may lose all both our own future & that of the world for hundreds of years to come.'[104] She worked with Neville, who controlled the Unionist organisation in Birmingham, to accommodate the women who were about to be enfranchised. All the Chamberlains, daughters and sons alike, had opposed votes for women, true to their father's insistence on that issue. But now they accepted it as one of the changes that the war made irresistible. Bea's attitude was also modified by her wartime experience. She was disgusted at the spineless male leadership of the Unionist party, particularly at Bonar Law. Like her sisters, she had come to think that women usually got things done while men gave themselves supervisory positions. She therefore fought for the retention of separate associations for women. Otherwise, she argued, the lively women among Unionists would find their way into 'the Women's Party, – or the Labour, or Liberal parties which are giving them place as organized bodies – or to bodies like the National Union of Women Workers, which is developing a strong tendency to become a sort of Women's Social Reform party, ostensibly outside politics, but in reality under Radical direction.'[105] Like Austen, Bea was less of a radical than Neville and his sisters.

Austen was the last of Joseph's children to air his public concerns to the family. He felt impelled to do so by the unanimity with which they had opposed his return to government office the previous autumn. The family were in full accord with his springtime denunciation of Lloyd George's gift of ministerial positions to the press barons who had attacked him. Austen still insisted that, 'With all his faults,' Lloyd George 'has certain great qualities specially valuable at this time & I want not to destroy him but to save him from his own folly & crookedness.'[106] Speaking for Hilda as well as herself, Ida would only concede 'that L.G. has great qualities which are most useful in their place, but he has equally great defects & the longer he remains in office the more obvious those defects become'. She concluded with a humorous revelation of all the offices she and Hilda had accumulated during their three years in Odiham: 'The above is the opinion not only of the Misses Chamberlain of the Bury House but of the Rural District Councillor, the Chairman of the School Dinners Association, the Secretary of the Food Economy Committee,

104  Beatrice to Neville, 24 Mar.1918, 35 Egerton Crescent, NC1/13/2/159
105  Beatrice to Neville, 10 Feb.1918, 35 Egerton Crescent, NC1/13/2/156
106  Austen to Hilda, 2 Mar.1918, Barton St. Mary, in Self, ed., *op.cit.*, 77

the Registrar of the Womens War Agricultural Association, the Secretary of the Surrey Hants & Berks Growers Ltd, the Secretary of the Infant Welfare Society, the School Manager & the Secretary of the Working Party. The gardener & the poultry woman entirely concur!'[107] Austen responded in a similar vein: 'You are far too experienced in the ways of men to be much surprised on learning that, having invited your advice & received it (you & Hilda are in truth veritable Pooh-Bahs), I am going to act in defiance of it.'[108]

His attack on the inclusion of the press barons in the government elicited enough sympathy in Parliament to disconcert Lloyd George. But the German assault in France only increased Austen's willingness to take office under the man he insisted was 'still the best War Prime Minister'. This time Austen took pains to win family approval for his course of action. He assured Neville that it would be 'quite another thing to suggest that we should take service under [Lloyd George] permanently or confide the fortunes of our Party or ourselves to a politician who is so erratic and so untrustworthy'.[109] He also kept Neville abreast of the discussions that preceded his return to office. Neville accordingly endorsed his acceptance of a place in the War Cabinet. Bea agreed that he had 'done his duty in going in again'. But she found it 'impossible to be glad for him personally; he must lose by it.'[110] Once back in office, Austen reverted to his former practice and refused to divulge his political concerns to anyone but Ivy. 'As regards politics he was in one of his most aggravatingly uncommunicative moods,' Ida complained after a visit: 'It was like extracting teeth to get any information out of him beyond "yes", "no" or a shrug of his shoulders.'[111] Nor did he welcome suggestions on political matters from his siblings. Neville wondered whether his father had so bombarded Austen with advice that he 'instinctively [took] up a defensive attitude'.[112]

The ferocity of the German assault on the western front deepened Austen's reluctance to discuss affairs of state with his family. They shared his anxiety about the military situation: 'we keep on losing ground bit by bit,' Ida wrote in alarm, '& though they say always territory does not matter, yet one does wish there was a little

107 Ida to Austen, 5 Mar.1918, The Bury House, AC5/2/87
108 Austen to Ida, 9 Mar.1918, Barton St. Mary, in Self, ed., *The Austen Chamberlain Diary Letters*, 77
109 Austen to Annie, 20 Mar.1918, 9 Egerton Place, NC1/27/147
110 Beatrice to Annie, 21 Apr.1918, 35 Egerton Crescent, NC1/13/5/24
111 Ida to Neville, 2 May 1918, The Bury House, NC18/2/108
112 Neville to Hilda, 20 July 1918, Westbourne, in Self, ed., *The Neville Chamberlain Diary Letters*, I, 278

more of it between the Germans & Amiens & the sea.'[113] Most of the family fell ill, pulled down by the deteriorating wartime diet as well as the depressing news. Ida and Hilda alone flourished. Ida was placed by the District Council on its housing committee: 'we go round on tours of inspection about once a week,' she reported with relish, 'poke our noses into all the most disgusting places we can find & get slanged for our pains by all the agents of the big estates in the neighbourhood.'[114] The sisters' experience wrestling with various departments of state for grants to meet local needs confirmed their reliance on local action: 'if there is not some de-centralization of powers soon,' said Hilda, 'it will be impossible to carry out any work.'[115] Later in the year the sisters agreed to set up branches of the recently established Women's Institute around Odiham.

The prolongation of the war wore Beatrice out. She showed signs of heart trouble along with broken blood vessels in ear and eye that made her 'look as if I had been fighting or drinking'.[116] Though informed of the cause, she would not tell her family. A month later she was 'apparently still cramfull of gout in all possible ways, except gout itself'. Yet she remained insistently optimistic: 'I always greet the day I was born with gratitude for all that life has brought me,' and wrote: 'Had I been consulted in limbo, I should have said: I wouldn't miss it for anything!'[117] And she continued to meet the demands of her increasing public commitments with excessive conscientiousness. Her father had once said to her, 'Of course you must do your duty, my dear, we all know that, but are you sure you are not making a duty where there isn't one?'[118]

Everyone but Beatrice felt better that summer as the German assault receded. September brought 'glorious news of the war': 'although we may not get appreciably further this Winter,' Ida dared to feel that 'there are boundless possibilities before us.'[119] 'We all feel breathless,' Hilda wrote a few days later, '& one hardly knows how to wait for one's morning paper.'[120] Austen revealed a little news going round in government circles. 'The air is full of rumours of further armistices or peace proposals ... & every demi-semi-official & unofficial busybody is whispering in any ears whose duty it is to listen, but I see no signs as yet of any authorized

---

113  Ida to Beatrice, 19 Apr.1918, The Bury House, BC3/3/84
114  Ida to Austen, 3 Apr.1918, The Bury House, AC5/2/95
115  Hilda to Austen, 28 July 1918, The Bury House, AC5/2/111
116  Beatrice to Annie, 28 Apr.1918, 35 Egerton Cresce3nt, NC1/13/5/24
117  Beatrice to Annie, 26 May 1918, Odiham, NC1/13/5/28
118  Beatrice to Neville, 16 Sept.1918, 35 Egerton Crescent, NC1/13/2/160
119  Ida to Mary, 29 Sept.1918, The Bury House, BC4/2/134
120  Hilda to Austen, 3 Oct.1918, The Bury House, AC5/2/123

approach from any quarter. Such may come at any moment ... Germany is in a tight hole'.[121] He also confided to Neville his unhappiness at the infrequency with which Lloyd George consulted the Cabinet. The pace of events at the end of October was too rapid for much letter writing. Hilda agreed with Austen that it was better to reach an armistice rather than invade Germany. 'I should think,' she added hopefully, that the war 'will have pretty effectually drained out the blood & glory spirit, & that whatever form her Govt. takes in the future, it will be a peace at any price govt, for the next generation.'[122]

Just before the war reached its end, Bea accepted her most important assignment in the public service: membership of the Women's Advisory committee for the Ministry of Reconstruction. But the cost of boundless commitment caught up with her. 'I have had a terrific cold in my head this week, not flue [sic],' she insisted, ' – & it isn't gone yet, but I don't feel pulled down by it ... It didn't prevent me from making a very good speech to women voters.'[123] She kept going throughout the day on which the armistice with Germany was signed. She spoke that morning to a committee of '"Industrial Women" of a pretty stiff type' and in the afternoon to a collection of South Kensington ladies. 'Oh that I could have been in the Abbey or in front of Buckingham Palace ... or with the crowds anywhere!' She longed to celebrate with her family. She attempted to dine with Mary, 'but couldn't get a vehicle ... I knew the trains were quite impossible, & my cold is too bad to try walking in the rain at night ... Austen & Ivy have gone to B'ham, so they are with Neville & Annie.'

So she spent the evening by herself, writing to her sisters.[124] 'I had up a bottle of Graves & drank to the men who have fought for us & the memory of the dead ... Do not your thoughts keep going to Norman & John? And to all those less known to us who went in their spirit?' Her mind turned to the political consequences of the armistice, in accord with Austen: 'my own belief is that we shall have the election at once. ... I don't think ... anyone has a dog's chance against Lloyd George & his men just now – & I say Heaven be praised for it. I'd sooner trust him, with my brother A. to watch that the needful points are secured, & a thumping majority to strengthen his hands – I'd sooner trust him to make the peace good & sure than any other available man. Oh! I am glad for the old who have seen this day, & for the young who are spared & for the women, whose hearts need not ache. For the others

121 Austen to Hilda, 4 Oct.1918, Thornhill, AC5/1/106
122 Hilda to Austen, 31 Oct.1918, The Bury House, AC5/2/127
123 Beatrice to Annie, 10 Nov.1918, 35 Egerton Crescent, NC1/13/5/35
124 Beatrice to Ida & Hilda, 11 Nov.1918, BC3/2/51

one can but say: It has not been in vain.' On the envelope in which she enclosed her message, Ida wrote: 'Beatrice's last letter.'

Ivy took charge when she discovered on her return from Birmingham that Beatrice was ill in bed. Still for a few days the family did not appreciate how ill. It was the dreaded Spanish flu, which led to pneumonia. When Hilda reached Egerton Crescent, she found Beatrice 'quite herself, but very weak'. She tried to encourage Bea with talk of taking her to the seaside once she was convalescent. 'It's all right either way,' Bea responded, and Hilda knew 'she felt that the War was over, and her work was done.'[125] She died just after midnight on November 19th surrounded by her brothers and sisters.

Tributes poured in from all over the country and beyond, from the organisations she had served and the individuals to whom she meant much. One came from Oliver Wendell Holmes, now Justice of the U.S. Supreme Court. The keenest expressions of loss came from the women in her extended family for whom she had 'always been such a "mother",' as one of them put it.[126] Her cousin Cecily could not 'imagine the world without Bea. Why one loved even her failings, they all sprang from her generous, overflowing nature. ... always before one – creating a precedent – setting one an example of high endeavour – public spirit & family devotion. It is as if a tree that had sheltered us had been up rooted.' 'You felt that you ought to be up & doing something when ever you met her,' wrote another cousin. 'It was the real fire of youth that burned in her & never died down,' wrote a third.[127] One woman who differed from Beatrice 'on all the questions of the day said that she considered her one of the greatest of Englishwomen ... her warm heart kindled many fires. She was a splendid antagonist, but, however sharp her blade, or however straight her home thrust, the wound was a clean one that quickly healed and left no scar.'[128] Men found it harder to understand that kind of strength in a woman. One male admirer told Ida, 'to me your sister Beatrice was just your Father in a womanly form'.[129] The front page of the service sheet at her funeral bore the inscription: 'The heart of a great woman, and mind of a great man.'

---

125  Hilda's memoir of Beatrice, BC5/10/2

126  Alice Beale to Ida and Hilda, 19 Nov.1918, Edgbaston, BC5/8/5

127  Cecily Debenham to Ida & Hilda, & Charlotte Chamberlain to Ida, 19 Nov., & Norah Kenrick to Ida & Hilda, 21 Nov.1918, BC5/8?6,7 & 16

128  'Beatrice Mary Chamberlain: An appreciation' from 'A correspondent', *The Times*, 22 Nov.1918

129  M. Austen Park to Miss Chamberlain, 1 Dec.1918, Earl's Court, BC5/8/25

*Austen and Ivy with their son Joseph at Twitt's Ghyll*

# 6

# Fraternal Division

In her last letter, Bea had thanked Heaven that Lloyd George looked likely to win the impending general election: she would 'sooner trust him to make the peace good & sure than any other available man' – so long, of course, as Austen was on hand 'to watch that the needful points are secured'. Lloyd George proceeded to win the 'thumping majority' Bea anticipated, and Neville joined Austen in the House of Commons. But the electoral triumph of Lloyd George opened up a division in sentiment among the Chamberlains between the older set – now only Austen, who, like Bea, had come to admire Lloyd George – and the younger trio, who still smouldered over Lloyd George's treatment of Neville. The division was exacerbated by the alliance Austen formed with Lloyd George and the contrary alliance that Neville formed with Austen's nemesis, Bonar Law. The division extended to policy: Neville and his sisters focused on health and housing, which they understood from their involvement in local government, while Austen guarded the national treasury as Chancellor of the Exchequer and lost touch with the grass roots of his party.

❦

The disagreement between the brothers surfaced even before the general election when Austen joined Neville in Birmingham to celebrate the armistice. Neville seized the opportunity to talk about housing, which he thought crucial to the post-war reconstruction. Austen agreed that the future seemed 'full of difficulty & danger, strikes, discontent & much revolutionary feeling'.[1] But when Neville

---

1 Austen to Ida, 9 Nov.1918, in Self, ed., *The Austen Chamberlain Diary Letters*, 99

proposed that the government set aside 'a very large sum for state housing', Austen took fright. 'It is what I always feared about my going into Parlt,' Neville confided to Ida, 'that he & I would disagree.'[2] The brothers had long taken 'rather different views of political affairs', and instead of discussing their differences 'fully & frankly', both men 'had a way of retiring into [their] shells'.[3] Their disagreement did not surprise Ida. Austen 'never will agree with you on social questions,' she replied to Neville, 'because at heart he is more of a Conservative than a Radical, whilst you are the other way about.' The surviving sisters lined themselves up with Neville: 'Hilda & I have come to the conclusion that we too are radicals at heart & get more so instead of less in our old age.'[4] Ida's survey of the housing stock around Odiham consolidated her alignment with Neville; and what she learned there enabled Neville to adapt his ideas on housing to rural areas, which they discussed during the election campaign.

Neville stood for election in the Ladywood division of Birmingham. Annie mobilised support for him there as Beatrice had for Austen in East Worcestershire, but in a different way. 'No one is safe from her,' Neville reported in adoring amazement. 'The innocent postwoman on her round is waylaid, the cabman is run to earth in his shelter, middleaged shopkeepers are dragged forth from the recesses of their back rooms ... all whisked off their feet & despatched as on a crusade to a Committee Room. ... Even the Committee couldn't help smiling as Annie addressing them in her earnest way declared that on the [polling day] they must "go out without waiting for breakfast, & standing at the street corners *drive* out the people from their homes to go and vote".' Neville and Austen, standing now for election in his father's former division of West Birmingham, shared in the victory that the combined forces of Unionists and Lloyd George Liberals won in this election. Despite their huge majority in the new Parliament, the implications of this victory were as obscure as Austen had feared. Neville thought Lloyd George might have more sympathy than Austen for his housing proposals, but neither brother trusted the Prime Minister, however much Austen had come to admire his leadership in wartime.

Once the votes were counted, the brothers and sisters alike turned their thoughts to the place that Austen might take in the post-war government. Here they found themselves in complete accord, appreciating Austen's better understanding of international than of domestic affairs. Ida urged him to think of the Foreign Office: 'he is far the best man for the post, – he has a much wider knowledge of foreign affairs

2  Neville to Ida, 16 Nov.1918, in Self, ed., *The Neville Chamberlain Diary Letters*, I, 297
3  Mary to Neville, 31 Oct.1923, aboard the S.S. Adriatic, NC1/20/1/17
4  Ida to Neville, nd because missing front page, NC18/2/140

than most of our statesmen.' And she doubted that he was 'equally well fitted for the great constructive work' of post-war reconstruction at home 'which is bound to be carried out on much more radical lines than I think he is likely to approve of'. She concluded bluntly: 'as I do not believe that there is now the least chance of his ever becoming Prime Minister, I should like to see him in a post where he would really find himself at home ... & which for the next decade or so, is bound to be of the greatest importance.'[5] Neville fully agreed.

Everyone in the family recoiled from the position that he was more likely to be offered: the Chancellorship of the Exchequer. Austen knew from experience that Chancellors are rarely popular figures. He recoiled from having to say 'no' in the name of financial responsibility to the plans for post-war reconstruction that the main domestic ministries were sure to propose. But Bonar Law wanted Austen to replace him as Chancellor so that he could concentrate his own energies as Leader of the House of Commons on maintaining the wartime alliance he had formed with Lloyd George. Lloyd George agreed only reluctantly to Austen's return. The terms on which Austen was offered the Chancellorship made brutally clear that Lloyd George and Bonar Law would treat it as a subordinate position. Still, they made their offer in terms that Austen could not turn down on public grounds, and he felt bound to accept.

Anxious that his family understand why, he sent full reports on the preceding discussions to Neville for transmission to Ida and Hilda. Austen did not disguise how shabbily he was treated. Lloyd George and Bonar Law denied him the Chancellor's customary residence at 11 Downing Street so that Bonar Law could stay there in constant touch with the Prime Minister. They even wanted to deny Austen a seat in the Cabinet. Austen angrily told Lloyd George that he had thrown him the offer 'like a bone flung to a dog',[6] and laid down two conditions for acceptance. The first had to do with financial policy. Here they agreed on cultivation of the resources of the empire – 'your father's policy in fact', as Lloyd George put it – and housing, to which Neville had made Austen more responsive. But on Austen's second condition, membership in the Cabinet, the talks came close to collapse. Bonar Law finally proposed placing Austen in the War Cabinet at least until conclusion of the peace talks in Paris. Austen accepted only 'on the clear understanding that if at any time [Lloyd George proposed] to make a Cabinet without the Chancellor of the Exchequer, I resign.'[7]

---

5  Ida to Neville, 27 Dec.1918, Thornhill, NC18/2/138
6  Austen to Neville, 11 Jan.1919, Thornhill, NC1/27/45
7  Austen to Neville, 13 Jan.1919, Thornhill, NC1/27/46

Austen's reports to his family brought them round. Neville feared that Austen's appointment to the Treasury would only 'make things more instead of less difficult for me'. He felt sure that Lloyd George would ultimately 'do the dirty' on his brother, yet did not 'see how he could very well refuse office on personal grounds'. Hilda wished that the Prime Minister 'had adhered to his resolution to exclude the Chancellor of the Exchequer from the Cabinet: Austen could then have refused with a clear conscience.' But she saved her sharpest words for Bonar Law. 'He always has been & always will be desperately jealous of Austen from the knowledge I believe in his heart of hearts, that he himself is a much inferior man'.[8]

۶৯

'I begin to feel that I can't bear it,' Austen cried within two months of his appointment. Tired at the best of times by the demands of office, Austen was also worried about Ivy, who came down with flu, though not of the dreaded Spanish variety: 'you know what she is to me ... I just look in for a minute once or twice a day, but she is best kept quite quiet & does not want to talk.'[9] His own health deteriorated. Neville 'met him in Palace Yard as white as a sheet and crawling slowly along. ... I am seriously afraid of his depriving himself of all chance of enjoyment of life if he goes on much longer.'[10] Hilda shared Neville's concern but held him back. 'I confess I don't see how he could go before the Budget unless he had a complete break down ... every one would feel his leaving at such a critical moment as a sort of desertion, & it would mean a complete end to his career, one which left a bad taste in the mouth. On the other hand I doubt very much whether he will think of getting out if he gets over the critical time of the Budget. He will then feel he has earned his holiday & can take one without relinquishing his position.' She continued to hope that he would soon resign. 'Austen could make himself perfectly happy out of political life if he did not feel that he was neglecting his duty.'[11]

Austen managed to introduce a small instalment of imperial preference into his Budget, a tribute to his father's dying dream. But that achievement did not revive Austen's spirits for long. He found more enduring relief from the purchase of 'a tiny but delightful old farm-house' in Sussex. 'It is just big enough for us to squeeze into

---

8  Hilda to Neville, 17 Jan.1919, The Bury House, NC18/2/141

9  Austen to Ida, 2 Mar.1919, 9 Egerton Place, AC5/1/121

10  Neville to Hilda, 13 Apr.1919, Westbourne, in Self, ed., *The Neville Chamberlain Diary Letters*, I, 320

11  Hilda to Neville, 25 Apr.1919, The Bury House, NC18/2/155

but not a bedroom to spare.' That limitation disposed of any obligation to accommodate guests. He loved the 'magnificent views' which the house commanded, and its 'small garden & a couple of paddocks'. He was not disconcerted by the name of the house: Twitt's Ghyll.[12] The only problem was that it cost more than he could afford. He 'spent a cruel night dreaming I was ruined. ... & we are setting to work to see what we can sacrifice to find it.'[13] Money that Ida and Hilda had made over for his children helped make the purchase possible. He sold some china, clearing over £3,000, and '£1000 worth of pictures'.[14] So he was able to spend Christmas at Twitt's Ghyll 'very snug', warmed by 'big wood fires ... resting mind & body in my accustomed way, a little digging & weeding rewarded by a bottle of beer at lunch & a nap after tea.'[15]

Though Austen was just six years older than Neville, the difference in their ages looked much greater in their first year together in the House of Commons. While Austen epitomised the tired old guard, Neville was reinvigorated by his entry into Parliament. He approached his maiden speech as apprehensively at the age of fifty as Austen had at twenty-nine, and enjoyed a similar success. His contribution to a debate on rent restriction induced the government to amend its proposal. His concentration on the problems of post-war reconstruction brought out his propensity to seek solutions in coordinated intervention by the national and local government. Hostile to socialism but attentive to what moderate spokesmen for labour had to say, he welcomed the prospect of some form of state control in the mining industry to give workmen 'a voice in the direction & a share of the profits'.[16] Ida fortified his radicalism on housing with her analysis of the situation in Hampshire, where many owners of slum-like rental housing could not afford to renovate it without financial help or a takeover by the Local Authority. She reported a need for '350 cottages to be built which at £500 apiece' would cost a total of £175,000, 'a big sum for a district in which a penny rate brings in only £500!'[17] Ida also sent this information to Austen as Chancellor to shock him into action, but to little avail.

The end of the war stimulated the sisters to extend local services in new directions. Hilda focused on the development of Women's Institutes. Ida represented

---

12  Austen to Neville, 22 Aug.1919, Thornhill, NC1/27/49
13  Austen to Ida, 23 Aug.1919, Thornhill, AC5/1/136
14  Austen to Ivy, 27 Sept.1919, 9 Egerton Place, AC6/1/354
15  Austen to Mary, 26 Dec.1919, Twitt's Ghyll, AC4/1/1202
16  Neville to Ida, 22 Mar.1919, Westbourne, in Self, ed., *The Neville Chamberlain Diary Letters*, I, 314
17  Ida to Austen, 29 Mar.1919, The Bury House, AC5/2/141

the District Council at a national Poor Law Conference of Guardians, where she came up against Bea's former friend and would-be fiancée of Joseph, now prominent in the Labour party, Beatrice Webb. Ida bristled at Webb's 'belief in the perfection of "officials". The "efficient" official is her God, & she turns down all voluntary effort without a qualm & also all local knowledge except that supplied by officials to officials.' Experience 'in this backward country district' around Odiham had taught Ida that District Councillors, though 'on the whole a pretty inefficient body', were familiar with the cases which came up for poor relief. The more Ida learned of Webb's ideas, the angrier she grew: 'what she wants is a vast bureaucracy which shall regulate all poverty ill health & immorality out of existence, & ... soon degenerate into the worst kind of inhuman machine smothered in red tape.'[18]

Ida hoped instead to build the welfare state at the local level. She persuaded the District Council to appoint a committee 'to consider the cost of living & draw up a scale of relief for our future guidance. ... at present it seems to me we have the very vaguest idea of how much it really costs to keep say a widow & three children adequately'. She and Hilda, who was elected to the Parish Council, also turned their attention to matters of public health including nursing and epidemics like the flu that killed Beatrice. Toward these ends, Ida persuaded her District Council to cooperate with neighbouring authorities and the County Council. The local chairman remarked that 'this was the first time in all his experience that the District Council had taken the initiative in working with other bodies, he thought they were to be congratulated upon it & it was all due to Miss Chamberlain!'[19] Ida and Hilda regarded Women's Institutes as an integral part of this effort. The Institute in Odiham discussed 'the desirability of cheaper milk' and 'the inclusion of medical benefit for the wife in Health Insurance' as well as 'the nature of the education that should be given to children in their last two years at school ... whether or not the ideal leaving age should be raised ... & if it were whether there should be maintenance grants'.[20]

This approach to public service carried the sisters far from Austen's concerns as Chancellor. Neville's entry into Parliament also accentuated the brothers' differing responses to the leaders of the coalition ministry. Austen was won over by an attack Lloyd George made on the press barons: 'I am not sure whether Neville was in the House – I did not see him – but if not ... he missed a treat. Lloyd George did his part admirably. He was grave, restrained & moderate in expression

18  Hilda to Austen, 25 Feb., & Ida to Austen, 26 Feb.1919, The Bury House, AC5/2/136–7
19  Ida to Neville, 2 May 1919, The Bury House, NC18/2/156
20  Ida's Diary, 18 May 1936, BC5/16

... showed good sense, reticence where reticence was required, & courage. I never liked him better'.[21] Austen was also impressed by the Prime Minister's conduct of the peace negotiations in Paris, and grew anxious only when Lloyd George rushed at international dilemmas without informing himself carefully about them beforehand. He was further gratified by the support that Lloyd George, alone among the members of the Cabinet, gave him in difficult budget discussions at the end of the year. But Neville never forgave the man who sacked him. Neville was also favourably impressed by Austen's nemesis, Bonar Law, 'struck by Bonar Law's adroitness & persuasiveness in leading the House'.[22] And while Neville was delighted by the success of Austen's budget speeches, he was irritated by Austen's refusal as Chancellor to grant even the smallest of his requests. Toward the end of the year, unbeknownst to Austen, Neville gathered together a small group of Unionists critical of Lloyd George.

Ida and Hilda reinforced Neville's dislike of the coalition. Ida argued that 'it would not be a bad thing to let the coalition go to pieces. By the nature of things its life must be one of continual compromise which is not exactly the sort of thing that appeals to the young & ardent ... Personally too, I shall never feel keen about politics as long as we have L.G. as leader. One does like to have some sort of confidence that all ones dearest principles won't be thrown over at a moment's notice on the ground of expediency, & without one's even being consulted'.[23] Hilda reinforced Neville's criticism of other ministers prominent in the coalition, particularly F.E. Smith now Lord Birkenhead and Winston Churchill, to both of whom Austen drew close. 'With all his genius,' said Neville, Churchill 'has got no judgement.' 'As you say,' Hilda echoed, 'a combination of the Lord Chancellor [Birkenhead] & Churchill fills one with as great distrust as the present regime.'[24] Neville and his sisters also resented Austen's reticence about what he was doing once back in office and his lack of curiosity about their activities.

Nevertheless, the family feeling between the sisters and both brothers remained strong. Ida and Hilda found themselves with an embarrassment of riches when Beatrice left her portion of the paternal inheritance to them. They resolved to share the most lucrative of their shares with Neville and Austen, as Hilda explained:

---

21 Austen to Ida, 18 Apr.1919, Thornhill, in Self, ed., *The Austen Chamberlain Diary Letters*, 112
22 Neville to Ida, 23 Feb.1919, Westbourne, in Self, ed., *The Neville Chamberlain Diary Letters*, I, 309
23 Ida to Neville, 23 Jan.1920, The Bury House, NC18/2/187
24 Neville to Ida, 11 Jan.1920, Westbourne, in Self, ed., *The Neville Chamberlain Diary Letters*, I, 354, and Hilda to Neville, 30 Jan.1920, The Bury House, NC18/2/188

'amongst Papa's things was the Colombo Commercial Co. which has turned out such a "plum" ... it would be only just to hand these shares over to you & Austen. ... we feel ourselves, & indeed are disgustingly rich for all our wants, & should be relieved to get rid at least of this small fragment of unearned income.'[25] Even after this gift, the sisters spent much of their time 'devising sink holes for the drainage of superfluous wealth ... We now have three beauties,' Ida reported: a recreation ground, a World War Memorial Hall, and 'most recent & most interesting ... a cottage ... as an experiment & demonstration' of affordable housing.[26]

❦

But there was no escape from the disagreement within the family on the future of the Lloyd George coalition. In 1920 Asquith's prospective return to the House of Commons made Lloyd George anxious to offset Liberal defections to the former Prime Minister by consolidating his support among Unionists. Neville's suspicions were awakened at the opening of Parliament when 'Ll.G. passed and came back specially to speak to me saying he hadn't seen me for a long time'.[27] His suspicions were confirmed by word that Lloyd George sought a fusion between the Unionists and his Coalition Liberals to guarantee his continued leadership, a fusion to which Austen proved sympathetic. 'What is to happen to me,' Neville asked Hilda; 'I shall try and stave it off but ... the thing is probably inevitable. I can never trust Ll.G. or follow him with any feeling of personal loyalty. ... If I refused to join the new party & stood out as an independent I should find myself probably in opposition to Austen ... We are rapidly approaching the moment when the decision will have to be taken one way or another and I can see no possible decision which can give me satisfaction.'[28]

Neville's quandary deepened when Bonar Law asked him to accept an under-secretaryship in the government: tantalisingly, perhaps at the new Ministry of Health. Neville saw the hand of Lloyd George behind the offer, but did not want to respond ungraciously to 'Bonar who has always been very nice to me'. When Neville told Bonar Law that he 'could not forget nor forgive Ll.G's treatment of me', Law agreed that Lloyd George 'had never done me justice' or treated him 'as one

---

25  Hilda to Neville, 26 Feb.1920, The Bury House, NC18/2/193
26  Ida to Neville, 5 Mar.1920, The Bury House, NC18/2/94
27  Neville to Annie, 10 Feb.1920, 35 Egerton Crescent, NC1/26/191
28  Neville to Hilda, 15 Feb.1920, Westbourne, in Self, ed., *The Neville Chamberlain Diary Letters*, I, 361

gentleman would another'. But he accompanied this assurance with a warning that 'if I did not take this chance I might not ever get another and he significantly asked my age.' When Neville tried to move the discussion away from his personal situation to the prospective fusion of the Unionists with the Coalition Liberals, Law replied 'that it was inevitable', that all the Cabinet approved, including Austen who 'was very strongly in favour of it'; and he advised Neville to consult Austen. But without doing so, Neville turned the offer down. As he told his sisters, 'I should be miserable with my head under [Lloyd George]'s arm again and am not so enamoured of office that I would sell my peace of mind for it.'[29] Austen pressed him to reconsider and called Bonar Law in to reinforce his efforts. They could not persuade Neville to take office but managed to lessen his hostility to a consolidation of the coalition.

Neville's rejection of office left him on the margins of the coalition to which Austen was increasingly committed. The praise that Austen's budget that year had won from the Cabinet and the Commons increased Lloyd George's respect for the Chancellor. Austen was deeply gratified: 'Certainly in this House I have a position quite my own & the pleasant feeling that men of all parties like & respect me.'[30] Neville agreed: 'Austen has still further improved his position in the House which now stands very high.' He added enviously, 'A long Parliamentary & administrative experience gives any man of ability a tremendous advantage in the House.'[31]

Economic depression and escalating unemployment that summer, which Austen's budgetary orthodoxy did nothing to alleviate, dimmed his reputation outside ministerial circles, but inside the Cabinet Austen took up a centrist position. He was convinced that continued adherence to old party divisions would deny the government the consistency in policy that he deemed vital in the postwar world. Neville gauged Austen's ascent in political esteem to be even higher than Austen did himself, and hoped that he might bid for the leadership of the Unionist party on his own: 'if Austen were ambitious of leading a party and chose to cut loose from the Govt he would have an enormously strong backing.'[32] But Hilda despaired of Austen pushing to the top 'for two reasons at any rate, first that nothing would induce him to supplant anyone, & secondly I doubt rather

29 Neville to Hilda, 13 Mar.1920, Westbourne, in Self, ed., *The Neville Chamberlain Diary Letters*, I, 366–7

30 Austen to Hilda, 30 Apr.1920, Twitt's Ghyll, in Self, ed., *The Austen Chamberlain Diary Letters*, 134

31 Neville to Hilda, 24 Apr.1920, Westbourne, in Self, ed., *The Neville Chamberlain Diary Letters*, I, 371

32 Neville to Ida, 1 Aug.1920, Westbourne, in Self, ed., *The Neville Chamberlain Diary Letters*, I, 382

whether he would ever have sufficient strength & energy'.[33] Austen brought Lloyd George to Birmingham to receive a cascade of honours. 'No living Englishman can compare with him,' Austen declared to Hilda, '& when the history of these times comes to be written can you doubt that he will stand out like the younger Pitt if not with the effulgence of Chatham!'[34]

He wrote those words under Neville's roof at Westbourne. Nothing better epitomised the difference between the brothers. Neville found the speeches of 'the little Welshman' in the Commons 'evasive & highly rhetorical'.[35] But the developing partnership between Austen and Lloyd George silenced Neville in the House of Commons; and he sought to make his mark outside in the surrounding committee rooms. He eventually immersed himself in eight committees, all on subjects pertinent to post-war reconstruction, including transport, industrial fairs, medical service, and slums. This work took place, however, away from the centre of attention; and Neville made less of a mark in his second year in Parliament than in his first.

He was depressed also by the costs of parliamentary life. 'For the first time in my life,' he admitted to Annie, 'I feel seriously concerned about finance. ... if things don't look any better by Christmas I shall have to reconsider our way of living' and perhaps exchange Bea's house in London, which they took over while Parliament was in session, for 'a service flat'.[36] The depressed economy and rising unemployment also eroded Neville's sympathy with labour. 'Workmen have got to realise that they can get no more increases, but on the contrary must suffer decreases if they are to keep their employment at all.'[37]

His uneasiness deepened the next year while Austen soared higher in the political firmament. Deteriorating health forced Bonar Law to resign his leadership of the Commons and the Unionist party. Austen was the obvious successor. Characteristically he recoiled at the prospect, and was 'inclined to say it was too late now'.[38] When Lloyd George asked him 'to step fully into Bonar's shoes', Austen mused: 'Ten years ago I ... resigned my chances not without regret ... I now accept as an obvious duty but without pleasure or any great expectations except of trouble

33  Hilda to Neville, 11 Aug.1920, Evian-les-Bains, NC18/2/218

34  Austen to Hilda, 6 Feb.1921, Westbourne, in Self, ed., *The Austen Chamberlain Diary Letters*, 145

35  Neville to Annie, 24 June, House of Commons, NC1/26/206, & to Ida, 26 June 1920, Twitt's Ghyll, in Self, ed., *The Neville Chamberlain Diary Letters*, I, 378

36  Neville to Annie, 10 July 1920, Westbourne, NC1/26/223

37  Neville to Ida, 21 Aug.1920, Overstrand, in Self, ed., *The Neville Chamberlain Diary Letters*, I, 385

38  Ida to Neville, 18 Mar.1921, The Bury House, NC18/2/245

& hard duty.' Another difference lay at the root of the troubles Austen faced. In
1912 he led the most uncompromising faction in the Unionist party. Now 'we are
no longer an independent Party with a clearly defined & perfectly definite policy
but part of a coalition bound necessarily to much compromise'.[39]

Yet Austen soon took 'a decent honest pride in being leader of my Party &
above all Leader of the House'.[40] The first hurdle he faced, an anti-dumping bill
which accentuated the difference between free-trading Liberals and tariff-reforming Unionists, did not prove troublesome. And he found that he could work well
with the Prime Minister on most issues. His siblings too were gratified by his
belated advancement. Neville reconciled himself to the probability of coalition
by reflecting that Lloyd George would 'inevitably be forced more to the Right' by
his reliance on Unionists. Wistfully Neville toyed with the possibility – 'I do not
think it very likely but it is not outside the bounds even of probability' – that Lloyd
George might 'temporarily retire for a rest and A[usten]. might become P.M.!' Still,
Austen's appointment as second-in-command was bound to make things difficult
for his brother. He had hoped to serve in office alongside Austen, but never under
Lloyd George. Neville was standing one day at the Bar of the House of Commons
when 'the P.M. came by and stopped to say a word with a very forthcoming smile.
It was evidently intended as an advance, but,' Neville still insisted, 'I don't like that
fellow.'[41] Nor was Neville likely to hold cabinet office in a government headed by
his brother: 'it is a handicap to have a near relation in high places & the nearer he
is to the highest place the greater the handicap.'[42]

Neville adjusted himself to his diminished prospects by supporting Austen as far
as he could without endorsing the leadership of Lloyd George. He refrained from
voicing criticism of the government, and gave more attention to his business concerns
around Birmingham. One of them, the Birmingham Small Arms Company, suffered
badly from the depression, though the others fared well, Hoskins spectacularly so.
Working again locally, Neville brought his ambitions for the City of Birmingham
Orchestra to fruition, luring Adrian Boult from Liverpool to be chief conductor.
Meanwhile Neville consolidated his grip on the Unionist organisation in the Midlands, intensifying his party affiliation. Ida and Hilda concentrated their attention

---

39  Austen to Hilda, 20 Mar.1921, 9 Egerton Place, in Self, ed., *The Austen Chamberlain Diary
Letters*, 154–5
40  Austen to Ida, 25 Mar.1921, Twitt's Ghyll, in Self, ed., *op.cit.*, 155–6
41  Neville to Annie, 11 May 1921, House of Commons, NC1/26/257
42  Neville to Ida, 19 Mar.1921, Westbourne, in Self, ed., *The Neville Chamberlain Diary Letters*,
II, 47

similarly on local concerns. The depressed economy turned Ida's attention away from social housing, for which governmental funding dried up, to public health. She let it be known that she wished to serve on the Health Committee of the District Council, which prompted compliance. Both sisters became president of local branches of the Women's Institute, Hilda in Odiham and Ida nearby in North Warnborough. Hilda was quite caught up in the Women's Institutes – 'I do so much believe in the movement'[43] – and was elected to the county-wide executive for Hampshire.

Though Austen was never as communicative as Neville with Ida and Hilda, he began to tell the family more about his doings in his new elevation. He wanted their understanding of his role, even if they could not bring themselves to admire the Prime Minister. The issue that made Unionists most uneasy was Ireland, now in the throes of guerrilla warfare. 'There is much restlessness & not a little discontent in the Unionist Party,' Austen explained to Mary: '... I think that we shall have a split over the Irish question ... it is difficult at present to judge its probable extent. Ireland will be the reason for some & the excuse for others. The pressure of taxation, the difficulty of reducing expenditure, & the unpopularity of cutting one's coat to suit one's cloth all combine to produce discontent.'[44] Austen, however, added to his difficulties over Ireland by prompting Lloyd George to make 'a last attempt at peace before we go the full lengths of martial law'.[45] This tactical shift enabled the government to enter negotiations with the Irish Nationalists, but also intensified opposition to the government from Tory diehards. Ireland nevertheless drew the Chamberlain brothers together. Neville recoiled from association with diehards who also opposed the constructive domestic agenda he wished to promote. He conceded that some felt that the government had gone too far to conciliate the Irish. 'But the majority ... would be apathetic. They are sick of the Irish, sick of murder & bloodshed, sick of expenditure & military expenditure above all, and sceptical about the danger of an independent Ireland. ... they wd. be inclined to back any plan that offered prospects of a settlement.'[46]

The skies were darkened for Austen in the autumn of 1921 by the same cloud whose disappearance had brightened them in the spring. Bonar Law returned to the fray. He claimed recovery of his health and was unhappy at his absence from the centre of activity. He had always been harder than Austen on Ireland; and his

---

43  Hilda to Neville, 11 Mar.1921, The Bury House, NC18/2/243
44  Austen to Mary, 25 Aug.1921, 11 Downing Street, AC4/1/1207
45  Austen to Hilda, 26 June 1921, 11 Downing Street, in Self, ed., *The Austen Chamberlain Diary Letters*, 161
46  Neville to Annie, 16 Aug.1921, 35 Egerton Crescent, NC1/26/262

return encouraged the diehards to stir up opposition at the Unionist party conference scheduled for the end of November in Liverpool. 'I am fighting for my political life,' Austen warned his sisters. 'What L'pool has in store I don't know.' Still he insisted that the agreement with Ireland which the government had in view was worth fighting for. 'I believe now that we shall carry a united Cabinet & get a solution in complete accordance with our pledges. If so, we shall have done the greatest service any body of men could render to the Empire at the present time.'[47]

The old contest between Bonar Law and Austen revived. It strengthened the bonds between Austen and the other Unionist members of the Cabinet who were ready to stand or fall alongside Lloyd George, especially F.E. Smith, Lord Birkenhead. Bonar Law meanwhile wooed the Unionists in the Cabinet who were least enamoured of Lloyd George, in particular Lord Curzon and Stanley Baldwin. For the moment this contest strengthened the bond between the Chamberlain brothers. Austen asked Neville to rally support for him at the party conference from the Unionists in Birmingham. Neville 'hustled round' and sent 'a body of 22 stalwarts prepared to vote down the Diehards'. He also induced the Unionist management committee in Birmingham 'to pass a resolution of confidence in the Govt'.[48] Austen asked Ivy, who was again convalescing on the Continent, for moral support. Better than anyone, she stiffened him to speak up for himself. 'My dearest,' he assured her, 'if I can carry the Party with me I ... do not intend to give way to Bonar again.'[49] On the eve of his speech to the party conference, Ivy wired, 'Am with you in spirit my soldier blood is up fight on.'[50]

Austen saved the day for himself. 'The Conference swayed back & forth,' he reported, 'The cheering gave no evidence of the proportions of the voting at the end, but the Die-hards were weakening even before the Conference opened ... I never spoke better ... I was easy, in complete control of myself & them, & all that had preceded gave me the fire that I usually lack. ... Today for them & for all there I am the leader, instead of merely bearing the title.'[51] It was his crowning moment as party leader. He did not forget to thank Neville 'for the part you played ... in sending men to Liverpool ... had the vote been taken before lunch it would very probably have gone the other way.'[52]

---

47 Austen to Hilda, 13 Nov.1921, 11 Downing Street, in Self, ed., *The Austen Chamberlain Diary Letters*, 171

48 Neville to Hilda, 19 Nov.1921, Westbourne, in Self, ed., *The Neville Chamberlain Diary Letters*, II, 84

49 Austen to Ivy, 9 Nov.[1921], 11 Downing Street, AC6/1/457

50 Ivy telegram to Austen, 17 Nov.1921, Madrid, AC6/2/266

51 Austen to Ivy, 19 Nov.1921, 11 Downing Street, AC6/1/466

52 Austen to Neville, 22 Nov.1921, 11 Downing Street, 'Personal & Secret', typed copy, NC1/27/58

But in the guise of Lloyd George, the worm turned and weakened Austen's grip on the Unionist party. As soon as the government secured treaty agreement with the Irish Nationalists, Lloyd George seized upon the good impression it made to press for an early general election in which the Unionists would fight alongside his Liberal supporters to renew the mandate of the coalition. Austen stood out against the proposal, fearful of the opposition that it would stir up among Unionists; and he sought support from the regional chiefs of the party organisation, including Neville for the Midlands. Neville was happy to support his stand. He even gave Austen reason to hope that, if the election were delayed for a couple of years, the two brothers might fight side by side in support of the coalition. But he warned Austen that 'there are a number of Unionists who would not agree to give up the old name and scrap the old machine and enter a new combination under a new name ... with Lloyd George accepted as the Leader of their party'. Neville placed himself candidly among that number, and left no doubt of his feelings about Lloyd George: 'by far the most popular and the soundest thing to do, would be to dissolve the Coalition and go to the country as a Unionist Party, but of course I fully realise that this is out of the question until somebody has the happy idea of "p'isoning Lloyd George's rum and water".'[53]

Austen welcomed Neville's support effusively. He encouraged Neville to join him frequently for lunch when in London: 'in all the chances & changes of life your love friendship & help are among the things I most care for.'[54] He was grateful for Neville's support because he found little elsewhere in the party. Lloyd George's call for an early election provoked uproar among Unionists. Neville gave his advice to his brother quietly. But the Unionist Chief Whip, George Younger, said in public what Neville said in private. Though the message from both men coincided with Austen's line of thought, Younger's statements won mutinous endorsement among the rank and file of the party and placed Austen's leadership in peril.

In view of the 'chaotic & uncomfortable state of affairs' at Westminster, Neville remained in Birmingham. Austen reached out to his sisters; Ida strove to keep her brothers in touch with each other. She was pleasantly surprised by Austen's apparent resilience in a situation which seemed to them gloomy: 'he has been a different man since he became Leader,' she told Neville: 'He feels ... that he can influence the course of things more than he was ever able to before, but he admitted to feeling

---

53  Neville to Austen, 29 Dec.1921, Westbourne, Private, AC32/2/13
54  Austen to Neville, 22 Mar.1922, 11 Downing Street, NC1/27/64

a great want of colleagues on which he could depend. Those who have brains are not trusted by the party, & those who are trusted by the party have no brains!'[55] But Austen's spirits crumbled under the weight of the discord in the party. 'The outlook seems to get more & more confused & unpleasant instead of less so,' Ida commented to Neville: 'I suppose now [Austen] will have to make a great effort to get the party to agree to support Lloyd George. If they do they will be more tied to him than ever. If they don't what then? L.G. threatens to retire, which is just what the bulk of the Unionists want, but would Austen under those circumstances undertake to form a Govt, – if he did would he succeed, & if he succeeded what would happen at the polls ...? And suppose Austen refused to try to form a Govt & went out with L.G. ... I confess I hate the idea of Austen's finding himself by the side of the P.M. in case of a rupture.'[56] Nothing, to the sisters' dismay, seemed to weaken Lloyd George's grip on the coalition ministry. As Hilda put it, 'the arch-fiend himself I fear there is no dispossessing.'[57]

Though well aware of the sentiments of his brother and sisters and of the damage that Lloyd George had done him in Unionist circles, Austen's commitment to the Prime Minister only deepened as the year advanced. He was impressed by the effectiveness of Lloyd George in foreign affairs. 'The Press reports, the official reports & private letters all show that he is at the top of his form & handling things & people with immense skill,' Austen insisted to his sisters: ' ... our reputation never stood higher, our influence was never greater.'[58] Austen's hopes fell, however, and his health crumbled when the Irish treaty produced civil war instead of stability in Ireland. The violence reached its climax with the assassinations of Field Marshall Sir Henry Wilson in London and the leading Nationalist signatory of the treaty, Michael Collins, in Ireland. Austen fled to Twitt's Ghyll. 'I really cannot write a letter,' he told Hilda: 'It makes me think & think & think all round what I would most wish to forget.'[59]

Supportive again on Ireland, Neville marshalled support for Austen in the Midlands. When he learned that 'some local Unionists were planning to get the Chairmen and secretaries of all the divisions to a supper at which they were to be

---

55  Ida to Neville, 3 Feb.1922, 36 Sloane Court West, NC18/2/287
56  Ida to Neville, 3 Mar.1922, The Bury House, NC18/2/290
57  Hilda to Neville, 10 Mar. 1922, The Bury House, NC18/2/291
58  Austen to Hilda, 18 Apr.1922, Twitt's Ghyll, in Self, ed., *The Austen Chamberlain Diary Letters*, 187
59  Austen to Hilda, 25 June 1922, 11 Downing Street, in Self, ed., *The Austen Chamberlain Diary Letters*, 194

induced to "show our members that we are fed up with this coalition" ... I arranged to invite them all myself to a private gathering of an informal kind to meet [Austen as] the Leader of the party & discuss the position of Unionists with him. I had light refreshments and Austen made them a speech after which they asked him questions for 2½ hours and went away in high good spirits.' After the meeting, Neville used his time with Austen to amplify the domestic programme he had previously described 'dealing with some neglected aspects of Social Reform such as the Poor Law, Laws affecting women and children, permanent provision for unemployment, agriculture etc.'[60] Austen responded sympathetically. Neville was also gratified when his usually mild-mannered brother mocked his Diehard critics in the Commons to prolonged cheers. But the civil war that erupted in Ireland undermined what faint hopes Neville had for the coalition. 'Ireland seems to have gone utterly to the bad,' he wrote dejectedly to Annie; '... I can see nothing but war in prospect there.'[61] Seeking temporary escape from the situation, he asked her 'what she would think if I proposed that we should go to Canada' in the autumn. She agreed with alacrity.

Their departure for Canada may have contributed to Austen's fateful detachment from Unionist opinion outside the Cabinet. Staying in Neville's vacated home to pay attention to his constituency, Austen sent his sisters an estimate of the outcome of a general election. It proved to his satisfaction that 'No Govt is possible without coalition'[62] and that continued combination with Coalition Liberals was possible only under Lloyd George. Austen knew that at the next party conference in November the Unionists might declare against any coalition except under a Unionist Prime Minister. But that did not hold him back. He ceased to communicate with his siblings for the next eight weeks – during which he was ousted as party leader.

Afterwards Austen told his sisters the story of his fall. The party had begun to fracture during the summer when the Unionist ministers below cabinet rank told him of their opposition to continued coalition under Lloyd George. Their protest only stiffened Austen's support for the coalition. He and the leading members of the ministry, Unionist as well as Liberal, reaffirmed their resolve to stay together. Paradoxically this decision heightened Austen's estimate of the Unionist opposition to the coalition. He pressed for an immediate dissolution of Parliament before

---

60  Memorandum of 29 Dec.1921, AC32/2/14
61  Neville to Annie, 24 May 1922, House of Commons, NC1/26/297
62  Neville to Ida, 24 Sept.1922, Westbourne, in Self, ed., *The Neville Chamberlain Diary Letters*, II, 197

the rot deepened, and the Cabinet agreed. The Unionist whips were dismayed at this decision; and when Austen insisted upon it, they 'proceeded to work against me'.[63]

He told the family that an early general election 'was quite on the cards' just as Neville left for Canada.[64] Out of touch thereafter, Neville heard nothing of the turmoil which engulfed the Unionist party. Ida brought him up to date in a letter that reached him after the storm broke. She could not, she said, 'see how the Coalition can in the present condition of affairs fight the election as a coalition ... wouldn't it perhaps be better in the long run if Labour did get in with a small majority. We might perhaps then be able to get something more approaching to two parties with real differences of policy between them.'[65]

Day by day the threat to Austen's leadership mounted. Yet he refused the whips' demand to wait for the party conference before precipitating a general election. The only compromise he offered was to summon Unionist MPs to a meeting at the Carlton Club. Thereupon his support among the Unionist cabinet ministers cracked. Baldwin at the Board of Trade declared against Lloyd George, while Curzon at the Foreign Office took refuge in diplomatic absence. Bonar Law kept his peace until the last moment. But Austen 'knew' that he would use the opportunity to regain his old position. Feeling the groundswell against him, Austen delivered an address at the Carlton Club that was 'wholly unyielding'. He refused 'to obscure the difference' with his opponents 'or to find any compromise'. The meeting rejected his advice emphatically, and hence repudiated his leadership of the party. Lloyd George immediately resigned as Prime Minister and Bonar Law took both positions.

Neville remained oblivious of these events until a telegram from Austen reached him in Toronto 'to say that a general election was to take place at once'. Hurrying to catch a steamer, Neville wrote in mounting confusion to his sisters.[66] En route he learned that Austen had called for the party meeting in London 'to endorse his policy'. Anxious for agreement with his brother, Neville mistook this to mean that Unionists and Coalition Liberals would campaign 'as separate parties under separate leaders but with the understanding that they wd co-operate afterwards'. He

63 Austen to Hilda, 20 Nov.1922, Twitt's Ghyll, in Self, ed., *The Austen Chamberlain Diary Letters*, 202–6
64 Ida to Mary, 21 Sept.1922, The Bury House, BC4/2/182
65 Ida to Neville, 10 Oct.1922, The Bury House, NC18/2/318
66 Neville to Hilda, 24 Oct.1922, on board SS Homeric, in Self, ed., *The Neville Chamberlain Diary Letters*, II, 126–8

told reporters that Lloyd George need not remain as Prime Minister, particularly if the Unionists picked up strength at the election in comparison to the Coalition Liberals. He was therefore taken aback to discover that the diehard opponents of the coalition were joined by a broad majority of the Unionists at the Carlton Club meeting to defeat Austen. Neville's 'last surprise' was to learn 'that Bonar Law had agreed to accept office'.

Neville sailed to England in dismay. 'Did Austen mean to follow Ll.G. and form a new party, and if so what was to be my position? To tie myself up to [Lloyd George] and to take opposite sides to Austen seemed equally disagreeable.' Yet Neville immediately resolved to align himself with the Unionist opponents of Lloyd George, hoping to do so without breaking with his brother. The more Neville thought of it, 'the more it became clear to me that with no fundamental difference of policy but only of personalities I could not see myself following Ll.G. and that if Austen were out of the question I should have no hesitation in remaining with the Unionists & even, if I were asked, joining the new Govt.' Neville hoped that Austen would 'remain outside the Govt as an independent Unionist, in which case I should hope we might keep the party united.' Two snippets of information strengthened Neville's hope. Bonar Law announced in his manifesto that he was 'going to call an Imperial Economic Conference if the Dominions are willing'; and from conversations Neville had with the Canadian Prime Minister, he was sure that Canada would respond favourably. 'Hurrah!' Neville ever the tariff reformer exclaimed, 'That's the stuff to give 'em.' He was heartened too by Austen's declaration that he had no quarrel with Bonar Law. Neville nevertheless hesitated to take Austen's declaration at face value, knowing that 'this was the second time Bonar had snatched the leadership out of his hands'.

Ida did not know how to advise Neville on his arrival in England: 'Personally,' she wrote, 'I feel I have no party left, for I certainly don't feel inclined to throw in my lot' with the diehards, 'nor do I feel special confidence in the fighting qualities of Bonar Law ... On the other hand I am no fonder of Lloyd George than you are ... & I fear the bulk of the Conservative party, having dissociated themselves from the Liberals will get more & more reactionary.'[67] Her use of the term 'Conservative' rather than 'Unionist' reflected her reluctant recognition that maintenance of the union with Ireland could no longer be the party's defining issue.

67 Ida to Neville, 28 Oct.1922, The Bury House, NC18/2/319

The change of government plunged the country into a general election and intensified the division between the brothers. Heartened by the burst of enthusiasm that the election generated for the Conservatives, Hilda encouraged Neville to join the new government if Bonar Law asked him. The new Prime Minister quickly indicated that he was so inclined. During the election, when poor health forced him to abandon a speaking engagement in Manchester, he asked Neville to fill in for him, and afterwards praised him on his performance. Neville was the more encouraged because he used the opportunity at Manchester to promote his own programme on housing and unemployment. Bonar Law then offered Neville the position of Postmaster General. Neville later learned that Law expected him to ask for something more important. But Neville welcomed the offer. It placed him in full charge of the Post Office, not subordinate to an overseeing minister; and he was content to prove his administrative abilities at a modest level away from the centre of debate.

But Austen responded badly. He called Neville's acceptance 'the last drop of bitterness in the cup'. Neville argued that it need not put the brothers in opposite camps. He hoped to form a link between Austen and the new government, 'facilitating [Austen's] acceptance as one of the leaders if not the leader in the event of B.L.'s being unable to carry on'.[68] What Neville feared was an irreparable breach between Austen and the Conservatives if he maintained his association with Lloyd George. But that was precisely what Austen was intent on: 'I shall try to keep the way open for a new coalition,' he told Ida, '... by not letting go of Lloyd George.'[69]

Neville then offered to turn the offer of appointment down, insisting that he 'cared more for our personal relations than for politics. But I felt bound to tell him that I should consider my political career as ended for one cannot go on refusing office when one does not differ on principles.' At that, Austen gave way, unwilling to 'carry such a responsibility. He declared that nothing should or could alter our personal relations and he begged me to accept.' Neville had given Austen such support at some cost to himself over the past two years that Austen could not refuse to do the same for Neville. Next day Austen 'rang up to say he was still of the same mind,' and left Neville 'assured now that he will feel no grievance against me' in accepting Bonar Law's offer. Ida and Hilda welcomed the agreement their brothers reached. Ever a progressive, Ida thought that 'if we are to have an all-Conservative

---

68  Neville to Hilda, 31 Oct.1922, Westbourne, in Self, ed., *The Neville Chamberlain Diary Letters*, II, 128–9
69  Austen to Ida, 21 Nov.1922, Twitt's Ghyll, in Self, ed., *The Austen Chamberlain Diary Letters*, 208

govt it is very desirable that it should include as many as possible of the advanced wing'. Hilda also recognised that Neville would 'have a freer hand & greater opportunity to make your mark with Austen outside the govt. than you could ever have whilst he was the head'.[70]

The offer nevertheless deepened Austen's sense of grievance against Bonar Law. Austen recognised more clearly than Neville how their rival alliances with Lloyd George and Law twisted their relationship to each other. 'What a tragedy it is for us two,' Austen wrote to Ida, 'that L.G. should have done the dirty by [Neville] & Bonar by me.' Replicating Neville's reaction to Lloyd George, Austen continued: 'I am not going to quarrel with Bonar, but I won't serve with him.' Nor would Austen return to the fold alone: 'I won't go back without my friends.'[71] He demonstrated who his friends were by standing on platforms beside Lloyd George and Lord Birkenhead, the Unionist former minister who turned most venomously on Bonar Law.

The brothers nevertheless helped each other when they stood for re-election in Birmingham. Austen had his work cut out for him, having rarely visited his working-class constituency. 'My people were thoroughly frightened.' They warned him that the Socialists had been hard at work on every street corner. He admitted that 'why anyone who lives in such slums should not be a Socialist, a Communist or a Red Revolutionary I am at a loss to say'. He was pleased by the difference he felt able to make: 'I am a biggish man when I get to work & if I get a hearing I think that my speeches will tell.' Even so, he was astonished at the majority he won, thanks to 'solid argument, personality & the revival of the old West B'ham feeling'. It had been his father's constituency for nearly fifty years. Now 'I have not only inherited but made personal to myself much of the old Chamberlain feeling.'[72] Gratification at his achievement in West Birmingham was accentuated by the narrow margin by which Neville held on to Ladywood, a result that galled Neville and Annie. Neville found some consolation, however, in the ability of the regional organisation which he supervised to carry all twelve Birmingham constituencies for the Conservatives.

Bonar Law's government secured a working majority in the new Parliament, and settled down to work. Austen's personal electoral victory and release from the cares of office raised his spirits. He adopted the same seat in the House of

---

70  Ida to Neville, 1 Nov. & Hilda to Neville, 3 Nov.1922, The Bury House, NC18/2/321 & 323
71  Austen to Ida, 18 Nov.1922, Twitt's Ghyll, in Self, ed., *The Austen Chamberlain Diary Letters*, 202
72  Austen to Ida, 18 Nov.1922, Twitt's Ghyll, in Self, ed., *The Austen Chamberlain Diary Letters*, 200

Commons that his father occupied in the early 1890s. Then he headed away for a prolonged vacation. He remained gloomy, however, about the political outlook. 'I am out of sympathy with the present mood of my party, irritated by the sight of B.L. & his smug complacency & very doubtful whether politics hold any future for me.'[73] His alienation was underscored by the need to find a new residence in London. He had given up Egerton Place on moving as Leader of the House of Commons into 11 Downing Street, which he had to leave when ejected from office. He found a rather depressing ground floor and basement flat at Morpeth Mansions within easy walking distance of Parliament. But he hoped to make Twitt's Ghyll his headquarters in the coming year.

Neville meanwhile took hold of his responsibilities as Postmaster General. There was immediate talk even from the Prime Minister about raising him to the Ministry of Health, for which he seemed particularly well fitted. But after his searing experience as Director of National Service, Neville wanted to begin in 'comfortable obscurity'.[74] He could not, however, fail to be flattered by the attention Bonar Law paid to him. Law took his advice on concerns of the Ministry of Health in preference to the recommendations of the Minister. And not only there: Law turned to Neville for advice on foreign affairs, on the French occupation of the Ruhr and the quarrel with the United States over reparations. 'If at any time you have any suggestions to make don't hesitate to come and see me,' he went on.[75] Neville thus rapidly acquired 'an influence in the Govt beyond what [his] office warranted'. He liked to think that it was 'ascribable to a general respect for my experience and judgement'.[76] Yet he could not but recognise that he owed it also to the inexperience of Bonar Law's Cabinet, which was much less distinguished than the one Lloyd George and Austen had led.

Though unimpressed by the performance of the new government, particularly in foreign policy, Austen was unwilling to throw himself into active opposition. He loved his newfound freedom. When, after a little weeding on the terrace at Twitt's Ghyll, 'it suddenly occurred to me that I now had all the years to finish my job I could have shouted for joy'.[77] In Parliament he threaded his way uncertainly

---

73 Austen to Ida, Sunday eve, Twitt's Ghyll, A5/1/256, in Self, ed., *The Austen Chamberlain Diary Letters*, 218

74 Neville to Hilda, 11 Mar.1923, Westbourne, in Self, ed., *The Neville Chamberlain Diary Letters*, II, 151

75 Neville to Annie, 23 Jan.1923, 35 Egerton Crescent, NC1/26/313

76 Neville to Mary Carnegie, 10 Mar.1923, 35 Egerton Crescent, NC1/20/1/122

77 Austen to Hilda, 21 Jan.1923, in Self, ed., *The Austen Chamberlain Diary Letters*, 218

between the two sides. He was uneasy about Lloyd George's movement toward Liberal reunion between his supporters and Asquith's. Ida welcomed the movement, hoping 'that it would put a greater distance' between Lloyd George and Austen: 'but what I fear is that ... at the present moment he feels himself more in sympathy with Lloyd George than anyone else.'[78] Austen voted with the government on his first visit to the Commons in the New Year; and he denounced Liberal reunion as 'either a sham or a negation of my policy'.[79] But he was quick to rejoice when the government lost a trio of by-elections: 'If Neville had not joined this Govt I'd have had them out in six months.'

&

These by-election defeats revolved around the Minister of Health, Arthur Griffith-Boscawen, who failed repeatedly to secure a seat in Parliament, partly because he also failed to devise an acceptable form of rent control for affordable housing. 'I hope that Neville will not be forced to take the M/Health & the Cabinet,' Austen commented uneasily, 'for I think that in his own interest he would be better out of it.'[80] But that was precisely what Bonar Law asked Neville to do. Shedding the scars from his failure with the National Service, Neville accepted the challenge, confident in this case that he knew what to do. He was gratified to find that this confidence was widely shared: his appointment was welcomed by the press and on both sides of the House of Commons. Bonar Law helped by releasing Neville from the commitments made by his predecessor: 'what a relief & contrast it is to have ... a P.M. who treats you like a friend,' Neville responded.[81]

His elevation precipitated a change in his housing arrangements. Annie and their children, Dorothy and Frank, were still in Birmingham, to which Neville returned every weekend. But that was hard on Annie, who extended her local commitments to strengthen Neville's electoral base after his narrow victory. Hilda gave Annie advice based on the family's earlier experience: 'If you really lived in London during the session & only went down to Westbourne as Papa went to Highbury – about once a month & for holidays, it would be a real relief to Neville ... you both

---

78 Ida to Neville, 16 Feb.1923, 36 Sloane Court West, NC18/2/3335
79 Austen to Hilda, 20 Feb.1923, Twitt's Ghyll, in Self, ed., *The Austen Chamberlain Diary Letters*, 220iH
80 Austen to Hilda, 4 Mar.1923, Twitt's Ghyll, in Self, ed., *The Austen Chamberlain Diary Letters*, 221–2
81 Neville to Mary, 10 Mar.1923, 35 Egerton Crescent, NC1/20/1/122

[are] burning the candle so hard at both ends & ... must find some way of lessening the strain.'[82] To Neville's surprise, Annie accepted Hilda's advice 'meekly'. He sold the small house that he had taken over after Beatrice's death and moved the family into spacious accommodation on Eaton Square. Meanwhile he tackled his new ministerial responsibilities with winning effectiveness. Hitherto uneasy on his feet in the Commons, he now had to speak frequently, and he relaxed into the task.

But the plaudits Neville won damaged Austen's prospects for a return to the fore. Perplexed, Austen stayed away from the Commons and spent as much time as he could at Twitt's Ghyll. Ivy too was pulled down by persisting threats to the health of little Lawrence. They welcomed an Easter vacation with Ida and Hilda in the Pyrenees. But the need to take the children along reduced the benefit of the holiday for Ivy, who spent the first night with Lawrence in her arms as he was wracked with croup. As for politics, Hilda thought that Austen was 'in a ... hopeless position ... his insistence on ... the necessity for all moderate parties to work together, may after all bring him back some day'. But 'as at present I can only see it likely if this Govt. fails, I cannot wish for it'.[83]

The situation in which the brothers found themselves was vexed further by the machinations of the press barons, Beaverbrook and Rothermere, to replace Bonar Law with Austen. He rejected their scheming, but Beaverbrook then used his newspaper 'like the scamp he is to denounce me & my friends as intriguers'.[84] Austen wrote to reassure Neville, who responded gratefully: 'only such frankness between us will keep us in sympathy with one another. I need not say that I have never suspected you of intrigue which is unthinkable in connection with you.' But Neville continued, 'There is a feeling that less respectable people shelter behind your name to carry on intrigues,' and he understood that Bonar Law 'could not hand over the leadership to you' so long as Austen insisted on bringing the likes of Birkenhead back with him. 'Personally I recognise that you could not join the Government in the near future and to attempt to bring about your immediate return to office would be futile.' Unionist dislike of the Lloyd George coalition remained too intense. Neville hoped that Austen would overcome this aversion by speaking well of the Conservative government. As a first step he pressed Austen 'to have a private talk with Bonar, not to negotiate terms, but simply to "have it out" and remove misunderstandings'.[85] Austen would have none of it: 'what good would

---

82  Hilda to Annie, 8 Mar.1923, The Bury House, NC1/15/4/34
83  Hilda to Neville, 25 Mar.1923, The Bury House, NC18/2/342
84  Austen to Ida, 22 Apr.1923, Twitt's Ghyll, in Self, ed., *The Austen Chamberlain Diary Letters*, 228
85  Neville to Austen, 23 Apr.1923, House of Commons, 'Secret', copy in Neville's hand,

it do,' he asked. 'What can [Bonar] have to say to me of the present or the future &
what good would it be to go back on the past? His ideas & mine on the obligations
of friendship & colleague-ship differ.'[86]

After this unpropitious exchange, Ida and Hilda moved swiftly to repair the
damage. Holidaying alongside Austen in the Pyrenees, they tried to gauge his cast
of mind and passed their impressions on to Neville, asking him to reply on separate sheets in his letters so that Austen would not notice. They found that Austen's
assessment of the situation differed completely from Neville's: 'all his thoughts are
directed to returning to politics & ... he believes it is likely not to be long. ... his
friends tell him that the Govt. is going rapidly down hill & ... he vaguely anticipates
a smash which may give him his chance.' Hilda wished that 'he saw things rather
differently for I fear otherwise it may be difficult for him to come back'.[87] Ida quite
agreed: 'it is amazing to me that he should think as he apparently does'. But she
also appreciated how perplexed Austen must be: 'at the back of his mind there is
always the possibility that a discredited & defeated party may turn to him as a last
resort ... but the moment he really looks this idea in the face he realises that there
is not the least probability of its ever coming to pass ... He cannot really make up
his mind that his career is ended & yet he cannot see any way out of the present
tangle.' Ida's sentiments were similarly mixed. She agreed with Austen that Bonar
Law had 'behaved to him personally in a dishonest & underhand way. ... However,
all that is past history ... The question is now what is to happen in the future.' And
on that she agreed with Neville that if Austen were 'to attend the House & <u>support</u>
the Govt ... then there might be a general call for him'. She deplored the company
Austen was keeping: he was 'at present much in the position of a King in exile – He
hears only the views of the discontented & dissatisfied.'[88]

Suddenly Austen's hopes were raised by the resignation of Bonar Law, only to
be dashed by his successor. Law's cancer recurred and forced him to retire. Urged
by his friends to return to England, Austen hurried north to Paris. But there he
stopped. His hopes of a return to high office depended on the selection of Lord
Curzon to be Prime Minister, for that would leave the Leadership of the Commons
to be filled. Stanley Baldwin, however, was appointed Prime Minister, disappointment enough for Austen, but made worse by Baldwin approaching Austen in
humiliating fashion. An embassy secretary gave him a note saying that, 'The Prime

---

NC1/27/70

86  Austen to Neville, 25 Aug.1923, Twitt's Ghyll, 'Secret', NC1/27/71
87  Hilda to Neville, 2 May 1923, Hotel du Portugal, Vernet-les-Bains, NC18/2/346
88  Ida to Neville, 9 May 1923, Hotel du Portugal, NC18/2/347

Minister wishes to see Mr Chamberlain at Chequers tomorrow.' Baldwin then used Neville to convey conflicting messages to his brother. The first led Austen to believe that he would be offered a position. The second told him that this could not be done because the diehard Tories forbade it. Baldwin added to the insult by offering Austen the Washington embassy, which would bring his career in politics to a close. Austen never forgot or forgave this treatment. Ivy poured oil on the flames: 'to say that I am a seething mass of indignation is to put it mildly! I am a volcano!'[89] Baldwin thus replaced Bonar Law as Austen's bête noire. The worst feature of the whole episode for Austen was the use Baldwin made of Neville: 'That was a dirty business & hit me in my tenderest spot.'[90]

The change of Prime Minister intensified the awkwardness between the brothers. Neville did not like Baldwin personally and had hoped that Curzon would become Prime Minister. Yet he felt some kinship with the new Prime Minister as a former metal manufacturer and accepted him as 'the nearest man we have to Bonar in the qualities of straightforwardness and sincerity'. Neville was also dismayed during the ministerial reconstruction to discover the extent of the Conservative hostility toward Austen. This hostility infuriated Hilda: they 'don't seem to recollect anything of what he has done for the party & all his work through the war,' she cried, '& solely because in the end he would not kick over Ll.G. (I admit I think he was wrong) they seem to feel that he is so low & so hopelessly out of things that only by humbly backing everything which is done by every member of the govt, can he hope to come back.'[91] Neville welcomed an invitation from Mary for dinner with Austen to restore the understanding between them. But nothing could assuage Austen's resentment at Baldwin's treatment of him. He pleaded with Neville 'as my brother ... not to facilitate my return' to the government, and 'if Baldwin at any time desires to approach me again, to prevent him from blundering into fresh offences or exposing me to further indignity'.[92]

The magnanimity with which the brothers continued to treat each other through these trying months was remarkable. The men with whom each brother allied himself seemed to conspire to set them against each other. But neither of them would allow this to happen. The bonds of family proved stronger than those of political alliance. Just as Neville applauded Austen's early successes as Leader of the Commons under Lloyd George, so Austen praised Neville's performance

---

89  Ivy to Austen, 26 May 1923, Paris, AC6/2/291
90  Austen to Neville, 18 Nov.1923, Twitt's Ghyll, NC1/27/82
91  Hilda to Neville, 14 July 1923, The Bury House, NC18/2/357
92  Austen to Neville, 1 June 1923, 2 Morpeth Mansions, 'Personal', NC1/27/72

under Baldwin in piloting a Rent Restriction bill through Parliament. 'I thought Neville's speech admirable,' Austen told his sisters, '& his style greatly improved. ... I hear on all hands that his management of the Housing Bill in Committee has been perfect. We can all be very happy in his success.'[93]

⁂

The bond between the brothers faced its most severe test that summer when Baldwin raised Neville from the Ministry of Health to be Chancellor of the Exchequer. Though this extraordinarily rapid promotion reflected well on Neville, it also reflected the lack of seasoned talent in the ministry. The Unionists with most ministerial experience had left office alongside Austen, who had first become Chancellor twenty years earlier, as he reminded Neville. It was hard to avoid other comparisons between the positions in which the brothers now found themselves. Baldwin made Neville his second-in-command, the same position Austen had held under Lloyd George.

Neville had no wish to leave the Ministry of Health. It gave him just the sort of work he was good at. Before he went on holiday, he spent some time with his principal officials at Health 'sketching in the outline of a programme for the next two or three years.' They sought assurance that he would remain with them that long. He replied 'that there was no certainty in politics ... but so far as depended on me I did not intend to move'. Rumour already had it that he might be offered the chancellorship, and he discussed the possibility with Annie. They agreed that, while he would 'rather like the compliment ... if the offer came I should of course refuse it'.[94] At that they parted for the holidays, Annie with the children to Wales, Neville for the usual fishing and shooting in Uncle George's Scottish lodge. It was there, in mid-August, that Baldwin's offer of the Exchequer arrived. 'It is very nicely put and I confess I am pleased,' Neville wrote to Annie, '...But ... of course ... I have written as nicely as possible to decline.'[95]

Baldwin would not take no for an answer. He repeated the invitation in terms that forced Neville to reconsider. He had already asked his sisters for advice. And they reacted 'with profound dismay! ... your removal from your present position would be a terrible blow to the Govt. ... their principal need in the country nowadays is a constructive domestic policy & you are the only person capable of doing

93  Austen to 'Hilda (or Ida)', 9 June 1923, Twitt's Ghyll, AC5/1/272
94  Neville to Mary (in Massachusetts), 8 Sept.1923, Harrogate, NC1/20/1/125
95  Neville to Annie, 16 Aug.1923, Loubcroy Lodge, NC1/26/325

that.' This policy was, after all, theirs as well as his. 'The scheme of the Housing Act was based upon the local authority,' as Ida wished: 'The Ministry deliberately divested itself of all the authority it could ... on the principle that the local authority ought to know its own conditions best.'[96] Social housing was as dear to Ida as to Neville. She and Hilda had used part of Uncle George's gift to fund the construction of six cottages to be let 'at a rent representing the usual rent paid by unskilled labour in the neighbourhood. ... We shall feel proud indeed if we have contributed [in this way] to the solution of the housing problem!'[97] Baldwin's offer of the chancellorship made them afraid that Neville would prove 'altogether too loyal & like Austen too anxious to assist your chief & to take his view instead of sticking to your own position'.[98]

Their fear was not unfounded. Annie lacked the sisters' gift for clear expression, particularly on paper. Her response to Neville's renewed request for advice was by her own admission 'rather tumultuous'. But she was more attuned to his state of mind than were his sisters. Neville did not know which way to turn. He reasoned that, if Baldwin had presented him with the offer 'in the shape of a reward for good service the matter would have been simple. But he says "You are the one man to whom I can safely entrust the job" ... The more I think of it the more disinclined to it I feel. Finance has no attractions for me, nor have I the temperament for perpetually clogging & checking the schemes of other people. ... On the other hand, while I don't carry loyalty to Austen's extremes, I do feel always that one must to some extent subordinate one's own inclinations to the interests of the team and the desires of the chief. Only, – if you feel that their interests are best served in the way you want & not in the way they want?'[99] Left with that uncertain query, Annie swung from side to side. Yet she grasped aspects of the offer that Neville had not identified. She pointed to international issues the Chancellor would have to deal with such as wartime loans and reparations and the stand-off between France and Germany over the industrial heartland of the Ruhr. She saw too that the chancellorship would probably involve leadership of the Commons whenever the Prime Minister was absent. And the Exchequer might give Neville the kind of constructive opportunities he liked. She and Neville would have to move out of the house they

96 Neville to Ida, 29 Sept.1923, Westbourne, in Self, ed., *The Neville Chamberlain Diary Letters*, II, 184–5

97 Hilda to Neville, 14 June 1923, Derby (at the National Women's Institute Conference), NC18/2/352

98 Hilda to Neville, 24 Aug.1923, The Bury House, NC18/2/360

99 Neville to Annie, 18 Aug.1923, Loubcroy Lodge, NC1/26/326

had just bought on Eaton Square, but she thought they could let it out at a profit.

Baldwin piled every available inducement on to his proposal. He said he had 'felt very much the absence of a colleague living [next door in Downing Street] with whom he could discuss affairs at any and every moment. ... and he would rather have me than any of his colleagues in the Cabinet'. At that, Neville's resistance crumbled: 'it appeared to me that I should be acting contrary to the principles which have hitherto always guided me in public matters if I declined to accept the responsibility.' He asked only 'to be allowed to discuss matters with Annie'. That afternoon they 'went back together' to accept.[100]

Acceptance left Neville with acute regrets. 'All my people ... are in despair,' he reported from the Ministry of Health: 'They have torn up their sketch programmes ... if I died tomorrow I should have left nothing behind but a vague suggestion of possibilities. ... There is one other thing that makes me uncomfortable,' he went on. 'I have had most affectionate and delightful letters from Austen but I can see that he still feels his position acutely and moreover ... thinks evidently that it is made even more difficult by the change in mine. ... One of my reasons in old days for not wanting to enter Parlt was a fear lest it might bring me into a difference with Austen. ... That is what has happened now.'

Austen indeed greeted the news of Neville's appointment with affectionate cordiality. 'I am sorry that fate has separated us instead of, as I once hoped, uniting us in the same Cabinet, but you are making a fine career & I am proud of your success.'[101] But the more Austen thought of it, the larger loomed the cost to himself of Neville's promotion. 'It is an immense regret to me,' he wrote again, 'that you & I do not see eye to eye and are no longer acting together. I do & say as little as I can, for politics are hateful to me since we two parted. I shall see this Parlt. out, but my position is very difficult & I think it not unlikely that I shall not stand again. The fact that you & I both sit for B'ham makes my position more difficult, for whilst I will not argue with you anywhere, B'ham is the last place I would choose for the theatre of our differences – & without B'ham I am nothing. Well, fate has so willed & it's no use kicking against the pricks, but it's d – hard that fate should separate the fortunes of two brothers who are to one another as you & I.'[102]

These reflections saddened Neville. Forgetting how his own hopes were blighted when Austen became co-leader of the coalition with Lloyd George, Neville thought Austen exaggerated the damage to his political future. He also insisted that Austen

---

100  Neville to Mary, 8 Sept.1923, *loc.cit.*
101  Austen to Neville, 28 Aug.1923, Eigg, NC1/27/73
102  Austen to Neville, 30 Aug.1923, Eigg, NC1/27/74

was damaging his own prospects through periodic public criticism of the government. The only place that Neville, like Ida, could think of for Austen was the Foreign Office, but he recognised that neither Austen nor his party were willing to consider that yet. What most concerned Neville meanwhile was lest 'the impression should become established in [Austen's] mind and that of his family that he gave up the career to which he had devoted himself on account of the difference with me.'[103]

Neville had Ivy rather than his sisters in mind when he referred to Austen's 'family'. Ida and Hilda were 'very sorry but hardly surprised' at Austen's response to the promotion. Ida recognised that Neville's presence in the government would indeed hamper Austen. But whether 'his personal position would be better if he had freer action is quite another matter ... there is not the slightest indicator that if he <u>were</u> to change his attitude there would be the smallest disposition [among Conservatives in the Commons] to welcome him back. ... I hate the idea of his going out of politics as a failure, & yet I can't see what prospect remains to him if he stays in.' Hilda put it even more bleakly: 'he is a war casualty. He was driven into a false position by the exigencies of the war, he lost touch with his party & ... made a great mistake in trying to force his party to keep in an outworn coalition.'[104]

⁂

Yet another twist in Austen's fortunes, and relationship with Neville, lay ahead. It began again with the raising of high hopes. Neville 'came away' from a weekend with Baldwin 'much encouraged' because he found that the Prime Minister was inclined to move a long way toward the Chamberlain family dream of imperial preference. 'I need hardly say,' Neville wrote excitedly to Hilda, 'that I warmly welcome this disposition & believe it will be the salvation of the country & incidentally of the party.'[105] He told Austen, hopeful that the news would draw them back together. Austen responded carefully. He had been fighting for imperial preference ever since his father first raised the standard, but the thought of continuing the fight under Baldwin's leadership awakened painful memories. There was an element of jealousy here. Austen would have liked to lead this fight himself when he was leader of the party, but had felt that the party then was unwilling to follow:

103  Neville to Hilda, 9 Sept. 1923, 35 Egerton Crescent, in Self, ed., *The Neville Chamberlain Diary Letters*, II, 181

104  Ida to Neville, 14 Sept.1923, Seaton, Devon, NC18/2/365

105  Neville to Hilda, 6 Oct.1923, 11 Downing Street, in Self, ed., *The Neville Chamberlain Diary Letters*, II, 187

'a good deal has changed since that time,' he remarked bitterly, 'and among other things the Party is much more inclined to support its leaders.' Experience had also taught Austen how fainthearted leadership could imperil the fight for imperial preference. Balfour's equivocations had broken Joseph's heart, and Bonar Law's abandonment of food taxes broke Austen's. He nevertheless assured Neville, 'If the Government should eventually decide upon such a policy as you indicated as possible, I am of course pledged by all my traditions to throw myself wholeheartedly into the fight and give them any support that I can.'[106]

He would not, however, commit himself unequivocally to Baldwin's course until Baldwin committed himself to the entirety of Joseph's programme, including a tariff on foodstuffs. Baldwin never spoke with such clarity on any subject, as Neville tried to explain: 'his very dullness is part of the character which appeals to the country'. Baldwin was also developing his policy on the hoof, so to speak, seeing how far he could go over tariff reform without reopening his party's divisions. He discussed his ideas with Neville, who conveyed them to Austen. In public Baldwin kept to generalities, and he applied his most precise commitments to himself alone rather than commit the whole party. Meanwhile lesser lights in the party also spoke for themselves. Neville and Leo Amery advocated full-blown imperial preference. The Cecils of Hatfield shied away from protectionism. Others abjured food taxes. This cacophony filled Austen with dismay: 'the gilt is off the gingerbread,' he cried. 'I thought the whole policy very bold, perhaps even rash, but for that I would have taken off my coat. But this is Father's policy with all that part left out for which he cared most.'[107]

Ida and Hilda pursued a middle course between their brothers, more appreciative than Austen of the constraints within which Baldwin had to work, but less absorbed than Neville in cooperation with Baldwin. The sisters looked forward to the day when their brothers might work 'side by side in the same Cabinet ... carrying to fruition the great ideas for which Papa sacrificed his health & his life'.[108] They therefore encouraged Neville to respond generously to the muted public welcome which Austen gave to Baldwin's movement toward tariff reform and they encouraged Austen to 'follow it up a little later with more emphatic declarations'.[109]

The sisters shifted sharply toward Austen over Baldwin's mistreatment of him during the general election, however. Baldwin asked Austen and Birkenhead to

---

106  Austen to Neville, 15 Oct.1923, 2 Morpeth Mansions, 'Confidential', & 22 Oct.1923, Twitt's Ghyll, NC1/27/78–9
107  Austen to Neville, 24 Oct.1923, Twitt's Ghyll, NC1/27/80
108  Ida to Neville, 26 Oct.1923, The Bury House, NC18/2/371
109  Hilda to Neville, 1 Nov.1923, The Bury House, NC18/2/372

meet him privately to explore the possibilities for their return to office. Baldwin approached Austen as a way to secure the services of Birkenhead whose use he valued more highly and whose tongue he feared. Austen and Birkenhead had formed a tight alliance, each contributing what the other lacked. Birkenhead was a brilliant orator and a regional power in the crucial electoral battleground of Lancashire, but he was personally dissolute and had turned the sharp edge of his tongue against Baldwin's Cabinet. Austen was the embodiment of the respectability Birkenhead lacked. Baldwin could not secure one man without the other.

However, opposition from the diehard Conservatives to early readmission of either man to the leading councils of the party kept Baldwin's offer offensively low. As Austen told Hilda, all Baldwin could say was 'that he hoped that if we fought together in the election it "might be found possible" for us to join the Govt. in unspecified positions after the election'. Sickened by Baldwin's performance, Austen responded with terms he knew Baldwin could not accept: detailed commitment to imperial preference, immediate appointment of Austen and Birkenhead to the Cabinet as ministers without portfolio, to be promoted if the Conservatives won the election to 'positions that showed clearly that we were accepted on our former footing'. Austen said 'frankly that [he] would not be treated as a boy on probation'.[110] Baldwin's behaviour infuriated Hilda, and she told Neville so: 'It is the worst move ... that Baldwin could make & done in the worst manner. If he were not prepared to make a firm offer he never ought to have asked for an interview at this juncture.'[111]

Deprived for the first time of reinforcement from his sisters, Neville floundered. Describing her 'outburst' as 'very one sided', Neville made matters worse by defending Baldwin. 'S.B. made an attempt to reunite the party and failed,' Neville argued, 'and you say if he was going to fail he ought not to have made the attempt.' Neville did not realise how half-hearted Baldwin's approach to Austen had been. 'No one would have made any difficulty if A. had been alone,' he told Hilda: 'But few people seem to realise, and I don't think you do, how profoundly [Birkenhead] has shocked the moral sense of the country. ... his reputation as a drunkard and loose liver ... has roused intense feelings of abhorrence and contempt ... Even if we win I am not sure that reconciliation will be possible – at any rate until [Birkenhead] has to some extent purged himself.'[112]

---

110 Austen to Hilda, 14 Nov.1923, Twitt's Ghyll, in Self, ed., *The Austen Chamberlain Diary Letters*, 236–7
111 Hilda to Neville, 16 Nov.1923, The Bury House, NC18/2/374
112 Neville to Hilda, 17 Nov.1923, Westbourne, in Self, ed., *The Neville Chamberlain Diary Letters*, II, 194–5

When Neville urged Austen not to be bitter, Austen could not contain himself. 'Have I no reason? You were unforgiving to Lloyd George for treatment not more crooked or offensive than Baldwin's of me. ... What hurts & what wounds me deeply is not the inevitable separation of a year ago but the things that have followed.' What hurt him most was the blow to his bond with his brother. 'Fate has dealt hardly with you & me. ... [Baldwin] has wounded me in every spot but most of all in making you an unconscious party to the proscription of your brother.' Even so, Austen concluded his letter with extraordinary magnanimity: 'There! I have had my say, & without saying it I should have felt always that there was something between you & me which we dared not touch. Burn this letter & don't let us speak of the matter again. In this fight I am on your side in spite of Baldwin & will do, as far as I can, all you ask.'[113]

The results of the general election added yet another twist to the tale. Though the Conservatives remained the largest party in the House of Commons with 258 seats, they lost the majority they had won barely a year ago. Baldwin's position was badly damaged. But who had won? Labour's 191 seats, substantially more than the Liberals' 159, pointed toward a minority Labour government, for the first time in British history, yet the results also revived hope for another coalition between Liberals and the Unionist supporters of Austen and Birkenhead, a prospect Birkenhead trumpeted. Austen advocated it less abrasively as the way to keep Labour out. He pleaded with Neville to advise Baldwin that 'irreparable harm' would be done if Ramsay MacDonald was 'allowed to form a Labour govt'.[114] Neville, however, refused to do so because he feared, once again in harmony with his sisters, that the worst outcome for the Conservatives would be 'to continue in office leading an absolutely maimed life',[115] dependent on Liberals for survival. In the event, Labour formed a minority government with precarious support from the Liberals.

The disagreements within the family were muted by concern for Ida who underwent emergency surgery in the final days of the election. Scheduled initially for an appendectomy, she eventually underwent three operations complicated by a weak heart and intolerance for chloroform. She remained in danger until mid-December. The New Year therefore began uneasily for everyone in the family; they turned their attention away from Westminster. Austen abandoned 'the desert air of politics'[116] for the pleasures of gardening at Twitt's Ghyll. Ida gave up her

113  Austen to Neville, 18 Nov.1923, Twitt's Ghyll, NC1/27/82
114  Austen to Neville, 8 Dec.1923, 2 Morpeth Mansions, 'Confidential', NC1/27/83
115  Hilda to Neville, Saturday, 17 Dean's Yard, NC18/2/380
116  Austen to Hilda, 4 Jan.1924, Twitt's Ghyll, in Self, ed., *The Austen Chamberlain Diary*

committee work for three months and headed for the Riviera with Hilda. The election left Neville 'a bit "nervy" and irritable and sometimes ... desperately depressed,' wishing he 'were out of politics'.[117] His sisters sent him a cheque for a fortnight abroad, which he accepted with alacrity.

But the opening of Parliament brought the brothers back to deal with their discontents. Austen had to be restrained from denouncing Baldwin in the opening debate. The speech he delivered instead 'heartened up our party immensely', Neville reported with relief. 'He had a very good reception when he got up and loud & long cheers when he sat down'. Neville was 'sure the psychological effect on himself must have been excellent.' But it was not. Neville could not persuade Austen to sit with the former Conservative ministers on the Opposition front bench. To do so implied membership in the Shadow Cabinet. Neville was sure Baldwin would include Austen on his own. But Austen insisted on the inclusion of Robert Horne, former Chancellor of the Exchequer, as well as Birkenhead.

Undaunted, Neville tried to persuade his outgoing colleagues that 'it was better to have [Birkenhead] in than Austen & Horne out.' [118] The next step was to bring Baldwin and Austen together. Neville 'carefully coached S.B. as to what he was to say', and then invited the two men to dinner. Austen approached the occasion in a prickly frame of mind, unwilling 'to repeat the last performance & be bowed out of the room with a "thank you" & no corresponding frankness on [Baldwin's] side.'[119] He arrived 'a bit stiff at first but gradually thawed,' as Neville recounted. 'I started in and called on S.B. He said what he had to say without any beating about the bush and after one moment's hesitation A. frankly accepted the invitation. After that all went like clockwork and very soon it was My dear Stanley & My dear Austen as if they had ne'er been parted.'[120] Still, all was not well. When the Shadow Cabinet met next day, Austen, Horne and Birkenhead 'were treated with marked affability & did more than their share of the talking,' as Austen admitted. 'But I am not happy, for I don't feel towards Baldwin as I like to feel towards my "leader" & do not think him competent for his position.' Austen nonetheless conceded that, 'unless he comes to understand that himself, it would be worse than useless to try to displace him.'[121]

---

*Letters*, 246

117  Neville to Ida, 12 Jan.1924, Westbourne, in Self, ed., *The Neville Chamberlain Diary Letters*, II, 203

118  Neville to Hilda, 24 Jan.1924, 11 Downing Street, in Self, ed., *op.cit.*, II, 204

119  Austen to Ida, 4 Feb.1924, Twitt's Ghyll, in Self, ed., *The Austen Chamberlain Diary Letters*, 248

120  Neville to Hilda, 9 Feb.1924, 37 Eaton Square, in Self, ed., *The Neville Chamberlain Diary Letters*, II, 207

121  Austen to Ida, 9 Feb.1924, Twitt's Ghyll, in Self, ed., *The Austen Chamberlain Diary Letters*,

Trouble erupted within a matter of days. Churchill, who had been the most conspicuous Liberal minister in the coalition aside from Lloyd George, lost his parliamentary seat in 1922 and had yet to regain one. In search of political survival, he drifted back toward the Conservatives whom he had deserted when Joseph Chamberlain launched his crusade for tariff reform. That tale of 'ratting' made him loathsome to Conservatives. Never daunted, Churchill decided to stand for election in a safe Conservative seat as an Anti Socialist. In doing so, he added himself to the number of leading men in politics who vexed the relationship between the Chamberlain brothers, in this case with the most fateful of consequences. Austen embraced Churchill's action as a step toward Liberal reunion with Conservatives. Neville opposed it as a return to the hated coalition: 'Let him stand as a Liberal for a Liberal seat, or even an anti Socialist if he likes, so long as he sits with the Liberals. Then let him come over with the others later & his ratting won't be so much objected to.'[122] The disagreement between the brothers risked becoming confrontational when Neville undertook to speak for the regular Conservative candidate. By threatening to campaign for Churchill, Austen forced Neville to back off. As fortune would have it, the Conservative candidate narrowly won.

Nevertheless, Austen's return to the Conservative front bench made the relationship between the brothers, if anything, more difficult. Hilda had long felt that Austen's position would be 'infinitely better inside the party than outside'. But she understood why Austen's return was hard on Neville: Austen would to a certain extent 'take what would otherwise have been your place'. But she argued that the Conservative party would be 'immensely stronger for the inclusion of the "old men",'[123] by which she meant those who had served under Lloyd George. They were better fighters, as Baldwin's lacklustre performance leading the Opposition reminded Austen: 'Stanley himself never fires more than a pop gun or a peashooter at critical moments.'[124]

One thing kept the disagreement between the brothers from widening: Neville lost patience with Baldwin's 'impenetrable silence, I see a good deal less of him than I did & he doesn't seem so much in need of council [sic] as when he was in office.'[125] Still,

122  Neville to Hilda, 23 Feb.1924, Westbourne, in Self, ed., *The Neville Chamberlain Diary Letters*, II, 211

123  Hilda to Neville, 20 Feb.1924, Grand Hotel d'Alassio, NC18/2/389

124  Austen to Ida, 18 Apr.1924, Twitt's Ghyll, in Self, ed., *The Austen Chamberlain Diary Letters*, 250–1

125  Neville to Ida, 7 June 1924, Taunton, in Self, ed., *The Neville Chamberlain Diary Letters*, II, 229

as discontent with Baldwin spread across the Conservative benches, another wrinkle developed in the brothers' relationship. Both were talked of as replacements for the party leader: 'it seems,' said Ida, 'as if you must inevitably stand in each other's way.'[126]

Austen did not improve his prospects by welcoming Liberals whose support might give Conservatives a parliamentary majority. His welcome confirmed the distrust of him among Conservatives: 'they say he still has a Coalition mind ... As a matter of fact,' Neville confessed, 'I agree with them ... [Austen] positively desires co-operation whereas' – like Neville – Baldwin only 'reluctantly accepts it.' This continuing cleavage between the brothers left a mark on Neville's sense of party. He had long shied away from the label of Conservative, sticking rather to Unionist; and he declined to deliver a lecture on the historical contributions of Conservatism: 'I was brought up a Radical so I should think I shd be the worst person in the world for such a subject.'[127] But his fight against coalition with the Liberals increased his acceptance of the Conservative label. While Austen looked to Liberals to produce the margin of victory, Neville looked to social reform to enhance the Conservative appeal.

That summer the sisters had other things on their mind. Shaken by her surgery, Ida was incapable of returning to work for the first half of the year. Hilda, on the other hand, rose rapidly in the hierarchy of the Women's Institute. No sooner was she elected County Chairman for Hampshire than the President of the federation asked her to become national treasurer. She turned the offer down, preferring to extend throughout the county the practical good she had done around Odiham.

September deepened the unsettlement in the wider parliamentary world, not however within the Opposition benches so much as for the Labour government and its Liberal allies. The government fell in October, precipitating the third general election in three years. Once again Austen and Neville responded differently. When Ivy was ordered by her doctor to head for warmer climes, Austen could have accompanied her and played only a distant part in the election. But he resolved to stay and fight: 'if I am to keep any hold on politics I cannot leave England now.'[128] Neville, on the other hand, foresaw nothing from the election 'but trouble for our party. We may be fairly well organised but we have no programme ready and the difficulties of forming a Cabinet are immense. Politics are really hateful in these days.'[129]

---

126 Ida to Neville, 14 Aug.1924, Harrogate, NC18/2/412
127 Neville to Annie, 10 Aug.1924, Loubcroy Lodge, NC1/26/335
128 Austen to Mary, 28 Sept.1924, Twitt's Ghyll, AC4/1/1257
129 Neville to Annie, 2 Oct.1924, 37 Eaton Square, NC1/26/341

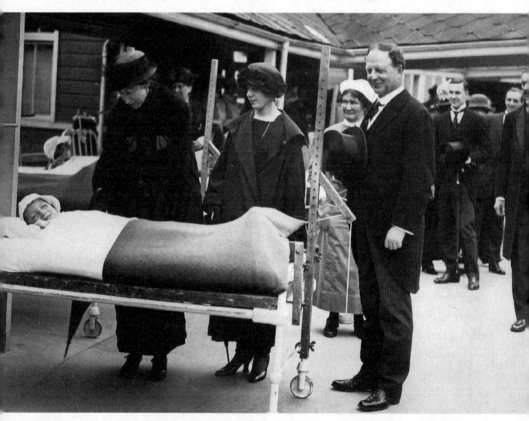

*The austere Minister of Health and his engaging wife visiting a hospital*

# 7

# Square Peg in Square Hole,
# Round Peg in Round Hole

The five years of tension between the Chamberlain brothers were followed by five years of fulfilment, working side by side in the same Cabinet as they had long hoped. The rival alliances which divided them, Austen's with Lloyd George and Neville's with Bonar Law and Baldwin, were overcome because Baldwin in his second term as Prime Minister allowed both brothers to focus on the work of their assigned ministries. These assignments, Austen to the Foreign Office and Neville back to the Ministry of Health, which both men found deeply congenial, carried them to the pinnacle of achievement from which, however, they would descend later in their lives.

❦

There was little sign of this prospective concord at the beginning of the general election campaign when the brothers looked to their constituencies. Austen had not lived in Birmingham for nearly twenty years, but he did not take kindly to remonstrations from Neville on this score. When Neville suggested that 'it might be necessary to do a little more than he had been doing,' Austen 'very testily replied that he *might* go down for a month, and he *might* take a house in the division, but he wasn't prepared to hold the seat on such terms and if his people thought he wasn't doing enough he was quite ready to place his resignation in their hands.'[1] Austen's mood was not improved by Ivy's departure to the spa town of Aix-les-Bains. 'I am so unhappy at not being able to be with you,' she wrote on arrival, 'but

---

1 Neville to Ida, 27 Sept.1924, in Self, ed., *The Neville Chamberlain Diary Letters*, II, 248

I do feel that I should not be much use ... the least thing tires me & I do not seem to have any reserve.' After a bath, she had to be 'carried back & laid on my bed like a mummy!'[2] Their daughter Diane headed for Birmingham to take her mother's place.

But the electoral outlook and some kindly treatment by Baldwin raised Austen's spirits. Before campaigning began, Baldwin encouraged Austen to expect high office in the event of a Unionist victory. Austen mulled over the possibilities happily: 'S.B. had thought of the F.O. for me or "would you like India?" ... the F.O. is one of the most exacting offices there is,' it would involve 'more entertainment & therefore expense'; it was 'the higher office in public estimation,' Austen told Ivy, '& one that, as you know, I have in past times thought I should have enjoyed. Now I dread a little the undertaking.' Ivy felt no such hesitation: 'it is essential that the Secretary should be some one whom everyone can trust & who has character & experience,' she said, '& there is no one who would inspire more confidence than you & from a patriotic point of view I think you ought to do it.'[3]

Austen's hopes were heightened by the rising size of the electoral victory he expected. His thinking began with the coalition he desired: 'though I don't suppose that we can get a working majority of our own, I think that we, with those Liberals who are whole-heartedly with us, shall be able between us to make things work.' His hopes soon rose. 'There may be a big swing,' he told Ivy. 'I think that we shall even get a majority &, with the Winstonians [Churchill and his friends], a working majority ... my present feeling is that we shall be in for four years at any rate. It is long since you have seen me in this hopeful mood.' He encouraged his sisters to 'count on another Baldwin Govt with 2 Chamberlains in the Cabinet instead of one only'. Austen even conceded that Baldwin 'in his quiet way' was doing 'very well'.[4] To produce the outcome he desired, Austen encouraged 'arrangements for withdrawing opposition of Lib. & Cons. & concentrating in doubtful cases on opposition to Socialists'.[5] Neville was less confident of success, nor did he desire the same outcome. He thought the Conservatives likely to emerge as 'much the strongest party'. But he feared that without a clear working majority on their own, they would be 'condemned to a further period of such doubts and uncertainties

---

2  Ivy to Austen, 10 & 12 Oct.1924, Hotel Thermal, Aix-les-Bains, AC6/2/333–4

3  Austen to Ivy, 10 Oct.1924, vi, Twitt's Ghyll, AC6/1/563, and Ivy to Austen, Aix-les-Bains, AC6/2/336

4  Austen to Hilda, 11 Oct., Twitt's Ghyll, & to Ida, 19 Oct.1924, Birmingham, in Self, ed., *The Austen Chamberlain Diary Letters*, 258

5  Austen to Ivy, 11, 13 & 14 Oct.1924, vii, ix & x, AC6/1/564 & 566–7

as we have now.' He wanted a Conservative government strong enough to 'leave behind a mark on social reforms'.[6]

Both brothers were confident of re-election in their constituencies. They proved right, though by smaller majorities than they anticipated. Neville barely survived a challenge from Sir Oswald Mosley, the mercurial candidate put up by Labour. On arrival at the Town Hall for the count on election night, Neville and Annie were warned 'that the voting papers seemed about equal and the issue entirely doubtful. What we were not prepared for was a 4½ hours wait while they were counted & counted again. Mosley was beside himself, walking up and down the tables, hectoring & bullying the officials & once even going out to address his friends in the square to whom he announced that he was in! The first count gave me a majority of 30, then it was said to be 15 then 7, then I was out by 2 & finally at 4:30 the Lord Mayor accounted that I was returned by 77.' Throughout the turmoil, 'Annie was splendid. She and I sat calmly by ... waiting for whatever the decision might be. Of course we hated the thought of being beaten especially by that viper.'[7] The stoicism with which Neville awaited the results may have accounted in part for the narrowness of his victory. Austen thought so: 'It is his coldness which kills,' he confided to Ivy. Neville 'hates any sign of feeling & all, I think, at bottom because he feels deeply & is afraid of letting himself fall to pieces.'[8]

Everywhere in Birmingham the Unionists did less well than expected, and for the first time in more than half a century they lost a seat in the city: Kings Norton, won by Labour: 'How they would have exulted if they had broken the B'ham unity for the first time by making a Chamberlain lose his seat.'[9] In the country at large the Conservatives swept to victory, winning a majority that assured them of a full four- or five-year term in power. 'I wish we had won fewer seats,' Austen confessed, 'that Labour had lost more & the Liberals less.' The question now was how Baldwin would construct a Cabinet from the embarrassingly large pool of men with ministerial experience from the governments of Lloyd George, Bonar Law and Baldwin himself. Hilda prayed, 'If only I can see Austen as Foreign Secretary & [Neville] as Health Minister I shall be quite happy.'

Baldwin kept both Chamberlains at bay in forming his ministry. He consulted

---

6  Neville to Ida, 11 Oct. & to Hilda, 19 Oct.1924, Westbourne, in Self, ed., *The Neville Chamberlain Diary Letters*, II, 250 & 255
7  Neville to Ida, 1 Nov.1924, Lytchett Heath, Poole, in Self, ed., *The Neville Chamberlain Diary Letters*, II, 256–7
8  Austen to Ivy, 31 Oct.1924, xxvi, 2 Morpeth Mansions, AC6/1/587
9  Hilda to Neville, 31 Oct.1924, The Bury House, NC18/2/423

Neville only with the utmost circumspection, and Austen scarcely at all. Neville knew that Baldwin 'would like me back at the Treasury'; but 'I remain convinced that I might be a great Minister of Health but am not likely to be more than a second rate Chancellor.'[10] Baldwin indeed asked Neville to become Chancellor again. But when Neville asked instead for the Health Ministry, Baldwin did not press the Exchequer on him. He had someone else in mind, a choice neither Chamberlain expected. Both of them thought of Horne, a former Chancellor and Austen's close colleague under Lloyd George. Neville hoped Horne would help overcome the rift between coalitionist and anti-coalition Conservatives.

But to Neville's dismay and Austen's delight, Baldwin had another coalitionist in mind: Churchill. Churchill's appointment plunged Neville into despair. He foresaw 'rifts splits & resignations not immediately but in the near future', and 'Just when all looked so rosy.'[11] But the appointment proved less provocative to Conservatives than Neville feared. His mood changed once he returned to the Ministry of Health, to the obvious delight of its officials. 'Tomorrow I start planning out a four years programme! The staff fairly fall on my neck!'[12] Still, Churchill's appointment blighted Neville's return to his chosen ministry. The two men might have formed a productive partnership. Churchill had a reputation as a social reformer from the days of Asquith's pre-war government. Both men were imperialists, though of opposing economic stripe. But they were fated to frustrate each other, paralysing Churchill for the next fifteen years and then terminating Neville's career with tragedy.

Though content with Churchill as Chancellor, Austen was unhappy about Baldwin's treatment of other leading coalitionists. But Austen at last reached the office which his family had long hoped he would receive: Secretary of State for Foreign Affairs. Ambivalent at the moment of success, he moaned to Hilda, 'my garden will go to ruin and you need not expect to get a letter from me for the next 4 years if I survive so long ... O how the collar galls. I feel no elation, but only a very sobering sense of great difficulties in my path.'[13] Hilda did not take him seriously: 'Of course Austen has the temperament which makes him regard with alarm the difficulties & responsibilities of any new position but I don't think I have seen him

10  Neville to Ida, 26 Oct.1924, Westbourne, in Self, ed., *The Neville Chamberlain Diary Letters*, II, 256

11  Neville to Hilda, 6 Nov.1924, 37 Eaton Square, in Self, ed., *op.cit.*, II, 258

12  Neville to Ida, 12 Nov.1924, 37 Eaton Square, in Self, ed., *op.cit.*, II, 258

13  Austen to Hilda, 9 Nov.1924, Twitt's Ghyll, in Self, ed., *The Austen Chamberlain Diary Letters*, 260

so happy & so generally pleased for more years than I can remember.'[14] It was Ida who best summed up the situation in which her two brothers were now placed: 'For once we have the square peg in the square hole & the round peg in the round hole. ... Oh isn't it delightful to think they are both in together & especially in those positions where they will each have a field of their own & their rather different points of view won't clash.'[15]

*

Austen's achievement over the next twelve months was meteoric. He strode onto the international stage with all the skills requisite for success in European diplomacy and with a clear sense of direction. His father had groomed him for this moment, directing him at Cambridge to the leading writers on geo-politics, then sending him to France and Germany to gain familiarity with their languages and cultures. Austen was fluent in French and knew enough German 'to follow practically all the Germans had to say ... & even to correct their interpreter.'[16] Since he first took junior office at the Admiralty, he had been drawn more to international than domestic concerns, unlike everyone else in his family. Austen hoped to shine in a field in which his father had blundered badly, though no one in the family dared say so. Austen had acquired an understanding of diplomatic developments on both sides of the Atlantic. He wrote about them at length in the family correspondence during his father's illness. After Joe's death, Mary continued, during her visits in Massachusetts, to elicit letters from Austen on Anglo-American concerns for transmission to her friends in Washington.

His aim at its broadest level upon becoming Foreign Secretary was to bring stability to Europe after the uneasy peace secured at Versailles. The treaty of Versailles left Germany deeply resentful without assuring France that its inveterate foe would not recover its strength. Austen focused his energies on stabilising the relationship between these two countries. While not at all sure of success, he did not doubt his ability to meet the demands of the task. Dining with Austen soon after his appointment, Ida could see that he felt 'a sense of mastery' in tackling the problems which awaited him. She was surprised to find that he also 'saw every prospect of the Cabinet working smoothly together'.[17]

---

14  Hilda to Neville, 14 Nov.1924, The Bury House, NC18/2/426
15  Ida to Mary, 9 Nov.1924, The Bury House, BC4/2/200
16  Ida to Neville, 4 Mar.1921, 36 Sloane Court West, NC18/2/242
17  Ida to Neville, 21 Nov.1924, Cadogan Hotel, NC18/2/427

Even so, Austen worked alone and rarely sought advice. Customarily the Foreign Secretary shared responsibility for the conduct of foreign policy with the Prime Minister, but Baldwin left Austen to get on with it. Austen talked only retrospectively with his siblings about the diplomatic problems he encountered, though he informed them of the results he achieved. He still conceived of his position in a familial context. He thought that his tombstone should 'bear the simple inscription

Fortunate in his family life
Thrice fortunate in his marriage
He spent many years in the Public Service
And sat in Cabinet
First with his father
And afterwards
With his brother'[18]

But he kept his own counsel. What he sought was not counsel but cooperation, in particular from his peers in the chancelleries of Europe. And he found cooperation in the countries that mattered most: from Gustav Stresemann of Germany, from Italy's Mussolini, and above all from Aristide Briand of France. Briand, he told Mary, 'is an admirable man to work with, bent on peace, broad minded, supple & courageous'.[19]

By the beginning of March 1925 Austen had 'got [his] policy clear & definite in [his] own mind'.[20] He sought alliance with France to allay French fears of Germany and hence to cultivate French willingness to address the legitimate grievances of Germany. He was, however, a declared and unrepentant Francophile, and the Cabinet whose approval he needed for the alliance bristled at his proposal as lopsidedly favourable to France. He turned therefore to another proposal, this one from Germany, which he moulded to reach the same objective. Stresemann proposed a mutual security pact for the Rhineland. Austen moved to turn that proposal to the general advantage of the Rhineland states; France and Belgium as well as Germany. Even at this the Cabinet baulked. Austen threatened to throw up

18  Austen to Hilda, 23 Dec.1924, 2 Morpeth Mansions, in Self, ed., *The Austen Chamberlain Diary Letters*, 272
19  Austen to Mary, 20 Sept.1925, Twitt's Ghyll, AC4/1/1264
20  Austen to Ida, 1 Mar.1925, Foreign Office, in Self, ed., *The Austen Chamberlain Diary Letters*, 274

his office unless Baldwin backed him up. Baldwin did so handsomely, the Cabinet fell into line, and Austen remained master of his office for the rest of the year.

Engrossed in his continental diplomacy, he sent only impressionistic remarks to Ivy when they were apart, and summary reports to his sisters. He gloried in what he was able to achieve by himself; and Ivy, Ida and Hilda applauded his accomplishment. 'I have won the battle here,' he told Ida at the end of June. 'It is rather a triumph, is it not? & though it is true that I could not have done it without my colleagues Neville would confirm that it would never have been done but for me. ... if the policy succeeds I shall feel some title to the reputation which [the American ambassador to Germany] assures me will be mine as the true author of European peace, & in that case my long and somewhat broken public career will not have ended without one solid & complete achievement.'[21]

He next had to win the consent of France to a settlement that would enhance its security in western Europe but do nothing to support French commitments to the states on the eastern flank of Germany, including Czechoslovakia and Poland. By mid-August he had Briand's approval. 'Now for the Germans!' he wrote to Hilda: 'I believe that we shall bring it off. Here I put great faith in Briand's reasonableness & persuasiveness.'[22] Austen remained anxious about the Germans for another six weeks. 'They & the Poles are the restless elements in Europe north of the Balkans.'[23] By now his colleagues in London were willing simply to observe his progress. Baldwin left him 'to go my own way, pursue my own policy & face my own difficulties'. Austen was content, 'tho' sometimes I wish that he showed a little more interest & gave a more active support'.[24]

Austen's accomplishment reached its height upon his arrival at the Swiss lakeside town of Locarno to conclude his European negotiations. The resulting treaties were signed on his birthday. The achievement thrilled his family. 'It has been a wonderfully successful conference,' Hilda exulted, 'going further & better I imagine than any of them expected when they went there.' She still underestimated the praise that the achievement would elicit at home. 'I don't suppose that his work can ever be "popularly" recognized for the public cannot understand the

21 Austen to Ida, 27 June 1925, 2 Morpeth Mansions, in Self, ed., *The Austen Chamberlain Diary Letters*, 277

22 Austen to Hilda, 16 Aug.1925, Twitt's Ghyll, in Self, ed., *The Austen Chamberlain Diary Letters*, 279

23 Austen to Hilda, 22 Sept.1925, 2 Morpeth Mansions, in Self, ed., *The Austen Chamberlain Diary Letters*, 279

24 Austen to Mary, 20 Sept.1925, Twitt's Ghyll, AC4/1/1264

complexity of these Foreign questions .... If he had not secured Briand's confidence without forfeiting that of Stresemann, he could never have brought the French to give up their claim to march troops through Germany to Poland or Czechoslovakia without the League's sanction ... We have had so many conferences & the result has often been only bitterness or disappointment that one cannot expect people to feel enthusiastic about Locarno, but I trust the results in a few years will lead people to look back & say, – this improved state of affairs dates from that moment. Anyway Foreign Secretaries in a peculiar degree get their recognition, – if they get it at all, from history & not in their own lifetime.'[25]

But a few days later Ida began to relish 'the gratitude not only of his fellow countrymen but of all Europe' that Austen received: 'he has done something which is worth all the previous struggles & anxieties & discouragements. ... Mussolini told Ivy that it was because Austen was there that he came! It was Austen who produced the atmosphere that made everything possible, & it was to him that everyone turned for advice & counsel. How proud Papa & Beatrice would have been of him! ... It is a wonderful achievement.'[26] The settlement reached at Locarno indeed constituted Austen's greatest achievement. Neville nevertheless remained 'a little puzzled at the réclame which [Austen's] success has aroused – not because it is not appropriate but because foreign affairs are usually too remote to be appreciated by the general public.'[27]

Though Hilda had underestimated the immediate acclaim, she overestimated the long-term appreciation that Austen's achievement at Locarno would receive. Its joints were soon probed, and its inadequacies exposed long before Hitler rendered it useless. Austen was himself 'astonished & a little frightened by the completeness of my success & by its immediate recognition everywhere'. He lapped up the praise he received in 'telegrams from the King & Prime Minister both recognising in such generous terms that it was *my* policy'. And he accepted it all at face value: the policy was indeed 'mine in conception & still more mine in execution, but I did not think that they would feel this. Still less did I suppose that all the world, beginning with the little community of Locarno & spreading to the U.S.A. would hail it as Great Britain's triumph.'

The more he thought of it, the higher the estimate he placed on his achievement. 'Of course I have had my luck & much luck; but I say for myself that I have

---

25  Hilda to Neville, 16 Oct.1925, The Bury House, NC18/2/471
26  Ida to Neville, 22 Oct.1925, The Bury House, NC18/2/473
27  Neville to Ida, 24 Oct.1925, Westbourne, in Self, ed., *The Neville Chamberlain Diary Letters*, II, 317

known how to use every bit of luck that came my way, that I am myself the author of some of my luck & that no one else ... inside or outside the [Foreign] office would have seen the importance of the early moves or made them, & that not another member of the Cabinets since the Peace [of Versailles] had understood the conditions of such a policy or could have carried it out.'[28] He looked for a historical parallel to his achievement. 'I was called to face a situation comparable to that which faced Castlereagh after the fall of Napoleon. I had to face it without having been, as he was, the representative of my country in the years which won victory for the Allies & without any of his acquired prestige & little, very little, of his personal knowledge of & intercourse with foreign rulers.'

He tried to rein in his euphoria. He reminded himself 'of the reaction & disappointments that are bound to come'. But the honours he was offered led him to breach the sober conventions of his family. His father, an austere Unitarian by upbringing, and proud of his achievement in industry, had scorned the titles through which monarchs rewarded their well-born servants. Joseph died proudly as he had lived, plain Mr Chamberlain. Austen struggled to come to terms with that legacy. But Neville's arrival in the Cabinet weakened its force since the two brothers now had to be identified by their first names: neither at the moment could be plain Mr Chamberlain. Austen toyed with the thought of the Order of Merit, the highest honour in the gift of the monarch that did not carry a title. But titles conveyed prestige in the world of diplomacy. And no title of honour had more lustre in Britain than the Knighthood of the Garter. It had never before been awarded to a commoner and was usually awarded only when a vacancy occurred in the Order. The King offered to award it to Austen immediately.

He accepted the offer before discussing it with his siblings. 'I hope you will not be too distressed,' he then wrote to Ida. 'I confess that that peculiar distinction attracts me, & I think it would be good business from the point of view of my standing with foreign countries.' As to receiving the Garter without waiting for a vacancy, he explained, 'If you knew all that this means to me you would appreciate the immensity of the favour.'[29] The last member of the family he told was Neville. 'I feel some little misgiving but the Garter conferred upon a commoner is so rare a distinction & it means so much – in foreign eyes especially – for the Minister & his policy that I have accepted gratefully.'[30] Neville would rather he had taken

28  Austen to Ida, Sunday night after 31 Oct.1925, Twitt's Ghyll, in Self, ed., *The Austen Chamberlain Diary Letters*, 282
29  Austen to Ida, 28 Nov.1925, 2 Morpeth Mansions, in Self, ed., *op.cit.*, 284
30  Austen to Neville, 26 Nov.1925, Foreign Office, NC1/27/87

a peerage: 'Austen would make an excellent peer and Ivy an admirable peeress,' he said with a hint of distaste. 'They are both naturally cut out for it, and a peerage would have the great practical advantage of relieving Austen from the worry (and expense) of a constituency.'[31] But Austen lacked the financial resources expected of a peer. Nor was he ready to exchange his seat in the Commons for the Lords. Prestige was the decisive consideration. With relish Austen pointed out that 'there is a swagger about being the only commoner in such an august body, more I think than if I had taken a peerage at the same time.'[32] 'It is absurd the pleasure I take in my Gartership,' he later confessed. 'I laugh at myself but ... admit that I am as pleased as a child with a toy which seemed absolutely beyond its reach.'[33] Churchill envied in Austen this unique distinction – it 'stands so apart'[34] – and chose the Garter himself a generation later.

Honours continued to be showered on Austen for the rest of the year. Birmingham gave him the freedom of the city, an honour he would have valued 'more if it had come a few years earlier'.[35] The City of London followed suit, as did two of the City Guilds. '"It rains gold boxes" once again!' he told Mary, remembering how the same happened to his father. 'Well, if at any time I have not had my full share of recognition, I have it now in more than generous measure. It is a double pleasure to reap the rewards which Father had.' Austen coveted another honour, 'the only "honour" beside the Garter that I should like to have'. The French government offered him the Grand Cross of the Legion of Honour. But 'alas I have felt bound to say no ... the Kings cattle should be branded only with his own mark.'[36]

&

While Austen soared to the pinnacle of his achievement, Neville dedicated himself with similar zeal and deeper roots in their paternal heritage to the Ministry of Health. He compared his choice of ministry to his father's choice of the Colonial Office. One morning 'as I was shaving I was thinking that though I should never

---

31 Neville to Hilda, 28 Nov.1925, 37 Eaton Square, in Self, ed., *The Neville Chamberlain Diary Letters*, II, 325

32 Austen to Ida, 28 Nov.1925, 2 Morpeth Mansions, AC5/1/370

33 Austen to Hilda, 9 Nov.1930, 58 Rutland Gate, in Self, ed., *The Austen Chamberlain Diary Letters*, 359

34 Churchill quoted by Austen to Ida, 28 Nov.1925, 2 Morpeth Mansions, in Self, ed., *op.cit.*, 284

35 Austen to Hilda, 26 Dec.1925, Hotel Bristol, Rapallo, AC5/1/372

36 Austen to Mary, Christmas 1925, Rapallo, AC4/1/1267

be a favourite with the press like Father was or Winston is, yet, if I have 4 or 5 years of office I may leave behind as ... great a reputation as Minister of Health as Father did as Colonial Secretary. Only it will probably take longer for the public to find it out and it will only be after I am dead that my administration will be talked of as the Golden Age at the Ministry!'[37]

The precedent that Neville selected from his father's career was, significantly, his tenure as Colonial Secretary rather than as Mayor of Birmingham. Though Joseph remained indeed the greatest of Colonial Secretaries, it was as Mayor of Birmingham and architect of 'gas and water socialism' that he showed how the powers of government could be used to enhance the wellbeing of an industrial society. Neville did not bring a similar vision to the Ministry of Health, and he would not leave as great a mark as his father. Neville's vision was also damaged during the 1920s by his disenchantment with labour. Masterful though his administrative transformation of the Ministry of Health was to prove, his tenure would not be remembered as its Golden Age.

The remit of the Ministry extended farther than its title suggested. It embraced public health in its broadest sense to include the immediately most pressing postwar problem, housing. Neville planned for a still more far reaching 'four year programme. Of course the public thinks of nothing but Housing, but ... I want to take the opportunity of dealing with the big questions of rating & valuation, Poor Law, Pensions & Health insurance, and the re-organisation of the medical services.'[38] The Ministry of Health gave Neville an opportunity, which he savoured, to exploit the failure of Lloyd George to put together a non-socialist but still social reforming alternative to the Labour party. In a watered-down version of his father's early strategy for Birmingham, Neville hoped to use the Ministry of Health to turn the Conservative party into the alternative to socialism that Lloyd George failed to deliver.

Neville walked at the Ministry of Health not so much in the footsteps of his father as in collaboration with his sisters. He turned to them for guidance in the spheres of responsibility which they were more familiar with than he, namely agricultural communities and County Councils. How could he make his plans for pensions and housing effective in rural communities? Pensions were particularly problematic in these areas because agricultural labourers were not covered by unemployment insurance. 'With other workmen I could perhaps relieve the extra burden of contributory pensions by lowering the unemployment contribution', but

37  Neville to Ida, 23 May 1925, Westbourne, in Self, ed., *The Neville Chamberlain Diary Letters*, II, 292

38  Neville to Hilda, 15 Nov.1924, Westbourne, in Self, ed., *op.cit.*, II, 260

that would not work for farm workers. Furthermore, housing too in rural communities 'required different treatment from urban'. Knowing that the scheme he had in mind would alarm his orthodox financial advisers, Neville looked to Ida who had done battle for years with 'economical' local councillors and guardians. But the assault that Neville intended to make on financial orthodoxy was not as adventurous as his father's, nor was he as much of a radical. How, he asked Ida, could he combine minimal cost to the public purse and minimal interference in private enterprise with protection of the tenant against increases in rent?[39]

Ida responded in detail from her experience in even smaller units of local government than Neville was familiar with in Birmingham. Though perhaps more of a radical than her brother, she too was an able manager whose response to social needs was closely informed rather than visionary. Her ability to help Neville increased with her election to the Hampshire County Council, for he was to make County Councils the basic building blocks of his administrative reform. She stood for election as an advocate of 'a forward policy ... It is quite time that something should be done towards educating the public as to the desirability of spending a little more on Public Health.'[40] At Hilda's urging, the Women's Institutes of the county rallied behind Ida's candidacy, and they deterred the Farmers' Union from fielding an alternative candidate. So Ida won without a contest. Neville welcomed her elevation: 'As my policy is to increase the activities and responsibilities of County Councils I shall expect to get a good deal of help from you.'[41]

Hilda added another dimension to the family cooperation from her position on the executive of the Hampshire County Nursing Association, where she did battle with the great Lord Salisbury's daughter Lady Selborne. Neville fed Hilda information about funding provided by his ministry to train midwives. 'You really are a perfect angel!' she replied. 'I hope by means of this information & with Ida's help ... we shall in time get ourselves put upon quite a good basis.'[42] Austen was out of the family loop on these issues: he confessed that he knew 'very little of Neville's business'. He was nonetheless impressed by all his family were up to. 'Here's Neville who, not content with having the biggest bill of the session [on pensions] on hand, must needs take up that hideously controversial subject rating & valuation at the

---

39 Neville to Ida, 8 Feb.1925, 37 Eaton Square, in Self, ed., *The Neville Chamberlain Diary Letters*, II, 209

40 Ida to Neville, 12 Mar.1925, The Bury House, NC18/2/442

41 Neville to Ida, 28 Mar.1925, Westbourne, in Self, ed., *The Neville Chamberlain Diary Letters*, II, 279

42 Hilda to Neville, 24 Apr.1925, The Bury House, NC18/2/448

same time. Here am I with rather more work than is good for any man & no visible chance of a holiday, & there are you & Hilda with a nice little house, a nice little garden & as one might suppose, the leisure to enjoy both as well as your books, &, instead of thanking heaven that you are not as your brothers are, you thrust yourselves into & onto more Institutes, Committees, Councils, Boards, &c. &c. &c. than any other two women in the County!'[43]

To achieve his ambitions as Minister of Health, Neville had to work with Churchill as Chancellor; and from the outset he found that difficult. Churchill's way of expressing himself struck Neville as 'so peculiar that I was left in doubt whether he had not invited me to join him in a secret plan not disclosed to any colleagues'.[44] Churchill, he complained, 'never sticks to anything for two minutes together and when you have had a conference in order to arrive at a final decision on doubtful points your one certainty is that the agreement arrived at will be thrown overboard a few hours afterwards.' The way the two men approached their work could scarcely have been more different. 'I always postpone my decisions to the very last moment possible,' Neville said, 'but once taken I very seldom go back upon them, because I have generally been pretty well all round the subject and new considerations therefore seldom arise.'[45] Churchill's approach, like that of Lloyd George, was intuitive and impulsive.

Unlike Lloyd George, however, Churchill learned to respect Neville's methodical approach. When they met to discuss the Health Ministry's proposals for Poor Law reform, Neville noted how things had changed. 'At first [Churchill] was inclined to be a little patronising and used to walk about & orate. This time he sat quietly in a chair and listened quite a lot to what I had to say. [Baldwin] told me that it was beginning to dawn upon [Churchill] that his new colleagues were not all duds after all!'[46] But Neville did not develop similar respect for Churchill: 'the more I get to know Winston the less I think of him. I don't mean morally; he doesn't strike me in the least as a villain though I think he is *a*moral and lacking entirely in some things that most of us think rather essential. But the fault with which he is generally credited is lack of judgement and there public opinion seems

43  Austen to Ida, 31 May & 11 July 1925, AC5/1/355 358

44  Neville to Hilda, 24 Nov.1924, Westbourne, in Self, ed., *The Neville Chamberlain Diary Letters*, II, 261

45  Neville to Hilda, 5 Apr.1925, 37 Eaton Square, in Self, ed., *The Neville Chamberlain Diary Letters*, II, 282

46  Neville to Hilda, 17 Oct.1925, 37 Eaton Square, in Self, ed., *The Neville Chamberlain Diary Letters*, II, 316

to me to be absolutely right. ... And with his courage and strong will and power of oratory he is a very dangerous man to have in the Govt.'[47]

While Churchill's term as Chancellor would not turn out to be his finest hour, Neville's transformation of the Ministry of Health would not be superseded until the creation of the National Health Service. He won praise on all sides for his Pensions Act even more quickly than Austen had at the Foreign Office. Annie was thrilled to hear her husband spoken of as the greatest social reformer since Disraeli. Even so, the compliments he received did not tempt him to set his sights higher than his current Ministry. He felt at home there and remained restlessly inventive. As Hilda put it, 'when you are not fighting a first-class measure through the House, you are heating one or other of your manifold irons at some public ceremony every day.'[48] Ida worried about the demands he placed upon himself: 'the strain would be less if you did not have so many ideas about everything.'[49] Neville took her concern as a compliment, which indeed it was. His sisters were cut of the same cloth. Hilda reported that she was 'very full of business ... schools, school dinners, Institute classes, Evening classes, Library, Women's Institute meetings, & Nursing affairs.'[50]

❧

The skies darkened for Austen even before the honour of his knighthood sank in. Ivy was found to have 'a slight adhesion of the heart' which meant that 'her heart does its work with so much extra fatigue'. She was also worn down by worry about Lawrence, whose illnesses remained alarming, and Diane too was slow to recover from an appendectomy. The doctor urged Austen to take the family to Italy for Christmas and then to Egypt for 'an idle fortnight'.[51] En route, however, Lawrence caught a bronchial cold. The holiday turned into 'a catastrophe of "flu", colds coughs & fevers'[52] that trapped Ivy in Rapallo and prevented any onward journey. The only bright light emanated from Mussolini who 'interrupted his journey southward to dine' with Austen. Austen 'always found [Mussolini] very pleasant. It was good to renew our very friendly relations & tho' ... no world shaking projects

47  Neville to Hilda, 1 Nov.1925, 37 Eaton Square, in Self, ed., *The Neville Chamberlain Diary Letters*, II, 319
48  Hilda to Neville, 27 Nov.1925, The Bury House, NC18/2/479
49  Ida to Neville, 17 Dec.1925, The Bury House, NC18/2/481
50  Hilda to Neville, 2 Oct.1925, The Bury House, NC18/2/470
51  Austen to Ida, 15 Nov.1925, Twitt's Ghyll, AC5/1/369
52  Austen to Ida, 21 Jan.1926, Rapallo, AC5/1/374

were discussed such free & open talks tend to the common understanding & policy which I think we most desire.'[53]

Gloom returned to Rapallo upon Mussolini's departure. The concord achieved at Locarno turned bitter, but that only deepened Austen's commitment to the policy he had pursued there. One provision of the Locarno settlement, Germany's return to the League of Nations, left France uneasy. Briand sought compensation by including the French ally Poland on the League Council, previously reserved for the great powers. Austen visited him en route home to England; and they had 'a very satisfactory talk roaming over a wide field, assuring ourselves of our common agreement on all fundamental matters, ... giving me the assurance that Briand has lost none of his faith in Locarno & none of his determination to pursue that policy.'[54] But in reaching this agreement, Austen distorted the Locarno settlement by siding unmistakeably with France vis-à-vis Germany, to the dismay of some in the Cabinet and the parliamentary party. Briand's proposal also set off a string of demands for inclusion in the Council of the League from lesser powers; first Brazil and Spain, then Belgium and China.

Without grasping how he had tarnished his reputation, Austen headed for Geneva 'to play as difficult a hand as ever fell to a man's lot'.[55] He left Neville to tell their sisters of the collapsing international concord. Neville stood by his brother with only the mildest of criticism. Any uneasiness Neville may have felt was removed when Lloyd George attacked Austen in the Commons. Lloyd George seemed to Neville 'just as reckless and mischievous and spiteful as he could be and he left nothing unsaid that could make things more difficult. "Poisoning the cup" "bullying Germany" "destroying his own masterpiece" "breach of faith" were among his phrases every one of which is no doubt seized upon and exploited by the German Nationalists. To me such a speech was no surprise; it is in character, but it must have cut Austen deeply.'[56]

Like Austen, Neville had concerns about the health of his wife. Annie 'got into a condition which borders on a nervous break-down', and fell repeatedly 'into the extreme of depression' which 'actually prevents herself from getting the repose which is what she needs'. She brought extraordinary gifts to Neville in public life:

53  Austen to Neville, 10 Jan.1926, Rapallo, NC1/27/88
54  Austen to Ivy, 30Jan.1926, i, 2 Morpeth Mansions, AC6/1/629
55  Austen to Ida, 5 Mar.1926, 2 Morpeth Mansions, in Self, ed., *The Austen Chamberlain Diary Letters*, 287
56  Neville to Hilda, 7 Mar.1926, Westbourne, in Self, ed., *The Neville Chamberlain Diary Letters*, II, 333

she touched audiences he could not reach and she thawed out his relations with individuals disconcerted by his stiffness. But these gifts came at high psychological cost to Annie. She managed best in Birmingham, where she and Neville spent weekends with their children, but she did not 'seem able to cope' with life in London.[57] Her doctor prescribed six weeks convalescence away from everyone – friends, political associates and family: 'exactly what she and I had felt was wanted.' So they complied. Neville said that, 'though I look forward to my lonely life with loathing and disgust I feel a reasonable confidence that the sacrifice will bring its reward and that I shall get rid of this uneasy shadow which has been getting gradually darker for some time. Annie ... rejoices in a prescription which abhors exercise but involves rest and sunshine!'[58] She headed that Easter for Biarritz while he headed north to the strenuous recreations which he loved, fishing and shooting in the Highlands.

As she settled into the sofa on the balcony of her hotel overlooking the Atlantic, Annie felt 'as if the lid which was shutting me in on top was lifted & thousands of things were gradually getting free ... I'm sure this wonderful view above the sea – & the sea itself are the <u>cure</u> – the space & freedom & nothing to do – and just what I wanted, & no-one to speak to one.' She reported every other day to Neville on her recovery, which proved slow. At night at first, 'if anyone moves above ... then back one goes to politics etc. for hours. ... I still feel I can't <u>bear</u> the thought of meeting people.' She craved light and sun: 'I had a sun bathe on the balcony this afternoon & have an electric light bathe to-morrow, & ... start sun roof baths next week.' Within two weeks the doctor reported that her 'blood pressure is now nearly normal, & he [was] sure the six weeks will set me up, though he does not want me to start "obligations" before June 1st.' A week later she felt that she had 'passed the stage of having any <u>bad</u> days' but 'My brain & memory is not right yet'.[59]

Annie's recovery was upset at the beginning of May, along with everything in Britain. All the organised labour in the country went on strike in support of the miners, who were confronted by a cut in their pay and an increase in their working hours. Annie longed to rejoin Neville as the government faced the crisis. He was uneasy, as well as relieved, at his exclusion from the group of ministers who took charge of negotiations with the trade unions. Baldwin nevertheless wanted him to stay near at hand. Everyone in the full Cabinet attended its daily meetings,

57  Neville to Ida, 13 Mar.1926, 37 Eaton Square, in Self, ed., *op.cit.*, II, 336
58  Neville to Ida, 27 Mar.1926, Westbourne, in Self, ed., *The Neville Chamberlain Diary Letters*, II, 339–340
59  Annie to Neville, 2, 5, 7 13, & 21 Apr.1926, Biarritz, NC1/25/193, 195, 199 & 203

except for Austen. He stayed at Twitt's Ghyll nursing his lumbago, confident that the strike would be 'better dealt with by my colleagues.' His estimate of Baldwin's ability on domestic matters had risen remarkably. 'Baldwin has the right character for the job since all men trust him & rightly ... he has developed amazingly since he became Prime Minister a second time.'[60] Neville was nonetheless critical of Austen's absence during the emergency.

But he was more concerned to keep Annie from cutting her convalescence short. He pleaded with her to stay in Biarritz: 'there is nothing that requires your presence here ... to return now would be to jeopardise & perhaps throw away the whole benefit of your "cure"', and he signed the letter, 'Your very own but rather-troubled-by-his-importunate-wife – Neville.'[61] Reluctantly Annie remained in Biarritz. The strike had in any case blocked travel between France and England. Still she 'felt very desperate', afraid 'lest I should get completely cut off from getting home if things got worse'. If that happened, she would 'be <u>utterly</u> miserable ... & ... think of nothing but getting home, & worrying myself <u>dreadfully</u>. Do you see Neville darling,' she pleaded, 'I <u>am</u> fit to come home now.'[62] Ida and Hilda reinforced her plea to Neville: 'we hope,' Hilda wrote, that 'you will let her come back, if she can return with reasonable safety. ... she has behaved with great self-control in not starting for home at once ... She wrote us a desperate note ... it is a horrid situation for her & she is likely to do herself more harm by remaining out now than by coming home.'[63]

The sudden collapse of the general strike enabled Neville to wire Annie to come back, to her ecstatic delight: 'To know fully where one's heart is, one ought to have these <u>horrible</u> separations. It will be <u>heavenly</u> to be back, & you will find me quite a different person. The "cure" is really finished.'[64] A month later she was 'quite herself again and ... enjoying life',[65] though she continued to refuse public engagements.

❧

The Chamberlains settled back into their differing forms of public service. Austen

60  Austen to Hilda, 25 Apr. & 8 May 1926, Twitt's Ghyll, in Self, ed., *The Austen Chamberlain Diary Letters*, 289–90

61  Neville to Annie, 3 May 1926, 37 Eaton Square, NC1/26/362

62  Annie to Neville, 6 May 1926, Biarritz NC1/25/209

63  Hilda to Neville, Sunday [9 May 1926], The Bury House, NC18/2/496

64  Annie to Neville, 11 May 1926, Biarritz, NC1/25/214

65  Neville to Ida, 20 June 1926, Westbourne, in Self, ed., *The Neville Chamberlain Diary Letters*, II, 352

kept 'almost out of sight,' Neville reported, 'but remains a great figure, gradually becoming more hazy and legendary as he is less familiar. He comes but little to the House and told me ... that he was very weary. It is however also true that he no longer has political ambitions beyond his present office and does not feel either inclination or duty calling him thither.'[66] The brothers had little contact with each other these days, and learned of each other's doings through their sisters. Ida blamed the demands of the Foreign Office for Austen's weariness. Neville was not convinced: 'to me an office which involves no legislation, very perfunctory attendance at the House, and hardly any speeches outside seems an old man's job! Not that I complain.'[67] He thrived on the demands of the Ministry of Health and took pride in the nine Acts of Parliament for which he claimed responsibility in 1926, 'not as difficult or as long' as his Pensions and Rating and Valuation Acts of 1925 but still 'a very useful & creditable little bunch'.[68]

Once Austen's difficulties over the Council of the League of Nations passed, he reaped more rewards from Locarno. Mussolini came up 'especially to see' him at Livorno and 'was most satisfactory politically & most cordial personally'. Austen proceeded to Paris, where he interrupted dreams by Briand and Stresemann of a rapprochement between France and Germany that ran beyond what Austen thought viable: 'but what an outcome since Locarno & what a justification of my policy!'[69] Like Neville at the Ministry of Health, Austen loved and took pride in the work of the Foreign Office: 'Not only is there so much of it, but the issues are so big & the consequences may be so serious if you decide wrongly. But it is fascinatingly interesting & it is really rewarding to find for how much we count & how high our influence now stands.'[70] Later he was awarded a Nobel Prize for his accomplishment at Locarno; but he valued it more for the accompanying money than for the honour. He settled for the moment into the Foreign Office as the height of his political ambition.

Neville, however, began to set his gaze a little higher, and thought of following his father's footsteps into the imperial arena as Colonial Secretary. He was earning a reputation at the Ministry of Health for 'sheer mental efficiency', in the words of the national and provincial press which singled him out as 'the most effective

---

66  Neville to Hilda, 10 Aug.1926, Inverness, in Self, ed., *op.cit.*, II, 363
67  Neville to Ida, 15 Aug.1926, Oykell by Lairg, in Self, ed., *op.cit.*, II, 364
68  Neville to Hilda, 11 Dec.1926, 37 Eaton Square, in Self, ed., *op.cit.*, II, 382
69  Austen to Hilda, 8 Oct.1926, Twitt's Ghyll, in Self, ed., *The Austen Chamberlain Diary Letters*, 293
70  Austen to Hilda, 20 Dec.1926, Twitt's Ghyll, in Self, ed., *op.cit.*, 297

member'[71] of the government. But his efficiency had its hard side. It reduced the understanding of the needs of labour which marked his mayoralty. He now found spokesmen for the trades unions unintelligible. 'They will never give you a straight answer to a straight question. They reply always at interminable length in sentences which have no grammatical ending and leave me in a hopeless fog.'[72] When the miners refused to abandon their industrial action after the collapse of the general strike, his attitude toward labour hardened further, and he chided his sisters for their kinder response. 'Of course it is a thousand pities that after all this loss and damage we haven't got any prospect of a more permanent peace among the miners. But that in my view is solely the fault of the miners leaders.'[73]

He dealt even more roughly with the Labour Opposition in Parliament, to the delight of Conservative backbenchers. He took pleasure in the hatred he generated on the Labour benches 'because of my nasty sarcastic way. Very few people can stand sarcasm; the Socialists so far lose control that they have taken to hissing me.'[74] Baldwin begged him 'to remember that [he] was addressing a meeting of gentlemen' and deplored the impression that he 'looked on the Labour Party as dirt.' 'The fact is,' Neville told Ida unrepentantly, 'that intellectually, with a few exceptions, they *are* dirt.'[75] But Hilda's heart ached at the lengthening lines of the unemployed. She recalled 'the extraordinarily painful impression made on me' in an earlier 'period of long unemployment, – I think in the 90s – & the awful desperate expression on the faces of the men in the back streets in London & B'ham.'[76]

This difference in feeling between Neville and his sisters did not affect their reliance on governmental action to deal with social problems. While the brothers served on the national and international stage, their sisters attended to the needs of Hampshire. Ida's focus in the County Council on housing and health continued to dovetail nicely with Neville's concerns at the Ministry of Health. She also used Hilda's influence as president of the Hampshire Federation of Women's Institutes to build up support for 'a very good Health service' and 'wring a little more money out of the County Council'.[77]

Hilda meanwhile launched a campaign to make the national executive

71  Neville to Hilda, 6 Apr.1926, Banchory, Scotland, in Self, ed., *The Neville Chamberlain Diary Letters*, II, 340

72  Neville to Hilda, 2 May 1926, 37 Eaton Square, in Self, ed., *op.cit.*, II, 344

73  Neville to Ida, 10 Oct.1926, Westbourne, in Self, ed., *op.cit.*, II, 367

74  Neville to Hilda, 3 Apr.1927, in Self, ed., *op.cit.*, II, 405

75  Neville to Ida, 19 June 1927, Sevenoaks, in Self, ed., *op.cit.*, II, 412

76  Hilda to Neville, 14 Oct.1926, Bell Hotel, Gloucester, NC18/2/516

77  Ida to Neville, 16 Dec.1926, The Bury House, NC18/2/525

committee of the Women's Institutes more responsive to the counties: 'the Nat. Executive Committee being practically a closed body working in London ... get out of touch with the work of the Counties, & more & more inclined to turn the whole thing into a ... distinctly feminist political body, working for social reform but dealing quite as much with town questions as with country ones.' The various county federations differed, however, to each other in their proposals for reform, which enabled the National Executive to maintain the status quo. Hilda therefore set 'to work to try & organize an opinion' in vintage Chamberlain fashion: 'if we could educate a certain number of people in different areas all over the country to work for the same main principles, we might win in the end.' Far from wishing to weaken the Women's Institute movement, she feared that 'the separation of the Nat. Fed. Executive from any direct relation with the County Executives is bound in the end to lead to trouble & probably a breaking up of the whole movement & large secessions which would be a very great pity.'[78]

The National Executive under its resilient chairman, Lady Denman, sought to lessen Hilda's reforming zeal by bringing her within its tent. They invited her to become a member of its organisation sub-committee. Hilda accepted the invitation, used her position on the sub-committee to woo support for the Hampshire proposals for reform, and drew representatives from twenty-one county federations together to agree on a resolution. As she marshalled support, she discovered that she had 'inherited something of Papa's power of clear statement'.[79] The National Executive, uneasy at her advance, invited her to join them as a co-opted member. She deferred acceptance for a year, anxious to put the Hampshire organisation in better shape. The National Executive then asked her to discuss her scheme for constitutional reform with them, an opportunity she welcomed: 'I must keep a tight hand on myself for my object is to convert them & not to score them off, but I think I shall have some fun.'[80] But she met her match in Lady Denman. Hilda was asked at the National Executive 'to explain various points but they did not discuss [them] before me as I had hoped they would'. Afterwards Lady Denham told her that, though the National Executive were not prepared to accept her scheme of reform, they would 'send a letter to the Counties recommending discussion'.[81] Lady Denman's circular precipitated a stream of requests for Hilda to make her case to the counties.

---

78  Hilda to Neville, 9 July 1926, The Bury House, NC18/2/506
79  Hilda to Neville, 24 June 1927, The Bury House, NC18/2/550
80  Hilda to Neville, 30 Sept.1927, The Bury House, NC18/2/561
81  Hilda to Neville, 25 Oct.1927, Ladies' Imperial Club, London, NC18/2/563

1927 proved to be a happier year for Hilda and Ida than for Austen and Neville. They sent self-congratulatory reports on their hard work to their sisters, searching for reassurance when it went unappreciated by their cabinet colleagues. Austen continued to rely on the legacy of Locarno and the methods of private consultation among foreign ministers by which it had been achieved. 'If anyone tells you that Locarno is dead, they are talking nonsense,' he told Ida at the end of a year marked by repeated setbacks. He doubted that British foreign policy had 'ever been quite as frank & confidential as in these days when your brother knows & talks with almost every foreign minister in Europe.'[82] But his experience did not bear out his claims. Methods that worked well in western and central Europe were less effective farther away, whether in China or Russia, or with the Americans who were paralysed by their frequent elections. Austen's search for diplomatic compromises was also obstructed by a truculent trio of colleagues, Amery, Birkenhead and Churchill, who could persuade a majority in the Cabinet to overrule him. 'I have been disappointed at receiving so little support from some of my colleagues &,' Austen added, 'having my informed & considered opinion swept aside so lightly by ... backbenchers who don't know what I know of the *state* of Europe & how thin the crust is on which I have to tread.'[83]

Yet he remained confident that he was the right man in the right office. He refused to let setbacks pull him down, and his physical resilience seemed to bear him out. When his doctors insisted that he was in good health, he jested, 'It is really disappointing to get such optimistic reports when you have felt that you were sacrificing your life to public duty!' He was heartened too by the endorsements he received from senior staff at the Foreign Office. When Baldwin enquired how long Austen, now sixty-four, might feel able to continue in his demanding position, he replied that he 'would go on for another Parliament!'[84] He ended the year exultant at the treaty of perpetual friendship with Egypt for which he secured Cabinet approval: it 'seems to me a prodigious achievement' and 'a great triumph for British diplomacy.'[85]

Neville ended the year in a gloomier frame of mind. The brothers were tormented in Cabinet by the same person: Churchill. He was ringleader of the hawks on foreign policy. The Chamberlains drew together in face of that threat. 'Seeing

---

82  Austen to Ida, 12 Dec.1927, Geneva, in Self, ed., *The Austen Chamberlain Diary Letters*, 320–1

83  Austen to Ida, 20 Feb.1927, Twitt's Ghyll, in Self, ed., *op.cit.*, 310

84  Austen to Hilda, 15 Oct.1927, 2 Morpeth Mansions, in Self, ed., *op.cit.*, 317

85  Austen to Ida, 6 & 12 Nov.1927, 2 Morpeth Mansions, in Self, ed., *op.cit.*, 318–9

what a rough passage Austen was having' over his negotiations with Russia, Neville sent him 'a suggested draft of a despatch which I thought might help'. The domestic legislator did not expect the Foreign Secretary to 'pay any attention' to his draft: 'so I was quite flattered when he sent me a note to say it was admirable & he proposed to adopt it.'[86]

The threat from Churchill to Neville was even greater than to Austen, for Churchill as Chancellor held the purse strings. It seems ironic in retrospect that Churchill focused his cost-cutting zeal on defence rather than on social reform. But when Neville outlined his plan to overhaul the Poor Law upon which the British system of social insurance depended, Churchill insisted on coupling it with an equally far-reaching scheme of his own to overhaul local government finance. Churchill's vaulting proposal shattered Neville's patient planning. He had already withdrawn the rest of his legislative programme for 1927 in order to reform the Poor Law: 'now,' he moaned, 'I have positively got nothing whatever.' 'Winston's alliance,' he concluded, 'is even more dangerous than his opposition.'[87]

Struggling to keep his plans for Poor Law reform alive, Neville tried to reduce Churchill's plans for local government finance to manageable proportions, meanwhile maintaining support from the Prime Minister and Cabinet for a complicated piece of legislation which none of them fully understood. The only support upon which he could regularly rely in the full Cabinet came from Austen. Churchill infuriated Neville by changing his plan 'like a kaleidoscope so that even now I don't know what form it will take when it comes before the Cabinet ... At this moment Winston is under the impression that he has squared me but till I see the final form I don't know whether he has or not.' Winston focused his powers of persuasion on the rest of the Cabinet committee, and won them over. Neville dug in, 'and after sustaining a prolonged barrage ... presented a minority report'. A tolerable compromise was devised, but it did not improve his spirits: 'I have got a horrible session in front of me. Winston will do all the prancing and I shall do all the drudgery.' By the end of April Neville felt confident that he had 'preserved the conditions which I consider vital and have lost nothing in weight or influence by what I have consented to surrender'. Still 'I shan't feel safe till the Bill is through'.[88]

---

86　Neville to Hilda, 19 Feb.1927, 37 Eaton Square, in Self, ed., *The Neville Chamberlain Diary Letters*, II, 394, and Ida to Neville, 25 Feb.1927, The Bury House, NC18/2/534

87　Neville to Hilda, 5 Feb., 37 Eaton Square, & 12 Feb.1927, Westbourne, in Self, ed., *op.cit.*, II, 391–3

88　Neville to Ida, 24 Mar. & 21 Apr., & to Hilda, 31 Mar. & 15 Apr.1928, Westbourne, in Self,

Aside from battling Churchill, Neville and Austen were drawn together by their anxiety regarding their straitened financial circumstances. Ministerial salaries, once munificent, no longer covered the costs of office-holding including dual residence in town and country. Austen was pressed further financially by his social duties as Foreign Secretary. He had to use hotels because his flat in London and his country house were small and unimpressive. The financial conditions of the brothers were put further at risk by the precarious health of their wives. Annie had not completed her rest cure in Biarritz. Nervous fatigue broke into her sleep and left her prone to colds and flu. Ivy was worn down by Lawrence's needs and suffered from recurrent neuritis. These illnesses necessitated costly cures for Annie at the spas of Harrogate and still costlier trips abroad for Ivy. Both women leapt at the idea of chauffeur-driven cars to carry them away from their cares at home. Ivy sold china she bought in Corsica in order to buy a Chrysler. Neville paid for Annie's vehicle. His pockets remained deeper than Austen's, though both suffered from the impact of the depression on the family business, Hoskins.

Ivy added to Austen's financial concerns by developing an appetite for gambling in the casinos built beside the better spas on the Continent. He tried to restrain her, without success. 'You will be glad to hear that I am losing my winning!' she sought to assure him: 'However it is my winnings. It's a sad heart that never rejoices & I have had great fun playing!'[89] She gambled with spirit. On one occasion she ran considerable risk by challenging some rich Americans at baccarat, to applause from her French friends.

Hilda meanwhile moved upward in the hierarchy of the Women's Institutes. Though her campaign for better county representation at the national level made her widely known, she failed in her first bid for a place on the National Executive. But on reading the constitutional amendment that the National Executive itself put forward, she discovered she 'had been a great deal more successful than [she] knew.... they are doing now what we begged them to do earlier'. She remained reluctant, however, to accept co-option on to the National Executive until a letter arrived saying that Lady Denman 'was anxious to propose me' and 'would also like to propose my serving on the sub-ctee which would be at once appointed to consider the constitution'.[90] At her first meeting with the National Executive, Hilda was pleased to find 'two of the youngest & most enthusiastic members on my side'. With their support, she secured 'a report which will give us the essential

ed., *op.cit.*, III, 77, 79 & 81–2

89  Ivy to Austen, 8 Sept.1926, Royat, AC6/2/436

90  Hilda to Neville, 25 May & 7 June 1928, The Bury House, NC18/2/586 & '8

representation which we were asking for, whilst safeguarding the independence of the Executive Ctee. ... Naturally I don't get what I wanted exactly in the form in which it was proposed, but ... we have secured the kernel in the shape of an advisory body with a representative from every county Federation ... to which the committees of the National Federation must report.'[91]

At the same time, however, Austen experienced the worst disaster of his Foreign Secretaryship. He was personally responsible for the setback, and it shattered his health. For months he had said little to his siblings apart from sighing with exhaustion. Suddenly he informed the House of Commons of an arms limitation agreement that he had privately concluded with Briand of France without prior approval from the Cabinet or notice to the other Locarno powers or the United States. The agreement offended the Cabinet, broke German faith in their Locarno allies, showed Americans that the European powers were up to their old tricks, and demonstrated to the Labour party and friends of the League of Nations that Austen was addicted to the kind of secret diplomacy which they held responsible for the Great War. Sensing the seriousness of his blunder, Austen suffered an immediate collapse, influenza turning into pneumonia, digestive disorder and rapid weight loss. An Acting Foreign Secretary was appointed to give him time to recover. Though Austen overcame the pneumonia after a month, he remained 'very depressed'.

His financial situation deepened his worries: 'he had paid so little attention to his own affairs, that he had not realized in the least the size of his overdraft.' Desperate, he put Twitt's Ghyll up for sale. Ida and Hilda offered to help. But Ivy insisted that the house was 'absolutely unsuited for their present requirements'. Hilda was horrified: 'to have nothing but that underground flat [in London] as a home seems to me ghastly.'[92] Austen's financial plight was only deepened by the rehabilitative trip Ivy planned to California. She assembled a party of seven including two of the three children, and helped pay for it by selling her car.

Austen's recovery was not complete when he returned to England. Neville had found the press reports of his departure from Liverpool 'most disturbing' and 'still more alarming were the photos published in various newspapers which made him look as if he had had a stroke'.[93] The reports Ivy despatched en route for the West Indies were scarcely reassuring. She wrote from Bermuda that Austen 'could now

91  Hilda to Neville, 22 June & 5 & 21 July 1928, The Bury House, NC18/2/590 & 592–3
92  Hilda to Neville, 17 Aug.1928, L'Ermitage d'Evian, NC18/2/598
93  Neville to Ida, 3 Sept.1928, Bamburgh, in Self, ed., *The Neville Chamberlain Diary Letters*, III, 103

walk all round the deck by himself!', which only showed Ida 'how bad he was to begin with'. A month later, Austen was 'wonderfully better', but 'still "inconceivably weak"'. And he was 'still very lame with sciatica!' Ida concluded that, 'it is not the pneumonia he is suffering from, that was merely an incident, but a regular nervous break down from prolonged over work & strain'.[94] 'He must be a perfect skeleton,' said Neville. He had already questioned whether Austen would be strong enough to stay on at the Foreign Office if the Conservatives retained power after the next general election. Neville now doubted that Austen would 'be fit to take on the strain of the F.O.' when he returned to England at the end of the year.[95]

§

But Austen had no thought of retirement. At Ivy's insistence, he took good care of himself after his return, promising to 'wrap myself up again in scarf & fur coat & be very careful not to get a chill' when he paid a pre-election visit to his Birmingham constituency.[96] He was shocked by what he saw there. 'Unemployment will make our fight a very hard one. Even the best arguments won't fill empty stomachs & in desperate cases men are apt to turn to desperate courses.' Foreign affairs attracted little attention among the electorate. But Austen remained confident of the respect he commanded on the Continent. He was also heartened by the house in London, 58 Rutland Gate, which Ivy found after their sale of Twitt's Ghyll, not far from the former family enclave around Egerton Crescent. 'I have been three times up to the roof to see my plants', Austen told Ivy happily.[97]

She encouraged his attachment to the Foreign Office, relishing her privileges as wife of the Foreign Secretary, especially in Italy, where Mussolini's 'powers of judgement & organisation' impressed her.[98] Ivy urged Austen to draw Mussolini into the inner circle of Locarno powers. To promote Anglo-Italian friendship herself, she used embassy facilities to assemble a collection of Italian masterpieces for display in England and the United States. She credited Mussolini with giving her 'full powers to do all'[99] that she wanted for the famous Italian artist Modigliani, ignoring the fact that he had been dead for almost a decade. Mussolini certainly

94  Ida to Neville, 25 Sept. & 18 Oct.1928, The Bury House, NC18/2/603 & 606
95  Neville to Ida, 20 Oct.1928, in Self, ed., *op.cit.*, III, 108
96  Austen to Ivy, 12 Feb.1929, xii, Birmingham, AC6/1/736
97  Austen to Ivy, 30 Mar.1930, 58 Rutland Gate, AC6/1/760
98  Ivy to Austen, 8 Feb.1929, v, Menton, AC6/2/488
99  Ivy to Austen, 11 Apr.1929, British Embassy, Rome, AC6/2/510

pulled out all the stops when Ivy visited Milan. She was 'comfortably installed' in a splendid hotel, with 'a nice bed & bath room & large sitting room', laden with bouquets from the Italian ambassador and city officials: 'A motor at my disposal & a loge at the Opera for the week!!' Her car was furnished with 'an Italian & England flag in front & a private detective ... all traffic is cleared for me! & all the police salute me!!'[100]

Neville remained riveted on the less glamorous business of reforming the Poor Law. The legislation that he and Churchill pushed upon each other brought out a difference between Neville and his sisters on the subject. Neville thought in terms of administrative efficiency, to which he believed large units of local government were conducive. But Ida thought that large administrative units bred bureaucrats, whom she regarded with contempt. She wanted to invigorate the smaller units of local government, and protested when Neville's proposals for Poor Law reform offered responsibility for roads and workhouses to County rather than District Councils. She praised District Councils as schools of good citizenship, and questioned the capacity of County Councils 'to undertake the immense amount of extra work which you are gradually imposing upon them. Will it not mean that more & more everything will get into the hands of the bureaucrats? From a business point of view I suppose the larger area must help to greater economy & efficiency, but from the point of view of encouraging local feeling & local patriotism, & getting people interested in the administration of their own affairs I deplore it. ... As soon as you get large areas you get caught in a complicated machinery which controls you & you cannot control.'[101]

Neville replied impatiently, 'you can't make omelettes without breaking eggs.'[102] But Hilda reinforced her sister's plea, arguing that administration by smaller local units 'would be more "human" & also more economical'. She proposed a compromise to turn District Councils into agents of the County Councils, subject to their general control 'but not interfered with unless big developments are needed, or unless they become reckless'.[103] Neville acted on this advice, and altered his bill to permit committees of local guardians and district councillors 'to visit & even manage' local institutions, under general supervision from the County Council. He also insisted that County Councils delegate the upkeep of unclassified roads to District Councils, subject to similar supervision. Ida thanked him for 'leaving

100  Ivy to Austen, 23 & 24 Feb.1929, Albergo Principe & Savoia, Milan, AC6/2/503–4
101  Ida to Neville, 29 June 1928, The Bury House, NC18/2/591
102  Neville to Ida, 15 July 1928, 37 Eaton Square, in Self, ed., *op.cit.*, III, 97
103  Hilda to Neville, 26 Oct.1928, NC18/2/607

plenty of work worth doing in the hands of the local people'.[104] It was the final achievement of the collaboration between Neville and his sisters.

With the passage of the Local Government Act in the spring of 1929, attention shifted to the approaching general election and the composition of the subsequent government. There was less interest in the question of Austen's retention of the Foreign Office than in the future of his brother. Neville's obvious command during the recent debates raised his stature. He was hailed half in jest at a luncheon with lobby journalists as a future Prime Minister, 'ruling alone or sharing the purple with Austen like the old Roman Emperors of the West & East, "Nevillius and Austinian" taking Home & Foreign Affairs respectively'. Neville had just turned sixty and had accomplished most of what he set out to do at the Ministry of Health.

His heart was nevertheless not set on the premiership. Remarkably for a politically ambitious family, the position of Prime Minister meant less to the Chamberlains than the causes for which they crusaded. Here as always, Joseph set the model for his family, firstly when he gave up the prospect of becoming Prime Minister in order to prevent disruption of the Union with Ireland, and secondly when he again sacrificed himself to crusade for imperial preference. Neville much preferred command of an important ministry to the manifold concerns of the premiership – until Baldwin demonstrated how exasperating an inert Prime Minister could be. When Hilda said to him that it was 'ten to one against my ever being P.M.,' he replied 'that does not trouble me a bit.' The only thing that led him to think more of the premiership was his desire to keep Churchill out. Anything would be better than 'a Churchillian domination'. [105] Otherwise Neville would have preferred to become Secretary of State for the Colonies. But when Baldwin indicated that he might have to accept the Chancellorship of the Exchequer, he no longer recoiled as in 1923. Baldwin quickened Neville's interest in the Exchequer by letting him know that the Conservative parliamentary party would prefer him to 'the present occupant', Churchill.[106]

Neville approached the general election with cautious optimism, hopeful that his legislative accomplishments would enhance the reputation of the government. He was still taken aback by the dissolution of Parliament. 'When I think that in less than four weeks from now it will be all over I feel inclined to gasp.' 'Nineteen days!' he wrote a week later; 'It is not very long, but it's like the Channel crossing; one thinks a lot about it before hand and the thoughts are not pleasant.' Yet once he

---

104 Hilda to Neville, 9 Nov., & Ida to Neville, 16 Nov.1928, The Bury House, NC18/2/609–10
105 Neville to Hilda, 31 Mar., & to Ida, 6 Oct.1928, in Self, ed., *op.cit.*, III, 78 & 106
106 Neville to Ida, 24 Feb. & 9 Mar.1929, 37 Eaton Square, in Self, ed., *op.cit.*, III, 124 & '7

was in the thick of electioneering, he enjoyed himself. He had changed constituencies in Birmingham since the last election, having barely retained Ladywood then. He stood now without anxiety for Edgbaston, the safest of Conservative seats. He loved watching Annie 'making hosts of new friends who will soon be as devoted to her as those in Ladywood'.[107]

However, he was in for a rude shock. The general election of 1929 exposed the shallowness of his accomplishment over the past five years. Paradoxically, this election also opened a chapter of accidents that would carry him high over the next five.

---

107  Neville to Hilda, 5, 11 & 25 May 1929, Westbourne, in Self, ed., *The Neville Chamberlain Diary Letters*, III, 136, 138 & 140

*Part III*

# OVERREACH

*Ida and Hilda, leaders in local government and Women's Institutes*

## 8

# Depression

'It is rather a shock to have one's whole outlook on life completely changed in 24 hours,'[1] Neville gasped. The results of the general election sent him reeling. Though he carried Edgbaston without difficulty, Austen hung on to West Birmingham by a mere forty-three votes. Breaking the grip that the Chamberlains and Unionism had held upon Birmingham for more than half a century, Labour won half of the city's twelve seats. Labour also emerged as the largest party in the new Parliament, though without a majority. The general election of 1929 thus brought the years of greatest achievement for Joe's sons to an abrupt end.

Austen saw the defeat coming. He had warned Ivy that he might lose the seat that his father had held for nearly forty years. West Birmingham had become 'one vast slum. The housing conditions are inexpressible – overcrowding, floors rotted into holes, paper falling off damp walls, plaster falling from the ceilings, stopped up drains, stenches & death.' Because he rarely visited his constituency, he had not known '<u>how</u> bad it is. ... Housing was the one & only question & the miracle is that I kept the seat at all.'[2]

The centrality of housing in the government's defeat placed responsibility for it at Neville's door. His attempt to renew the reputation of Conservatives as capable social reformers had alienated right-wing activists in the party and left the working-class electorate quite unconvinced. Neville faced up to the fact that his efforts over pensions and housing had lost the government more votes than they gained. 'No one has voted for us on account of these things who would not otherwise have

---

1  Neville to Mary, 1 June 1929, Westbourne, NC C1/20/1/147
2  Austen to Mary, 31 May 1929, Midland Hotel, Birmingham, AC4/1/1297

done so but thousands have voted against us because they or their relations or even some one they knew had not got a pension or a house.' That recognition deepened Neville's discouragement. 'My pleasure is in administration rather than in the game of politics ... To me it makes all the difference to be in office. If I were told that I could never hold office again I should prefer to go out now.'[3]

And he feared that the Conservatives were likely to be out of office for at least seven years. Labour, as the largest party in Parliament, could 'carry on for 2 years in such a way as to establish their ability to govern ... Then they would frame an attractive Budget & appeal to the country to give them a majority', able to carry on for another five years. By then Neville would be sixty-seven: 'how far shall I have travelled down the hill' he asked bleakly. 'On the most favourable supposition I cannot expect to have either the energy or the physical strength I have now. Now was my chance when I still retain plenty of physical vigour and when my mental powers are at their zenith. ... But,' he continued, grasping for hope, 'there is no certainty in politics ... The most unexpected things may happen and we may return to office sooner than seems possible now.'

The Conservatives had been driven from office by their inability to satisfy the hopes raised by Britain's costly victory in the First World War and to alleviate the subsequent depression. The country soon found itself in a worsening situation. Four months after the general election, a crash on the New York stock exchange threw the United States into depression. It took two years before that depression rocked the economy of the Old World, and another two before the economic deterioration was matched politically by the rise of Hitler. The worth of Austen's handiwork in foreign affairs as well as Neville's in domestic was now in question. But this twofold upheaval had reverse consequences for the two brothers. The economic slump, as the British called it, shattered the Labour government and installed Neville as the workhorse in a new National Government. Austen, on the other hand, was denied the opportunity he craved to continue his work at the Foreign Office.

&

The years ahead worked out far differently than any scenario Neville had envisaged. But they began as badly as he feared. The defeated Conservatives fell out with each other over how to regain power and hence about who should lead them.

---

3 Neville to Ida, 2 June 1929, Westbourne, in Self, ed., *The Neville Chamberlain Diary Letters*, III, 143–4

This squabbling and jockeying for position within the party might have repelled Neville, who found little pleasure 'in the game of politics'. But his determination to get things done and, if at all possible, to advance the familial cause of tariff reform enabled him to push his way forward without the appearance of self-seeking which so damaged Churchill. Neville saw tariff reform not as a crusade but as a practical way of dealing with the country's most pressing economic problems, in particular the soaring cost of unemployment insurance and the slump in trade. But after the general election his focus on tariff reform pushed the concerns he had displayed for social reform as Minister of Health far down his immediate order of priorities.

Defeat in the general election brought Conservatives back to the issues that had divided them before 1924: tariff reform and relations with the free-trading Liberals. Neville was afraid that Labour might take up some version of tariff reform before the Conservatives could adopt it in ampler form. But he was embarrassed by the keenest tariff reformer among the ex-Ministers, Leo Amery, who insisted on all or nothing. Amery's stance prompted an equally aggressive riposte from Churchill, the most insistent free trader among the former ministers. This quarrel reawakened Austen's desire to cooperate with free-trading Liberals, pre-eminently Churchill. When the former ministers reconvened, they had, according to Austen, 'a very quiet and friendly discussion which showed a quite satisfactory measure of agreement amongst us for the present at least, with the possible exception of Amery'.[4] But Neville reacted with disgust to Churchill's behaviour. 'Winston is shoving very hard, with an eye to the leadership it is said, and ... wants us to do a deal with [Lloyd George] over electoral reform and I am afraid Austen is also disposed in the same direction.'[5]

Removal from office thus revived the vexing triangular relationship of the Chamberlain brothers with Churchill. Though Churchill had persistently criticised Austen's foreign policy, Austen continued to admire him as second only to Lloyd George in brilliance. The Chamberlain brothers also reacted differently on another issue, though in this case it did not trouble their relationship. Both looked to the private sector to supplement their financial resources; but they differed in the acuteness of their need. Austen simply had to secure remunerative directorships. If, he said, a good one was offered to him 'on condition that it should not be given up for [political] office he would accept'. Neville could pick and choose; he

---

4 Austen to Hilda, 13 July 1929, 2 Morpeth Mansions, in Self, ed., *The Austen Chamberlain Diary Letters*, 339
5 Neville to Ida, 13 July, Westbourne, & to Hilda, 21 July 1929, Dorchester, in Self, ed., *The Neville Chamberlain Diary Letters*, III, 149–50

turned down the chairmanship of British Steel in order to 'be free to do as much political work as [he] wanted'.[6]

With the brothers for the moment in political eclipse, it was the sisters' turn to shine. Ida fought to make District Councils responsible for local roads, as she had persuaded Neville to allow in his legislation. But the County Clerk frustrated her campaign. Undeterred, she took over the chairmanship of the county's Public Health Committee, which involved membership in crucial sub-committees on finance and public assistance. From her place on the public assistance sub-committee, she made sure that the management of the institutions under its supervision was entrusted as far as possible to committees of local guardians. 'It is terribly sad,' she wrote to Neville, 'to think that just when things are getting so interesting for me, politics are so very depressing for you & Austen.'[7] Hilda used her place on the National Executive of the Women's Institutes to curb the influence of the feminists in the movement and keep it in line with Conservative policy on agricultural questions. Her election as Vice-Chairman of the National Executive consolidated her power.

The brothers, however, were at sea over the direction and leadership of their party. Its plight worsened because Baldwin, whose performance in his recent term as Prime Minister had satisfied Austen as well as Neville, proved hopeless as Leader of the Opposition. Both brothers were 'very dissatisfied' with his 'passivity'. Austen talked of producing an unauthorised programme such as Joseph had issued when fed up with the party leadership in his day. Neville tackled Baldwin directly. Walking him around St James's Park, Neville spoke 'of the criticisms ... that were being so widely propagated'. Baldwin admitted that he 'was not a good leader of opposition', that 'temperamentally he was not made that way'. Neville could sympathise with that response but insisted that 'he must do violence to his instincts, give a lead and attack the enemy'. Baldwin agreed 'rather ruefully'. Neville still regarded him as 'my friend as well as my leader' and did not want to undermine him. But everyone told Neville of Baldwin's 'failings and many suggest that I should do better in his place'. Neville did not covet the job of party leader, 'a thankless one at any time & never more so than now when the party is all to pieces'. Only one thought gave him reason to reconsider: if Baldwin threw up the leadership, 'the succession would come either to Winston or myself & I don't know which I should dislike most!'[8]

---

6  Neville to Hilda, 23 June, to Ida, 29 June 1929, in Self, ed., *The Neville Chamberlain Diary Letters*, III, 146–8

7  Ida to Neville, 31 Oct.1929, The Bury House, NC18/2/656

8  Neville to Annie, 22 Oct., NC1/26/416, & to Hilda, 13 Oct.1, Swinton, & 26 Oct.1929, 37 Eaton Square, in Self, ed., *The Neville Chamberlain Diary Letters*, III, 157 & 160

Baldwin stumbled badly that autumn. Without consulting colleagues, he approved of a declaration by Lord Irwin, the new Viceroy of India, that India could look forward to Dominion status. Edward Wood, as Irwin was known before his ennoblement, was a good friend of Neville as well as Baldwin; and Neville could understand why Baldwin approved of Irwin's declaration. Neville nonetheless understood that Baldwin had 'put his foot in it'. Austen reacted more strongly. He knew from his experience as Secretary of State for India that Dominion status was understood in one sense by the British Government but 'in a different sense by what is called "moderate" Indian opinion'; and that that difference was 'certain to lead to charges of breach of faith in the future'.[9] Neither brother foresaw that the Irwin declaration would find its fiercest critic in Churchill.

&#10086;

Neville escaped from these Conservative quarrels at the turn of the year by visiting East Africa. Discontent with Baldwin deepened while he was away. Austen was impatient for Neville to return: 'I see no one but him in our ranks capable of developing a constructive policy & winning confidence.' Abandoning any thought of the position for himself, Austen looked to his younger brother to give the party the leadership it needed. 'I hope it may come to him before it is too late.'[10] Hilda welcomed Neville back in March to 'the sea of troubles'. The only good thing she saw in the situation was that the sea engulfed all parties. The majority on which Labour could rely in its parliamentary alliance with the Liberals fell to single figures. But the Conservatives could not exploit the opportunity so long as they remained 'in a welter of conflicting opinions'.[11] Neville returned from East Africa full of ideas. He hoped to give the party direction through two agencies: one 'a sort of inner Shadow Cabinet called the Committee of Business' which Baldwin had been forced to set up, the second the Research Committee at party headquarters, which Neville undertook to chair. But these plans developed into a more direct challenge to Baldwin than Neville desired; and it delayed his ascent in the party, though without doing Churchill any good.

Despite his admiration for Churchill, Austen was eager to promote his

---

9 Neville to Annie, 22 Oct.1929, 37 Eaton Square, NC1/26/416, & Austen to Hilda, 6 Nov.1929, 2 Morpeth Mansions, in Self, ed., *The Austen Chamberlain Diary Letters*, 341
10 Austen to Hilda, 19 Jan.1930, 2 Morpeth Mansions, in Self, ed., *The Austen Chamberlain Diary Letters*, 343–4
11 Hilda to Neville, 2 Mar.1930, 105 Cadogan Gardens, NC18/2/671

brother, sometimes tactlessly, and he embarrassed Neville more than he helped him. He gave Neville 'useful' assistance on the Committee of Business in handling Churchill. When Neville found Winston 'too intolerable', Austen intervened 'with those calm and measured utterances which bring the discussion back to earth and common sense'.[12] But Neville's plans to make Baldwin more decisive reminded the other Chamberlains of their father's frustration under Balfour and of Austen's frustrations under Bonar Law. Hilda warned Neville that it was 'a thankless task', but added bleakly, 'I suppose you too, must suffer.'[13] Neville was, however, encouraged by the growth at home and in the self-governing dominions of interest in imperial trade. Protectionism in the United States turned Canadian eyes toward the British market. In Britain the press lords, Beaverbrook and Rothermere, mounted a campaign for what they called 'Empire Free Trade'. Neville made contact with Beaverbrook, 'Max' as he was familiarly known, and found him 'extraordinarily forthcoming and confidential'. Even Austen sensed that 'we are not far from a landslide' of opinion in favour of protective tariffs: 'the whole side of the mountain is beginning to move & when a crack once appears, who shall say where it will stop.'[14]

Baldwin was nevertheless acutely aware of his party's continuing divisions over tariff reform, and he used them to fortify his position. He did not like being hustled, nor did he have any wish to surrender the leadership. As Hilda caustically observed, 'Men who have occupied positions such as his, are often very modest about taking them, & say they won't stay, but they always do.'[15] Baldwin was protected as leader of the party by its chairman, J.C.C. Davidson. So long as Davidson remained in place, Neville's attempt to give the party clearer direction was unlikely to succeed. Close associates of Neville pushed him to take over as chairman; and he was willing. After weeks of dithering, Baldwin was similarly pushed by advisers into offering the post to Neville; and he accepted.

But his siblings wrung their hands. Neville's acceptance of the party chairmanship reminded them painfully of how Joseph and Austen had been frustrated by the party leadership in times past. They recalled how the Central Office, as party headquarters was known, had frustrated Joseph's attempt to commit the party to tariff reform. Austen too had 'been constantly sacrificed to someone else & he does

---

12 Neville to Ida, 22 Mar.& 6 Apr.1930, Westbourne, in Self, ed., *The Neville Chamberlain Diary Letters*, III, 169–70 & 177

13 Hilda to Neville, 18 Mar.1930, The Bury House, NC18/2/674

14 Austen to Hilda, 14 June 1930, 58 Rutland Gate, in Self, ed., *The Austen Chamberlain Diary Letters*, 347

15 Hilda to Neville, 24 Oct.1929, The Bury House, NC18/2/655

not see why you should be the same'. They all hoped that Neville would eventually become Prime Minister. But they knew that this was not his driving motivation. Hilda warned him that if he convinced Baldwin to give the party a stronger lead toward tariff reform and then carried the country, he 'would also confirm Baldwin's position & as usual you would do the work whilst others got the kudos'. Even so, she believed that the chairmanship gave Neville 'the only chance to secure an Empire policy & tariff reform'.

It was at this point that Hilda began to compose her family litany: 'with Papa ... the position was just the same: – a leader who would not lead, & the [Central Office] really hostile & forever urging the P.M. not to go ahead.' 'If you are successful', she concluded uneasily, Neville would accomplish 'what no one else could have done. If you fail you will at least have done your best & gone down fighting as Papa did.'[16]

While Neville wrestled with the consequences of Baldwin's lacklustre leadership, Annie suffered from recurrent 'symptoms of mental disturbance'.[17] Baldwin's indecision was sometimes put down to depression, which Annie could understand. 'I do feel awfully sorry for Stanley, the more I think of his depressed feelings,' she told Neville with perceptive sympathy. 'His faults as a leader are probably due to his having these other qualities – of a mystic & poet – whatever one may call it, which make one so admire him in some other respects & which make some of his speeches so inspiring. And I'm sure this temperament helps him to get more tired in the stress of political life & it therefore becomes harder than ever for him ever to take a decision about <u>anything</u>. ... I mustn't feel distressed as I sometimes do that the good schemes come from you, & that someone else so often gets the credit.'[18] Her understanding of Baldwin helped Neville where he could not help himself.

His misreading of people became painfully apparent during Annie's convalescent absence in Switzerland. He was approached by Lord Beaverbrook, whose campaign for Empire Free Trade was directed against Baldwin. Neville, in his new position as party chairman, sought to quell the infighting by devising some formula for imperial preference to which Baldwin, Beaverbrook and he himself could agree. A small dinner was arranged at which Neville outlined his terms to Beaverbrook. And thereby began a devious tale which exposed Neville's naïveté. Beaverbrook 'listened attentively' to his proposal, 'put a number of questions to get it all clear',

---

16 Hilda to Neville, 27 May, 6 & 20 June, & Ida to Neville, 29 June 1930, NC18/2/683, '5 & '7–8
17 Neville to Hilda, 15 Nov.1930, Sevenoaks, in Self, ed., *The Neville Chamberlain Diary Letters*, III, 222
18 Annie to Neville, 10 Oct.1930, 37 Eaton Square, NC1/25/284

and finally 'said "If I were alone I should jump at these terms but I cannot separate myself from Rothermere. ... I shall go and see him at once & will then communicate with you again."' Neville was overjoyed.[19] Baldwin, however, gave his account of the conversation only a guarded welcome.

This 'affair with Max' was immediately complicated by the death of the Conservative M.P. for Bromley. The press barons looked for a supporter of Empire Free Trade to stand in the by-election. Beaverbrook said nothing of this to Neville: 'but various would be candidates kept coming to me for advice', and he grew 'more & more uneasy'.[20] Slow to make out the aim of the press barons, Neville eventually gathered that they were thinking of a coup to replace Baldwin with Neville himself. He was disgusted but also tantalised. 'The plot thickens, doesn't it,' he reported to Annie: 'I must see Max & tell him to drop that idea. But I fear he may not be willing to pick up any other.'[21] Beaverbrook flattered him into 'feeling more confident than at any time that things were coming right', and also appeared to accept Neville's policy formula.

But that illusion was shattered by a letter from Beaverbrook to say that he and Rothermere had decided to nominate Rothermere's son Esmond for election at Bromley. Beaverbrook 'recognised that I should regard this as a renewal of hostilities & regretted that we had to separate'. At last Neville recognised that Beaverbrook was 'a crook after all and that he has been tricking me ... war has begun'. Neville took Beaverbrook's betrayal hard. 'I had trusted him and been fooled. The fact is that by temperament I am trustful and in consequence I have been taken in more than once. But I cannot recollect having been taken in twice by the same man and I shan't trust Max again.'[22] Fatefully, Neville failed to take his own lesson to heart. He came to trust Beaverbrook again, and later proved unwilling to withdraw his confidence from a more formidable adversary, whose cooperation he sought, but who betrayed him far more seriously than Beaverbrook.

Neville's immediate response to Beaverbrook's betrayal was nevertheless swift and strong. Throwing all his weight as party chairman into the contest, Neville made sure that the candidate he favoured for Bromley 'would stand firm'. Neville also assured the constituency party that if Rothermere's son became a candidate, he would receive no support from party headquarters and, if elected, would be denied the party whip. At that, the press barons dropped his candidacy. 'So we have won

19  Neville to Annie, 20 July 1930, 37 Eaton Square, NC1/26/430
20  Neville to Annie, 24 July 1930, 37 Eaton Square, NC1/26/431
21  Neville to Annie, 27 July 1930, Westbourne, NC1/26/432
22  Neville to Annie, 30 July & 4 Aug.1930, NC1/26/433–4

the first round,' Neville told Annie proudly, 'and I was heartily congratulated by my colleagues particularly by Winston who greatly admired what he called my firm handling of the situation.'[23]

Still the outcome at Bromley did not lessen the problems raised by Baldwin's chronic indecision. The Empire Free Trade candidate at Bromley, though defeated, did well enough to deepen discontent with Baldwin. Austen and Neville were also dismayed by Baldwin's feeble commitment to tariff reform and his desire for a referendum before a tariff on wheat and meat could be imposed. Neville hammered out a policy statement that made a tariff on foodstuffs and hence a referendum unnecessary; and Baldwin consented. Austen still feared that Neville's future chances were 'being seriously jeopardised by his new office [as party chairman] & his old leader'.[24] And by now Neville was inclined to agree that Baldwin was too badly damaged by his performance in opposition to survive as leader for long. He only hoped that the 'air of decision' which Baldwin acquired by endorsing Neville's formula might save his 'bacon long enough to enable him' to resign later with dignity. 'I have given him another chance,'[25] said Neville beneficently, failing to foresee how Baldwin would exploit that chance.

While Neville remained preoccupied with the situation at home, Austen looked anxiously abroad. A former British ambassador to Germany alerted him to the mounting appeal in Germany of Hitler, 'not dangerous, he thought, if there were a *man* to fight him, but since Stresemann's death Germany had no man. What a troubled world it is! ... Briand's position is much shaken in France by Hitler's success.' Austen dreamt of returning to the Foreign Office. It would be a less promising assignment than last time: 'Mussolini's attitude has changed & not for the better; Germany lacks the strong guiding hand of Stresemann & France, frightened by Hitler's success & Mussolini's flirtations with Hungary & Bulgaria has reacted violently against the policy of appeasement.' He spoke of appeasement admiringly, in the then widely accepted sense of removing perceived injustices left by the treaties that ended the war. 'There is good work to be done at the F.O. but there is no easy success & perhaps no success at all to be reaped.' Though Austen believed himself 'still fitted to do good work in the sphere of foreign policy', better than anyone else 'on our side', he began 'to see that youth is getting not unnaturally impatient & to

---

23  Neville to Annie, 4 Aug.1930, NC1/26/434
24  Austen to Ida, 4 Oct.1930, 58 Rutland Gate, in Self, ed., *The Austen Chamberlain Diary Letters*, 354
25  Neville to Ida, 11 & 18 Oct.1930, Westbourne, in Self, ed., *The Neville Chamberlain Diary Letters*, III, 212–4

suspect that it would prefer my room to my company.'[26] Yet he failed to see that Baldwin shared that impatience.

Forces beyond these personal considerations were shaking the ground on which all statesmen stood. Austen felt the tremors in Europe. But it was the fallout at home from the Wall Street Crash and what Americans called the Great Depression that captured the attention of most politicians in Britain. They felt the ground cracking under their feet and struggled to strengthen their standing. But none of them fully comprehended the profundity of the twofold earthquake that threatened them.

Austen was no better able than most to see beyond the squabbling in his party, and he brought it to a head with a precipitate challenge to Baldwin. With quiet support from Neville at party headquarters, Austen confronted Baldwin at a meeting of the Business Committee. The chief staff officer there, Sir Robert Topping, had provided Neville with 'a memorandum on the feeling in the Party about the Leadership', conveying the 'general feeling that the Party could not win the election with S.B. as leader'. Before forwarding the memorandum to Baldwin, Neville toned down 'a couple of phrases which I thought were too wounding for S.B. to read', and consulted a range of leading figures in the party including at least one Baldwin sympathiser, Lord Bridgeman. 'Everyone without exception agreed that I was in duty bound to show the document to S.B. Every one confirmed the view expressed by Topping of the rapid decline in S.B.'s position. Every one I think, except Willie Bridgeman was of the opinion that S.B. would have to resign.' The men Neville consulted were also united in their determination to keep Churchill out of the leadership.

Initially taken aback by this consensus, Baldwin decided to resign. But Bridgeman had no difficulty persuading him to stand and fight. The press barons gave him a good opportunity to do so. They carried their campaign for his removal into another by-election, this one in the fashionable London constituency of St. George's. Their intervention prompted Baldwin to deliver the most memorable speech of his career. What the press lords were aiming at, he declared, was 'power, and power without responsibility – the prerogative of the harlot throughout the ages'. Baldwin then turned on those who had pressed for his retirement, particularly on Austen. Neville escaped Baldwin's wrath but not his resentment. Realising that he could no longer serve his intended purpose as party chairman, Neville offered to resign. Baldwin barely acknowledged the resignation. He did not thank Neville for

---

26 Austen to Ida, 20 Sept. & 4 Nov., & to Hilda, 9 Nov.1930, 58 Rutland Gate, in Self, ed., *The Austen Chamberlain Diary Letters*, 354 & 358–9

his service. And he proceeded to change the direction at Central Office without reference to the departing chairman. Neville exploded, determined to have 'some frank not to say brutal talk' with him. Baldwin 'made no attempt to hit back', and agreed to a discussion with the malcontents. Neville thought it 'a painful ordeal' for Baldwin: 'Austen in particular showed him little mercy'.[27] Both Chamberlains failed to grasp how far they had offended the party leader and how tenacious his grip on power remained. The only thing Neville gained from his tussle with Baldwin was 'a new attitude on Austen's part. He has never before quite abandoned the elder-brother manner. But now he treats me as an equal and as a result I feel much more sympathetic than at any time since we have been in the House together.'[28]

⁊❧

The Great Depression struck Britain with full force in the summer of 1931. Neville responded with consummate dexterity, all the more effective because it was not evidently self-promoting, regaining Baldwin's confidence. Austen, on the other hand, was sidelined by the crisis. Though alarmed at 'accounts of distress, food queus [sic], unemployment & even starvation',[29] he did not recognise their political impact until the end of July. Thoughts of inter-party alliance or a national government gripped the inner circles of the Conservative party, to which Neville was central but to which Austen was not privy. Baldwin kept his distance, entrusting Neville to stay in touch. Before Parliament broke up for the summer, Neville briefed his closest associates, including Austen at last.

None of them, not even Austen, wanted a coalition. But they agreed, as Neville reported to his sisters, 'that it might be unavoidable though only on condition that tariffs were accepted'. Fortified by this agreement, Neville 'intended to make a strong attack on the Government, but ... found the City ... nervous that that sort of line ... might have precipitated a flight from the £'. So he arranged instead, with the Labour Chancellor of the Exchequer, Philip Snowden, to issue an appeal for economy. Snowden was happy to cooperate, for he recognised 'that sooner or later the country had got to face up to the realities'. The way in which Neville and Snowden reinforced each other satisfied the Bank of England; 'the City plucked up

---

27  Neville to Ida, 18 Mar., & to Hilda, 28 Mar.1931, in Self, ed., *The Neville Chamberlain Diary Letters*, III, 246 & 249–50

28  Neville to Hilda, 25 May 1931, Salisbury, in Self, ed., *The Neville Chamberlain Diary Letters*, III, 260

29  Austen to Ivy, 3 Feb.1931, 58 Rutland Gate, AC6/1/786

spirit again'; and the press began to sing Neville's praises.[30] His pleasure was complete when he heard that Lloyd George had to undergo an operation that would keep him out of commission for months. Neville left for his holiday in the Highlands in good heart.

But two weeks later the Deputy Governor of the Bank called him back, saying that 'the position was desperate'. Baldwin returned from France; and the two Conservatives met straightaway with Snowden and the Labour Prime Minister, Ramsay MacDonald. In 'an astonishing change', the Labour ministers reported themselves ready to cut national expenditure by £100 million a year, and offered to make detailed proposals to this end in a few days. Though they 'went further than many expected,' Neville still 'felt bound to say that in my opinion they were inadequate'. He found to his surprise that both MacDonald and Snowden agreed with him and 'had put the same arguments before their colleagues!' 'To secure such a measure of relief and to do it through a Socialist Govt' seemed to Neville 'so important in the national interest that we *must* give it our support provided the proposals for "equal sacrifice" do not imperil British credit or too brazenly affront ordinary rules of justice & fair play.'[31]

Baldwin fully agreed with his deputy – and promptly returned to France. He was 'chiefly anxious to be gone before he was "drawn into something"' and 'prayed that he might not have to join a National Government'. Neville shared his uneasiness and interpreted the current manoeuvrings 'as part of Ramsay's game to put pressure on his Cabinet. My belief,' he reported, 'is that they will accept & throw the blame on the Bankers & the Tories.' In that case the crisis would be over, and Neville could return to Scotland. Meanwhile he was content to remain in London and 'carry the responsibility'. He was delighted 'to be <u>doing</u> something'. From talks with Baldwin and other Conservative colleagues, he knew 'pretty well what are the limits within which I can promise support'. At last the party was at one: 'My colleagues have been splendid & united all through.'[32] Neville still hoped to 'concentrate on tariffs & Imp[erial] Preference as the restorers of prosperity'. But it was becoming clear 'that retrenchment was the vital thing and that we must, to begin with, concentrate entirely on that'.

---

30  Neville to Hilda, 2 Aug.1931, Perthshire, in Self, ed., *The Neville Chamberlain Diary Letters*, III, 272

31  Neville to Hilda, 16 Aug.1931, Perthshire, in Self, ed., *The Neville Chamberlain Diary Letters*, III, 274–5; Neville to Annie, 21 Aug.1931, Conservative Research Department, NC1/26/446

32  Neville to Annie, 23 Aug.1931, 37 Eaton Square, NC1/26/447

He was in a strong position as he waited for MacDonald and Snowden to present their proposals. The disarray in the Labour Cabinet and party stood in contrast to the cohesion the Conservatives had suddenly acquired. MacDonald and Snowden found more sympathy from Neville than from their Cabinet colleagues and nominal supporters. Still Neville kept up the pressure, dismissing the first set of proposals as inadequate. When MacDonald and Snowden could not secure assent from the Cabinet for more, 'it appeared that nothing could stay the financial catastrophe'. At that, the Conservative negotiators '& the Liberals consulted together & went again ... to see the P.M.' and 'told him that if that were the last word we would combine to kick him out as soon as Parlt met. If however he could reconstruct his Govt so as to be able to put forward adequate proposals we would do all we could to support him. Nothing was said about a Nat. Govt. but it was obviously not excluded. He said he intended to make his own proposals to the Cabinet & those that didn't like them would have to take their own course.' Neville's blow-by-blow account to his sisters went on: 'We are now waiting for this final decision.'

He broke into his report with word that MacDonald could carry neither 'his colleagues nor his party. So unless they change their minds in the next few hours this Govt will come to an end and S.B. will be sent for tomorrow. I have just wired Austen to come back.' Neville regarded his own role to this point with satisfaction: 'I have had a strenuous time these last few days but have nothing to regret & no reason to be dissatisfied with the part I have played. It looks ... as if a much more strenuous time was ahead, but I shan't mind that if we are *doing* something.' His only concern was lest, in putting a new government together, Baldwin should work primarily with the Liberals, of whom Neville remained suspicious. He advised Baldwin 'to make every effort first to get Macdonald & one or two other Labour men in with him. In that case I have little doubts the Libs would play & we could carry the Economy Bill and – then dissolve.'[33] Things turned out even better than Neville hoped. Next day he was able to report that MacDonald had 'decided to form a Nat. Govt. himself. This is the best thing that could have happened ... It is understood that it will be temporary cooperation to carry through the necessary measures and will be followed by a dissolution. ... I shall probably go back to Health.'[34]

Despite the flurry around Neville, the heart of the work of Cabinet construction fell to Baldwin. It was the one kind of work he enjoyed. The task this time was particularly hard for the Conservatives. They would provide the National

33 Neville to Ida, 23 Aug.1931, 37 Eaton Square, in Self, ed., *The Neville Chamberlain Diary Letters*, III, 276

34 Neville to Annie, 24 Aug.1931, 37 Eaton Square, NCI/26/448

Government with the bulk of its support in the Commons, since the parliamentary Labour party deserted MacDonald en masse. Yet places in the Cabinet had to be divided three ways to accommodate the remaining Labour ministers and the Liberals. Neville returned happily to the Ministry of Health 'as if I had never been away'.[35] He did not look for more, content with the improvement in his position over the past few weeks. Ida could see that 'no one now would dispute his place as second in command after Baldwin'.[36]

But two Conservative aspirants were deeply unhappy. One was Leo Amery. Baldwin refused to send him back to the Colonial Office where he had served in the previous Conservative ministry. Amery poured out his grievance to Neville, arguing that the Conservatives should have 'refused all cooperation unless a tariff was agreed to in which case ... we need not have bothered about economy'. Neville knew that other ardent tariff reformers were unlikely to go that far.

The other unhappy Conservative of eminence was far more serious: for it was Austen. He fell victim to the tripartite construction of the Cabinet. An emergency Cabinet of ten was decided upon, to include four each for the large parties in the Commons, Labour and Conservative, and two Liberals. Austen was not entirely surprised to find that he was not among the Conservative quartet: 'You can't have two Chamberlains out of four.'[37] It bothered him more to find the post of Foreign Secretary assigned to a Liberal, Lord Reading. Baldwin wanted to give Austen the leadership of the Lords, but Austen did not want to leave the Commons. He found some consolation when assigned the First Lordship of the Admiralty, though without a seat in the Cabinet. He had loved the Admiralty since his first posting there as a junior minister. He sent a telegram to Ivy, who had remained on holiday in Scotland, to say 'that "I am returning to my first love"', which he hoped she would 'remember was the Admiralty'. He was also relieved by Baldwin's assurance that he would not have to give up the directorships on which he was financially dependent until a general election was held and a more durable government could be appointed. Neville assured Austen 'that I could only help by joining. My name alone, especially abroad, was worth much. ... Also N. said he wanted me to be in – the Govt. might last longer than expected – once out was out completely.'[38]

'Beloved,' Ivy wrote back in ecstatic misunderstanding of Austen's telegram,

35  Neville to Annie, 26 Aug.1931, 37 Eaton Square, NC1/26/450
36  Ida to Mary, 26 Aug.1931, Kinloch Bannock, BC4/2/218
37  Austen to Ivy, 24 Aug.1931, Oxford & Cambridge Club, AC6/1/801
38  Austen to Ivy, 25 Aug.1931, Oxford & Cambridge Club, AC6/1/802

'have just received your wire & cannot tell you <u>how</u> delighted & relieved I am.'
The newspapers had encouraged her to hope that he would return to the Foreign
Office. 'I spent a sleepless night wondering whether [Baldwin] <u>could</u> ignore your
claims in such a crisis as this, & my heart sank! This morning Diane rushed into my
room with papers saying, "Papa is Foreign Secretary" But I had to calm her & say
that it was only what the papers thought & <u>not</u> official! However just as they were
leaving ... your telegram came & she has gone off radiant! She would not believe
that anyone but you <u>could</u> be made F.S. Oh! darling how much I have longed for
it for you these past two years.'[39]

Her delight cut Austen 'to the heart to think how I raised your hopes only to
dash them. ... I am in fact going through some bitter moments,' he confessed, '& it
is no use pretending to you that I am not.' He tried to persuade Ivy that he had done
right in accepting the Admiralty; but his attempt was half-hearted[40] and she was
not convinced by it. She found his exclusion from the Cabinet galling, particularly
in view of Neville's inclusion: 'you cannot expect me to think that Neville is better
in Cabinet than <u>you</u> ... N. is clever & able to a point but I do not believe that his
judgement is anything like as sound & he will never be a <u>big man</u> – in the broad
sense, his outlook is too parochial.'[41] Austen insisted that Neville was 'essential to
the Cabinet at this moment. But I could have been useful in Cabinet & if S.B. had
been different I should have been there as Foreign Secy. But the last people S.B.
considers are his supporters.'[42]

At dinner with Neville, Austen 'burst out that he was humiliated and treated as
a back number. His lips trembled & tears came into his eyes ... Of course,' Neville
told Annie, 'he does absurdly exaggerate the position but there is enough truth
in his idea to make it very galling and I hate his being so unhappy about it.'[43] The
brothers gave themselves a short fishing holiday together during which Austen
'didn't mention his troubles again'. This encouraged Neville to hope that Austen's
sense of injury might lessen 'as he gets interested in his department & sees things
in better perspective.'[44]

Austen was indeed impressed by the spirited reception which the Conservative
parliamentary party gave to the National Government. 'There was no discordant note'

39  Ivy to Austen, 24 Aug.1931, Aberdeenshire, AC6/2/545
40  Austen to Ivy, 26 Aug.1931, Oxford & Cambridge Club, AC6/1/803
41  Ivy to Austen, 26 Aug.1931, Warthill House, AC6/2/546
42  Austen to Ivy, 27 Aug.1931, Admiralty, AC6/1/805
43  Neville to Annie, 29 Aug.1931, Moor Lane House, NC1/26/452
44  Neville to Annie, 30 Aug.1931, 37 Eaton Square, NC1/26/453

at the party meeting, he told Ivy; '... at the end there was round after round of cheering & then someone in the hall started "God save the King" & it was sung impressively.' He also insisted to Ivy that 'Neville, my Beloved, is a much bigger man than you think'.[45] But Austen's wound healed slowly, if at all. He continued 'going through a mental hell ... I was asked to accept a sacrifice & to help by example. How was I to refuse. But the net result is that I am a cypher & worse than that; except to a few people I appear not as someone who gives all he can to help in a crisis but as an old party hack who might be dangerous outside & so must have his mouth stopped with office. ... It is all very bitter to me ... I have to think of this as the last act of my political life.'[46]

The creation of the National Government did not rescue the country from its financial crisis. The situation only worsened, and Britain was driven off the gold standard. Here again, Austen was hit hard. The cuts in pay which the government demanded to reduce its yawning deficit triggered a mutiny in the Atlantic fleet at Invergordon. The mutiny undermined confidence in the government's ability to bring the financial crisis under control. But it did not undermine Austen's self-confidence, even though he was caught unawares by the discontent brewing below deck. When an attempt to deal with the worst cases of hardship among the sailors failed to stop the rumbling, the Cabinet felt obliged to reduce the cuts in salary for all the armed forces plus the teachers and police. 'We have all been humiliated,' Neville moaned, 'and our whole scheme of economy jeopardised.'[47] Austen, however, minimised the setback. He told his sisters on the eve of the abandonment of the gold standard that the 'trouble at Invergordon was lamentable' but '... there was not a single act of disrespect to officers ... the general spirit was not revolutionary or Bolshevist'.[48] He called it 'a "down-tools" movement by men who were really frightened for their wives & homes & who were swept off their feet by the suddenness & severity of the cut. ... On the whole good men gone wrong.'[49] And he was content with his handling of the affair. 'If I have had a very painful experience at the Admiralty,' he said afterwards, 'I can at least feel that my experience & authority have been useful & have helped to give confidence in the Admiralty itself & the House.'[50]

45  Austen to Ivy, 28 Aug.1931, Oxford & Cambridge Club, AC6/1/806

46  Austen to Ida, 31 Aug.1931, United University Club, in Self, ed., *The Austen Chamberlain Diary Letters*, 383–4

47  Neville to Hilda, 26 Sept.1931, Westbourne, in Self, ed., *The Neville Chamberlain Diary Letters*, III, 280

48  Austen to Hilda, 20 Sept.1931, 58 Rutland Gate, in Self, ed., *The Austen Chamberlain Diary Letters*, 385

49  Austen to Mary, 27 Sept.1931, Dorking, AC4/1/1312

50  Austen to Ivy, 1 Oct.1931, House of Commons, AC6/1/814

The Invergordon mutiny nevertheless deepened Austen's discontent with his position. No one in the government but Neville had consulted him during the past month about the other issues with which it was confronted. A general election had to be called without delay; and only through Neville was Austen privy to the arguments in Cabinet about the platform that the government would present to the electorate. Those arguments, particularly over trade policy, accentuated the determination of MacDonald to keep the Liberal contingent in his Cabinet, and thus weakened the Conservative friends of tariff reform. Austen's prospects in a post-election reconstruction of the government worsened accordingly. Ivy's health also gave way again, and she headed for the Riviera. 'You know how much I hate to leave you & especially at such a time', she wrote back, 'but I know that I will return stronger & able to face things better, after the rest & quiet here.' She was slow to recover. But convalescence had its compensations. 'We went into Monte Carlo by train yesterday afternoon,' she reported, '& had a gamble after tea, & I won another 1000 francs!'[51]

While the economic and political upheaval did nothing to improve Austen's position, it nudged Neville upwards. MacDonald asked him to represent the Conservatives in inter-party talks with Snowden for Labour and Reading for the Liberals on 'the adverse trade balance & what should be done about it'. Neville felt 'pretty sure' that MacDonald was ready to accept tariff reform. But Snowden and Reading as free traders were sure to reject it. Snowden did not 'matter so much' since he seemed ready to retire.[52] What worried Neville was the number of Liberals who might join the campaign for free trade which Lloyd George wanted to launch from his sickbed. A large Liberal defection would place the national character of the government in jeopardy by accentuating MacDonald's dependence on Tory support.

Neville now believed that 'the only way to secure the sort of majority which would give the world confidence is to go as a National Government, perhaps even as a National Party carrying Macdonald and his colleagues with us together with as many Liberals as we could get'.[53] Departure from the gold standard increased Neville's desire for a speedy election to confirm the government in power before prices began to rise. He won support from the principal Conservative newspapers and the Business Committee of the party for 'a prompt election and a national appeal … with Macdonald as P.M. & in the event of victory the formation of a National

51 Ivy to Austen, 28 Sept. & 11 Oct.1931, Cap Martin, Menton, AC6/2/553 & 567

52 Neville to Hilda, 12 Sept.1931, 37 Eaton Square, in Self, ed., *The Neville Chamberlain Diary Letters*, III, 278

53 Neville to Ida, 19 Sept.1931, Westbourne, in Self, ed., *The Neville Chamberlain Diary Letters*, III, 278–81

Government *under him.*' Ida laughed when she remembered all the intrigues of the past year 'as to who should be the next Conservative Prime Minister' only 'to find out that it is to be Mr. Macdonald!'[54] Neville recognised that Baldwin's leadership of the Conservative party was indispensable to the National Government because of his willingness to work under MacDonald. At the same time, Baldwin's willingness to leave the nitty-gritty of inter-party negotiation to Neville raised his spirits. He was gaining recognition as the real if not formal leader of the Conservative party: 'people come to see me when they want things done.'

No matter how strong his wish to maintain the three-party ministry, Neville wanted to give it a coherent policy. Coherence in policy, however, proved much harder to achieve than the creation of the National Government; and it took far longer. To Neville, the only policy capable of coming to terms with the economic emergency was tariff reform. But that had been the most divisive issue in British politics since his father first proposed it at the beginning of the century. Neville had not yet discovered how to approach it with any subtlety. He demanded that the Liberals either 'swallow the whole programme or go out'.[55] Gradually, however, he grew flexible, ready for instance to drop mention of a tariff so long as he secured recognition of the need to check imports.

Austen pushed him on impatiently, infuriated by Baldwin and MacDonald. 'It really is hard lines,' he wrote to Hilda, 'that after being led for these two years by a man so unhelpful and inert as S.B., Neville should now be driven in the bitterness of his heart to exclaim to me that Ramsay is "infinitely worse".'[56] Whenever Neville seemed about to secure the resignation of the free-trading Liberal ministers, MacDonald backed away, fearful of ending up in the hands of the Tories. Eventually the Cabinet agreed to call an immediate general election as a supposedly united government but with each of its component parties issuing its own manifesto. MacDonald called for 'a free hand', Baldwin for tariff reform in a manifesto which Neville wrote, and the Liberals for free trade. Neville reacted to this programmatic disarray with dismay: 'I never fought an election under such a difficulty.'[57]

There was no knowing the likely electoral response. Ida reported from Odiham

---

54  Ida to Mary, 3 Oct.1931, The Bury House, BC4/2/220
55  Neville to Ida, 4 Oct.1931, 37 Eaton Square, in Self, ed., *The Neville Chamberlain Diary Letters*, III, 282–3
56  Austen to Hilda, 3 Oct.1931, 58 Rutland Gate, in Self, ed., *The Austen Chamberlain Diary Letters*, 387
57  Neville to Hilda, 10 Oct.1931, Westbourne, in Self, ed., *The Neville Chamberlain Diary Letters*, III, 284

that 'Everyone I meet just round here takes a most gloomy view ... they are terrified of the unemployed, & whilst they know that ... most, if not all the seats, in Hampshire are perfectly safe they regard the great towns as all unknown quantities where millions of unemployed are likely all to cast their votes for those who promise them most.' She tried 'to explain to them that in the North & Midlands there are still vast numbers of genuine unemployed who care far more for the chance of getting work than for a cut of 2/- when they are out of work.'[58] But she was not sure she was right.

Once the campaigning began, the auguries turned encouraging. 'It will be a disagreeable election,' Austen predicted, 'but our people in Birmingham are hopeful and think they may win back three if not four seats.'[59] After spending two hours on 'one of our black spots last time', he found that many people 'who voted Socialist are now saying that they will never be caught by them again'.[60] Encouraged, he plunged into a wash house where he 'was photographed with my coat off, shirt sleeves rolled up, taking a hand at the wash-tub! The women were delighted.'[61] Neville grew optimistic: 'everyone of my meetings has been packed out', he reported. 'I have never before had such crowds to address nor so little interruption. People seem to want to hear every word that may enlighten them and even the Socialists remain quiet and subdued.'[62]

The prospect of electoral victory did not improve Austen's assessment of his personal prospects. 'For thirty years I have been at the very heart & centre of public life,' he scarcely needed to remind Ivy; 'for the last few weeks I have been outside the circle – a glorified Under-Secretary. I can't adjust myself with any comfort to this position ... I shall have done my duty during these fateful days & can walk out with dignity & contentment.' She concurred: 'I would not have you take a subordinate position in any Government & am sure that you would be happier if you were free & able to express your views, than as you are now, with no knowledge or say in what is going on. Don't worry about me darling you know that I can be just as happy in a small flat, as long as I have you & the children.' Even so, 'if there were the least chance of your being offered the F.O. of <u>course</u> you must take it'.[63] But Austen could see that even if Reading did not return to the Foreign Office,

---

58  Ida to Neville, 16 Oct.1931, The Bury House, NC18/2/754
59  Austen to Ida, 7 Oct.1931, 58 Rutland Gate, in Self, ed., *The Austen Chamberlain Diary Letters*, 388
60  Austen to Ivy, 15 Oct.1931, Birmingham, AC6/1/836
61  Austen to Ivy, 20 Oct.1931, Birmingham, AC6/1/840
62  Neville to Ida, 18 Oct., & to Hilda, 24 Oct.1931, Westbourne, in Self, ed., *The Neville Chamberlain Diary Letters*, III, 285–6
63  Ivy to Austen, 4 & 8 Oct.1931, Menton, AC6/2/560 & 565

neither MacDonald nor Baldwin wanted him there again: 'the fact that neither of them thought it worth an effort to bring me into their counsels in these critical days is a sign I cannot disregard. I do not wish to outstay my welcome or to sit on as a survival with lessening influence. I have, therefore, practically made up my mind that, unless something quite unforeseen happens, I shall not again take office after this election. ... Neville ... genuinely regrets but does not, I think in his heart disapprove my decision.'[64]

The results of the election enabled Austen to depart in good heart. 'Oh, my Beloved, now I can sing my Nunc Dimittis politically. I could not have borne to have left W. B'ham with a Unionist majority of only 43' – like last time – 'but 11,900 is a different story.'[65] In Birmingham the Unionists regained all the seats they lost to Labour in 1929. Repeating the declaration his father made in 1906, Austen declared, '"We are twelve." I had not hoped to see that again.'[66] Nationally the general election reduced Labour to a mere 57 seats in the Commons, and removed almost all its leaders. Austen also found himself in better circumstances financially, for Mary contributed not only to his election costs, as did his sisters, but gave him enough to cover all his political expenses for more than a year. The act of retirement still left a bitter taste in his mouth. Austen let Baldwin know of his willingness to go. 'Why do you always make [Baldwin's] task easier?' Ivy asked irritably: 'he has never considered you & always takes advantage of you!!'[67] And indeed when Baldwin acted on the intimation, Austen treated it as another betrayal.

❦

The Chamberlain brothers had worked together well through the crisis. But the ensuing reconstruction of the government made it hard for them to stay in step with each other. Neville welcomed his continued participation in the National Government with surprising cordiality for one who hated coalitions. He did not, however, think of the National Government as a coalition, but rather as truly national. Nor did he regard its leaders as unprincipled, as he had Lloyd George.

---

64 Austen to Ida, 11 Oct.1931, Westbourne, in Self, ed., *The Austen Chamberlain Diary Letters*, 390
65 Austen to Ivy, 28 Oct.1931, Birmingham, AC6/1/847
66 Austen to Neville, 1 Nov.1931, 58 Rutland Gate, in Self, ed., *The Austen Chamberlain Diary Letters*, 391–2
67 Ivy to Austen, 30 Oct.1931, Menton, AC6/2/588

He thought MacDonald and Baldwin were simply weak. He also welcomed the stories he heard from every canvasser 'of Socialists declaring themselves "fed up" with their own people and determined to vote "National".' Like his father who never called himself a Conservative, Neville hoped 'that we may presently develop into a National Party and get rid of that odious title of Conservative which has kept so many from joining us in the past'.[68]

Neville regarded the less ideological label of National as entirely compatible with his determination to commit the government to tariff reform. The best position from which to advance that policy would be as Chancellor of the Exchequer. Since Snowden did not stand for re-election to the Commons, Neville was expected to take that place. But he cautioned his sisters not to count on it. He thought that MacDonald, 'terrified of being made the servant of the Conservative Party',[69] would prefer a Liberal who was flexible on trade policy. The increased preponderance of Conservatives among the supporters of the government in the new House of Commons only exacerbated Neville's difficulties and delayed his appointment as Chancellor. Austen hoped that his own withdrawal from office would 'make Neville's accession to the Chancellorship easier to secure'.[70] But Hilda saw how the family name worked against Neville. She observed 'how truly hampering to your career it has been to be the son of your father! ... the fact that you are his son & Austen's brother is brought up at every stage ... as a reason against your having what is obviously your due.'[71] Neville disagreed: 'I have to a large extent escaped the handicap which certainly afflicted Austen in being his father's son. The fact that they were for a long time actually in the House together made comparison inevitable.' But 'to the majority [of] my contemporaries in the House Father is a name only and they judge me on my own record'.[72]

He also believed that the way in which Austen had left office demonstrated that Austen had 'his own personality apart from Father's'. Many people 'from the King downwards' paid tribute to Austen for the manner of his going. But no tribute moved Austen as much as the one from Neville, who said that 'his latest action [had] greatly strengthened the "legend" that was already growing up of the "great

68 Neville to Hilda, 24 Oct.1931, Westbourne, in Self, ed., *The Neville Chamberlain Diary Letters*, III, 286

69 Neville to Ida, 18 Oct.1931, Westbourne, in Self, ed., *The Neville Chamberlain Diary Letters*, III, 285

70 Austen to Ida, 1 Nov.1931, in Self, ed., *The Austen Chamberlain Diary Letters*, 392

71 Hilda to Neville, 6 Nov.1931, The Bury House, NC18/2/758

72 Neville to Hilda, 7 Nov.1931, Moor Lane House, in Self, ed., *The Neville Chamberlain Diary Letters*, III, 287–8

gentleman" and model of chivalry' – terms of praise never applied to old Joe. Austen recognised that Neville 'must have felt much to write so warmly, for you know how tongue-tied in matters of sentiment he usually is':[73] and he responded by handing on to Neville the torch of tariff reform which their father had raised. When Neville was at last made Chancellor, his appointment gave Austen 'the deepest satisfaction. I was the first Chancellor to introduce in a very humble way imperial Preference into a Budget; you will be the Chancellor to complete the building for which I laid the first brick in 1919. Father's great work will be completed in his children.' In contrast to Neville's first appointment in 1923 as Chancellor, this time Austen regarded Neville's elevation with 'some thing more than a brotherly interest; it is an immense love & a possessive pride'.[74]

That outpouring was the high water mark in the relationship between the brothers. The different levels of responsibility which they now held were bound to produce different responses. Out of office without prospect of return for the first time in thirty-five years, Austen had no intention of retiring. Politics remained his consuming interest. And he was determined 'to keep my interest in life alive. I think I may play sometimes a useful part in debate but,' he added soberly, 'I suspect that the first lesson I shall have to learn will be to keep my hands off the wheel when the navigation of the ship is the business of a junior.' That was easier said than done. Austen had long experience of the issues in international trade which were now Neville's responsibility. But Austen was now cut off from the flow of information vital in public life. And the demands of office no longer kept the brothers in touch. The pressures on Neville as workhorse of the ministry kept him away from the Commons. He was 'so busy in the afternoons that I am generally not in the House & so don't even hear [Austen's] speeches'.[75] Austen relied on the letters his sisters received from Neville 'to tell me the news'.[76] The importance of those letters indeed increased, for Neville began to recount his ministerial discussions in considerable detail. Hilda could hardly wait for each instalment of his 'marvellous weekly!'[77]

As soon as he became Chancellor, Neville was confronted with a pair of issues close to his heart. Britain was threatened with a flood of cheap imports from

73  Austen to Ida, 8 Nov.1931, 58 Rutland Gate, in Self, ed., *The Austen Chamberlain Diary Letters*, 393

74  Austen to Neville, 5 Nov.1931, 58 Rutland Gate, NC1/27/99

75  Neville to Hilda, 6 Dec.1931, 37 Eaton Square, in Self, ed., *The Neville Chamberlain Diary Letters*, III, 295

76  Austen to Hilda, 28 Nov.1931, 58 Rutland Gate, in Self, ed., *The Austen Chamberlain Diary Letters*, 395

77  Hilda to Neville, 4 Dec.1931, The Bury House, NC18/2/762

trading partners made desperate by the depression. At the same time Britain and its major self-governing colonies were preparing for a conference the next summer in Ottawa on their trading relationships. The resulting sets of issues matched the two sides of tariff reform: protection and imperial preference. Outmanoeuvring the free traders with newfound deftness, Neville directed the attention of the Cabinet to the precarious position of the pound and the adverse balance of trade. The free traders felt obliged to accept a motion from the Prime Minister to refer the situation to Neville as Chancellor and Runciman, a Liberal pragmatist, as President of the Board of Trade. Swiftly Neville secured Cabinet approval for a bill to allow the Board of Trade to impose a duty on excessive imports of up to 100 per cent. He conveyed his jubilation discreetly to his sisters: 'Comic, isn't it, to think of the Free Traders giving power to two Ministers to put a 100% duty on any mortal manufactured article they like!'[78] Then he secured similar treatment for agricultural goods. He was astonished at what the National Government could accomplish. 'We have witnessed a political revolution in 3 months and though bloodless it is none the less effective.'[79]

Having won the anti-dumping battle, he turned his attention to the instructions for Britain's representatives at the Ottawa conference. Neville insisted on 'Treaties with each Dominion, to be afterwards ratified by the Empire as a whole'.[80] When he talked to representatives of the self-governing dominions, the Canadians warned him that Britain must move swiftly: 'if a Democrat should be returned at the next Presidential Election (by no means impossible) he would at once make an offer of Reciprocity so attractive that no Canadian Government could afford to refuse it.'

That warning accentuated Neville's awareness of the international implications of his responsibilities. He looked at the international arena through economic spectacles, as was expected of a Chancellor. Unlike Austen, the power that worried Neville was France rather than Germany. The punitive policies which the French pursued toward Germany kept 'the whole of Europe in a state of nervous anxiety and [were] thereby precipitating the advent of Hitler to power'. The problem, as Neville saw it, revolved around post-war reparations. The French were 'making it impossible for Germany to pay any reparations. The only chance of her ever doing

---

78  Neville to Ida, 15 Nov.1931, St Neots, in Self, ed., *The Neville Chamberlain Diary Letters*, III, 289

79  Neville to Ida, 29 Nov.1931, Sevenoaks, in Self, ed., *The Neville Chamberlain Diary Letters*, III, 292

80  Neville to Hilda, 21 Nov.1931, Westbourne, in Self, ed., *The Neville Chamberlain Diary Letters*, III, 291

so [was] to be put in a position to trade so as eventually to provide the surplus from which alone Reparations can come.' But France did its best to prevent any revival of German trade. The Americans were not much better than the French in Neville's eyes. Like Austen in this case, he regarded the United States as enfeebled by endless preoccupation with elections, at the moment the presidential election due in 1932. Any settlement of the French demand for reparations from Germany would have to be 'accompanied by a corresponding settlement or adjustment' of the debts incurred among the wartime allies to the United States. The incumbent President 'Hoover knows it but daren't say so. Unless he says so France daren't move and so we are all locked in a suicidal embrace which will probably drown the lot of us!'[81]

Even so, Neville ended the year of his return to office 'well pleased with the way things have gone'. He found himself 'in a different position in this Cabinet from any other that I have sat in. ... I carry more weight. ... the P.M. shows much deference to what I say and as S.B. mostly remains silent our people look to me for the lead and I see that they get it.'[82] There were nevertheless clouds on Neville's horizon. He could not avoid painful reductions in his personal costs. Unable to use the customary residence for Chancellors at 11 Downing Street because that went to Baldwin as the government's second-in-command, Neville had to slash the running costs of his London home on Eaton Square: 'so Annie has given notice to all the servants & is going to try and manage with a different kind of staff.' He even toyed with the idea of giving up his home in Birmingham.

The other cloud on his horizon came in two year-end letters from Austen. Though the brothers saw little of each other these days, they cooperated amicably in their separate spheres. Relishing the praise he heard of Neville's performance as Chancellor, Austen sought other subjects of concern on which to make his mark. He worked behind scenes to head off a rebellion among Conservative MPs about the bearing of the new Statute of Westminster, which defined the status of the self-governing dominions, on the treaty arrangements with southern Ireland. After lunch together in mid-December, Austen 'sat & talked with Neville till 4 o'clock & heard all his news. On the whole I found it very reassuring.'

But he pursued the conversation in two letters that annoyed Neville and left Austen painfully aware of their altered standing. The first stemmed from a meeting of the Highbury Trustees in Birmingham which Neville alone attended. Highbury was

---

81  Neville to Hilda, 6 Dec.1931, 37 Eaton Square, in Self, ed., *The Neville Chamberlain Diary Letters*, III, 296

82  Neville to Ida, 12 Dec.1931, Westbourne, in Self, ed., *The Neville Chamberlain Diary Letters*, III, 298–9

serving as a home for old-age pensioners. After the meeting Neville spoke to the Lord
Mayor to suggest treating the great hall and rooms on the ground floor 'as a memorial
to Father'.[83] Hilda welcomed the idea, which Neville mentioned during his luncheon
with Austen. But the more Austen thought of the suggestion, the less he liked it; and
he 'found when dining with Mary [later] that she shared all my misgivings'. Austen
had allowed most of his father's books, china and furniture at Highbury to be sold.
'Of what then is the memorial to consist?' he asked, '– three rooms in a poor-law institution with a few show cases. Frankly the idea fills me with horror.'[84] Austen's other
letter raised objections to the general tariff which Neville had outlined for him.

Neville's response left Austen in no doubt of his annoyance. Austen accepted
the plan for Highbury because the Lord Mayor was already acting to ensure that
all Neville's 'suggestions are faithfully carried out'.[85] As for the tariff, Austen assured
Neville that 'all my hopes & good wishes are with you'. He went on to explain that,
'It is not very easy to adapt oneself to the role of onlooker after being for so long
in the very centre of events & divisions. I am genuinely anxious not to be a bore
or an unhelpful critic & you will, I know, have patience with me if my keen interest sometimes makes me a little tiresome. I am grateful to you for having given
me your confidence so freely.'[86] Neville responded gracefully: 'I do want your help
and advice in political matters in which I recognise that I am still but a child in
comparison with your vast experience of responsibility. ... there is no one whose
judgement I value and respect more than yours.'[87] The moment of disharmony was
swiftly concluded. But it left Austen depressed.

The sisters too had their differences. Ida took her political discussions to heart
too much for her sister's liking, and got 'terribly worked up' over her arguments on
the Hampshire County Council about the public health budget. 'I shall be glad
when it is over,' Hilda confessed. She was nonetheless delighted at Ida's election as
the first woman alderman for Hampshire. Ida was gratified by this recognition of
the position she had made for herself in the county. There was a dividend in it for
Hilda too. Ida's new responsibilities took her away from the Bury House 'for two
nights,' as Hilda reported to the other music lover in the family, '& by good luck
there has been a Symphony concert on the Wireless each night. I can't say how

---

83  Neville to Hilda, 21 Nov.1931, *The Neville Chamberlain Diary Letters*, III, 291
84  Austen to Neville, 21 Dec.1931, 58 Rutland Gate, NC1/27/101
85  Neville to Hilda, 3 Jan.1932, Westbourne, in Self, ed., *The Neville Chamberlain Diary
Letters*, III, 300
86  Austen to Neville, 27 Dec.1931, Polesden Lacey, Dorking, NC1/27/103
87  Neville to Austen, 28 Dec.1931, Westbourne, AC39/3/53

much I enjoyed them. ... It is a pity that Ida dislikes it as noise or I should certainly make more use of it as the tone is wonderfully good.'[88]

§

Regardless of the disagreements within the family, Austen fully agreed with his sisters in anticipating great things for Neville. Hilda sent him momentous New Year greetings: 'what a pride & pleasure it is to us to see you in the position to which your work & your abilities entitle you ... though you are faced with an almost superhuman task I have a great belief that your sane counsels & power of getting your own way, will slowly draw us & other nations out of our slough of despond. That ... in so doing you [may] also carry out Papa's great policy is just what was needed to make the whole thing perfect.'[89] Neville accepted her predic-tion soberly: 'this is going to be a very momentous year for me. Probably it will be ... the critical point in my political career. If I don't make a success of it I shall slowly drop back.'[90]

Few outside the family as yet saw Neville's position in quite this way. His ascent over the past six months had taken place largely behind closed doors in consulta-tion with colleagues, and was made possible by the anomalous agreement among the parties in the National Government to campaign in the general election on markedly different platforms. That approach not only won a huge endorsement from the electorate, but also enabled Neville to secure a wide measure of Cabinet agreement on the subject over which its members were most sharply divided: foreign and imperial trade. Three things accounted for this achievement: the size of his party's support in the Commons, his position as Chancellor, and his sense of purpose. Neville knew what he wanted more clearly than the Liberals, divided as they were between firm free traders and pragmatists.

Even so, it took Neville another month of negotiation in Cabinet before he could reveal the extent of his accomplishment to the public. First he had to over-come the resistance that a quartet of free traders in the Cabinet, three Liberals plus Snowden, put up to his demand for a general tariff. To divide them, he suggested a small development in the anomalous approach of the National Government to the general election: Why not allow Snowden, now in the Lords, 'to express his dissent

---

88  Hilda to Neville, 4 Dec.1931, *loc.cit.*
89  Hilda to Neville, 1 Jan.1932, NC18/2/764
90  Neville to Hilda, 3 Jan.1932, Westbourne, in Self, ed., *The Neville Chamberlain Diary Letters*, III, 300

in public & still remain in the Cabinet'? After all, the House of Lords had lost its veto in financial matters twenty years ago.

The dissident quartet frustrated this manoeuvre by resolving to stand together. The Conservative Leader of the House of Lords then took Neville's suggestion one step farther, and proposed extending permission to express dissent in public from Snowden in the Lords to the dissident Liberal Cabinet ministers in the Commons. 'I had not thought it possible for members of the House of Commons to take such a course,' Neville admitted to his sisters. But the dissident quartet accepted this proposal. All that remained was for Neville, in concert with the Liberals, to draft a communiqué for the press. The Cabinet's agreement to disagree on the most important issue it faced won acceptance as 'a sensible arrangement which will be approved by all practical men'. It gave Neville substantially what he wanted: a general tariff upon which his family's plans for tariff reform and imperial preference could be constructed. The procedural agreement freed the dissenters in the Cabinet to speak their mind in public but prevented them from doing anything more 'to obstruct or hamper the proposals approved by the majority' in the House of Commons. The agreement also protected Neville from extreme tariff reformers such as Amery who might otherwise say that he had 'sold the pass'.[91]

In crab-like fashion, these agreements moved Neville into the first tier of statesmen. As he told Austen, the agreement gave 'us all we should have done if the Govt. had been formed from our Party only'.[92] But that outcome could only be reached obliquely, through negotiations in Cabinet. That was a new route to success for Neville. He had long been recognised as an able administrator; now he had shown surprising ability in the thickets of intra-ministerial manoeuvre to give the government clarity in policy and a sense of direction which it would otherwise have lacked. Delighted by the achievement, he was content to serve under the formal leadership of MacDonald as Prime Minister and Baldwin as leader of the Conservative party, so long as he himself set the government's pace.

He interpreted his accomplishment as a vindication of his whole family: of Joseph who dreamed the imperial dream, of Austen who was denied entry to the Promised Land, and of his sisters, remembering particularly the imperial Beatrice. That was his rendition of the Chamberlain litany. The surviving family gathered to hear him present his Import Duties Bill to the House of Commons. Austen sat in his father's former seat below the gangway. Mary sat beside Hilda in the Ladies

---

91  Neville to Ida, 23 Jan.1932, Westbourne, in Self, ed., *op.cit.*, III, 303–4
92  Austen to Ida, 30 Jan.1932, 58 Rutland Gate, in Self, ed., *The Austen Chamberlain Diary Letters*, 405

Gallery. The House of Commons sensed the occasion. But neither of Joseph's sons had risen to his heights as a speaker. Afraid that his voice would break with emotion, Neville hesitated to express the family loyalty he felt strongly. But 'by going slow' he was able to conclude his presentation of the bill on a 'personal note'. In the cadences of the litany, he directed attention to his father, who 'would have found consolation for the bitterness of his disappointment if he could have foreseen that these propos-als, which are the direct and legitimate descendants of his own conception, would be laid before the House of Commons ... in the presence of one and by the lips of the other of the two immediate successors to his name and blood.'

Afterwards everyone 'from the King to my tailor' congratulated Neville. But the congratulations that moved him most came from the family. 'All the time,' wrote Joseph's widow, 'I was seeing two scenes before me, hearing two voices ... At last to have the policy for which he practically laid down his life brought forward in a House eager for its fulfilment was a hope to which I have clung through long years of expectation and disappointment.'[93] Hilda found 'moments when you were rounding off a sentence when I could have thought it was Papa'.[94] It all left Neville rather dazed: 'I suppose we shall gradually realise that the great chance has come and is not a dream but it is hard to believe it yet.'[95]

Ida and Hilda directed more attention to Austen, anxious that he receive credit for the familial accomplishment. Ida wrote 'to say how much I feel that this great result is a joint achievement of all three of you. Papa initiated it, Neville has carried it to a successful issue, but you took up the fight at the hardest moment & carried it on under the most trying & adverse conditions. You handed on the torch & your share of the work though not so spectacular was equally important.' Hilda added: 'For so many years I did hope that it would be you who would have the reward of bringing into force the policy for which you too had worked so hard, but the war cut out that, & still I felt it must have been very hard for you yesterday in one way, though I know no brother could have a more generous appreciation of another than yours of Neville.' She also noted how 'curious' it was 'that having been for so many years associated with Papa's policy yet your greatest work should after all have been in another sphere', in foreign affairs.[96]

In spite of this reassurance, Austen floundered despondently for the rest of the

93  Mary to Neville, 5 Feb.1932, NC1/20/2/27
94  Hilda to Neville, 5 Feb.1932, NC18/2/767
95  Neville to Ida, 6 Feb.1932, 37 Eaton Square, in Self, ed., *The Neville Chamberlain Diary Letters.*, III, 305–7
96  Ida to Austen, & Hilda to Austen, 5 Feb.1932, The Bury House, AC4/2/278–9

year. It was not easy to live with the contrast between his fallen star and the rising star of his brother. He thought Neville had 'every reason to be' happy. 'As to me,' however, 'I am bored stiff & the time I spend at the House hangs very heavy on my hands.'[97] His judgement, normally oversensitive to the slightest suggestion of self-advancement, was weakened by his financial plight. Neville was horrified when Austen asked for appointment as chairman of the Import Duties Advisory Committee, a body that advised Neville as Chancellor on adjusting the tariff to meet the threat of foreign competition and realise the promise of imperial trade. Neville asked his sisters, 'does it not strike you as very extraordinary that Austen of all people should not see the gross impropriety of such an appointment. ... how could I give this well paid post to my own brother ... It makes my blood run cold to think of the cynical comments which would burst out everywhere.'[98] Hilda admitted that she found it 'difficult ... sometimes to understand the workings of Austen's mind whereas I feel so entirely in sympathy with yours.'[99] Eventually Austen found a more acceptable way to meet his needs when, following Churchill's example, he signed up for a lecture tour in the United States. 'It will be an appalling grind but as Winston says I know no easier method of earning money.'[100]

Disturbed by the reversal of position between the brothers, Neville preferred to think of comparisons with his father. 'I have surely been extraordinarily fortunate. Although I was 10 years older when I entered the House than Father when he was first elected I have already held office almost as long as he had at my age and I have been far more comfortable with my colleagues than he was.' Neville was happier with 'this mixed lot' in the National Government than in Baldwin's one-party ministries. His contentment had much to do with MacDonald's increasing reliance upon him. Neville in return looked upon MacDonald as 'the keystone of our arch' and convinced himself that their relationship was growing 'more confidential every day!'[101]

The outlook was shadowed, however, by the toll that his work took first on Annie's health and then on his own. The higher Neville rose in the political firmament, the more Annie expected of herself. When she fell short, she suffered from what Neville learned to call an 'inferiority complex'. It turned into something 'like

97  Austen to Ida, 28 Feb.1932, 58 Rutland Gate, in Self, ed., *The Austen Chamberlain Diary Letters*, 407

98  Neville to Ida, 20 Feb.1932, Westbourne, in Self, ed., *The Neville Chamberlain Diary Letters*, III, 310

99  Hilda to Neville, 26 Feb.1932, NC18/2/770

100  Austen to Ida, 15 Apr.1932, 58 Rutland Gate, in Self, ed., *The Austen Chamberlain Diary Letters*, 409–10

101  Neville to Mary, 19 Mar.1932, Westbourne, NC1/20/1/157

a nervous breakdown', which left Neville 'rather in despair to know what to do with her'.[102] Then, after presenting the Budget, he was himself laid low by lumbago followed by 'a sharpish attack of gout', which turned into 'the worst I have had for many years'. He could not 'avoid the conclusion that it is a sign of overwork on the machine'. For Neville as for Annie, illness had psychological dimensions. 'The worst of it is that it (or the medicines they give you) do depress one so & make one's inside such a burden that life seems insupportable at times.'[103] Unable to supervise the passage of the Finance bill through the Commons, he contemplated 'the possibility of my retirement from politics'. But at that, Annie 'developed very definite ideas of her own'. She persuaded Neville to join her in Harrogate for the different treatments their ailments called for.[104] What was left in the Finance Bill could not compare in importance with the international conferences Neville would have to attend, first in Lausanne on war debts and reparations, then in Ottawa over imperial preference. Harrogate soon had the two invalids feeling better than they had for years.

৯৯

Neville made his debut on the international stage at Lausanne. He did not seek advice from Austen partly because the subject was economic. But also he 'could not help feeling that Europe had already changed' since Austen's time as Foreign Secretary, 'and that his advice ... could not really be of much help except after a fresh term of service in touch with what is going on'.[105] Even so, he took a leaf from Austen's book. Remembering with envy the introduction that his father had given Austen to the languages and culture of France and Germany, he sent his son Frank to Bonn. 'The great thing,' he coached Frank, 'is ... to talk as much as possible with Germans even if you make mistakes.' Neville hoped to profit soon from Frank's experience: 'as you get more fluent I hope very much that you may be able to give me some report on how Germans think and talk about the topics of the day.' He told Frank what to look for: 'I should like very much to know what the ordinary middle class German in a place like Bonn thinks about the future of his country.'

---

102  Neville to Hilda, 27 Feb., & to Ida, 5 Mar.1932, 37 Eaton Square, in Self, ed., *The Neville Chamberlain Diary Letters*, III, 311 & 314

103  Neville to Hilda, 23 Apr., 37 Eaton Square, & to Ida, 30 Apr.1932, Chevening, in Self, ed., *The Neville Chamberlain Diary Letters*, III, 320–2

104  Neville to Ida, 21 May 1932, Salisbury, in Self, ed., *The Neville Chamberlain Diary Letters*, III, 324

105  Neville to Ida, 17 Apr.1932, 37 Eaton Square, in Self, ed., *The Neville Chamberlain Diary Letters*, III, 319

As in England, the people central to Neville's concerns came from 'the ordinary middle class ... the average German who is no doubt very heavily taxed and also alarmed at the increasing numbers of unemployed.'[106]

He wrote on departure for Lausanne to tell Frank how he hoped the conference would deal with its assignment of reparations for wartime loans. 'We here have always held the view that apart from questions of morality it was impossible to make these huge payments from one country to another without any corresponding return, without serious injury to international trade. Whether the payments are called Reparations or War Debts makes no difference, the results are the same and they are responsible for much of our troubles today. We would therefore like to cancel them all and of course Germany would not object to that. ... France & America have held out against it ... However things have got so much worse lately that the French have moved pretty rapidly towards our view. The American Congress is as bad as ever ... What I hope for at Lausanne is first a general expression of view that all Debt & Reparations should be cancelled and then an agreement among the European nations only that they will cancel all payments as between themselves. Such an agreement could not be finally & definitely binding unless the Americans accept cancellation. They certainly wouldn't do that now but if we adjourn Lausanne till the autumn and then wait to approach the Americans till after ... their Presidential Election ... I think there is a good chance that we may find them more reasonable. Meanwhile a European agreement on the lines I have suggested would go a good way towards restoring confidence. Germany would then be able to borrow money to develop her industry.'[107] Restoration of confidence among trading partners and development of industry: these were the way to meet the needs of ordinary people and overcome the resentments exacerbated by the war.

Neville pursued this agenda at Lausanne to considerable effect, despite a recurrence of gout that disabled him for several days. He got along better than he expected with the French finance minister whose English was no better than Neville's French. Neville also consolidated his rapport with MacDonald, who led the British delegation. 'He has a good deal of difficulty in following the more technical side,' Neville reported to his sisters, 'and he doesn't understand French, so he likes to have me about and in fact he won't now conduct any conversations with the other delegations without having me there too.'[108]

In the midst of the conference, Neville capped his achievement by slipping back

---

106  Neville to Frank, 19 May 1932, Salisbury, NC1/23/16
107  Neville to Frank, 12 June 1932, Westbourne, NC1/23/17
108  Neville to Ida, 4 July 1932, Lausanne Conference, in Self, ed., *op.cit.*, III, 333–4

to England to announce a conversion of Britain's war loan to a rate reduced from 5 to 3½ per cent. His sisters had half expected this announcement, which took nearly everyone else by surprise. No one was more impressed than Austen. 'It is a prodigious operation such as has never been presented before ... a triumphant result of the Government's policy.'[109]

Soon after he returned from Switzerland, Neville left for Ottawa, buoyed up by 'being able to leave behind me two such successes as the Conversion and Lausanne'. He took particular pleasure in the 'terms of mutual liking and confidence' that he established at Lausanne with the French Prime Minister Herriot. Privately they worked out an agreement that brought the conference to a happy conclusion, though it would not amount to much until the Americans ratified it. Neville hoped to deal with the premiers of the British dominions as he had with Herriot. Yet he tried not to pitch his hopes for Ottawa too high: 'so much has been said & written about what it may or should accomplish that I fear disappointment is inevitable. Moreover, the Dominions are likely to be very exacting.'[110]

He was right to be apprehensive. The proceedings began well enough. The British delegation sailed for Canada aboard the appropriately named *Empress of Britain*. Neville used the opportunity to set the delegation in running order. Baldwin was its formal head; and he set the tone for the conference in a series of speeches delivered after arrival in Canada 'in his best style full of the deeper things'.[111] These speeches gave Neville 'a bad attack of inferiority complex' because Baldwin was 'admirable as he always is on such occasions'.[112] Neville tried to accomplish something similar with 'a series of general propositions ... to give the lead to the Dominions and the outside public and ... form a test to which every proposition afterwards put forward could be submitted'.[113] The British delegation endorsed Neville's set of propositions 'with enthusiasm'. But it fell flat at the conference: 'not a single delegation would accept it and the South Africans made it clear that they did not want anything which suggested that the Empire as such had either principles or policy.'[114]

---

109 Austen to Hilda, 2 July 1932, 58 Rutland Gate, in Self, ed., *The Austen Chamberlain Diary Letters*, 414
110 Neville to Mary, 13 July 1932, NC1/20/1/159
111 Neville to Hilda, 30 Aug.1932, Westbourne, in Self, ed., *The Neville Chamberlain Diary Letters*, III, 345
112 Neville to Annie, 22 July 1932, Ottawa, NC1/26/468
113 Neville to Ida, 17 July 1932, R.M.S. Empress of Britain, in Self, ed., *The Neville Chamberlain Diary Letters*, III, 335
114 Neville to Ida, 21 Aug.1932, Ottawa, in Self, ed., *The Neville Chamberlain Diary Letters*, III, 344

Still when it came to concrete proposals, Neville took charge. As in the National Government at home, so for the British delegation in Ottawa, he provided executive leadership. When Baldwin had to speak on concrete matters, Neville wrote the speech and had it typed to ensure that it was read out word for word. Yet he resented the impression thus conveyed to the public that Baldwin was in charge. Neville got along as well with the leading Labour minister in the delegation, J.H. Thomas, as he had with MacDonald at Lausanne. 'If we had all been in the same party all our lives our relations could not have been more harmonious.'[115] Though the free-trading quartet in the Cabinet was excluded, the delegation contained two pragmatists, the Liberal Runciman as well as Thomas. They reduced Neville's room for tariff bargaining more narrowly than Amery as the truest of tariff reformers thought tolerable; and Amery encouraged the dominion premiers to demand more. Even so, the early indications from most of the self-governing dominions and India buoyed Neville up.

The premier who worried him was Richard Bennett of Canada. Neville had worked well with Bennett the previous autumn in London. But Bennett now kept the Canadian position very much to himself. He rarely consulted the rest of his Cabinet and listened instead to his brother-in-law, Canada's representative in Washington, who shared American suspicions of the British. When Bennett finally presented Canada's proposals to the conference, Neville 'wanted to bite someone very badly ... but by an effort controlled myself. Bennett's offer which he trumpeted so loudly in the Press and to us turned out even worse than I had anticipated. For example the concessions on iron & steel which he said were worth forty million dollars to us proved actually to mean a loss of existing trade to the extent of some two hundred thousand dollars.'[116] As Bennett's relationship with Neville deteriorated, he relished 'the observation of an American that Bennett had the "manners of a Chicago policeman & the temperament of a Hollywood film actor".' Their worsening relations affected other delegations and strained the cohesion of the British delegation almost to breaking point. Neville counted the days till he could sail for home: 'I never want to see Canada again', he swore.[117]

The conference managed to close with an agreement. Neville signed the section that applied to Canada at 1:30 a.m. on the day of his departure 'after a prolonged and desperate battle with Bennett' and 'fighting all day almost every delegation in

115 Neville to Annie, 10 Aug.1932, #7. Imperial Economic Conference, NC1/26/473
116 Neville to Annie, 10 Aug.1932, #7, Imperial Economic Conference, NCI/26/473
117 Neville to Hilda, 11 Aug.1932, Ottawa, in Self, ed., The Neville Chamberlain Diary Letters, III, 342

turn'. He had 'no complaint to make of the Australians or the New Zealanders ... if they drove rather a hard bargain with us they were quite straightforward about it. Bennett was a different proposition ... he lied like a trooper, and ... alternatively blustered, bullied, sobbed, prevaricated, delayed and obstructed to the very last moment.'[118] Bennett's only saving grace for Neville was to ask him as son of the prophet of imperial preference to sign the Canadian treaty.

Neville still insisted that the agreements reached at Ottawa were 'excellent. The Indians ... have accepted the principle of Imperial preference. The South Africans have given us considerable concessions and will denounce the German treaty so as not to give them equally to the Hun. The Australians & Canadians have agreed by progressive reductions of duties to put the British manufacturer in the position of a domestic competitor ... Both of them have given us considerable advantages against the foreigner.' These were nevertheless meagre achievements, more a matter of aspiration than of substance.

The main dividend for Neville emerged after he returned to England. Without accomplishing much by way of imperial preference, the Ottawa agreements strengthened his position in the National Government by driving out the free traders. When the agreements were presented to the Cabinet, the leader of the Liberal free traders, Herbert Samuel, 'asked many carping questions and reserved his position until he had consulted his friends'. Neville was in no mood for 'another agreement to differ' to keep the Cabinet together: if Samuel 'were to go I should rejoice ... and I believe his departure would draw the rest of us closer together'.[119] It did not work out that simply. Snowden and another Liberal dissident, Sinclair, joined Samuel in resigning from the Cabinet over the Ottawa agreements; and the losses were amplified by resignations from a handful of Under Secretaries. They left MacDonald 'very lonely and dispirited', vulnerable to the accusation that he was 'more than ever the slave of the Tories' and had 'sold his soul for office'.

Neville seized the opportunity to assure MacDonald that the rest of the Cabinet 'looked to him not to be the leader of the Tory Party but as the symbol of our faith that until prosperity returned country must come before party'. Neville hoped that the now 'far more homogenous' Cabinet would 'move towards the

---

118 Neville to Ida, 21 Aug.1932, aboard the Empress of Britain, in Self, ed., *The Neville Chamberlain Diary Letters*, III, 344
119 Neville to Hilda, 30 Aug.1932, Westbourne, in Self, ed., *The Neville Chamberlain Diary Letters*, III, 345

fused party under a National name which I regard as certain to come'.[120] It was a remarkable outcome, 'the more miraculous' to Neville when he recalled all that had 'come about in one short year'. Barely a year ago under Baldwin's limp leadership, Conservatives were at each other's throats. Now Neville sat in the driver's seat of a government with a political complexion more to his liking. Content to forget Bennett's bullying, he joined Ida and Hilda 'to rejoice in the fulfilment of Father's policy'.

But the autumn that Neville found so sweet plunged Austen to the depths of despair. Unable to find 'anything in public affairs to console me', he poured out his bitterness to his sisters. 'If I felt older & less able to work, it would be easier to reconcile myself to the place on the shelf to which I have been relegated. As it is ... I eat out my heart in idleness & uselessness & see my work [in foreign affairs] undone & feel myself unwanted & unregretted. All this is very bitter – forgive me & destroy this screed. I shall recover my equanimity one of these days, but just now I am in despair. ... After giving up everything to public life, it is hard to feel that you are in your coffin before you are dead.'[121]

120  Neville to Hilda, 18 Sept.1932, Ayrshire, in Self, ed., *The Neville Chamberlain Diary Letters*, III, 348
121  Austen to Hilda, 11 Sept.1932, 58 Rutland Gate, in Self, ed., *The Austen Chamberlain Diary Letters*, 416–7

*The Chancellor and his adoring wife, Budget Day, 17 April 1934*

# 9

# Rearmament

Less than a year after that *cri de coeur*, the fortunes of both brothers changed yet again. Both felt their age. Austen turned seventy: and Neville in his early sixties wondered how many more years of effective work he had in him. Their positions in the political order remained the same. But their spirits moved in different directions. Austen found new purpose in his liberation from office, while Neville settled in soberly for the long haul. Neville felt by the spring of 1933 that 'most of what I have worked for has been done ... now the chief task is to keep the ship steady in the course till she can make port again.'[1] Austen looked forward to the day when Neville could join him on the back benches as an 'elderly moralist'.[2]

But MacDonald's replacement as Prime Minister in 1935 by Austen's nemesis, Baldwin, disturbed both brothers. Baldwin's unending inertia in face of mounting international threats, above all from Hitler, exasperated Neville, always impatient for action: at the same time, it kindled Austen's sympathy for Neville's still more impatient rival, Churchill. Ironically, what put the Chamberlain brothers and Churchill at odds with each other was what all three wanted to accelerate: rearmament.

The role of armed force in international relations lay outside the experience of most Chamberlains. But Austen was the exception. During his political apprenticeship, he had acquired some understanding of international relations. He was

---

1 Neville to Hilda, 29 Apr.1933, Westbourne, in Self, ed., *The Neville Chamberlain Diary Letters*, III, 388–9
2 Austen to Ida, 24 June 1933, 58 Rutland Gate, in Self, ed., *The Austen Chamberlain Diary Letters*, 445

also impressed as a young man by the writings of the American authority A.T. Mahan on sea power; and he learned more during his first stint in office at the Admiralty about the weight in international affairs that Britain gained from its navy. He knew enough to appreciate, during the increasingly turbulent 1930s, that Churchill had a stronger intuitive grasp of these issues than he. Neville, however, saw only the lack of balanced judgement in his brilliant rival.

As the pace-setter in the National Government, Neville grew more self-reliant. He did not welcome advice from those who lacked the up-to-date information he possessed, including Austen. The tenor of Neville's correspondence changed even with his sisters. Their experience in the local government of Hampshire and the Women's Institutes had served him well when he was Minister of Health, but it had little bearing on the darkening international scene. Neville no longer looked for informed advice from them but for approval, even applause.

The fortunes of even the most powerful men of state rarely lie in their own hands. And the Chamberlain brothers were not among the most powerful. No one had ever said of Austen or Neville what Churchill had said of their father, that '"Joe" was the one who made the weather'.[3] In the opening months of 1933, two men of considerably greater power than old Joe rose to the head of their respective countries: Hitler in Germany and Roosevelt in the United States. They changed the political climate in ways to which Neville and Austen could only react. Roosevelt was the first to move. In the first hundred days of his presidency, he challenged the prevailing orthodoxy about political management of the economy. Hitler posed a graver challenge to the global order, though it took longer to reveal itself. With a cunning mixture of peace-seeking diplomatic gestures and aggressive military action backed by rapid rearmament, Hitler sought to make Germany the dominant power over the Eurasian landmass. Austen and Neville did not initially differ in their response to these challenges, but they eventually pushed Austen towards an alignment with Churchill that posed danger for Neville.

🙠

Austen chanced upon a new role in public life in an unlikely way. No longer bound to a desk in London, he saw more of his Birmingham constituency and of the slums that shocked him at the last election. He spoke of that shock in a housing debate in the Commons, and was gratified by the 'great impression' his speech made in the House. It had a wide impact, 'judging by the flood of letters it has brought me from

---

3 W.S. Churchill, *Great Contemporaries* (London 1937), 57

all over the country. I am now trying to follow it up.' But he confessed, 'my trouble is that I know so little'.[4] His sisters saw the difficulty. 'It is rather new for him to take an active part in discussing social legislation.'[5] Housing had been Neville's subject, as he testily observed. The brothers had 'some good talk' when they met at the annual dinner of the Jewellers' Association in Austen's constituency. 'Egged on' by Austen, Neville spoke to the Minister of Health and then 'sketched out a possible slum policy' for Austen. 'He seemed very much attracted by it and, as it were, relieved. For, he said, he was in agreement with all my ideas ... But he had not been able to put them together and make a picture of them as I had.'[6]

Austen turned his newfound effectiveness as a speaker to a subject where he was better able to put his thoughts together. Six weeks after Hitler's election as Chancellor of Germany, Austen spoke in the Commons about the dire state of affairs there. It was not Hitler that worried Austen so much as the brutality of the Nazis. They epitomised everything he had learnt to loathe as a student in Berlin. Nazism, as Austen saw it, was an essentially German phenomenon. He did not associate it with the Fascism of Mussolini, whom he continued to admire, encouraged by Ivy. She accentuated the Italian dimension of his Locarno policy: 'I do feel so strongly that something big might be accomplished between France & Italy, & that you are the only person to help them & bring them together.'[7] Mussolini reinforced her efforts and tried to persuade Austen that 'he was carrying out the Locarno policy'.[8] Thereupon Austen headed to Rome and 'had an hour's very friendly & interesting conversation' with Il Duce.[9]

He only wished that Britain's current Foreign Secretary, Sir John Simon, would pursue the path laid down at Locarno as well as the Italians: 'it is odd to see Mussolini understanding & believing in my policy more than my own Govt.'[10] Austen had welcomed the appointment of Simon in place of Reading as Foreign Secretary when the government was reconstructed after the election. But this confidence did not last long. 'I wonder whether Simon will do anything,' he asked Ivy impatiently, 'whether indeed he has any policy beyond drifting.'[11] A year later Ida echoed the

4 Austen to Hilda, 18 Dec.1932, 58 Rutland Gate, in Self, ed., *op.cit.*, 421

5 Ida to Neville, 16 Dec.1932, The Bury House, NC18/2/811

6 Neville to Ida, 29 Jan.1933, Westbourne, in Self, ed., *op.cit.*, III, 372

7 Ivy to Austen, 14 Sept.1932, 58 Rutland Gate, AC6/2/626

8 Austen to Hilda, 24 Apr.1933, 58 Rutland Gate, in Self, ed., *The Austen Chamberlain Diary Letters*, 437–8

9 Austen to Hilda, 3 Sep[t.1933, Hotel Royal, Rome, in Self, ed., *op.cit.*, 447

10 Austen to Ida, 12 June 1933, 58 Rutland Gate, in Self, ed., *op.cit.*, 442

11 Austen to Ivy, 16 Sept.1932, Corsica, AC6/1/890

'very strong feeling in the public that Simon is not equal to his job'.[12] Neville kept his distance from this disenchantment, but offered only a muted defence of the Foreign Secretary. Austen reciprocated by criticising the government only on its conduct of foreign policy.

He was confident that he and Neville thought alike on foreign affairs. That was certainly true over war debts and reparations. Both Neville and Austen were exasperated by the refusal of the United States, preoccupied as ever with the next election, to abate its demand for full repayment of its loans to wartime allies. 'Oh dear,' Hilda chimed in, '– it is a terrible thing that the world is now so small that we cannot be independent of America, & yet that America is so wretchedly self centred & so provincial that she can never see further than her own nose.'[13]

The agreement between Austen and Neville extended to Germany. Neville was pleased to find that Austen's attack on the Nazis 'made the Germans very cross'. Echoing Ivy, Neville maintained that Austen 'is the one man whose name is known abroad who can say those things. And they certainly wanted saying.' Yet the brothers also agreed that, as Neville put it, Hitler 'has really been the best of the bunch since he has been in office'. Austen regarded Hitler initially as 'a figurehead'. Even after Hitler pulled Germany out of the Disarmament Conference and the League of Nations, Austen continued to assert that he 'would sooner deal with Hitler himself than with von Papen', the former Chancellor, or with Joseph Goebbels or Hermann Goering.[14] Ida reflected a good deal of informed opinion in Britain when she told Neville that the 'only encouraging factor' she could find in the situation on the Continent was 'Hitler's repetition of his assertion not only that he wants peace, but that Germany has definitely given up all claim to Alsace Lorraine, in fact that he holds by the Locarno agreement'.[15]

The slight differences that emerged between the brothers on overseas matters in 1933 had more to do with their levels of governmental responsibility and access to information than with their individual opinions. Austen voiced the opposition of the Jewellers' Association in his constituency to the commercial treaty that the Board of Trade concluded with Germany. Neville privately agreed but could not say so, and envied the influence Austen gained through his freedom to speak out.

---

12  Ida to Neville, 24 Nov.1933, The Bury House, NC18/2/857
13  Hilda to Neville, 23 June 1933, The Bury House, NC18/2/839
14  Austen to Ivy, 14 Feb.1933, 58 Rutland Gate, AC6/1/949; Neville to Hilda, 16 Apr.1933, Aberdeenshire, in Self, ed., *The Neville Chamberlain Diary Letters*, III, 387; & Austen to Hilda, 11 Nov.1933, in Self, ed., *The Austen Chamberlain Diary Letters*, 453
15  Ida to Neville, 24 Nov.1933, The Bury House, NC18/2/857

'He has quite eclipsed all the other ex-Cabinet Ministers just by being himself and he is greeted with general cheers whenever he gets up. ... I fancy there is a large measure of truth in his own remark that [this reception] would not survive 3 months on the Treasury Bench.'[16]

Austen had found a way to benefit from his loss of office. But Neville found satisfaction in public life only when in office, in a position to do, and not just to say, something. The National Government enabled him to make a difference in many spheres of policy-making, foreign as well as domestic. Other members of the Cabinet looked to him for a lead. Ironically the Labour Prime Minister MacDonald depended on Neville to save him from the appearance of subservience to the Tories. Baldwin had little to say on most issues except 'that this is a most difficult question and he sees no way out' – 'the dormouse', Hilda called him[17] – though on the rare occasions when he expressed an opinion, Neville acknowledged that he was 'generally right'.[18] Most members of the Cabinet owed their position less to their aptitude for the work of their departments than to their previous political affiliation and willingness to serve in a government that prided itself on rising above party.

Even so, in his weekly reports to his sisters Neville exaggerated all this ministerial dependence upon him. Neville reported that Simon came to him 'in despair' on disarmament, confessing that 'he was stumped' on the subject. 'It amuses me to find a new policy for each of my colleagues in turn and though I can't imagine that all my ideas are the best that can be found, most of them seem to be adopted faute de mieux!'[19] The approach to disarmament that Neville devised was simplistic and did not impress those in Cabinet who were better informed, including MacDonald and Simon himself. It did impress the others, however, and Neville deemed it a breakthrough. 'It is really very simple,' he explained to Ida: '... since the difficulty about disarmament lies in the fears of France & her Allies lest Germany should take advantage of it to re-arm we should all agree that disarmament should take place in successive stages, each stage being dependent upon the good behaviour of Germany during the preceding period.' When Baldwin had this scheme outlined for him, 'he remarked that it was so simple that he couldn't think why nobody had thought of it before. But I believe,' Neville added blissfully, 'that was the comment

---

16  Neville to Ida, 3 June 1933, Salisbury, & 30 July 1933, Westbourne, in Self, ed., *op.cit.*, III, 393 & 401

17  Hilda to Neville, 29 June 1934, The Bury House, NC18/2/883

18  Neville to Ida, 4 Dec.1932 & 25 Feb.1933, in Self, ed., *op.cit.*, III, 364 & 378

19  Neville to Hilda, 30 Oct.1932, 37 Eaton Square, in Self, ed., *op.cit.*, III, 353

upon a celebrated solution by the late Christopher Columbus!'[20] This report went to Ida, not to Austen who could have punctured Neville's illusion.

Neville also failed to appreciate that his colleagues' dependence upon him in so many areas reflected a grave weakness in the National Government. The Cabinet was composed of solid, respectable men. It excluded the men of brilliance who proved unreliable, men like Lloyd George, Mosley and Churchill. Lloyd George grew ever more erratic as his party disintegrated. Mosley discredited himself by bewildering changes in party allegiance. Churchill later looked back on himself in these years as a voice crying in the wilderness against Hitler and the Nazis. But it was against Gandhi and Indian nationalism that Churchill directed most of his verbal venom in the early 1930s, and though he won a lot of support among the Conservative rank and file in doing so, he alienated all the leaders of the National Government.

Austen was irritated by Churchill's way of 'finding fault with everything & certainly not contributing to make the next steps easier'.[21] But Austen shared his anxiety about dominion status for India, and was, if anything, quicker than Churchill to take alarm at the rise of the Nazis. Neville seized every opportunity to draw attention to Churchill's unreliability and lack of judgement. But Austen accepted Churchill's invitation to lunch, along with Anthony Eden, the rising Conservative star on foreign affairs whom Austen called 'my protégé',[22] to discuss their common interests.

Churchill then invited Austen to his country home, Chartwell, for the weekend. Austen found the weekend 'very pleasant but on the tiring side, for both Winston & [his son] Randolph roar when excited in argument'.[23] Austen remained guarded: 'We differed about India without quarrelling ... felt equally free from any obligation to [Baldwin] & [MacDonald] & viewed the future with equal anxiety but with opposite hopes. [Churchill] anticipates that he & his Indian Die-Hards will continue to hold about 1/3rd of the Party, that the India Bill will be carried but that the fight will leave such bitter memories that the Govt. will have to be reconstructed.' MacDonald, Baldwin and two or three of the Conservatives closely identified with the India Bill would have to go. Simon as a Liberal 'could stay &

---

20  Neville to Ida, 5 Nov.1932, Westbourne, in Self, ed., *The Neville Chamberlain Diary Letters*, III, 356

21  Austen to Ivy, 11 July 1932, House of Commons, AC6/1/876

22  Austen to Ivy, 4 Mar.1933, 58 Rutland Gate, AC6/1/966

23  Austen to Ida, 22 October 1933, Chartwell, in Self, ed., *The Austen Chamberlain Diary Letters*, 451

it would still be a National Government, but,' Churchill asked, 'who is to lead it?' He turned to Austen: '& so he led me up into a high place & showed me the kingdoms of the world. I was not greatly tempted. I told him that I saw the situation developing differently ... We must fight out our Indian battle as friends & bury the hatchet as soon as it was over. I did not see any reason for resignations. I was not anxious, indeed was wholly averse to becoming P.M. at 70 or 71 ... At the same time,' he added to Hilda, 'as long as I was in politics, I was not going to say that I would not serve again in any capacity, if the necessity arose, or wipe my name finally off the slate.'[24]

Though Austen's rejection of the proffered leadership was firm, he was gratified by the overture and found the notion of removing Baldwin sweet. 'This is the second approach made to me on the same lines, & I get from all quarters more flattering testimonials than I have ever enjoyed in my life.' He would have been happy to take Simon's place at the Foreign Office, a possibility Churchill did not raise. Neither Churchill nor Austen spoke of Neville, though Churchill did not include him among the men he wished to remove from the Cabinet. The brothers met only intermittently these days. Still 'we understand one another,' Austen assured Neville: '... nothing shall come between us.'[25] They kept in touch through their sisters, who served as the family clearinghouse.

⁊⬤

Initially Churchill's courtship of Austen did not bother Neville. What else could you expect of a born intriguer? Neville had other things on his mind; above all, the economy. He had secured tariff reform and a modest instalment of imperial preference upon which he relied to lift the economy out of depression. The depression was also eased by Britain's ejection from the gold standard. Neville sought to consolidate those benefits by balancing the budget, restoring confidence in the City, and steadying the pound, a thoroughly conservative policy consonant with current orthodoxy. It was challenged on two fronts, at home by Keynes and abroad by Roosevelt. Keynes called for deficit finance including loans for public works to put people back to work with money in their pockets. He expounded his ideas publicly in *The Times* and privately to Neville, who was about to present his Budget. Neville did not argue with the brilliant economist 'but did succeed in elucidating

24 Austen to Hilda, 28 Oct.1933, 58 Rutland Gate, in Self, ed., *The Austen Chamberlain Diary Letters*, 451–2
25 Austen to Neville, 23 Mar.1933, House of Commons, NC1/27/113

his ideas which,' he reported to Hilda, 'were even worse than I had supposed. He does definitely want to unbalance the Budget'. Austen, though more conservative than Neville, was momentarily attracted by Keynes, whom he found 'extraordinarily clever & marvellously lucid ... he was the one man who at the moment of the peace negotiations made a true estimate of Germany's capacity to pay'. But Austen soon concluded that, while Keynes excelled in theory, 'his theories are too finespun to stand the wear & tear of work-a-day practice'.[26]

'Neville's budget has not excited anyone,' Austen observed when it was presented, 'but I think it is generally approved. Certainly in the City they would have been aghast if he had taken Keynes' advice.'[27] The reception of the Budget nevertheless left Neville down at heart: 'it is a depressing business to be in politics at present and I get very weary of it sometimes, seeing nothing ahead to look forward to, but only long struggles against a gradually more & more disgruntled public opinion. I wonder whether it will seem worth while to go on after the next Election. ... I have not Father's joy in battle and intense conviction that whatever he was pursuing was vitally important.'[28]

Keynes's theories did not cause Neville as much concern as Roosevelt's practice. Roosevelt strode into the presidency with a bold set of initiatives to give his depressed country a New Deal. 'Roosevelt seems to have begun well & to have already in a large degree restored confidence in America,' said Ida on the day he was inaugurated. She compared his actions with the formation in Britain of the National Government followed by the adoption of tariff reform and imperial preference. 'It looks as if it was as good for America as for us to find themselves suddenly on the verge of a precipice. At least it does make people ready to accept strong measures.'[29] But Neville did not see the similarity. 'If Roosevelt pulls off his policy,' he warned, 'it will be embarrassing because people will want to know why I haven't done the same. If, as I think more probable, it presently comes to grief, he will throw us all into frightful confusion.'[30] The steps Roosevelt took toward a competitive devaluation of the dollar deepened Neville's dismay. Evidence, however, of

---

26  Austen to Hilda, 26 Mar.1933, 58 Rutland Gate, in Self, ed., *The Austen Chamberlain Diary Letters*, 434

27  Austen to Ida, 30 Apr.1933, 58 Rutland Gate, in Self, ed., *The Austen Chamberlain Diary Letters*, 438

28  Neville to Hilda, 29 Apr.1933, Westbourne, in Self, ed., *The Neville Chamberlain Diary Letters*, III, 388

29  Ida to Mary, 3 Mar.1933, The Bury House, BC4/2/222

30  Neville to Hilda, 24 June 1933, Westbourne, in Self, ed., *The Neville Chamberlain Diary Letters*, III, 396

falling unemployment in Britain 'came in most opportunely to show that we were holding our end up'.[31] Better still, Neville could not 'help chuckling over ... the awful slump on the N.Y. Stock Exchange': it 'absolutely silenced the critics who were asking why our Chancellor could not be brave as well as wise like the American President'.[32] The New Deal accentuated but also seemed to validate the conservatism of Neville's economic management. Ida saw 'continued evidence of the success of [Neville's] financial policy as a whole' when 'return after return shows the same story of a steady increase of trade & decrease of unemployment ... The Tariff policy is justifying itself all along the line.'[33]

The Chamberlains consolidated their respective positions in the public service, Austen as elder statesman, Neville as Chancellor, Ida as alderman – all but Hilda. She was busy; too busy for Ida's liking, away from home several nights a week on Women's Institute business. She was a practiced speaker by now, and could 'pretty well count on finding the right words at the right moment', to Ida's amazement.[34] Like Neville outside the House of Commons, Ida rarely spoke in public without careful preparation. Neville and she were alike also in their tendency to lose themselves in administrative detail. But Hilda looked for the underlying pattern. She was fascinated to discover during a speaking tour that 'up in the North they have been successful in running their [Women's] Institutes with very little help from the "upper classes". ... They were chiefly small farmers, or small holders, shopkeepers, Teachers, etc. & I must say they were wonderfully keen.'[35]

This warmth of understanding made Hilda popular across the country and commanded the respect of the Women's Institute staff. Hence the dismay when she was not re-elected Chairman of the National Executive's finance committee. She had assumed that, in endeavouring to serve the public, ladies would treat each other like gentlemen. When another candidate was nominated for the chairmanship of the committee, Hilda shrank from voting; but the other candidate voted for herself and won. 'Result that the Treasurer is ready to tear her hair ... & the staff at the office ... have all been individually to say how desperately disappointed they are.'[36]

Austen had moved beyond that sort of setback and relished the respect he

31 Neville to Hilda, 10 July 1933, 37 Eaton Square, in Self, ed., *The Neville Chamberlain Diary Letters*, III, 396

32 Neville to Hilda, 23 July 1933, Moor Land House, Briantspuddle, in Self, ed., *The Neville Chamberlain Diary Letters*, III, 400

33 Ida to Neville, 13 Oct.1933, The Bury House, NC18/2/851

34 Ida to Neville, 19 May 1933, The Bury House, NC18/2/833

35 Hilda to Neville, 29 June 1934, The Bury House, NC18/2/883

36 Hilda to Neville, 15 June 1934, The Bury House, NC18/2/881

commanded as a former Indian and Foreign Secretary. He gave a lot of attention to the Joint Select Committee on India, a large body reflecting the many differing standpoints on the subject. Austen rallied the moderates who were willing to move India toward self-government but on terms that minimised the risk to the integrity of the Empire. He kept in touch with the Secretary of State for India, Samuel Hoare, but maintained enough independence to convince the Conservative rank and file that their concerns were taken into account. The committee finally recommended a much modified version of the arrangements for self-government favoured by the government. A Conservative party conference was convened to consider it. Baldwin spoke for the government, Salisbury and Churchill for the diehards.

By all accounts the voice that clinched the argument for acceptance of the report was Austen's. He 'had a reception which does ones heart good and must have delighted him,' Neville reported: '...Austen's ... reasoned & weighty arguments consolidated the votes satisfied the people that they were right in their decision & sent them away happy & confident.' Neville welcomed the contrast between Austen's reception and 'a strong disposition to resent the persistent opposition & obstruction of the minority' led by Churchill.[37] Austen placed an even higher estimate on his achievement. The government 'ought to be grateful to me, for if I had gone against them, there isn't a doubt but that they would have been beaten & indeed, unless I had exerted myself, I don't think they could have obtained a working majority' in the House of Commons. His achievement was poignant because it saved the man who supplanted him as party leader: 'what fun it would have been' to pull the rug from under Baldwin's feet 'if only it were not all so damnably serious.'[38] Ida recognised the 'bitter irony in the situation, when [Austen's] influence increases by leaps & bounds as soon as his power of executive action is taken away. ... he must be feeling all the time how much he could still do at the F.O. & how hard it is for him to see opportunity after opportunity thrown away for want of a definite policy.'[39]

※

37  Neville to both sisters, 9 Dec.1934, Briantspuddle, Dorset, in Self, ed., *The Neville Chamberlain Diary Letters*, III, 105

38  Austen to Ida, 15 Dec.1934, 58 Rutland Gate, in Self, ed., *The Austen Chamberlain Diary Letters*, 471

39  Ida to Neville, 7 Dec.1934, The Bury House, NC18/2/906

The economic improvement that Ida observed in the autumn of 1933 continued into the following spring when Hilda was on hand to hear Neville present his next Budget to the Commons. Neville treasured being told that 'no Budget in recollection had so good a reception' in the House, the country, and the press. This response helped to offset the irritation he felt at advocates of radical policies, whether proposed by Keynes, implemented in Roosevelt's New Deal, or promoted by uncompromising imperial protectionists. Amery described his Budget as 'timid'; and the word rankled. Neville listed all the plans he had initiated as the National Government's man of ideas, whether on unemployment or slums: 'every one of these things shows that I can be both bold & original when I believe that those qualities are called for'. He insisted, however, that in finance, 'at any rate in the times in which we are living, I believe confidence is the great essential, and all my efforts are directed to building it up'.[40]

The results of his budgetary orthodoxy enabled him to address the other area of mounting concern: rearmament. Three weeks after presenting the Budget, Neville announced to his sisters, 'I have practically taken charge now of the Defence requirements of the country.'[41] He combined this effort with a demand for clarification of Britain's commitments in Europe and Asia. The prospect of a substantial increase in the air force alarmed his sisters because Odiham was the site of one air base and close to another at Farnborough. But Neville refused to be deflected. 'I hate to think of the possible developments at Odiham,' he told Hilda; but 'in the absence of security other nations won't give up aircraft or bombing and we shall be more likely to deter Germany from mad dogging if we have an air force which in case of need could bomb the Ruhr from Belgium.'[42]

The Nazi assassination of the Austrian Chancellor, Engelbert Dollfuss, reinforced Neville's resolve. Dollfuss was killed soon after the anniversary of the assassination of the Austrian archduke that precipitated the Great War. '... what an ominous tragedy, with Austria once again the centre of the picture' and 'with Germany once more behind instigating, suggesting, encouraging bloodshed and assassination for her own selfish aggrandisement and pride. ... That those beasts should have got [Dollfuss] at last & that they should have treated him with such

---

40  Neville to Hilda, 21 Apr., Westbourne, & 10 Nov.1934, 37 Eaton Square, in Self, ed., *The Neville Chamberlain Diary Letters*, IV, 66–7 & 99

41  Neville to Ida, 12 May 1934, 37 Eaton Square, in Self, ed., *The Neville Chamberlain Diary Letters*, IV, 70

42  Neville to Hilda, 1 July 1934, 37 Eaton Square, in Self, ed., *The Neville Chamberlain Diary Letters*, IV, 77

callous brutality makes me hate Nazi-ism and all its works with a greater loathing then ever.' Yet he added, 'Fortunately Hitler seems to be keeping his head.' Accelerated rearmament was, as Neville saw it, quite compatible with, indeed the other side of, equally insistent exploration of the possibilities for peaceful resolution of post-war tensions. He was pleased that Mussolini moved troops to the Austro-Italian border to warn Germany of Italian support for Austrian independence. Equally Neville welcomed the swing of opinion that this episode was likely to produce in favour of rearmament. More for the air force, however, than for army or navy; the main need for increased naval spending had to do with the Pacific, and Neville thought that this theatre could best be handled by improving relations with Japan. He expected no real help here from the United States, and remarked with foresight that, 'We ought to know by this time that U.S.A. will give us no undertaking to resist by force any action by Japan short of an attack on Hawaii or Honolulu.'[43]

Neville's stiffening stance on defence made it likely that his next Budget would not receive as cordial a reception as his last. His sisters welcomed his opinion that Germany was not ready for war. But he insisted that 'our information shows that she is arming and training as fast as she can ... Whatever happens we shall have to spend large sums on defence.'[44] His budgetary anxieties were deepened in the New Year by Roosevelt's 'spectacular pronouncement' of the second instalment of his New Deal. It provided deficit financing for public relief projects and as well as social insurance for unemployment, illness and old age. These measures emboldened Neville's critics. Lloyd George led the critical chorus; but it extended to the Conservative back benches and even produced 'faint hearts among the brethren in the Cabinet'.[45] Austen defended his brother's management of the economy and rejected Lloyd George's alternative of a New Deal for Britain. Nevertheless, anxiety about Britain's international position prompted Austen to look to Churchill for support. He welcomed Churchill's signature on a letter to the Prime Minister calling for an enquiry into British defences against night bombing.

The differences between the brothers disappeared when, in response to the rearmament of Germany and at Neville's prompting, the government paved the way for increased expenditure on defence. The need for this step was only accentuated when Hitler reacted by cancelling a visit to Berlin from the British Foreign

43 Neville to Hilda, 28 July 1934, Westbourne, in Self, ed., *The Neville Chamberlain Diary Letters*, IV, 81–3

44 Neville to Ida, 4 Aug.1934, Perthshire, in Self, ed., *The Neville Chamberlain Diary Letters*, IV, 85

45 Neville to Ida, 6 Jan.1935, in Self, ed., *The Neville Chamberlain Diary Letters*, IV, 110

Secretary and announced the creation of an army of half a million in defiance of the Versailles settlement. In the ensuing parliamentary debate, the most effective speech in the government's support came from Austen. Neville described it to Ida as 'a clear and courageous exposition of sound policy'.[46] She shared Neville's delight. 'It is satisfactory to see you & him taking it turn & turn about in the House, & I swell with sisterly pride.'[47] She reinforced their solidarity: 'In negotiating with Germany there is no finality & the more you give the more she claims.'[48] Austen said the same: 'To a people who believe in nothing but force, force is the only answer.'[49]

This familial solidarity withstood a pair of developments that might easily have shaken it. In May 1935 Mussolini called for a conquest of Abyssinia. In doing so, he violated a friendship that Austen valued and placed the National Government in a quandary over how to maintain international order. At the same time the leadership of the government passed from MacDonald to Baldwin. That change might have jeopardised Neville's position. There was talk of moving Simon from the Foreign Office to the Leadership of the House of Commons. But Baldwin became Leader of the Commons as well as Prime Minister. Simon moved to the Home Office, making room at the Foreign Office for Neville's Conservative friend, Samuel Hoare, in whom Austen too had considerable confidence. Neville remained the moving spirit of the ministry. And the direction in which he moved cemented his agreement with Austen by placing rearmament at the centre of the National Government's appeal in the run-up to a general election.

Austen and Neville spoke in identical terms to condemn Mussolini's 'determination to have a quarrel with Abyssinia'.[50] Neville feared that Mussolini's insistence on conquest would 'render him useless as an ally against Germany' and thus undermine the whole point of the friendship that Austen had cultivated with Italy. The question now was how Germany would react. Here the brothers began to divide. Neville was 'intensely relieved' by Hitler's response. Austen was more cautious, accepting the response as 'good in parts' but in need of 'very careful examination'.[51]

46  Neville to Ida, 16 Mar.1935, Westbourne, in Self, ed., *The Neville Chamberlain Diary Letters*, IV, 121
47  Ida to Neville, 15 Mar.1935, The Bury House, NC18/2/919
48  Ida to Neville, 3 May 1935, The Bury House, NC18/2/926
49  Austen to Hilda, 5 May 1935, Exeter, in Self, ed., *The Austen Chamberlain Diary Letters*, 482
50  Austen to Hilda, 18 May 1935, 58 Rutland Gate, in Self, ed., *The Austen Chamberlain Diary Letters*, 482
51  Austen to Ida, 25 May 1935, 58 Rutland Gate, in Self, ed., *The Austen Chamberlain Diary Letters*, 483, & Neville to Hilda, 26 May 1935, Westbourne, in Self, ed., *The Neville Chamberlain Diary Letters*, IV, 137

For while Hitler defended Germany's rearmament in defiance of the Treaty of Versailles, he proposed expanding the German navy to no more than thirty-five per cent of the British. Neville regarded the proposal as 'a definite détente', though he recognised that Hitler had 'laid himself out to catch British public opinion and if possible to drive a wedge between us and France'.[52] The thirty-five per cent offer provided the basis for a naval agreement which Britain and Germany proceeded to reach. Neville grossly exaggerated the worth of the agreement which he interpreted as giving 'us the control of their Navy'.[53]

He was less confident about the Abyssinian affair, which went 'from bad to worse'.[54] Neville reinforced the desire of the British government to work with France and other powers to curb, if not to prevent, the Italian assault on Abyssinia. He and his colleagues were willing to use all means short of war, including economic sanctions. They would even threaten war, though only if a grand alliance, including Germany and the United States as well as France, backed them up. This threat was therefore empty because the British knew that Germany and the United States would not join them, nor would France do anything that might push Italy into the arms of Germany. Neville and Austen met before the House of Commons debated the Italian threat to Abyssinia, and found themselves 'in very close agreement'. Neville dismissed Austen's willingness to 'go to war with Italy if others will do so' as 'Quixotic', but was no more willing than Austen to face up to the dilemma.[55] Even so, he took the weakness of the British position to heart, and it steeled his resolve 'to fight the election on a defence programme'.[56] He won an endorsement of sorts from the Prime Minister, the Cabinet and the Conservative party conference for such a programme. Then he proclaimed it from the electoral housetops. His only dismay was to see how eagerly Churchill joined the campaign.

The general election drew the Chamberlain brothers back to the city of their birth. The newfound respect that Austen won as an elder statesman induced him to stand one last time for re-election. Ida and Hilda resented Neville's position in the

---

52  Neville to Hilda, 26 May 1935, Westbourne, in Self, ed., *The Neville Chamberlain Diary Letters*, IV, 137
53  Neville to Hilda, 22 June 1935, Westbourne, in Self, ed., *The Neville Chamberlain Diary Letters*, IV, 141
54  Neville to Ida, 6 July 1935, Westbourne, in Self, ed., *The Neville Chamberlain Diary Letters*, IV, 143
55  Neville to Hilda, 14 July 1935, 37 Eaton Square, in Self, ed., *The Neville Chamberlain Diary Letters*, IV, 144–5
56  Neville to Hilda, 7 Sept.1935, Aberdeenshire, in Self, ed., *The Neville Chamberlain Diary Letters.*, IV, 151

National Government as hewer of wood and drawer of water for Baldwin. But Neville felt 'bound to recognise that if I supply the policy and the drive S.B. does also supply something that is perhaps even more valuable in retaining the floating vote'. Neville appreciated that 'it will be the non-party men & women who will decide the nature of the Governments'.[57] Hilda was reluctant to accept this reading of the electorate, and again cautioned Neville by reciting a verse from the family litany: 'It is like Papa over again; – your colleagues all know that you are the moving spirit, & somehow the public gets an inkling of it, – but still the solid forces of conservatism stick to the mediocre in which they see their salvation.'[58] Grateful for her reaction, Neville noted how Baldwin 'supplied to this election neither policy, nor drive, nor fight, and doesn't see ... why he shouldn't accept the result as a purely personal triumph.'[59]

The National Government indeed triumphed. The majority it won in the House of Commons was not quite on the scale of 1931 but still handsome, and again included all the seats for Birmingham. Baldwin kept Neville as Chancellor and conferred upon him another benefit to which the Chamberlains were sensitive. Now that Baldwin had replaced MacDonald at 10 Downing Street, Neville moved into Number 11. Even so, he was not sure that he would ever move into Number 10. Baldwin intended to remain Prime Minister for another two years, until he turned seventy, and he was just three years older than Neville. The next general election would be due in 1940, when Neville would himself be seventy. He wondered whether at that age he would 'care much ... for the strenuous life of leader even if some one else hasn't overtaken me before then'.[60]

&.

The outcome of the election confirmed Neville in his belief that 'the deciding factor was the unattached vote.'[61] He did not dwell on the contribution he made by placing national defence at the centre of his appeal to the electorate. But the importance of that contribution became apparent immediately afterwards when

57  Neville to Hilda, 9–10 Nov.1935, Westbourne, in Self, ed., *The Neville Chamberlain Diary Letters*, IV, 159
58  Hilda to Neville, 22 Nov.1935, The Bury House, NC18/2/949
59  Neville to Ida, 17 Nov.1935, Sevenoaks, in Self, ed., *The Neville Chamberlain Diary Letters*, IV, 160
60  Neville to Ida, 8 Dec.1935, 37 Eaton Square, in Self, ed., *The Neville Chamberlain Diary Letters*, IV, 165
61  Neville to Hilda, 23 Nov.1935, 37 Eaton Square, in Self, ed., *The Neville Chamberlain Diary Letters*, IV, 163

it was torpedoed by an agreement that Hoare as Foreign Secretary reached with his French counterpart, Laval, to settle the conflict in Abyssinia. Before the election Hoare publicly complemented Neville's demand for strengthened defence by committing Britain over Abyssinia to 'collective resistance to all acts of unprovoked aggression'. No sooner was the general election over than Hoare concluded a secret agreement with Laval to bring the war to an end by surrendering Abyssinia to Italian control. The agreement was leaked to the French press.

Neville was horrified. He was already embarrassed by Britain's inability to take a stronger stand on Abyssinia. 'If only our defences were stronger I should feel so much happier but though we are working night & day they aren't what I should like.'[62] He was afraid meanwhile that extension of the economic sanctions against Italy to oil might prompt Italy to take advantage of the weakness of Britain's forces in the Mediterranean and attack them. When Hoare left for Geneva by way of Paris, Neville thought that his purpose was to persuade the League of Nations not to impose 'a particularly provocative extra sanction at this moment'. Hoare was not authorised to discuss peace proposals with the French, let alone conclude an agreement. 'Our whole prestige in foreign affairs at home and abroad has tumbled to pieces like a house of cards,' Neville moaned. 'If we had to fight the election over again we should probably be beaten & certainly would not have more than a bare majority.' He laid some of the blame on Baldwin for lax supervision of the Cabinet and resolved, if he ever became Prime Minister, to oversee the conduct of foreign affairs vigilantly.

Baldwin's efforts to reduce the damage to his government only made matters worse from the Chamberlains' point of view. Recognising that Hoare must resign, Baldwin asked Austen for advice on replacing him. He knew quite well that Austen had hoped to return to the Foreign Office when the National Government was formed and had been disappointed when that hope was repeatedly dashed. The way in which Baldwin discussed the appointment of a new Foreign Secretary with Austen only poured salt into the old wounds, as he reported bitterly to Neville. Baldwin said that he 'would have "loved" to offer the post to me but felt that at my age I could not last out a Parlt. & that no one would consider my appointment as more than a stopgap. He ... said that men often failed to recognise when their powers failed, illustrating this danger by the example of Ramsay MacDonald whom he had had to "carry" for two years &c. Having thus made clear that in his opinion I was not fit, he asked what I thought about it. I replied: "if that is your opinion, it is conclusive." He then asked my opinion about Eden's fitness.' When

---

62 Neville to Ida, 8 Dec.1935, 37 Eaton Square, in Self, ed., *The Neville Chamberlain Diary Letters*, IV, 165

Austen spoke well of Eden, Baldwin 'thanked me & I withdrew'. Austen closed this report by recalling Queen Victoria's famous remark: '"We were not amused".'[63]

Baldwin tried to repair the damage next day. He told Austen that he had 'done another "24 hours hard thinking"' – which 'must be an unusual task for him,' said Austen. Having asked Eden to be Foreign Secretary, Baldwin 'asked me to "render another great public service" by joining the Cabinet as Minister of State i.e. without a department. My experience would be useful in foreign affairs & in the great & urgent questions of defence.' No questions interested Austen more than these. But Baldwin spoke again 'of the uselessness of Ramsay MacDonald, of his inability to make up his mind on any subject, of the tragic spectacle offered by a man whose faculties it was evident to everyone except himself had failed'. When Austen asked diffidently about the salary for the proffered Ministry of State, Baldwin suggested £3000, forcing Austen to refer to his financial necessities; and only then did Baldwin agree to the £5000 customary for statesmen of Austen's stature.

Austen declined to answer Baldwin straightaway. 'I already knew my own mind, but I put the proposal to Ivy ... as objectively as I could, & she at once said she thought I should refuse'; whereupon he did so. 'After he had taken such pains to explain & emphasise that he thought me physically unfit for hard work & that he feared I may become as much of an incubus as MacDonald, I could only infer that what he really wanted was not my experience or my advice but the use of my name to patch up the damaged reputation of the Govt.' Baldwin made acceptance 'impossible for a man with any self-respect'.[64] Austen had accepted Baldwin's replacement of MacDonald as Prime Minister without demur. He also recognised the debt that the National Government owed Baldwin for its resounding re-election. But Baldwin's behaviour this time wounded Austen beyond forgiveness. He hissed a denunciation of Baldwin 'as self-centred, selfish & idle, yet one of the shrewdest not to say slyest of politicians but without a constructive idea in his head'.[65]

Recoiling, Austen looked for statesmen with constructive ideas. For most purposes that meant Neville, whom he longed to see as Prime Minister. But to strengthen Britain's military defences, Austen turned to Churchill. While there is no reflection in the family correspondence of Austen's alleged assertion that Neville did not know anything about foreign policy, Austen clearly believed that

---

63  Austen to Neville, 20 Dec.1935, The Goring Hotel, Belgravia, 'Secret', NC1/27/124
64  Austen to Hilda, 22 Dec.1935, Goring Hotel, in Self, ed., *The Austen Chamberlain Diary Letters*, 495–7
65  Austen to Ida, 28 Dec.1935, Polesden Lacey, in Self, ed., *The Austen Chamberlain Diary Letters*, 497

Neville lacked adequate appreciation of Britain's needs in defence. Neville was not the only one in the family who disagreed strongly. When Winston's son Randolph spoke out to reinforce his father, Ida exclaimed, 'How extraordinarily true to type that family remains. Here is the third generation, equally clever, equally bumptious, equally bent on getting into the limelight. They all admire each other & fail to see how much more they would achieve in the world if only they had principles to which they would stick or could subordinate self a little more.'[66]

Ida's voice rings through with particular force at this time because she began to record the family conversation. In February 1936 she came down with a chill which turned serious. The doctor warned that 'if she goes on it would mean a stroke, & therefore she must not put in so much work in future'. Hilda feared that the injunction meant 'stepping out of a good deal' in which they were keenly interested and would force them to 'remake our lives on rather different lines'.[67] They did not want to do so. Hilda had at last become national Treasurer of the Women's Institutes. Ida dreaded departure from 'the seats of the Mighty' in the Hampshire County Council: 'I hate the idea of having to scramble for a seat with the common herd!'[68] Unable to contemplate complete idleness, she resolved to keep 'some sort of diary'. She intended to record 'the everyday happenings of country life'.[69] But what she actually wrote about was her family communications.

The day after the diary began, Ida and Hilda received 'Letters from Austen & Neville, both referring to the debate [in the Commons] ... on the necessity for the coordination of the Defence Forces, & Austen's very weighty criticism of the PM's action, or rather want of action, in the past'.[70] Austen seized upon a motion for the creation of a Ministry of Defence to shake the Prime Minister 'out of his self-complacency'. Austen wanted to do more than deflate the Prime Minister. The humiliating treatment he received from Baldwin drove Austen to Churchill: 'In my view,' he wrote to Hilda, 'there is only one man who by his studies & his special abilities & aptitudes is marked out for [the Ministry of Defence], & that man is Winston Churchill. I don't suppose that S.B. will offer it to him & I don't think that Neville would wish to have him back, but they are both wrong. He is the right man for that post & in such dangerous times that consideration ought to be decisive.'[71]

66  Ida to Neville, 17 Jan.1936, The Bury House, NC18/2/954
67  Hilda to Neville, 8 Feb.1936, The Bury House, NC18/2/958
68  Ida to Neville, 28 Feb.1936, The Bury House, NC18/2/960
69  Diary entry for Sunday, 16 Feb.1936, BC5/16
70  Diary entry for 17 Feb.1936, BC5/16
71  Austen to Hilda, 15 Feb.1936, Goring Hotel, in Self, ed., *The Austen Chamberlain Diary*

Since the general election Neville had kept 'very busy over defence'. But his efforts were frustrated by Baldwin's endless foot-dragging. Neville tried to convince himself that, 'By continually bringing up the subject again I am making some progress and I don't despair of getting something done'. He particularly wanted a strong air force: 'if we can keep out of war for a few years we shall have an air force of such striking power that no one will care to run risks with it.'[72] At the same time he appreciated the need for a Ministry of Defence to coordinate the armed forces. The person Neville had in mind for the post was the fallen Foreign Secretary Samuel Hoare, whose abilities Neville still rated highly. He pressed Baldwin to place Hoare in charge of a preliminary 'enquiry into our present methods of coordination', hoping that, 'if, as I expected, there emerged from the enquiry a proposal for ... a Minister of Defence, Sam would naturally fall into that place. Of course that was moving much too fast for S.B. who delayed & did nothing but talk it over ... I then suggested Austen to take the enquiry ... S.B. liked this idea ... but still it got no further.'[73]

At that point, unaware of Neville's efforts, Austen launched his assault in the Commons on Baldwin's inertia. While he was speaking, Baldwin muttered to Neville, 'This is an unexpected attack.' It eliminated the selection of Austen to lead the defence enquiry. Baldwin continued to drag his feet. But at last Neville secured Cabinet approval for proposals on defence; and they won a blessing from Austen. The urgent thing now was to choose a Minister of Defence to implement them. Both brothers were considered for the position. But neither wanted it for himself or for the other. Austen urged Neville to stick to the Exchequer: 'work at the Exchequer is going to become not less, but more, important, and more difficult, by reason of the new [defence] programme'. He added less tactfully that the public 'never associated you with Defence' and 'know nothing of your active interest in that matter'.[74] Neville was similarly reluctant to see Austen take on the Ministry of Defence. 'He has such a wonderful position now that I don't much want to see him descend into the arena, and I believe he is more valuable to the country as an independent critic who can accord or withhold his approval with overpowering effect.'[75]

The brothers spent a weekend amid these discussions in markedly different

---

*Letters*, 499.

72  Neville to Hilda, 9 Feb.1936, 11 Downing Street, in Self, ed., *The Neville Chamberlain Diary Letters*, IV, 175

73  Neville to Ida, 16 Feb.1936, Westbourne, in Self, ed., *The Neville Chamberlain Diary Letters*, IV, 176–7

74  Austen to Neville, 18 Feb.1936, The Goring Hotel, 'Strictly Personal', NC1/27/125

75  Neville to Ida, 16 Feb.1936, Westbourne, in Self, ed., *The Neville Chamberlain Diary Letters*, IV, 176–7

settings. Neville drove down to the Bury House, where he talked to his sisters about 'armaments & defence. He thinks', Ida recorded, that 'the next war will be decided mainly in the air & that our object should be to have a "striking" air force, formidable enough to enable us to attack Berlin with as much ease as the Germans could attack London. The knowledge that we had such a force would act as a more powerful deterrent to Germany than anything else & would be more likely to lead them to consent to limitations of armaments.' Neville explained that he put up with Baldwin's listless leadership because the Prime Minister 'consults him much more than he did & treats him much more openly than he did as his second in command & probable successor'. But the sisters had doubts about Baldwin's intentions. In Ida's eyes, because Baldwin 'still talks of resigning only in "about two years" it seems more than doubtful as to whether N. will ever actually be P.M.'[76]

Austen meanwhile spent the weekend with Churchill at Chartwell. 'It is a man's party', Austen explained to his sisters, full of Churchill's friends and associates. 'Is it a Cave?' Austen asked, a gathering of the discontented? 'Well some would like to make it so, but I am not a cave man.' Austen's recent attack on Baldwin had, he hoped, achieved its purpose: 'now I mean to lie low for a time & give the Govt a fair chance to do what urgently needs doing. ... next year will be a dangerous one for Europe'. Austen wanted the government to act urgently on defence. But he feared that Baldwin would 'not follow things up. ... We were a merry party last night & the talk was good. There were almost as many opinions as men, but on one thing we were all agreed – that Germany was a danger, the one danger that might be fatal to us, & that that danger had been too long neglected.'[77]

On one point Austen proved wrong. The time of danger for Europe lay not a year but less than a month away. On March 7th Ida heard on the wireless 'that Hitler had denounced the Locarno agreement ... marched his troops into the de-militarized zone, & at the same time announced his willingness to make a non aggression pact for 25 years with France & Belgium, re-enter the League of Nations & negotiate for a limitation of air armaments'.[78] Hitler's diplomatic gestures clouded the significance of the reoccupation of the Rhineland and produced a mixed response even among knowledgeable observers.

Each of the Chamberlains responded differently. Ida oscillated between consternation at the German action and fear of the French reaction, before she hardened

76  Diary entry for 23 Feb.1936, BC5/16
77  Austen to Ida, 23 February 1936, Chartwell, in Self, ed., *The Austen Chamberlain Diary Letters*, 500
78  Diary entry for 7 Mar.1936, BC5/16

against Germany. Hilda balanced these concerns. 'I suppose the French will be extremely difficult,' she wrote; but 'their intense nervousness & suspicion' was 'only too well justified by the past & by the words & actions of Goebbels & Co'.[79] Austen came down firmly on the side of France. Neville 'contrive[d] to remain not too pessimistic & still hopes that Hitler may make some advance which will render negotiations possible'.[80] He clung to the belief that 'Hitler really, himself, wishes for peace'. All the Chamberlains agreed that the aggressiveness of the German government did not emanate from Hitler. Even Austen regarded him as a centrist who nevertheless made the critical decisions in Germany. On this occasion, Austen believed that Hitler had acted 'against the advice of the more moderate elements in his Govt' and '... marched into the Rhineland to escape from an internal crisis urged on by Goering & Goebbels'.[81]

Germany's reoccupation of the Rhineland cracked the consensus that had grown up among the Chamberlains on overseas policy over the past year. They differed less on the way to handle the Germans than over defence. Lining himself up ever more closely with Churchill, Austen reacted contemptuously to Baldwin's choice of the Attorney-General, Sir Thomas Inskip, 'a man with no experience in administration who has never given a thought to problems of defence, as the new Minister' of Defence. Austen felt 'driven into opposition or nearly so', and blamed Baldwin for the appointment. But Baldwin in fact acted on Neville's advice. Shaken by Hoare's repeated ineptitude in debate, Neville abandoned him as a candidate for the new ministry, and proposed Inskip as someone who, though not ideal, was 'strong & sound and will make no friction with either the Chiefs of Staff or the Service Ministers'. That was scarcely a ringing endorsement. Neville admitted to his sisters that he wanted to keep Churchill out. Churchill was, he said, 'in the usual excited condition that comes on him when he smells war, and if he were in the Cabinet we should be spending all our time in holding him down instead of getting on with our business.' [82]

Neville was not bothered by Inskip's inadequacy because he was himself assuming the formative role in defence and foreign as well as domestic policy. Austen welcomed his brother's ascent 'into the light as the dominating mind of the government

---

79 Hilda to Neville, 3 Apr.1936, The Bury House, NC18/2/965
80 Diary entry for 1 Apr.1936, BC5/16
81 Austen to Hilda, 15 Mar.1936, Goring Hotel, in Self, ed., *The Austen Chamberlain Diary Letters*, 502–3
82 Neville to Ida, 14 Mar.1936, 11 Downing Street, in Self, ed., *The Neville Chamberlain Diary Letters*, IV, 179–180

& the only possible successor to Baldwin'.[83] Neville won Cabinet approval for an agreement with Germany that 'avoided all sanctions, military or otherwise, and rather limited than extended our commitments under Locarno'.[84] Austen was pleased that 'the net result ... is to throw us more & more back on the essence of the Locarno policy – a definite guarantee of peace in the area where we are vitally interested & the restriction of our obligations elsewhere'. Meanwhile he was content to retain the position where Neville hoped he would stay, saying what 'needs saying & can be better said by one like me who will never again hold office with a freedom & plainness that Ministers & potential ministers would be unwise to use'.

Surprisingly, this stance enabled Austen to be more outspoken than Churchill. Anxious to get back into office, Churchill supported the government 'handsomely' over its handling of the reoccupation of the Rhineland. Neville dismissed his 'unexpected friendliness to the Government' as evidence that Churchill was 'playing up for another chance with another P.M.'.[85] Neville kept to his chosen path, paying for rearmament as far as the canons of responsible finance would allow. He funded this expenditure with the taxes on income and tea when most people expected him to get 'some of the money for armaments by way of loan'. He insisted that 'even when we have brought our forces up to date we shall have to spend more to keep them up & that therefore the time for a loan has not come yet'.[86]

The Chamberlains had other things beside politics on their minds. The financial position of the entire family was threatened by the poor performance of Hoskins. Austen was already in trouble and had told Neville that his financial position was 'desperate. Nearly all my capital has gone ... we shall have to change our whole way of life, let or dispose of this house & move into something – flat or house – much smaller. ... It is a sorry story & I am much to blame for not having faced the facts earlier.'[87] Hoskins was supposed to provide the family with supplementary, if not indeed basic, income. The steep losses at Hoskins had little impact on Ida and Hilda who were 'still fortunate enough to be able by the exercise of a little care to live within our income'.[88] But Neville and Mary were hit hard. And Austen, now

83  Austen to Hilda, 28 Mar.1936, Goring Hotel, in Self, ed., *The Austen Chamberlain Diary Letters*, 503

84  Neville to Hilda, 21 Mar.1936, 11 Downing Street, in Self, ed., *The Neville Chamberlain Diary Letters*, IV, 181

85  Neville to Ida, 28 Mar.1936, Westbourne, in Self, ed., *The Neville Chamberlain Diary Letters*, IV, 182–3

86  Diary entry for 22 Apr.1936, BC5/16

87  Austen to Neville, 13 Jan.1935, 58 Rutland Gate, 'Personal', NC1/27/120

88  Ida to Neville, 11 Sept.1936, The Bury House, NC18/2/987

living in a hotel, was hit hardest. 'Hoskins is the last straw to me,' he cried. 'I may have to leave Parlt.'[89]

His anxiety about the deteriorating situation abroad nevertheless overrode his financial concerns, and he remained in the Commons. He used his place there with some effect when the Italians overran Abyssinia. Their conquest induced him to advocate abandonment of the economic sanctions against Italy 'on the ground that their maintenance could in no way serve Abyssinia'. Ida knew that Austen had dined with Neville and Eden before he spoke; and she hoped 'that his outspoken declaration may strengthen their hands' and prepare 'the ground for subsequent acquiescence by the Govt in such a course'.[90] But Austen had not in fact discussed the subject with Eden and Neville beforehand, and his stance took them by surprise. Neville believed that 'public opinion here would be greatly shocked if we showed ourselves in too great a hurry to throw up the sponge'.[91] Austen accepted that assessment of the public mood. But still partial to Italy, he continued to insist that 'the only wise policy' was to call off the sanctions against Italy, unite the powers who were willing to stand up to the Germans '& then to try to come to terms with Germany if possible & to fortify peace against her if it is not'.[92]

It took Austen only a matter of weeks to bring Neville round. Then, in language more startling than Austen had employed, Neville publicly described the continuation of sanctions against Italy as 'the very midsummer of madness'. Austen kept up the pressure to accommodate Italy. He warned Neville that 'we are in danger of reaching a deadlock with Italy, Mussolini declaring that he could do nothing until sanctions are removed and we declaring that sanctions cannot be removed until he has given undertakings. Is not this a case for conversations through the ambassadors to try to find a way of making the two announcements simultaneously,' he asked.[93] Neville acted on his advice. The Cabinet fell into line. Mussolini cooperated, writing what Neville called 'a nice letter' to the League of Nations.[94] Neville followed it up with another increase in defence expenditure 'to fortify peace', as Austen put it, against Germany.

The accord with Italy narrowed but did not overcome the divergence in policy

---

89 Austen to Neville, 13 June 1936, Goring Hotel, 'Personal', NC1/27/126

90 Diary entry for 7 May 1936, BC5/16, and Ida to Neville, 8 May 1936, The Bury House, NC18/2/970

91 Neville to Ida, 10 May 1936, 11 Downing Street, in Self, ed., *The Neville Chamberlain Diary Letters*, IV, 191

92 Austen to Hilda, 10 May 1936, Hever Castle, Kent, in Self, ed., *The Austen Chamberlain Diary Letters*, 507

93 Austen to Neville, 13 June 1936, Goring Hotel, 'Personal', NC1/27/120

94 Neville to Annie, 18 June 1936, 11 Downing Street, NC1/26/518

between Austen and Neville which the reoccupation of the Rhineland had opened up. Neville feared that Austen was 'getting more and more tied up with Winston's crowd'.[95] Baldwin pushed him there, infuriating Austen as much by delay in making way for Neville as by differences on overseas policy. Neville felt the frustration: 'as I slave over my papers into the small hours I think a little bitterly of [Baldwin] snoozing comfortably away next door'.[96] Neville took comfort from his continued good health despite his multiple burdens as Chancellor and general workhorse of the government. But at the beginning of August his health gave way to 'a baddish bout' of gout: 'my doctor says the worst he has seen for years'. At the same time Annie took to her bed, 'exhausted by endless chores and worries'.[97] She refused, however, to stay there long enough to do her good. Nor did the August holiday bring either of them real recovery. Neville's gout flared up again in October: 'the foot is all swelled up and the colour of a Victoria plum and it will certainly take several days before I can walk on it'. He found it 'all very disappointing & disheartening', yet was reluctant to accept the doctor's 'short explanation' that he was exhausted. He wondered whether 'by the time S.B. makes up his mind that his King & Country can do without him there will be anything left of me except an enormous toe!'[98]

&

The only Chamberlain to enjoy good health that autumn was Austen. But the regrettable explanation was lack of work: 'Everyone seems to lead a busier life than I do at the present time.' Ida and Hilda were always at committees or meetings of some sort while 'I sit at home and read ... I have lunched out most days ... & generally [take] a short walk ... there is a picture of my life. News I have none & you must find Neville's letters nowadays much more nourishing than mine.'[99] He also found a way to ease his financial concerns. Again following Churchill's lead, he agreed to write books of reminiscence and 'gloomy articles on the state of Europe' for the

---

95  Neville to Ida, 4 July 1936, Westbourne, in Self, ed., *The Neville Chamberlain Diary Letters*, IV, 199

96  Neville to Hilda, 11 July 1936, 11 Downing Street, in Self, ed., *The Neville Chamberlain Diary Letters*, IV, 201

97  Neville to Ida, 2 Aug.1936, 11 Downing Street, in Self, ed., *The Neville Chamberlain Diary Letters*, IV, 204

98  Neville to Hilda, 14 Nov.1936, 11 Downing Street, in Self, ed., *The Neville Chamberlain Diary Letters*, IV, 218

99  Austen to Ida, 31 October 1936, Goring Hotel, in Self, ed., *The Austen Chamberlain Diary Letters*, 511–2

*Daily Telegraph*. The resulting income enabled Ivy to look for a proper home in London: 'she wants a three storey house that can be run by four servants, & it must have a good third sitting room for Austen & be near the Tube so that he can get easily to the House'.[100] They found what they wanted on Egerton Terrace, 'the old neighbourhood',[101] down the street from Beatrice's former house.

Austen and Ivy were preparing to move and Neville was down with gout when the first hint of scandal touching the new King Edward VIII reached the governing elite. Neville heard, as so often, before the Prime Minister; and the news added another twist to the delayed transfer of power between them. Baldwin wanted to preside over the scheduled springtime coronation. But that plan 'may not pan out as he thinks,' Neville confided contentedly to his sisters, 'for tomorrow morning he will hear that a certain Lady (who shall be nameless except that her initials are Mrs S – n) intends on *Friday next* to begin proceedings for the purpose of obtaining a divorce from her husband. S.B. will be informed that the most alarming consequences would or might ensue & that it is his duty to stop it.'[102] The news reached Austen two weeks later. Neville assured him that Baldwin 'had done his duty as P.M. in warning the Monarch of the risks he was running'. Mrs Simpson had by now received her divorce. Neville thought that she and Edward understood that the divorce did 'not remove obstacles to a regularisation' of their relationship.[103] But he was mistaken, and they pushed ahead. Neville feared that 'at any time there may be an explosion of feeling. ... The difficulty, as usual, is to get the P.M. to make a move'.[104]

The task was complicated by Neville's nemesis. Churchill championed the cause of the King. Austen believed that Churchill was 'moved solely by his affection for the King & his innate chivalry'.[105] Neville knew better. 'Winston', as he told Hilda, '... had gorgeous visions of a clash between the Sovereign & his Cabinet, the resignation of Ministers, general consternation and then in a flash of glory a champion stepping forth to defend his King in shining armour. I am told he had gone a long way in the formation of his Cabinet.'[106] Churchill's intervention heightened the

---

100  Diary entry for 25 July 1936, BC5/16
101  Ida to Neville, 24 Sept.1936, The Bury House, NC18/2/989
102  Neville to Hilda, 17 Oct.1936, *loc.cit.*
103  Neville to Hilda, 31 Oct.1936, Westbourne, in Self, ed., *The Neville Chamberlain Diary Letters*, IV, 216
104  Neville to Hilda, 14 Nov.1936, 11 Downing Street, in Self, ed., *The Neville Chamberlain Diary Letters*, IV, 220
105  Austen to Hilda, 6 Dec.1936, Goring Hotel, in Self, ed., *The Austen Chamberlain Diary Letters*, 515
106  These were Neville's rueful words which Baldwin indeed acted upon. Neville to Hilda, 13

drama. But the public response was not what Churchill desired. Hilda voiced a common reaction: 'it has finally damned Winston in my eyes'.[107] Still it was Baldwin, not Neville, who 'reaped a rich harvest of credit' from the abdication crisis, and it fortified his resolve to remain in office until the coronation, this time of George VI.

Churchill's response to the abdication crisis had more serious consequences because it compromised Britain's international position, particularly with regard to defence. His judgement lay badly damaged, and his cries of alarm about German rearmament were discredited, not least in Neville's estimation. Neville developed an alternative assessment of Britain's needs, one that questioned the need for all-out rearmament and accentuated its industrial cost. 'If the menace of attack from Germany is as imminent as Winston would have us believe,' he argued, 'there is nothing we could do which would make us ready to meet it. But I do not believe that it *is* imminent. By careful diplomacy I believe we can stave it off, perhaps indefinitely, but if we were now to follow Winston's advice and sacrifice our commerce to the manufacture of arms we should inflict a certain injury upon our trade from which it would take generations to recover.'

Even so, Neville did not rely simply on 'careful diplomacy' and maintenance of a strong economy to save Britain from German aggression. For the past two years he had done his best to strengthen Britain's armed forces. But his efforts were endlessly impeded by the procrastination of the Prime Minister. Neville could press his colleagues to do as he wished, but he could not insist upon it. He told Inskip 'that I must have an early decision as to the future of the army & the Territorials and I have told him what in my view that decision should be'. But he could only hope 'that there won't be any further delay'.[108]

The New Year nevertheless found all the Chamberlains in good heart. Austen and Ivy settled happily into their new home. Neville returned from a much-needed holiday in better health. Though never in as straightened financial circumstances as Austen, he had been living beyond his income for a long time. But in mid-February George Kenrick, Neville's now octogenarian uncle, gave him another large portion of the wealth that he would otherwise inherit. Neville poured out his thanks in large capital letters for the old man to read: 'THE COMMUNICATION YOU MADE TO ME ON SATURDAY WAS SO UNEXPECTED THAT I HAVE ONLY GRADUALLY BEGUN TO APPRECIATE WHAT IT MEANS TO ME, BUT SINCE THEN I HAVE

---

Dec.1936, Westbourne, in Self, ed., *The Neville Chamberlain Diary Letters*, IV, 229
107  Hilda to Neville, 11 Dec.1936, The Bury House, NC18/2/1000
108  Neville to Ida, 10 Oct. & 14 Nov. 1936, 11 Downing Street, in Self, ed., *The Neville Chamberlain Diary Letters*, IV, 211 & 220

FELT AN EASE OF MIND THAT I HAVEN'T KNOWN FOR YEARS. ... I COULD HAVE
GONE ON LIVING ON MY CAPITAL FOR A LONG TIME. BUT THERE HAS ALWAYS
BEEN AN ANXIETY ABOUT THE FUTURE WHICH HAS MADE ME UNCOMFORT-
ABLE OVER EVERY ITEM OF EXPENDITURE AND HAS HUNG OVER ME LIKE A
SHADOW. ... WHEN I LOOK BACK OVER MY LIFE, I AM ASTONISHED TO THINK
HOW MUCH OF THE BEST OF IT I OWE TO YOU. ... IN ENTOMOLOGISING,
IN SPORT, IN GAMES, AMONG FLOWERS AND IN CONVERSATION YOU HAVE
SHARED AND ENCOURAGED MY TASTES AND YOU HAVE TREATED ME MORE
LIKE A YOUNGER BROTHER THAN A NEPHEW.'[109]

Meanwhile Neville took his unsettled political situation in hand. Baldwin had 'not said a word' to Neville but had intimated to others that he intended to resign as soon as the coronation was over. That enabled Neville to open discussions on the succession with the Chief Whip. Together they agreed 'that May 27 would be a suitable date for the change'. Neville then turned his attention 'to the various consequential decisions which will really have to be arrived at before that date'. He did not mind that Baldwin wanted to stay in 10 Downing Street until the summer's end. 'This would really suit us very well,' said Neville, 'as it would ... avoid the tiresome move in the middle of the session.'[110]

Rearmament remained his highest priority. At last he secured 'a decision about the Army [which] practically gives me all I want'. The Regular Army would be fitted out fully 'with the most modern equipment ... ready to go anywhere at any time'. The Territorials, on the other hand, would be equipped 'only in sufficient quantity to enable them to train'. Two Divisions of Territorials would be ready 'to go out and reinforce the Regulars in four months after the outbreak of war'.[111] Neville put together the necessary financing to spend £1500 million over the next five years on rearmament, including protection against air raids. He emphasised that these preparations 'were not directed against anyone in particular'. Europe was, he thought, 'a little less uneasy' than it had been after the reoccupation of the Rhineland. He wanted to confront the dictators, not with irritating words of defiance, but with 'a demonstration of strength and determination' that 'would bring about some hard thinking'.[112]

---

109  Neville to George Kenrick, 14 Feb.1937, 11 Downing Street, NC1/12/2
110  Neville to Ida, 16 Jan.1937, Westbourne, in Self, ed., *The Neville Chamberlain Diary Letters*, IV, 230
111  Neville to Ida, 6 Feb.1937, 11 Downing Street, in Self, ed., *The Neville Chamberlain Diary Letters*, IV, 233
112  Neville to Ida, 20 Feb.1937, 11 Downing Street, in Self, ed., *The Neville Chamberlain Diary Letters*, IV, 236

Austen admired his brother's stand. 'Neville spoke well this week,' he told his sisters in what proved to be his last letter.[113] Though at seventy-three Austen was the oldest of Joseph's surviving children, over the past few months he had shown few signs of the strain that dogged his years in office. He enjoyed his influence as an elder statesman and looked forward with confidence to his brother's appointment as Prime Minister. Austen's sudden death was, therefore, 'a great shock to us all', as Neville recorded for his son Frank: '…He had been in bed with lumbago and had a short attack of pain at the end of last week but he seemed much better and was in good spirits all yesterday till after tea. He then decided to get up and have a bath and in answer to Aunt Ivy called from his bath to say he was all right.' But while dressing, he suffered a heart attack 'and died almost immediately. … I wish he could have lived a few years longer to enjoy his new house and garden and great & unique position he had attained in the House and the country. But he was fortunate' – unlike his father – 'in passing away so quickly without knowing that the end was so near and we are fortunate in having had him with us so long.'[114]

His death hit Neville harder than this account suggested. He came down with 'one of the worst colds I have ever suffered from with a touch of lumbago into the bargain', followed by gout. He felt 'thoroughly good for nothing and shaken up. I am not a superstitious man,' he tried to convince himself, 'and indeed I should not greatly care if I were never to be P.M. But when I think of Father & Austen and reflect that less than 3 months of time and no individual stands between me and that office I wonder whether Fate has some dark secret in store to carry out her ironies to the end.'[115] Would he too fail to become Prime Minister? Neville was not afraid of what might befall him once in the highest office, able swiftly to implement the policies he deemed wise.

He treated the political legacy of his brother with fateful selectivity. Like Austen, in foreign affairs Neville preferred to work alone and rarely sought advice. He embraced Austen's policy of wooing Mussolini away from Hitler, and he built upon the pattern Austen had set at Locarno of depending upon personal negotiations with foreign counterparts to preserve the peace of Europe. Neville, however, misread Hitler even more egregiously than Austen had Mussolini. He adopted a weakened and distorted version of the policy Austen had initiated at Locarno of

---

113  Austen to Hilda, 7 Mar.1937, 24 Egerton Terrace, in Self, ed., *The Austen Chamberlain Diary Letters*, 518

114  Neville to Frank, 17 Mar.1937, 11 Downing Street, NC1/23/10

115  Neville to Ida, 21 Mar.1937, Westbourne, in Self, ed., *The Neville Chamberlain Diary Letters*, IV, 242

conciliating concessions to Germany. Neville was heavily preoccupied with the Germans without any of Austen's overriding concern for the French. And though insistent on rearmament to strengthen Britain's negotiating position vis-à-vis the Continental dictators, Neville never acquired Austen's concern of how armed force could override diplomacy. Nor would Neville ever acquire Austen's ability to admire brilliance in others that he did not possess himself.

Neville's fear of what fate might have in store for him had less to do with Churchill than with the financial package he introduced to pay for his build-up of the armed forces. The package included a tax on the profits that businessmen made from rearmament. Neville called it the National Defence Contribution or N.D.C. He considered it 'the bravest thing I have ever done in public life, for I have risked the Premiership just when it was about to fall into my hands'. The storm of abuse that the proposal aroused left him 'feeling a bit low and depressed'. Yet he remained 'supremely confident that it is right and that in the long run it will be generally recognised to have been wise and far sighted'. He put a good deal of thought into the proposal. 'Prices are bounding up now and as new factories come into operation built with the capital supplied by the Govt the profits are bound to increase rapidly ... All the elements of danger are here, increasing cost of living, jealousy of others profits, a genuine feeling that things are not fairly shared out ... we might easily run, in no time, into a series of crippling strikes, ruining our programme, a sharp steepening of costs due to wages increases, leading to the loss of our export trade', and eventually 'a crisis as severe as that of 1931. I don't say that N.D.C. will prevent all this but I feel sure that it enormously diminished the danger'.[116] He saw benefit even in the uproar his proposal provoked, for it would teach the armed forces that there were limits to what taxpayers would pay for rearmament.

The uproar continued past the coronation. But it did not cost Neville the premiership. 'Every now & then' Ida would 'wake up to the fact that the great moment is nearly here when my brother will actually be Prime Minister of England!' Neville felt 'just a little solemn' on his last day as Chancellor, 'conscious of the many troubles which, as my friends cheerfully assure me, are in waiting for me. Nevertheless I am in good health and good spirits, and not without confidence in my ability to discharge my task. The general situation is not bad & looks as if it might be made better. But above all just now I rejoice in the love & trust of my own family – what is left of them.'[117]

116  Neville to Hilda, 25 Apr.1937, 11 Downing Street, in Self, ed., *The Neville Chamberlain Diary Letters*, IV, 246–7
117  Neville to Mary, 27 May 1937, 11 Downing Street, NC1/20/1/175

*Ida and Hilda (in front) holidaying in Egypt*

# 10

# Munich

'So the great day has really come at last.' A little surprised as well as delighted at Neville's delayed attainment, Hilda embellished the family litany: 'You have had the handicap of Father & Austen before you ... both failing to reach the highest position largely owing to their loyalty & their total inability to fight for their own hand.'[1] That was a strange thing to say about Joseph who fought hard for the causes with which he identified himself. Neville put it better. He thought of his achievement as making 'amends to Father and Austen'. As Neville saw it, they failed to become Prime Minister because they were forced 'to choose between their natural ambition and their principles' whereas he was not. Even so, Neville was surprised at reaching the prize 'without my raising a finger to obtain it' and without even a 'breath or whisper of any rival'. He suggested that he gained it 'perhaps because' – unlike Churchill – 'I have not made enemies by looking after myself rather than the common cause'.[2]

Neville played down the determination with which he had sought the premiership ever since Baldwin replaced MacDonald as Prime Minister. Previously Neville had displayed little appetite for the position, his interest in it piqued mainly by desire to keep Churchill out. But Baldwin's refusal to give Britain vigorous leadership, particularly over rearmament, showed Neville what only a Prime Minister could do. He was impatient to take charge at the top. As Ida announced, 'The sleepy days of S.B. are over.'[3]

---

1 Hilda to Neville, 28 May 1937, The Bury House, NC18/2/1019
2 Neville to Hilda, 30 May 1937, 11 Downing Street, in Self, ed., *The Neville Chamberlain Diary Letters*, IV, 253
3 Ida to Mary, 31 July 1937, The Bury House, BC4/2/225

Over the next sixteen months, Neville proved himself very much his father's son. The startling thing about the Munich conference was the speed with which it took place. Aged sixty-eight when he became Prime Minister, Neville was 'an old man in a hurry'[4] in his search for peace, just as his father had been at the age of sixty-seven in his demand for imperial preference and tariff reform. No action that old Joe ever took was as daring as Neville's first flight to meet Hitler. Nor was old Joe more insistent on every feature of his demand for tariff reform than was Neville on his particular form of appeasement. His sisters, Hilda with particular enthusiasm, urged him on; and Austen was not there to hold him back. Ironically, the most serious difference between Joseph and Neville in their concluding missions was that Neville secured his immediate objective whereas Joseph did not.

❧

But he began his premiership hesitantly. His proposal as Chancellor to tax the profits businessmen made from rearmament went down badly in the City. He recognised on becoming Prime Minister that his government could be 'wrecked at the start either by pig-headed obstinacy or by too great haste to abandon a threatened position'. He resolved his dilemma by agreeing to accept any other way industry might prefer to pay for rearmament. And he emerged from his embarrassment 'with, if anything increased credit & popularity'. No one congratulated Ida on Neville's becoming 'Prime Minister without at the same time expressing their sense of the immense debt of gratitude the nation owes you for having saved our finances from ruin!'[5]

His reception in Birmingham took him back to the palmy days of his father. He was surprised by the crowds that greeted him there on his first appearance as Prime Minister, and thought 'at first there must be a cricket match going on ... It was a most touching experience to see all those ugly, honest faces shining with perspiration in the heat but positively beaming with pride & joy and to hear the shouts of Good Old Neville. ... It reminded me of old days when the people used to run after Father's carriage & cry "God bless you Joey". One woman yesterday would not let go my hand but kept on repeating Bless yer, Bless yer, my *darlin* Premier.'[6]

Another blessing accrued to Neville in his new office. Chequers, the country

---

4 Lord Randolph Churchill's famous phrase about Gladstone's demand at the age of seventy-seven for Home Rule

5 Ida to Neville, 18 June 1937, The Bury House, NC18/2/1024

6 Neville to Ida, 4 July 1937, Westbourne, in Self, ed., *The Neville Chamberlain Diary Letters*, IV, 257–8

residence for prime ministers, lay within easy reach of London. It was 'a perfect godsend' for Annie, with 'no household cares and no one to be responsible to and where she can just sink into bed and into oblivion till her weary mind and body recover themselves'. The grounds of Chequers gave Neville also things he loved. He came upon one of the biggest tulip trees in England, and 'an elm said to have been planted by King Stephen! ... also a large tree of a species quite unknown to me which I must find out about. This morning I walked up the hill behind the house and found an uncommon plant the Houndstongue (Cynoglossum). I believe it's also a good place for birds.'[7] So during his three years as Prime Minister it would often be from Chequers that he wrote his Sunday reports to his sisters.

Weekends at Chequers assumed ever greater importance for him in view of the mounting turbulence on the Continent. From the outset of his premiership the international scene proved far more troubling than the domestic. 'The Germans and Italians are as exasperating as they can be,' he lamented, 'and it is rather difficult to reconcile their professions of desire for our friendship with the incredible insolence and license of their press.' Nevertheless, he differentiated between the chauvinistic press in the two countries and their governments. Surely the heads of state were too rational to want war. Neville accordingly wanted to play for time, meanwhile rearming until Britain was in a position to reject unreasonable demands. 'I believe the double policy of rearmament & better relations with Germany & Italy will carry us safely through the danger period.'[8]

He also sought to avoid taking on both fascist powers at once. Following Austen's preference, he tackled Italy first, hoping to 'restore Anglo-Italian relations to what they were before the Abyssinian adventure. ... a very important step forward towards European appeasement'. He therefore favoured recognising the Italian conquest of Abyssinia 'while we can still get something in return for it'.[9] Grandi, the Italian ambassador, responded by flattering Neville's already exaggerated 'sense of the wonderful power that the Premiership gives you. As Ch. of Ex. I could hardly have moved a pebble; now I have only to raise a finger & the whole face of Europe is changed!'[10] Hilda fostered her brother's illusion: 'before long your position on the

---

7 Neville to Hilda, 26 June & 1 Aug.1937, Chequers, in Self, ed., *The Neville Chamberlain Diary Letters*, IV, 256 & 262

8 Neville to Hilda, 1 Aug.1937, Chequers, in Self, ed., *The Neville Chamberlain Diary Letters*, IV, 262

9 Neville to Hilda, 29 Aug.1937, Balmoral Castle, in Self, ed., *The Neville Chamberlain Diary Letters*, IV, 267

10 Neville to Ida, 8 Aug.1937, Lochmore, Scotland, in Self, ed., *The Neville Chamberlain Diary Letters*, IV, 265

Continent will be as good as any of the dictators ... they also appreciate the strong hand & the clear mind. Decision I believe, helps more than anything else in these foreign affairs, where it is so rare for any country to be able to stick to anything.'[11]

But Neville's courtship of the Italians ran into difficulties. At first they came from the Foreign Office, which persisted to his dismay 'in seeing Musso only as a sort of Machiavelli putting on a false mask of friendship in order to further nefarious ambitions'. Furthermore Eden, who remained Foreign Secretary, 'never really believed in Musso's sincerity'. Neville insisted that, 'If we treat [Mussolini] like that we shall get nowhere with him and we shall have to pay for our mistrust by appallingly costly defences in the Mediterranean.' The Italians shook but did not shatter Neville's faith in his 'détente with Italy' by involving themselves in the Spanish civil war. Thereafter Spain remained 'a constant source of anxiety' to him: 'we have still to see whether Mussolini will be ready to agree to the withdrawal of any of his "volunteers".'[12]

The close supervision that Neville exercised over foreign as well as domestic policy took its toll on him. His doctor tried vainly to dissuade him from speaking to the party conference in October. Digestive trouble – was it the first hint of the colon cancer that eventually killed him? – gave Neville a night of nausea followed by a headache and repugnance at food. He took aspirin before his address, and his headache wore off as he spoke. But two weeks later he fell victim to his old enemy, gout, and found it hard either to work or sleep. In these circumstances he could not always keep his eye on the Foreign Office. Nevertheless, he continued to elaborate 'far reaching plans ... for the appeasement of Europe & Asia and for the ultimate check to the mad armaments race, which if allowed to continue must involve us all in ruin'.[13] Though still vigorous in his funding of defence, he grew anxious about the costs of the armaments race. It threatened the things he thought fundamental to every country's wellbeing: taxation, trade and the standard of living. He knew that conditions in Italy were 'deteriorating greatly. Taxation is terrific there are no fats available & no foreign imports can be bought.' Hence he was puzzled by the absence of 'any lessening of Mussolini's personal influence & I hear just the same about Germany & Hitler'.[14] Hilda reinforced Neville's line of thought: 'if you can

---

11  Hilda to Neville, 30 July 1937, The Bury House, NC18/2/1029
12  Neville to Hilda, 12 Sept., Inverness-shire, & to Ida, 19 Sept., Westbourne, & 26 Sept.1937, Chequers, in Self, ed., *The Neville Chamberlain Diary Letters*, IV, 270–2
13  Neville to Ida, 30 Oct.1937, Chequers, in Self, ed., *The Neville Chamberlain Diary Letters*, IV, 280
14  Neville to Hilda, 9 Oct.1937, Harrowby, in Self, ed., *The Neville Chamberlain Diary Letters*, IV, 274–5

prevent the world from flying to pieces in the next few years it does not look as if we should be suffering from bad trade & in that case people are never so anxious to fly to extreme measures.'[15]

He refused to heed the very different assessment of the situation from Austen's protégé, Eden. Eden bristled at sabre-rattling statements, whether from Rome or Berlin. Neville admitted that 'Mussolini had been more than usually insolent with his offensive remarks about "bleating democracies" and his outrageous allusion to the Colonies. But Anthony should never have been provoked into a retort which throws Germany & Italy together in self defence when our policy is so obviously to try & divide them'.[16] Hilda knew that Neville would react this way. She found his quest for peace 'terribly thrilling', and hoped, turning to Germany, that Britain's new ambassador, Nevile Henderson, would induce Hitler 'to pause & see whether after all there may not now be a way of appeasement opened, which would be ... the beginning of a real chance for Germany to be able safely to check her military development & give more thought to the increase of her domestic prosperity'.[17]

The floundering détente with Italy turned Neville's thoughts, like Hilda's, to a détente with Germany. The first step was an exploratory visit to Berlin which his friend the former Indian viceroy, now the leading peer in the Cabinet, Lord Halifax, undertook. 'I should imagine that Lord Halifax is as good an emissary as you could get,' Hilda wrote approvingly, '& it remains to be seen what mood he will find Hitler in, & if he really does wish for appeasement under reasonable conditions.'[18] The reception Halifax received in Germany encouraged him to take what Neville envisaged as 'my second step',[19] inviting the German foreign minister Konstantin von Neurath to London. Neville praised Halifax for 'creating an atmosphere in which it was possible to discuss with Germany the practical questions involved in a European settlement. ... What I wanted [Halifax] to do was to convince Hitler of our sincerity & to ascertain what objectives he had in mind ... both of these objects have been achieved. Both Hitler & Goering said repeatedly & emphatically that they had no desire or intention of making war and I think we may take this as correct at any rate for the present. Of course they want to dominate

---

15  Hilda to Neville, 7 Oct.1937, The Bury House, NC18/2/1039

16  Neville to Hilda, 6 Nov.1937, Chequers, in Self, ed., *The Neville Chamberlain Diary Letters*, IV, 281

17  Hilda to Neville, 4 Nov.1937, The Bury House, NC18/2/1043

18  Hilda to Neville, 19 Nov.1937, The Bury House, NC18/2/1045

19  Neville to Hilda, 21 Nov.1937, Basingstoke, in Self, ed., *The Neville Chamberlain Diary Letters*, IV, 284

eastern Europe; they want as close a union with Austria as they can get without incorporating her in the Reich and they want much the same things for the Sude- tendeutsche as we did for the Uitlanders in the Transvaal.'

Putting it this way, Neville equated Hitler's concern about the Sudeten Germans in Czechoslovakia with his father's determination at the time of the Boer War to keep the English residents of the Transvaal within the British Empire. Neville looked at relations with Germany in an imperial frame. He wondered whether a colonial arrangement to extend Germany's presence in Africa might help to bring about in return a peaceful settlement in Europe: 'here it seems to me is a fair basis of discussion'. He suggested saying to Germany, 'Give us satisfactory assurances that you won't use force to deal with the Austrians & Czecho-Slovakians & we will give you similar assurances that we won't use force to prevent the changes you want if you can get them by peaceful means.'[20] Here was the kernel of the foreign policy that Neville pursued for the next twelve months: he was willing to give Hitler much of what he wanted so long as Hitler did not use force to get it. Neville did not minimise the difficulties that lay ahead: 'even if all goes well it will be a long time before we get to the position of being able to make definite proposals to the Germans and their mentality is so different from ours that they may easily upset the applecart by some folly before then'. His approach to the Germans as to Hitler was psychological, an attempt to understand a 'mentality ... so different from ours.'[21]

&

Eden headed abroad for a much needed holiday at Christmas, freeing Neville, who remained at home with Annie, to take charge of foreign policy. Like Eden, the Chamberlain women aside from Annie spent the season abroad, a coincidence that bode ill for the Foreign Secretary. Mary headed for Italy to recover after the death of her second husband, Canon Carnegie. Ivy was already in Rome follow- ing Austen's death to 'make a more thorough break between the old & the new life'.[22] Ida and Hilda headed farther afield. Ida had been warned by her doctor to lessen her service work; and Hilda developed an intractable cough after adding the presidency of the Hampshire County Nursing Association to her duties as national treasurer of the Women's Institutes. Hilda's doctor urged her to go somewhere

---

20 Neville to Ida, 26 Nov.1937, Westbourne, in Self, ed., *op.cit.*, IV, 286–7

21 Neville to Hilda, 5 Dec., Tiverton, & to Ida, nr Newbury, 12 Dec.1937, in Self, ed., *op.cit.*, IV, 289 & 292

22 Hilda to Neville, 3 Dec.1937, The Bury House, NC18/2/1047

warm for the winter. He suggested Madeira or Tenerife. But those places were too relaxing for the restless Chamberlains. 'Fancy being marooned at Madeira for five weeks with nothing to do,' Ida protested. 'No, hang it all – if we are to spend all that time out of our country lets go a bust & do something worth while. – I've always wanted to go to Egypt again ... and Hilda agreed.'[23]

Ivy was soon caught up in the whirl of a city where Austen had had many friends. 'I have been entertained to lunch & dinner every day since my arrival ... & am full up to Xmas!' she reported happily to Neville. He planned to visit Rome in the New Year, and Ivy found herself at the centre of the preceding diplomacy. Hitherto she and Neville had been guarded towards each other. But now, as the person closest to Austen in his final ruminations about the troubled world, Ivy seized the opportunity to do what she was sure he would have wished; Neville welcomed her assistance. An Under Secretary at the Italian Foreign Office told her that the ministry regarded Neville as well disposed toward Italy, but believed that he faced opposition inside his Cabinet, particularly from Eden. The American ambassador urged her to ask Neville to start conversations with the Italians 'at any cost'; and the British ambassador, Lord Perth, reinforced this advice. 'I find that the Berlin-Rome Axis is not popular with the people,' Ivy told Neville, 'they think it means war & they distrust the Germans. They want friendship with England because they feel it means security.'

She was invited to see Il Duce himself, Mussolini. When she did so, he 'took both my hands & kissed them ... saying how glad he was to see me again & recalling past days & all the times we had met ... he said "Those were happy days. ... If we could only go back to Locarno. Sir Austen, he knew, he understood. How much I miss my dear friend, hèlas how he is needed now for Europe ... I want friendship with England ... I want peace' ... I was there three quarters of an hour,' Ivy continued her report to Neville, '& I found him just the same as he had always been to us kindly & human & genuinely glad to see me.'[24] Later, after the wedding of his niece at St. Peter's, Mussolini saw Ivy standing in the crowd and broke away to speak to her in the 'most cordial & friendly' fashion.[25]

She circulated other letters round the family telling 'much the same story – The Italians' deep distrust & dislike of Eden, & her own persistent efforts to dispel this idea & make them understand how much their anti-British propaganda adds to the difficulty. But she says "we are in a vicious circle. We say we can't begin negotiations

23  Ida to Neville, 30 Dec.1937, The Goring Hotel, Belgravia. NC18/2/1051
24  Ivy to Neville, 16 Dec.1937, Grand Hotel, Rome, NC1/17/5
25  Note enclosed by Mary in her letter to Neville, 5 Feb.1938, Grand Hotel, Rome, NC1/20/2/38

till they call off their propaganda & they say they can't call off their propaganda till we recognise their conquest of Abyssinia.'" All so like Austen's counsel in the past. Passing the information to Neville, Ida added her own hope that 'you may succeed before long in breaking through that circle some how'.[26] In the New Year she met Mussolini's son-in-law, the Italian Foreign Minister, Count Ciano, who greeted her with 'a smiling face & outstretched hands!' This reception encouraged her to read to Ciano an encouraging letter she had from Neville. 'I am convinced,' she wrote back to Neville, 'that once we start conversations they will be as charming as possible! Hitler is coming to Rome in May & it is essential that we should come to some agreement before then, otherwise I fear that 2 dictators together must do or say something dramatic!'[27]

Ivy's attempts to improve relations with Italy reinforced the approach that Neville already favoured. Discouraged by the deteriorating outlook in Germany, he wrote her an encouraging letter of which she made full use. 'I happened to see Ciano & he asked me if I had heard from you again', she reported. 'I replied "yes" & that your letter had pleased me, & he asked if he might know what was in it?' She was 'glad to read it to him'. After spending the next day outside the city, she 'returned back ... to find that Rome was being combed for me, as ... the Duce wished to see me at 7 pm.!' Escorted by Ciano, she read Neville's letter to Mussolini, who responded warmly. He talked of a wide-ranging agreement with Britain, '"as I should like to pay a tribute in memory of Sir Austen".'[28]

These highly irregular conversations ruffled Eden at the Foreign Office and he asked Neville 'to beg [Ivy] to desist from further interviews'. Rather than comply, Neville 'thought it best to stop writing [to Ivy] lest this vexation should lead to sabotage of the conversations'.[29] Astonishingly, Neville continued to believe that he and Eden were in full agreement, 'more complete perhaps than we have sometimes been in the past'.[30] Neville's eyes opened when the Foreign Office tried to postpone the Anglo-Italian conversations and prevent the Italian ambassador from talking to him. Angered, he concluded 'that the time had come when I must make my final stand & that Anthony must yield or go'. Rather than yield, Eden tendered his resignation, which Neville promptly accepted.

---

26  Ida to Neville, 30 Dec.1937, The Goring Hotel, Belgravia, NC18/2/1051
27  Ivy to Neville, 2 Jan.1938, Hotel des Temples, Agrigento, NC1/17/4
28  Ivy to Neville, 2 Feb.1938, Grand Hotel, Rome, NC1/7/7
29  Neville to Ivy, 3 Mar.1938, 'secret and confidential', 10 Downing Street, copy, NC1/17/9
30  Neville to Hilda, 13 Feb.1938, Chequers, in Self, ed., *The Neville Chamberlain Diary Letters*, IV, 302

There was some uncertainty among the public as to why Eden resigned. But there was no question for Neville, who expanded its significance. 'I rather doubt,' he wrote to Hilda, 'whether till the last moment [Eden] realised that the issue between us was not whether we should have conversations now but whether we should have them at all.' Neville concluded that 'at bottom Anthony did not want to talk either with Hitler or Mussolini'.[31] After dismissing him, Neville thanked Ivy for her 'invaluable help, which has certainly contributed materially to create the atmosphere in Rome necessary for the opening of conversations'.[32]

Eden's resignation crystallised Neville's commitment to thoroughgoing appeasement. But he still had to convince the Cabinet, Parliament and the public to follow him in pursuing this policy. The Cabinet fell into line. After a bitter debate in the Commons marked by a venomous attack from Lloyd George, Neville maintained his commanding majority. Sympathy for his efforts spread still wider, so far as one could tell, in the country. Eden's departure nevertheless fortified Neville's critics. Their arrows could not, however, cut through Neville's assurance: 'it was,' he told Hilda, 'now or never and must be now if we were to avoid another Great War.'

Ivy brought him reassurance from the grave. She reminded Neville of how Austen had worried about the 'needless misunderstanding' between Britain and Italy. 'Just before he died he ... said "what are we doing? Nothing but pin pricks to Italy. If we are not careful we will push her into the arms of Germany & you may take on one dictator but not two"!! So you can imagine how pleased he would be that you should be the person to carry on his policy of "peace in our time".'[33] It was these last words from Austen that Neville would repeat on his return from Munich. Ida, journeying back from Egypt, gave Neville more sombre encouragement: 'it still remains to be seen what can be done in a war-haunted Europe by one man who knows his own mind, who has no selfish ends of his own to serve & who is ready to face facts. You may succeed or you may fail, but in the latter case you will at least be able to feel that the failure is not due to your having allowed any opportunity to slip & that you have exhausted all possible means to maintain peace.'[34]

31  Neville to Hilda, 27 Feb.1938, Chequers, in Self, ed., *The Neville Chamberlain Diary Letters*, IV, 303
32  Neville to Ivy, 3 Mar.1938, 'Secret and confidential', 10 Downing Street, copy, NC1/17/9
33  Ivy to Neville, 11 Mar.1938, Grand Hotel, Rome, NC1/17/10
34  Ida to Neville, 28 Feb.193[8], S.S. Burma, NC18/2/1061

The storm signals shifted from Italy north toward Austria as the sisters journeyed home. The shift promised to strengthen the rapprochement Neville sought with Italy, which he assumed to be fearful of a German presence on its north-eastern border. Ivy reported that Mussolini was 'furious with Hitler over Austria'.[35] But that news lost credibility when the German army marched with impunity into Austria. Neville received the news just minutes after 'talking earnestly to Ribbentrop', the prospective German foreign minister, 'about a better understanding and mutual contributions to peace by Germany & ourselves'. He called Ribbentrop back; and Halifax, who had replaced Eden at the Foreign Office, talked to him 'most gravely and seriously begging him before it was too late to ask his chief to hold his hand'.

Neither Halifax nor Neville 'expected any result to follow'. They 'had had many indications during this present year that fresh developments in the process of swallowing Austria were imminent'. But – and here was their crucial point – they had hoped that Germany's absorption of Austria 'might be accomplished without violence'.[36] Hilda was sobered by Hitler's use of the army to take over Austria. 'You always said,' she wrote to Neville, 'that your hopes of a possible appeasement were conditional on the Dictators not kicking over the traces first, but alas Hitler has done so with a vengeance, & I fear this means a greater tension than ever & less & less chance of evading war.' She poured out her sympathy to her brother: 'your courage is great & I know you will be gathering yourself together to pick up the pieces, but it is heart breaking to feel that any chance of settlement in Europe is further off than ever'. And she recalled Austen's warning about German insistence on a 'brutal display of force when everything might have been gained with a little patience & with the approval of other nations, but they are not satisfied unless they can flaunt their power in the face of the world'. Presciently she concluded, 'It is a bad lookout for Czecho Slovakia & Poland.'[37]

Neville refused to accept Hilda's estimate of the setback and insisted, as he told his daughter, that 'the only thing is to set to work patiently on new ideas to get the same thing by a different road'.[38] His one regret was that he had not changed Foreign Secretary sooner. Examining the options with regard to Czechoslovakia, he thought of forming some kind of alliance which would not 'require meetings at Geneva and resolutions by dozens of small nations who have no responsibilities'.

---

35  Ivy to Annie, 27 Feb.1938, Grand Hotel, Rome, NC1/17/25
36  Neville to Hilda, 13 Mar.1938, Chequers, in Self, ed., *The Neville Chamberlain Diary Letters*, IV, 304–5
37  Hilda to Neville, 13 Mar.1938, The Bury House, NC18/2/1063
38  Neville to Dorothy, 19 Mar.1938, Chequers, NC1/23/63

Like Churchill, he thought of a 'Grand Alliance' with France and Russia, only to dismiss the notion. 'It is a very attractive idea; indeed there is almost everything to be said for it until you come to examine its practicability. From that moment its attraction vanishes. You have only to look at the map to see that nothing that France or we could do could possibly save Czecho-Slovakia from being over-run by the Germans if they wanted to do it. ... Russia is 100 miles away.'[39]

He fell back on his policy of accelerated rearmament while 'quietly & steadily [pursuing] our conversations with Italy. If we can avoid another violent coup in Czecho-Slovakia, which ought to be feasible, it may be possible for Europe to settle down again and some day for us to start peace talks again with the Germans.'[40] He hoped eventually to reach agreement with the Germans for a peaceful settlement over Czechoslovakia. He wanted to say to Hitler, "The best thing you can do is to tell us exactly what you want for your Sudeten Deutsch. If it is reasonable we will urge the Czechs to accept it and if they do you must give assurances that you will let them alone in future". I am not sure that in such circumstances I might not be willing to join in some joint guarantee *with Germany* of Czech independence.'[41]

But first he had to secure a salient increase in Britain's rearmament. He carried his Cabinet with him, won some understanding from the leaders of the Trades Union Congress, and then wooed Churchill. Neville spoke to Churchill privately 'because some of the considerations which had weighed most heavily with me could not be mentioned except in private, meaning of course military considerations. Winston was terribly pleased at being thus taken into confidence and ... assured me that he had not and would not intrigue against me.' Neville accepted the assurance with a pinch of salt: Churchill 'doesn't want office as long as he knows he can't have it, & though he won't intrigue himself he doesn't mind others doing it provided they are successful. But all the same I can't help liking Winston although I think him nearly always wrong and impossible as a colleague.'[42]

Neville's announcement of increased expenditure on rearmament won resounding endorsement in the House of Commons. He won an even dearer accolade from his sisters, whose faith was restored after being shaken by Hitler's armed takeover of

39 Neville to Ida, 20 Mar.1938, Chequers, in Self, ed., *The Neville Chamberlain Diary Letters*, IV, 307

40 Neville to Hilda, 13 Mar.1938, Chequers, in Self, ed., *The Neville Chamberlain Diary Letters*, IV, 304–5

41 Neville to Ida, 20 Mar.1938, Chequers, in Self, ed., *The Neville Chamberlain Diary Letters*, IV, 307

42 Neville to Hilda, 27 Mar.1938, Cliveden, in Self, ed., *The Neville Chamberlain Diary Letters*, IV, 311–2

Austria. Hilda wrote, 'you are the only man who could have handled the situation created by Germany in such a way as to, at once produce a certain feeling of calm & confidence, without either threatening the wrong doer or disguising your opinion of his action'.[43] 'I need hardly say that your letter was very gratifying to me,' he replied. 'My sisters are not mere "Yes-women", they have minds & brains of their own and I know that if they approve what I am doing it is not because it is I who am doing it.'

They wanted to keep in close touch with each other. The sisters understood that Neville's responsibilities might well prevent him from sustaining their weekly correspondence. Ida wrote 'to say once again how very much Hilda & I appreciate the regularity & fullness of your letters in these strenuous times. Of course they cannot entirely take the place of that personal intercourse, the possibility of which seems to fade more & more into the remote future. ... But they do keep us in touch & help us to draw the right conclusions from what we see in the papers. And they are a constant proof of the strong affection which binds us together & leads you to give up so much of your valuable time to us. All the same we don't want to add unduly to your fatigue & if any week you feel like missing the post we hope very much you will do so.'[44] Neville was reluctant to do as his sisters suggested. He explained his reluctance in terms of their interests: 'now that Austen has gone I am the only link you have with political activities which have been such a lifelong interest to you both'.[45] But his Sunday letters to his sisters also met his needs. Free for a few hours from the accelerating pace of events, he could set out the reasons for the policies that he was pursuing and mull over the challenges that lay ahead.

The three surviving Chamberlains recoiled from Nazi rule in practice. 'I feel positively sick when I think of what is going on in Austria, the veritable reign of terror that is being inaugurated there,' Ida wrote anxiously to Neville on his birthday. 'No doubt ... there are many that welcome German rule & the reign of Naziism, but what of the minority & of the unfortunate Jews. ... how many of the smaller nations must be asking themselves "How long before it is our turn"'. The one mystery the Chamberlains could not fathom was Hitler personally. Ida thought that he was 'being pushed as from behind – Either that or he is thoroughly dishonest & never means what he says.'[46] All three Chamberlains were reluctant to accept this latter possibility. Nor could they believe that Hitler actually desired war.

43  Hilda to Neville, 25 Mar.1938, The Bury House, NC18/2/1065

44  Ida to Neville, 31 Mar.1938, The Bury House, NC18/2/1066

45  Neville to Ida, 3 Apr.1938, 11 Downing Street, in Self, ed., *The Neville Chamberlain Diary Letters*, IV, 312

46  Ida to Neville, 17 Mar.1938, The Bury House, NC18/2/1064

But otherwise they did their best to look at the state of affairs in Germany without blinkered eyes. Ida and Hilda pored over a recently published account by a well informed Australian scholar, Stephen Roberts, of *The House that Hitler Built*, and found it 'most depressing. The whole policy is directed to suppressing free thought & making an absolutely united nation whose whole aim is to fit themselves for making war or swallowing the rest of Europe & assimilating them without war.' After reading more of Roberts' book, Ida reached conclusions closely akin to Austen's in the 1880s: 'The Germans are a strange people but there is no doubt that firmness & force are the only things that really appeal to them.' According to Roberts, 'Hitler has completely captured the youth of the nation & they revel in their chains. ... [the] worst of it is,' Ida concluded, 'that whilst I feel fairly confident that Mussolini if we make an agreement with him will keep his word we know from Hitler's own lips that in his opinion agreements are only valid as long as they suit him, & that he sees no reason for keeping them as long as he is strong enough to be able to defy the other Power'.[47] Neville never absorbed this message.

Roberts' book made a different impression on him. Neville was taken by Roberts' essentially psychological and sociological treatment of Hitler and the German people. Unlike Ida who was shocked at Hitler's willingness to renounce agreements whenever it suited him, Neville concentrated on Hitler's psychological instability. As for the German people, Neville hoped to bring them down to solid economic earth. Neville copied out long passages from *The House that Hitler Built* for insertion in his own copy of *Mein Kampf*.[48] 'Emotional & unbalanced he (H) gave way to delusional manias about everybody with whom he came into contact – Jews or capitalists or labourers. It is one of the ironies of history that world affairs today depend on the accidental contacts of a spoilt down & out in the Vienna of 30 years ago.' And: 'The Germans are a politically retarded race. They are still in the "myth" stage of development. ... H survives because he has deliberately built up the most showy, the most perfect myth of modern times.' On a more alarming note, Neville quoted Roberts to the effect that, 'The whole teaching of Hitlerism is to justify war as an instrument of policy in certain contingencies & there is hardly a boy in G. who does not view the preparation for ultimate war as the most important aspect of life.' 'The nation has been ... launched along a road that can only lead to disaster. ... unless it learns the habit of political & economic collaboration

---

47 Ida to Neville, 15 Apr.1938, The Bury House, NC18/2/1068
48 I owe this discovery to Martin Killeen on the Special Collections staff of the University of Birmingham Library.

in international matters.' That kind of collaboration was basic to Neville's way of thinking, and he refused to lose hope that it would prevail.

The agreements that he made with Ireland as well as Italy and France strengthened his faith in face-to-face negotiations with his counterparts in other countries. The crucial agreement was with Italy. In an exchange of letters, Neville formally recognised the Italian conquest of Abyssinia, in return for which Mussolini agreed to withdraw the Italian forces fighting for Franco in Spain. Although it took half a year to do so, that withdrawal finally took place. Meanwhile Hitler's courtship of the Italians proved less than successful. Neville thus had something to show from his attempt to separate the dictators of central Europe. His womenfolk rejoiced. Mary was delighted 'that you have so much to encourage you in the courageous & wise efforts you are making to "seek peace & ensure it". It is no small achievement to have been able to bring such varied personalities & questions to agreements which may very well stem the tide which has threatened to overwhelm Europe.'[49] Neville was also heartened by the support his policy won in Canada.

The Anglo-Italian agreement acquired further importance as Neville persuaded the new French ministry led by Edouard Daladier to fall into line. The significance of these talks for Neville had as much to do with the personal way in which they were conducted as with the power politics of the Mediterranean. 'The French conversations came out all right in the end,' he confided to Ida, 'but they were pretty difficult. Fortunately the papers have had no hint of how near we came to a break over Czecho-Slovakia. ... Daladier was saying to his own people that it was no use going on ... I arranged to change the places so that Daladier should sit next me at lunch. Unfortunately he does not speak a word of English, but I mustered what French I could to win his confidence & before we separated I could see that he had mellowed considerably. ... I made some new proposals. ... Daladier countered with some unacceptable modifications, I chipped in with a restatement with variations, Daladier found my suggestions "interesants" [sic] and asked for a further adjournment. ... When we rejoined the French they had translated my words into their own language & reading them out asked if that was correct; I said it was and thereupon they accepted them and our work was done.' The Anglo-French accord enabled Neville on behalf of both countries to apply his policy to Czechoslovakia; and 'as in accordance with the French it is left to us alone to ask the Germans what they want in Czecho-Slovakia,' he was 'not without hope that we may get through without a fresh demonstration of force'.[50]

---

49  Mary to Neville, 1 May 1938, 41 Lennox Gardens, NC1/20/2/40
50  Neville to Ida, 1 May 1938, 10 Downing Street, in Self, ed., *The Neville Chamberlain Diary*

The agreement Neville reached with Eamon de Valera of Ireland was of similar character. Neville thought that, by ridding Britain of a longstanding embarrassment on its western flank, the agreement 'would produce an excellent effect in Berlin'.[51] There was a specifically military dimension to the Anglo-Irish agreement. In order to secure 'a friendly Ireland', Neville gave up the rights of access to Irish ports which Britain enjoyed under the treaty of 1921. Churchill attacked that as a dangerous concession. But Neville was confident that 'Winston as usual is backing the wrong horse. The country approves the settlement and is not disposed to question the details. De Valera was most cordial and twice repeated to me "If you had not been here we could never have made this agreement".'[52] Neville failed to notice the ambivalence of this tribute.

The agreements with Italy, France and Ireland sharpened parliamentary criticism of Neville's policy from the Labour opposition, led by Clement Attlee. The Labour party was particularly infuriated by the implications for Spain, wracked by a civil war in which Neville refused to become involved, regardless of Franco's bombing of British ships. 'I have been through every possible form of retaliation,' said Neville, 'and it is abundantly clear that none of them can be effective unless we are prepared to go to war with Franco, which might quite possibly lead to war with Italy & Germany and in any case would cut right across my policy of general appeasement.'[53] Attlee's 'violent personal attack' on Neville as a friend of Fascists and enemy of the League of Nations did not shake his confidence that 'the country wants peace and appreciates the fact that this Govt is delivering the goods. If we could get a peaceful solution of the Czech problem this would still further add to our reputation.'[54]

His efforts seemed all for naught, however, when word arrived of troop movements on the Czech border and Germany accused a Czech officer of killing two Sudeten

*Letters*, IV, 317–9

51 Neville to Hilda, 9 Apr.1938, 11 Downing Street, in Self, ed., *The Neville Chamberlain Diary Letters*, IV, 314

52 Quoted in Neville to Ida, 1 May 1938, 10 Downing Street, in Self, ed., *The Neville Chamberlain Diary Letters*, IV, 317–9

53 Neville to Hilda, 25 June 1938, Salisbury, in Self, ed., *The Neville Chamberlain Diary Letters*, IV, 330

54 Neville to Hilda, 8 May 1938, 10 Downing Street, in Self, ed., *The Neville Chamberlain Diary Letters*, IV, 320

Germans. Neville cried, 'These are the sort of days that make you feel inclined to say Why should I go on in the face of criticism and discouragement and hasn't the time come for me to hand over. ... All I can say about the situation at this moment is that nothing has yet occurred to make it hopeless. The German Ambassador has given us all sorts of assurances.' And yet the German press attacked Britain for supporting the Czechs, 'entirely omitting any reference to our efforts to induce them to meet the Sudeten Germans more than half way'. Neville wrung his hands. Until the British forces were as strong as the German, 'we shall always be kept in this state of chronic anxiety'.[55]

Ida wrote back reassuringly: 'the one common reaction amongst the vast majority of your fellow countrymen is a sense of intense thankfulness that we have at the head of affairs a man of cool head, & clear vision, with a definite policy & the determination to carry it through undeterred by whatever other people may say. ... if any man can do it you are that man, & if you fail [your fellow countrymen] will at least have the comfort of feeling that everything that was humanly possible had been done.' This time at any rate the German forces had not already marched in; 'this time it has been possible to start negotiations before we are presented with a fait accompli, – & although unfortunately the Germans know that we are not yet ready & armed at all points, yet it seems quite on the cards that they are not altogether prepared & are not anxious to precipitate a conflict which they have been warned may easily bring in us as well as France & Russia against them.'[56]

The following Sunday, Neville could report some success. When Britain warned Germany that an attack on Czechoslovakia might lead to British involvement, Germany denied that there had ever been a crisis to respond to. The episode left Neville convinced 'that the German Government made all preparations for a coup' but decided 'after getting our warnings that the risks were too great'. Accordingly he stuck to his course: 'if only "incidents" whether spontaneous or deliberate can be avoided we begin to see our way to some suggestions which might offer a stable future for Czecho-Slovakia and the sterilisation of another danger spot.'

Assessing his first year as Prime Minister, he was satisfied that on balance he had achieved something. Italy's uneasiness at the annexation of Austria and the agreement that thereupon Neville reached with Mussolini had 'given the Rome-Berlin axis a nasty jar and in ... future ... we may hope for a good deal of quiet help

---

55  Neville to Hilda, 22 May 1938, 10 Downing Street, in Self, ed., *The Neville Chamberlain Diary Letters*, IV, 324
56  Ida to Neville, 23 May 1938, The Bury House, NC18/2/1075

from Italy.'[57] He was 'disposed to think that [the Germans] have missed the bus' – a metaphor to which he was fatefully addicted – 'and may never again have such a favourable chance of asserting their domination over central & Eastern Europe'.[58]

Though comparatively quiet, the next couple of months did not ease the strain that Neville was under. Mussolini struck him as 'behaving just like a spoiled child', and with the Germans it was 'difficult to be sure what the game is'. Neville found comfort in having 'Halifax instead of Anthony at the F.O.', for Halifax remained calm and compliant: 'I have only got to make a suggestion and he carries it out with sympathy and understanding.'[59] The reports on Czechoslovakia were not, however, encouraging, though Neville grasped at the most tentative overtures from Berlin. No sooner had he reached Scotland for his annual summer holiday than he was laid low with sinusitis, which forced him back to London.

He arrived in Downing Street to find the prospects for a settlement on Czechoslovakia deteriorating rapidly. Germany apparently planned to mobilise its army in September. Neville did not at first 'feel pulled down or depressed' by the news. It was 'rather fortunate' to be in London, able discuss the situation with Halifax 'and decide on our own policy by conversation instead of by correspondence'.[60] But the sinusitis was slow to lessen its grip, and the prescribed remedies were nauseating. When told to abandon all hope of returning to Scotland, Neville 'gave way to depression ... Every thing seemed to fall on my head'; and he fled to Chequers feeling 'very low'. But a weekend at Chequers did its magic. Although unable to see any improvement in the European situation, he felt 'more able to cope with it'. He clung to the hope that if only they could 'get safely through September', they could 'see light'.[61]

As his health recovered, his spirits revived. He warned his sisters toward the end of August that 'the Germans seem determined to make the worst of everything'.[62]

57 Neville to Ida, 28 May 1938, Chequers, in Self, ed., *The Neville Chamberlain Diary Letters*, IV, 325

58 Neville to Ida, 18 June 1938, Chequers, in Self, ed., *The Neville Chamberlain Diary Letters*, IV, 328

59 Neville to Ida, 9 July 1938, Chequers, in Self, ed., *The Neville Chamberlain Diary Letters*, IV, 335

60 Neville to Hilda, 13 Aug.1938, 10 Downing Street, in Self, ed., *The Neville Chamberlain Diary Letters*, IV, 339–40

61 Neville to Ida, 21 Aug.1938, Chequers, in Self, ed., *The Neville Chamberlain Diary Letters*, IV, 340–1

62 Neville to Hilda, 27 Aug.1938, Great Durnford, in Self, ed., *The Neville Chamberlain Diary Letters*, IV, 341

But the bleak outlook brought out his daring. Everything seemed to hinge on a speech Hitler was to make at a Nazi rally in Nuremberg on September 6th. 'Is it not positively horrible to think that the fate of hundreds of millions depends on one man and he is half mad.' If only Neville could meet Hitler face to face, he might be able to fathom the mental workings of the dictator, bring out the rational side that earlier visitors found convincing, and persuade him to take what he wanted of the Sudetenland by diplomatic agreement rather than by force.

Neville raised with Annie the possibility of flying to confront Hitler in Germany before he pushed Europe over the brink of war. 'Plan Z' he called it, to be used only 'if all else failed'.[63] Neville then discussed the idea with his most trusted advisers on Anglo-German relations, Halifax and Nevile Henderson, the ambassador. The plan was 'so unconventional and daring that it rather took Halifax's breath away,' Neville told his sisters elliptically: 'But since Henderson thought it might save the situation at the 11th hour I haven't abandoned it though I hope all the time that it won't be necessary to try it.'[64] The sisters had no trouble guessing that Neville had in mind 'getting into personal touch with Hitler'.[65] So like their father! As Mary later put it, 'His quick inspiration of how to act, his "flaire" [sic] for what might save a situation, & the daring to act on his intuition without delay! How well [Joseph] would have understood & commended your action.'[66] Ida and Hilda responded to Neville's idea more positively than Halifax. The storm warnings from Germany made it look 'only too probable that your last minute plan might have to be put into execution ... it is indeed unconventional & daring but with such a man as Hitler it is quite possible that it might have a chance of success'.[67]

Duty to attend the King at Balmoral took Neville back to Scotland. The situation in central Europe hung over him 'like a nightmare all the time'.[68] But he seized the opportunity to demonstrate his recovery after his summertime debility 'to stand the moors without fatigue ... to be neither tired nor stiff after a long walk which wore out some of the others ... the only one to do without a pony and always leading the way'. He extended his holiday in Scotland, strengthening his hopes as well as his body. 'I have a feeling that things have gone in such a way as to make it

63  Annie to Mary, 12 Oct.1938, The Hirsel, Coldstream, Annie Chamberlain correspondence in the possession of James Lloyd
64  Neville to Ida, 3 Sept.1938, Balmoral Castle, in Self, ed., *The Neville Chamberlain Diary Letters*, IV, 342
65  as Hilda later put it: Hilda to Mary, 30 Sept.1938, The Bury House, BC4/2/235
66  Mary to Neville, 10 Oct.1938, Danvers, Mass., NC1/20/2/42
67  Ida to Neville, 9 Sept.1938, The Bury House, NC18/2/1090
68  Neville to Annie, 2 Sept.1938, Balmoral Castle, NC1/26/530

more and more difficult for [Hitler] to use force and I hope it may yet be possible to avoid even the unprecedented step to which I alluded.'[69]

The following week was 'pretty awful'.[70] Though Hitler did not 'commit himself irrevocably' to invade Czechoslovakia,[71] the Germans fomented unrest in the Sudetenland and undermined the efforts of the Czechs to negotiate a settlement. 'You have no conception what the atmosphere is,' Neville reported from Downing Street, '– every ten minutes someone comes in ... bringing some new and disturbing communication.' It was 'enough to send most people off their heads, if their heads were not as firmly screwed on as mine'. Neville moved with assurance in the centre of the storm. He was irritated only by the 'busybodies of all kinds [who] intrude their advice, and the papers [which] do their best to ruin all one's efforts'. The one person he wanted at hand was Annie: 'it is a great comfort ... to be able to unburden myself to her at all hours'. Annie was 'terribly torn' that weekend between her desire to remain with Neville in Downing Street and to be with her daughter Dorothy, who was about to give birth in Birmingham. Hilda headed for Birmingham to free Annie to stay with Neville.

Throughout this anxious period, Neville used his letters to his sisters to survey the situation. 'I fully realise that if eventually things go wrong and the aggression takes place there will be many, including Winston, who will say that the British Government must bear the responsibility and that if only they had had the courage to tell Hitler now that if he used force we should at once declare war that would have stopped him. By that time it will be impossible to prove the contrary, but I am satisfied that we should be wrong to allow the most vital decision that any country could take, the decision as to peace or war, to pass out of our own hands into those of the ruler of another country and a lunatic at that.' Neville was painfully aware of Britain's military weakness despite his efforts to fund rearmament. His anxiety on this score was heightened by a study of Britain's Foreign Secretary after the Napoleonic Wars, George Canning. 'Again and again,' Neville told Ida, 'Canning lays it down that you should never menace unless you are in a position to carry out your threats and although if we have to fight I should hope we should be able to give a good account of ourselves we are certainly not in a position in which our military advisers would feel happy in undertaking to begin hostilities if we were not forced to do so.'

69  Neville to Hilda, 6 Sept.1938, Forfarshire, in Self, ed., *The Neville Chamberlain Diary Letters*, IV, 343

70  Neville to Ida, 11 Sept.1938, 10 Downing Street, in Self, ed., *The Neville Chamberlain Diary Letters*, IV, 344–5

71  Ida to Mary, 14 Sept.1938, The Bury House, BC4/2/234

Plan Z looked ever more attractive to Neville. He was afraid that Hitler might act so fast as to forestall it. 'That is a risk which we have to take but in the meantime I do not want to do anything which would destroy its chance of success because if it came off, it would go far beyond the present crisis and might prove the opportunity for bringing about a complete change in the international situation.' Here lay the genesis of 'the scrap of paper' that Neville brought back from Munich. He hoped for much more than a settlement on Czechoslovakia.

Hitler quickened the pace by striking a warlike note in his next address at Nuremberg. Neville immediately 'saw that the moment had come & must be taken if I was not to be too late'. He had intended to consult the Cabinet before setting Plan Z in motion. But he sent 'the fateful telegram' to Hitler straightaway and secured Cabinet approval the next morning: 'then followed hours of waiting for the answer ... At last during the afternoon my anxiety was relieved. Hitler was entirely at my disposal.' The response of the German leader and 'others who were with him,' as reported to Neville, showed him 'a side of Hitler that would surprise many people in this country.'[72] It lessened Neville's suspicions and heightened his expectations.

The public announcement of his impending flight – misunderstood to be his first – to meet Hitler in Germany on the brink of war evoked exclamations of relief everywhere. The relief only accentuated the continuing anxiety. Ida reopened a letter she was writing to Mary, who was with her family in Massachusetts: 'By the time you get this you will know the result. Whatever it may be we shall feel that no stone has been left unturned to avoid catastrophe. If [Neville] succeeds what will the world not owe to him! How wonderful to have such a brother.'[73]

❧

As Neville's plane neared Munich, it 'entered a storm' with foreboding.[74] But a pilot plane led the descent safely to the aerodrome. There Neville 'was delighted with the enthusiastic welcome of the crowds who were waiting in the rain' and clustered at crossing points along the route toward Berchtesgaden where Hitler was waiting. Their meeting began awkwardly. Neville found Hitler 'rather disagreeable'

---

72  Neville to Ida, 19 Sept.1938, 10 Downing Street, in Self, ed., *The Neville Chamberlain Diary Letters*, IV, 346–8

73  Ida to Mary, 14 Sept.1938, The Bury House, BC4/2/234, now dated 15 Sept.

74  Neville to Ida, 19 Sept.1938, 10 Downing Street, in Self, ed., *The Neville Chamberlain Diary Letters*, IV, 346–8

in expression and 'entirely undistinguished' in appearance: 'You would never notice him in a crowd & would take him for the house painter he once was.' The house was sparsely furnished with little ornament apart from paintings of Italian nudes which Neville found disconcerting. But after tea the two men got down to business. 'H. asked abruptly what procedure I proposed. Would I like to have two or three present at our talk. I replied that if convenient to him I would prefer a tête-à-tête. Thereupon he rose & he & I & the interpreter left the party' for 'his own room' where 'we sat & talked for 3 hours'.

Neville's immediate attempt to size up the man and the situation was accurate, if inadequate. 'I did not see any trace of insanity but occasionally he became very excited and poured out his indignation against the Czechs ... I soon saw that the situation was much more critical than I had anticipated. I knew that his troops & tanks & guns & planes were ready to pounce and only awaiting his word, and it was clear that rapid decisions must be taken if the situation was to be saved.' Neville refused to be browbeaten. 'At one point he seemed to be saying that he was going in at once so I became indignant saying that I did not see why he had allowed me to come all this way and that I was wasting my time. He quieted down, then said if I could assure him that the British Government accepted the principle of self determination (which he had not invented) he was prepared to discuss ways & means. I said I could give no such assurance without consultation' and proposed to 'break off our talk now, go back & hold my consultations & meet him again.' Hitler agreed to this procedure and suggested meeting Neville 'somewhere near Cologne. Then I asked him how the situation was to be held in the meantime & he promised not to give the order to march unless some outrageous incident forced his hand.'

Despite the uncertainty of that proviso, this procedural agreement gave Neville essentially what he had come for: postponement of the resort to arms to allow time for negotiation. But his retrospective assessment of Hitler contained the seeds of disaster. Neville accepted third-hand reports that he had made a very favourable impression on Hitler. The Führer was reported to have said, 'I have had a conversation with a *man* ... one with whom I can do business.' Adopting Hitler's reported words, Neville left Munich under the impression that 'in spite of the hardness & ruthlessness I thought I saw in his face ... here was a man who could be relied upon when he had given his word'. He forgot – or did not wish to remember – Ida's springtime warning from Stephen Roberts' book that Hitler by his own admission regarded agreements as valid only as long as they suited him and would not hesitate to repudiate them when he felt strong enough to do so.

She did not remind him of that warning when she welcomed him back to England and congratulated him 'on what you have so far accomplished'. Ida knew that he did not return triumphant: 'Of course I realise that there is still a terribly difficult time before you'; but 'whatever happens in the end, you will have made your effort to preserve the world from another Armageddon!' There was no denying the sensation his flight to see Hitler had made: 'Everywhere you hear the same thing. "What courage! what a man! it is wonderful. Hope has sprung up again in our hearts."' Ida also recognised the risks that Neville still ran and the criticism he would inevitably face. 'No doubt if you <u>do</u> succeed in coming to an understanding with Germany, there will be many criticisms of your methods, but who cares if the result is achieved.' She also appreciated that it was his sisters that he wanted to hear from upon his return home: 'I hate to think that you have to spend this evening talking to your colleagues.'[75]

Hilda was less circumspect in her welcome. 'I don't know how to express all the feelings which rush about in my mind & all that I want to pour out to you, – but they all resolve themselves into a great thankfulness for your existence, & an immense pride in my brother & the son of my father! So often in these days I have felt ... that our father was the only other man, whom I could imagine either conceiving it or carrying it out! ... it is heartening to hear the worldwide admiration ... I don't think even in your most sanguine moments you could have anticipated such an immense success for your gesture, as that it should have been so spontaneously welcomed & recognized for what it was, – a last bold chance to remove this spectre of war which had come so near.' That response by the public was an achievement in itself for it showed 'how all the world fears & dreads a European war as never before'.[76]

'Thank you & Hilda ever so much for your letters,' Neville replied to Ida. 'Hilda is quite right. It was an idea after Father's own heart.' Astonished to hear from him so soon, Ida could not help wondering about his assessment of Hitler. 'I hope you are right in thinking that if he once gives you a promise he will keep it.' She detected the avenue for escape that Hitler had given himself with his promise 'not to give the order to march unless some outrageous incident forced his hand'. 'The outrageous behaviour of the Sudeten Germans ... gives the impression,' she observed, 'that they are trying to force the issue but of course they could do nothing if they had not Hitler behind them.'[77] Hilda swept her sister's anxieties aside and reinforced her brother's self-confidence: 'I have always felt in you an extraordinary latent force,' she wrote; '... When you became P.M. I rejoiced that at last the opportunity had

75  Ida to Neville, 16 Sept.1938, The Bury House, NC18/2/1093
76  Hilda to Neville, 16 Sept.1938, Westbourne, NC18/2/1091
77  Ida to Neville, 21 Sept.1938, The Bury House, NC18/2/1094

come for full development, although I never dreamt that such frightful responsibilities were to be thrust upon you. What a test of your fortitude & self control those long hours of waiting [for Hitler's response to your overture] must have been, even greater than the 3½ hours wrestling for the soul of Hitler at night. ... that you must have singularly impressed him is shown by the fact that he thanked you for your attempts to keep the peace in Czechoslovakia, instead of resenting your interference. Nobody else would have achieved that.'[78]

Ten days of increasingly difficult discussions followed Neville's return from Munich. It took him five hours with the Cabinet to overcome his 'critics, some of whom had been concerting opposition beforehand'. Then 'an exhausting day' with the French Ministers: 'That also resulted in unanimity & we have sent our proposals to the Czechs.' They acquiesced 'with many bitter reproaches,' as Neville expected. Much worse lay ahead at Bad Godesberg where Neville next met Hitler, for Hitler repeatedly reneged on his promises.

Ida and Hilda stayed with Annie in 10 Downing Street while Neville was away. Outside the crowds jostled each other with conflicting reactions. Some sent flowers, everything 'from the little spray of half withered Michaelmas daisies left by some poor woman in passing, to the most wonderful baskets of lilies & roses & orchids'. But demonstrators along Whitehall shouted 'Down with Chamberlain' within earshot of the women in Number 10 who were waiting for news of the reception he would receive from Hitler. The International Peace Campaign and the League of Nations Union handed out placards that read 'Peace and Security', 'Help the Czechs', 'Down with Chamberlain'. Hilda was disgusted: 'Could one conceive three more self contradictory statements? ... Naturally one did not pay any attention to an unimportant rabble but still a howling mob when your nerves are strung to breaking point is not soothing.'[79]

The women were not optimistic about the outcome of the negotiations at Bad Godesberg. Ida left a note to await Neville on his return: 'I only want to say how deeply I feel for you in that your valiant efforts seem destined not to succeed.'[80] Mary too sent 'a word of love sympathy & admiration for the courageous action you have taken & your untiring effort to preserve Peace in Europe & the world. ... whatever the outcome your part will stand out as that of a great Prime Minister.'[81] Neville admitted upon his return that 'events seemed to be closing in and driving us to the

---

78  Hilda to Neville, 25 Sept.1938, The Bury House, NC18/2/1095
79  Hilda to Mary, 30 Sept.1938, The Bury House, BC4/2/235
80  Ida to Neville, Saturday, 10 Downing Street, NC18/2/1092
81  Mary to Neville, 27 Sept.1938, Danvers, Mass., NC1/20/2/41

edge of the abyss with a horrifying certainty and rapidity.'[82] When Hilda heard his report on the radio, she 'felt hope die within me,' for he sounded 'heart broken!'

On the day German troops were expected to march into Czechoslovakia, Neville 'decided on one last appeal to Hitler & also to Mussolini to use his influence'. It was Neville's 'last desperate snatch at the last tuft of grass on the very verge of the precipice'. That afternoon he delivered a sombre report to the House of Commons. Back in Odiham Ida and Hilda readied their gas masks and considered 'how to darken our windows & secure the best protection against incendiary bombs'.[83]

As Neville was concluding his report to the Commons, a note was passed along the front bench to him. 'Oh Annie, Annie, Can it be true?' Ida exclaimed, 'I can hardly believe it yet. I was finishing my tea thinking there could be nothing on the wireless before 6 o'clock, when [my housemaid] hurried in to ask if I had heard the news & told me Neville is to meet Hitler & Mussolini & she thought Daladier in Munich tomorrow. ... I have been thinking so much of ... all the myriads whose lives & happiness war threatened & had given up all hope of any other issue. But if this meeting has been arranged it must be because the dictators have quailed at the last moment. Surely once they have drawn back from the brink of the precipice they cannot return to it! – And it is to Neville's superhuman courage & resource, judgment & firmness that we owe this reprieve. What millions of blessings must be being called down upon him. ... Have all our prayers been answered – It seems too soon to rejoice but oh how grateful I feel for even a reprieve & the new hopes that come with it.'

Neville's daughter was even more ecstatic. 'I really do think you are the most marvellous man that ever lived,' she wrote from Birmingham, 'and so does every body else! ... Everyone here is nearly off their heads with joy & all work on dug-outs has been suspended for the time being anyway!'[84] Annie was sitting in the Ladies Gallery of the Commons between Queen Mary and the Duchess of Kent while Neville spoke. When he read out the announcement he had just received, Annie saw tears pouring down the royal faces, 'the Archbishop of Canterbury was pounding the rail in front of him & Lord Baldwin using his stick whilst even some of the Ambassadors joined in, ... the whole House rose, to cheer him,' even Lloyd George, 'though rather reluctantly!'[85]

---

82  Neville to Hilda, 2 Oct.1938, Chequers, in Self, ed., *The Neville Chamberlain Diary Letters*, IV, 349–51
83  Ida to Annie, Wednesday 28 Sept.1938, The Bury House, NC1/16/4/17
84  Dorothy to Neville, 28 Sept.1938, 57 Calthorpe Road, Edgbaston, NC1/23/19
85  As she reported to Hilda: Hilda to Mary, 30 Sept.1938, The Bury House, BC4/2/235

Despite their jubilation, neither Ida nor Dorothy thought that more than a reprieve, a suspension of war, had yet been achieved. But Neville aimed for much more. The next forty-eight hours 'entailed terrific physical and mental exertions' for him, beginning with an early rising and the long flight to Munich. 'The rest of that day till after 2 o'clock next morning was one prolonged nightmare ... Hitler's appearance and manner when I saw him appeared to show that the storm signals were up ... Yet these appearances were deceptive. His opening sentences when we gathered round for our conference were so moderate and reasonable that I felt instant relief. Mussolini's attitude all through was extremely quiet & reserved. He seemed to me cowed by Hitler but undoubtedly he was most anxious for a peaceful settlement and he played an indispensable part in attaining it.' Hilda commented, 'it was a master stroke to bring in Italy & it finally did succeed'.

Neville used the opportunity to talk to both dictators about their involvement in the Spanish civil war. He suggested that the four powers at the conference – Britain and France, Italy and Germany – should call on the two sides in the civil war 'to observe a truce while we helped them to find terms of settlement'. The fate of Czechoslovakia seemed a secondary concern for Neville, since he was willing to give Hitler most of what he wanted so long he did not grab it by force of arms.

Neville was more concerned about his further agenda; and he asked Hitler for a private talk next day. Hitler 'jumped at the idea & asked me to come to his private flat'. There Neville 'pulled out the declaration which I had prepared beforehand and asked if he would sign it. As the interpreter translated the words into German Hitler frequently ejaculated Ja! Ja! And at the end he said Yes I will certainly sign it. When shall we do it. I said "now", & we went at once to the writing table & put our signatures to the two copies which I had brought with me.' The statement spoke to the heart of Neville's endeavour, the way of dealing with international conflict which he inaugurated in Munich and hoped to extend across Europe to the Far East. The two men declared that their previous day's agreement was 'symbolic of the desire of our two peoples never to go to war with one another again. We are resolved that the method of consultation shall be the method adopted to deal with any other questions that may concern our two countries.'[86] Neville waved this piece of paper triumphantly on his return to London. Hitler signed it with scarcely a glance.

Hilda began a report to Mary as Neville flew home. She interrupted it to announce, 'Neville has arrived! I have just heard his address! Thank God for his

---

86 A copy of the Anglo-German Pact concluded between the Prime Minister and Herr Hitler – 30th September [1938], NC16/52

arrival Thank God for all he has done, Thank God that the prayers of the people have been heard, that he has rolled back that menace of war which has hung over us so long!' At that she brought the Chamberlain litany to its triumphant conclusion. 'Oh Mary what a time for us & how proud one feels of the whole family! That it should have been given to Neville to complete first his Father's work & then Austen's. Austen's great effort at Locarno was for the same end & had nations & governments been saner it might have produced a durable result but it seemed to need this actual bringing us to the very brink of war, this gazing into the abyss, to make possible what indeed we hope with Neville is the dawn of a new day for Europe.' Hilda's interpretation of Munich as the completion of Austen's handiwork at Locarno was not as farfetched as it seems in retrospect, for both agreements involved concessions to Germany in the interests of peace.

Ivy joined the jubilant chorus, writing to tell Annie 'from the fullness of my heart my admiration & thankfulness of Neville's wonderful courage & statesmanship. He will be remembered for all time. How proud Austen would have been!'[87] But no one was prouder than Hilda. She praised Neville in Christ-like terms. 'Millions bless your name today, & your happy sisters are uplifted beyond words, by the thought of all that you have been able to do! I know you have been upheld by the prayers of all the peoples, but all know & feel that only through you could their salvation come. You have accomplished the impossible, you have indeed snatched victory from the jaws of death. We lift up our hearts in thankfulness for you, for your character, trained & disciplined all through your life so that the great emergency found you armed at all points.'[88] Neville accepted her tribute with gratitude. 'The letters which you and Ida sent me on Friday, the day of my return, were what I wanted.'

---

87  Ivy to Annie, 30 Sept.1938, 24 Egerton Terrace, NC1/17/17
88  Hilda to Neville, Friday [30 Sept.1938], The Bury House, NC1/15/3/160

*In whose shadow? The War Cabinet, September 1939*

# 11

# In Face of Failure

Neville was driven from the pinnacle on which Hilda placed him by mounting evidence that the policy he followed at Munich was fatally flawed. His undeviating adherence to that policy even after the outbreak of war only deepened his discredit. Even his sisters came to recognise his failure. But Neville refused. For there were elements of success in his achievement at Munich, elements he misunderstood and hence misused.

He surrendered nothing at Munich that he was not prepared to concede, and he came away with everything he asked for. He was ready to give Hitler all of the Sudetenland that he wanted so long as he did not use armed force to get it. And Hitler agreed. Neville returned from Munich with Hitler's pledge to use the methods of consultation rather than of war to deal with any other questions of concern to their two countries. But he failed to grasp that Hitler had longed to use armed force, and was dissuaded from doing so on this occasion only because he obtained everything he asked for without it. Neville had done his best under his sisters' tutelage to fathom Hitler's way of thinking. Ida had warned him that Hitler by his own admission would honour agreements only as long as they suited him. Neville placed in his copy of *Mein Kampf* Stephen Roberts' statement that, 'The whole teaching of Hitlerism is to justify war as an instrument of policy.' Neville wrote it out in his own hand. But he could not quite credit it. The Munich agreement convinced him that Hitler was a man who could be persuaded to accept peaceful settlements if treated with a careful balance of diplomacy backed up by increased rearmament.

Neville also fatefully misjudged another person. He was slow to discover what Austen had long insisted: that Churchill was a man with whom he could usefully collaborate, particularly on matters of defence. He refused to bring Churchill into the Cabinet until war broke out, and continued thereafter to retard Churchill's widening command of the war effort. Only after Churchill replaced him as Prime Minister did Neville discover how well they could work together; Neville focusing on the home front while Churchill concentrated on the war. And this time Neville overestimated the cordiality of their cooperation. He was hurt by the alacrity with which Churchill accepted the resignation that cancer forced Neville to tender. Right up to his death a few weeks later, he underestimated the force of the indictment that Churchill, even more powerful as historian than as war leader, would pronounce upon him once the war was over.

*

The trajectory of Neville's brief premiership was as steep after Munich as before. London gave him a jubilant reception upon his return, but criticism mounted quickly. Exhausted, he 'came nearer ... to a nervous break down than I have ever been in my life'.[1] He pulled himself together to face the ordeal that awaited him in the House of Commons. Ida, who sat in the Speaker's Gallery, felt her blood boil 'at the way the Opposition kept interrupting & jeering when it was evident how tired he was'.[2] He had to win over wavering members of his ministry and parry the efforts of Churchill, who 'was carrying on a regular conspiracy ... with the aid of Jan Masaryk, the Czech Minister'.[3] Anxious to join rather than defeat the government, Churchill smiled at Neville while fomenting unrest behind him. These machinations infuriated party regulars in the House and shocked Churchill at the extent of the hostility he aroused. At the same time Neville had to deal with a threat from Italy to strengthen the axis between Rome and Berlin unless Britain conceded more to secure the withdrawal of the Italian forces still in Spain. Neville had to resist the Italian pressure for fear of intensifying the opposition to his policy at home.

His speech at the close of debate proved effective. Hesitant ministers fell into line. Notable critics found him impressive. Amery confessed that the speech 'very very nearly persuaded him' to vote with the government. Word reached Neville of Eden's comment that 'he was 90% with me on my last speech and when told that I had not found Hitler personally attractive declared that that brought his

---

1 Neville to Hilda, 2 Oct.1938, Chequers, in Self, ed., *The Neville Chamberlain Diary Letters*, IV, 351

2 Ida to Miss E.M. Leamon, Dorothy and Frank's former governess, NC1/23/29

3 Neville to Ida, 9 Oct.1938, 10 Downing Street, in Self, *The Neville Chamberlain Diary Letters*, IV, 351–4

agreement up to 100%'. Eden called for national unity in foreign policy. But Neville had no wish to carry conciliation that far. He knew that Eden would not have condoned the overture to Mussolini that led to the Munich conference: 'the difference between Anthony & me is more fundamental than he realises. At bottom he is really dead against making terms with dictators and what makes him think it possible to get unity is my insistence on the necessity for rearmament ... He leaves out or chooses not to see for the moment that the conciliation part of the policy is just as important as the rearming ... what I want is more support for my policy and not more strengthening of those who don't believe in it.'[4]

But first he needed rest. Alec Douglas-Home, his parliamentary private secretary, had witnessed his 'brief mental disturbance' on the return from Munich and offered the hospitality of his northern estate. It looked out over 'green lawns and fields dotted with the big Cheviot sheep and then up again to the corner of a lake [backed] by high dark woods'. Annie accompanied Neville to this retreat. She had held up well during the crisis, but now that relief had come she went 'to bits;'[5] and they both relished the opportunity to recover. Neville had time to ponder 'the countless letters and telegrams which continued to pour in expressing in most moving accents the writers heartfelt relief and gratitude. All the world seemed to be full of my praises except the House of Commons.' Tributes came in 'from all over the world ... such as no man & woman can ever have received before. ... From Germany itself there are great numbers from women who thank me for saving their sons but also from men and young men too' – apparently belying Stephen Roberts' assertion that 'there is hardly a boy in Germany who does not view the preparation for ultimate war as the most important aspect of life.' Neville was showered with gifts of things he was thought to love: 'fishing rods, stacks of flies, books, pictures, umbrellas, watches & clocks, scarves slippers & gloves cigars & cigarettes and flowers by the arm load – all accompanied by the most touching messages, often anonymous'.[6] 'I have also been given by Dutchmen 4000 tulips 500 hyacinths 500 daffodils and 1000 crocuses. So', he told Ida: 'if you would like some you can make your choice.'[7] Here were the Munich tulips.

Neville and his sisters accepted these tributes at face value. Ida told him of

---

4 Neville to Hilda, 15 Oct.1938, The Hirsel, Coldstream, in Self, ed., *The Neville Chamberlain Diary Letters*, IV, 356

5 Annie to Mary, 12 Oct.1938, The Hirsel, Coldstream, Annie Chamberlain correspondence in the possession of James Lloyd

6 Neville to Mary, 5 Nov.1938, Chequers, NC1/20/1/186

7 Neville to Ida, 24 Oct.1938, Chequers, in Self, *The Neville Chamberlain Diary Letters*, IV, 358

letters 'from friends in France ... speaking of the intense gratitude & admiration shewn to you by the French people & the "almost adoration" with which the poor people, fisher folk, market women, shopkeepers etc. speak of you.'[8] This response from ordinary folk convinced her that Neville had accomplished at least 'One great thing ... gaining time, to allow the people of all countries & especially the totalitarian states to show their hatred of war. One hopes it may make even the dictators hesitate a bit how far they push things in future. Of course the leopard cannot change his spots all in a minute nor will Hitler & Mussolini give up their offensive methods, but one does hope that by degrees we shall approach a more general appeasement & that in a better atmosphere they may moderate their ways.'[9]

Neville echoed and amplified Ida's hope: 'when all the world views the prospect of war with such horror it encourages me to believe that even dictators would find it difficult to plunge their people into it and survive'. He now placed more emphasis on 'the work of peace making' which 'is but just begun' than on accelerating rearmament. 'What I want is a restoration of confidence that would allow us all to stop arming and get back to the work of making our world a better place to live in.' One threat to this search for peace that both Ida and Neville found particularly annoying came from 'our own dissidents'[10] who 'constantly provoked and insulted' the dictators. 'All this makes life very strenuous,' Neville said, closing his mind to his critics, 'but I shall go on trying, for I feel confident that I have world public opinion behind me.'[11]

His next move along this post-Munich trajectory was to initiate a succession of meetings with the men he had worked with in Munich. He began with Daladier in Paris 'to give French people an opportunity of pouring out their pent up feelings of gratitude and affection, – to strengthen Daladier and encourage him to *do* something at last to put his country's defences in order ... and, finally to make it possible for me to go to Rome ... Rome at the moment is the end of the axis on which it is easiest to make an impression ... An hour or two tete-a-tete with Musso might be extraordinarily valuable in making plans for talks with Germany.' Neville relied on himself in these face-to-face encounters. 'Of course I should take Halifax with me to Rome but the important talks would be between Musso and myself.'[12]

8  Ida to Neville, 9 Oct.1938, The Bury House, NC18/2/1096

9  Ida to Mary, 10 Oct.1938, The Bury House, BC4/2/236

10  Ida to Neville, 21 Oct.1938, The Bury House, NC18/2/1097

11  Neville to Mary, 5 Nov.1938, Chequers, NC1/20/1/186

12  Neville to Hilda, 6 Nov.1938, Chequers, in Self, ed., *The Neville Chamberlain Diary Letters*, IV, 361

Though he encouraged the French to strengthen their defences, he gave conciliation a higher priority. 'A lot of people seem to me to be losing their heads and talking and thinking as though Munich had made war more instead of less imminent,' he complained.[13] He resisted calls for the appointment of a new Minister of Supply to build up the armed forces, and saw no need for 'huge additions to the programme now being put into operation'.

❦

But the dictators responded very differently to their experience at Munich. Neville found it 'difficult to believe that another crisis could arise so acute and dangerous within at any rate a considerable period'. But Hitler scoffed publicly at 'umbrella carrying' peacemakers. Within days, what Ida called 'disgraceful fresh attacks on Jews' took place across Germany 'under the immediate inspiration of Göbbels', the rash of attacks known as Kristallnacht, the night of breaking glass. 'Hitler does indeed make it difficult for those who wish to keep friendly relations with him,' she sighed.[14] Neville too was 'horrified by the German behaviour to the Jews. There does seem to be some fatality about Anglo-German relations which invariably blocks every effort to improve them.' Even so, he muted his public response to the Nazi barbarities, explaining to Ida that he did not want to voice 'such criticism as may bring even worse things on the heads of these unhappy victims'.[15]

Then the Fascists of Italy laid claim to parts of France and French North Africa, threatening to treat them the way Germany had the Sudetenland. 'What fools the dictators are!' Neville exclaimed[16] – as if the dictators did not know what their henchmen were up to. He refused to adjust his search for peace in light of these developments. Nor would he abandon the hopes he vested in his forthcoming visit to Mussolini: 'the fact that Mussolini sent word to us ... that he would like to publish the date of the Rome visit today shows I think that it may be possible to keep him quiet between then & now'. The maddening behaviour of Nazis and Fascists abroad and critics at home only confirmed Neville's commitment to

13  Neville to Ida, 24 Oct.1938, Chequers, in Self, ed., *The Neville Chamberlain Diary Letters*, IV, 357

14  Ida to Neville, 11 Nov.1938, The Bury House, NC18/2/1099

15  Neville to Ida, 13 Nov.1938, 10 Downing Street, in Self, ed., *The Neville Chamberlain Diary Letters*, IV, 363

16  Neville to Ida, 4 Dec.1938, Chevening, in Self, ed., *The Neville Chamberlain Diary Letters*, IV, 366

appeasement. 'At my age & in my position there can be nothing more for me to want. Personal ambition therefore does not count. The only thing I care about is to be able to carry out the policy I believe, indeed *know* to be right.'

The popular praise showered on Neville after Munich diminished unmistakeably after Kristallnacht. But this wavering of support at home did not deflect him from his course. He would have liked to strengthen his Cabinet through promotion of junior ministers and recruitment from the back benches. But nowhere could he find the unquestioning support he craved. The only way he thought likely to 'produce an improvement' was 'to get rid of this uneasy and disgruntled House of Commons by a General Election'. But he recognised that 'doubts about my foreign policy owing to the behaviour of the dictators' and doubts raised by Churchill about the adequacy of the rearmament programme made an appeal to the electorate risky. After barely eighteen months as Prime Minister, Neville looked at his beloved Chequers and wondered 'how much longer I shall be here'.[17] He did not relish his isolation as Prime Minister. He bemoaned the fact that while Baldwin 'had me to help him ... I have to bear my troubles alone'. Yet he could not accept even the friendliest criticism. Lord Halifax saw an advance text of the address Neville was to deliver to the Foreign Press Association, and commented that 'it laid too much stress on appeasement & was not stiff enough to the dictators'. Neville refused to make any change. After he delivered the address, 'Halifax passed me a note of congratulation adding "I think I was wrong and I am glad". This was handsome', Neville admitted, but went on to complain that Halifax 'didn't realise how upsetting it was to receive that sort of message just as I was going into action.'[18]

He approached his visit to Rome in the New Year well aware that there were plenty of people at home ready 'to misrepresent, crab, distort or minimise anything that I do'. He had his own doubts 'as to the possibility of bringing off any tangible result'.[19] The omens across western and central Europe were not good: Franco's successes in Spain, Italian provocation of France, the stiffening French reaction, 'and German general bad temper and mischievousness',[20] all boded ill. Even so, Neville

17  Neville to Hilda, 11 Dec.1938, Chequers, in Self, ed., *The Neville Chamberlain Diary Letters*, IV, 368

18  Neville to Ida, 17 Dec.1938, Farnham Park, in Self, ed., *The Neville Chamberlain Diary Letters*, IV, 370–1

19  Neville to Mary, 9 Jan.1939, 10 Downing Street, NC1/20/1/188

20  Neville to Ida, 8 Jan.1939, Hever Castle, in Self, ed., *The Neville Chamberlain Diary Letters*, IV, 372

had 'no shadow of doubt that I am right to go'. He clung to reports that 'Musso is most anxious for Anglo-Italian friendship to develop'. Neville nevertheless pitched his hopes low to guard against disappointment: 'personal contact with Mussolini is bound to be helpful in gauging his future actions even if one were to get nothing else to bring away'.

The response Neville received from the Italians sent these hesitant hopes soaring; and he came away convinced that the visit had 'definitely strengthened the chances of peace'. Mussolini struck him as 'straightforward and considerate', muting his demands upon France and emphasising his resolve 'to stand by his agreement' with Britain. He assured Neville 'that he wanted peace and was ready to use his influence to get it'.[21] Neville welcomed signs of uneasiness in Mussolini's relationship with Hitler, and was encouraged by the crowds who cheered him in Rome and Turin.

On his return to England, he gave similar credence to a succession of reports that 'Hitler was not planning any aggressive moves but was chiefly concerned with Germany's economic position'.[22] Changing omens in the international arena appeared to vindicate Neville's course of action over the past six months. He concluded that at Munich Hitler had 'missed the bus' – again that fateful metaphor: 'once you have done that in international affairs it is very difficult to reproduce the situation.' Britain had further strengthened its defences since Munich: the dictators 'could not make nearly such a mess of us now as they could have done then, while we could make much more of a mess of them'. All this added 'to the weight on the peace side of the balance'.[23] Ida, always the least confident of the sisters, welcomed his assurance: 'It was very pleasant to ... know that you really feel that your policy is making way.'[24] Electoral opinion was also swinging in his favour.

Dining at the German embassy 'in an atmosphere of great cordiality,' Neville was delighted to hear from the Italian ambassador 'that Rome was still talking & thinking of little else than my visit and that all Italy was rejoicing in it'. His hopes soared still higher. 'I think we ought to be able to establish excellent relations with [Spain's] Franco who seems well disposed to us, and then, if the Italians are not in

21 Neville to Hilda, 15 Jan.1939, 10 Downing Street, in Self, ed., *The Neville Chamberlain Diary Letters*, IV, 373

22 Neville to Ida, 28 Jan. & 12 & 26 Feb.1939, in Self, ed., *The Neville Chamberlain Diary Letters*, IV, 376, 380 & 387

23 Neville to Hilda, 5 Feb.1939, Chequers, in Self, ed., *The Neville Chamberlain Diary Letters*, IV, 377–8

24 Ida to Neville, 9 Feb.1939, The Bury House, NC18/2/1110

too bad a temper, we might get Franco Italian conversations going and if they were reasonably amicable we might advance towards disarmament ... and if I am given three or four more years I believe I really might retire with a quiet mind.'[25] Ida chimed in, 'It is really remarkable, the change of feeling in the country during the last few weeks. In January every one you met was saying "It does look as if war was coming. Do you think it <u>can</u> be avoided", & now the opening remark always is "You know I <u>don't</u> believe there is going to be war."'[26] Her approval emboldened Neville to quote the eighteenth-century Prime Minister in Britain's duel with France: 'Like Chatham "I know that I can save this country and I do not believe that anyone else can"'. Gleefully he watched his critics fall into line: eulogies from Churchill, approval from Eden, 'Even poor Leo Amery is eating humble pie.'[27]

Two days later the Germans marched over what remained of Czechoslovakia.

☙

Ida was staggered, but recognised the severity of this setback. 'I cannot tell you,' she wrote to Neville, 'all I feel about the bitter blow which Hitler has dealt to your policy at a moment when it seemed at last to be moving towards success.' Hitler 'has now belied every statement & promise that he made', confirming her early foreboding. He had put a stop to 'every possibility of further negotiation with Germany so long as his rule continues. ... sooner or later, unless something happens to Hitler, war is inevitable ... nothing else is likely to stop him from over-running the whole of Europe.' And 'a stand must be made somewhere'. In drawing these conclusions, she accepted that in this instance Neville's policy had failed. She refused, nevertheless, to say that the policy had been misconceived from the start. 'Germany <u>had</u> grievances' from the peace treaty imposed upon it at Versailles, she insisted, '& it could not be right to go to war in order to perpetuate them.' Further-more, Britain still derived substantial benefit from Munich: 'if war should come, at least we shall be far better prepared to meet it than in September.'[28]

Hilda displayed more confidence in Neville's handiwork. She could not yet bring herself to face failure. 'It is something to feel amidst the ruin around us that

25 Neville to Ida, 19 Feb.1939, Chequers, in Self, ed., *The Neville Chamberlain Diary Letters*, IV, 382–4

26 Ida to Neville, 24 Feb.1939, The Bury House, NC18/2/1112

27 Neville to Ida, 12 Mar.1939, Chequers, in Self, ed., *The Neville Chamberlain Diary Letters*, IV, 392–3

28 Ida to Neville, 16 Mar.1939, The Bury House, NC18/2/1116

you have nothing to regret in what you have done during the last year.' Like Ida, she stressed the 'tremendous value' of the six months of continued rearmament that Britain gained from Munich. She emphasised another benefit from Munich: 'the knowledge of the whole world that ... if war is to come there can be no question as to the justice of our cause. ... I know,' she concluded with some assurance, 'that you will go forward steadfastly even in these terrible times & I believe that somehow or other whether war comes or does not come that you will lead this nation through to better times.'[29]

Neville did not respond to Hitler's takeover of Czechoslovakia as swiftly or as firmly as his sisters. Obliged to make a statement in the Commons while German troops were still on the march, he deplored the invasion without any display of anger. When he spoke two days later in Birmingham, however, he denounced the invasion with vigour. The next day he turned seventy. Plans had been made to cel-ebrate the birthday in style, but he curtailed them and returned to London. There he moved speedily to put together an international response to the German aggres-sion. But nothing came of these efforts. And he remained reluctant to take 'a stand ... somewhere', as Ida thought he would have to. 'As always,' he insisted, 'I want to gain time for I never accept the view that war is inevitable.'[30]

Ida and Hilda did not know quite what to make of this response. Both sisters looked for an economic explanation of Hitler's behaviour. Like Neville, Ida had expected concern about the economic situation to deter Hitler from risking war. Now she wondered whether 'it was Germany's economic situation that has driven them into this last mad act of aggression'.[31] Neither sister shared Neville's assurance that war could be avoided. Hilda swung back and forth, torn 'between feeling that the end must be war, & another feeling that it simply can't happen; but I suppose if Hitler does not die or some unforeseen internal crash come in Germany, he may be forced into the last ultimate provocation in order to avoid a financial crash'.[32]

The sisters wrote to Neville sometimes more than weekly these days; and he responded at increasing length. 'From your letter,' he told Ida, 'I think you have realised that this has been a grim week though how grim even you couldn't know.'[33]

29  Hilda to Neville, 17 Mar.1939, The Bury House, NC18/2/1117
30  Neville to Hilda, 19 Mar.1939, 10 Downing Street, in Self, ed., *The Neville Chamberlain Diary Letters*, IV, 394
31  Ida to Mary, 20 Mar.1939, The Bury House, BC4/2/239
32  Hilda to Neville, 31 Mar.1939, The Bury House, NC18/2/1119
33  Neville to Ida, 26 Mar.1939, Chequers, in Self, ed., *The Neville Chamberlain Diary Letters*, IV, 395

He was harassed by rumours of further military movement. Word was whispered to him during a state banquet that 'the Germans have mobilised 20 divisions on the Western frontier'. He was less fearful of an attack by the German army in Continental Europe than by air directly on Britain: 'with this fanatic you can't exclude entirely the conception. He might well say ... I am justified in breaking all unwritten or written rules if I can deliver a knock out blow before the other fellow has had time to prepare.' Neville ordered guns and searchlights to be placed in position to defend London. He thus accelerated Britain's preparations against aerial attack, which he thought of as purely defensive rearmament, in contrast to a build-up of the army to fight abroad.

Once 'the clouds thinned out a bit', Neville recognised that the area of danger in Europe had shifted eastward to Poland. That was problematic territory for him. Britain needed allies to act effectively that far from home. He tried to secure a declaration from France and Russia as well as Britain and Poland to 'act together in the event of further signs of German aggressive ambitions. ... But it soon became evident that Poland would find great difficulty in signing and I could readily understand why.' Poland was wedged between Russia and Germany, two powers that had long denied it independence. Neville's proposal would have thrown Poland into the arms of the first to escape from the second.

That fact brought him face to face with the question that nagged at him for the next five months: what to do about Russia? He knew what he felt. 'I must confess to the most profound distrust of Russia. I have no belief whatever in her ability to maintain an effective offensive even if she wanted to. And I distrust her motives which seem to me to have little connection with our ideas of liberty ... Moreover she is both hated and suspected by many of the smaller states notably Poland Rumania and Finland ... who would much more effectively help us if we can get them on our side.' Accordingly Neville abandoned his proposal of a declaration by four major powers and looked instead to a lesser quartet; Rumania joining Britain and France to reinforce Poland. He also approached Mussolini, hoping that he would intervene with Berlin over Poland as he had over Czechoslovakia. Neville welcomed even the faintest hint of a favourable response from Rome.

Even so, he sensed that he was grasping at straws. If the Rumanians proved as reluctant as the Poles to stand up to Germany, 'if the small states won't face up to this sort of penetration even when backed by us', Britain would simply have to go on strengthening its capacities for self-defence. If need be, Britain could defend itself alone. But it could never command enough military might to defeat Germany elsewhere in Europe. Neville refused to contemplate a military challenge to Germany on the Continent. Any British ultimatum to Germany, he told Ida, would 'mean war and I would never be responsible for presenting it. We should just have to go on rearming & collecting what help we could from outside in the hope that something would happen to break the spell, either Hitler's death or a realisation that the defence was too strong to make attack feasible.'

Over the following week, events again moved faster than Neville expected. Reliable reports reached London 'that Hitler had everything ready for a swoop on Poland'.[34] Neville 'thought that we might wake up on Sunday or Monday morning to find Poland surrendering to an ultimatum'. He therefore hurried to announce a unilateral guarantee of assistance to Poland in the event of a threat to its independence, taking care, however, not to rule out an adjustment of its borders to satisfy the Germans. When the German attack failed to materialise, Neville concluded, as he had done after Munich, that his diplomatic action had averted war. He had given Hitler 'a definite check'.

Ida eulogised her brother's achievement: 'It must be a great satisfaction to you to see how completely you have the nation, & the whole non-totalitarian world behind you.' She credited him with choosing 'precisely the right moment' to make his 'declaration of support to Poland': it 'may stop further aggression, & once more postpone the danger of war'.[35] Her confidence increased during the week. 'If Hitler does not commit any further aggression within a very short time he is likely to find it more & more difficult to do so & we shall grow relatively stronger & stronger.' Yet she still lacked Neville's assurance that war was not inevitable. 'If [Hitler] does decide to risk everything then we are bound to have war, but horrible as that will be I cannot believe it will last long or that it will not precipitate a crisis in Germany itself.'[36]

Neville's confidence was slightly shaken by belligerent gestures from Italy. 'Musso has behaved to me like a sneak and a cad,' he admitted in antique Victorian terms to Hilda.[37] But to her relief, Neville refused to respond by tearing 'up the Anglo-Italian Treaty in a burst of indignation, – in which you would of course have been thoroughly justified, but you still give Musso one other chance & after all, – a possibility even of the faintest kind, of evading war is worth every effort.'[38] Neville

---

34 Neville to Hilda, undated, probably 1–2 Apr.1939, Chequers, in Self, ed., *The Neville Chamberlain Diary Letters*, IV, 400–2

35 Ida to Neville, 2 Apr.1939, The Bury House, NC18/2/1120

36 Ida to Neville, 6 Apr.1939, The Bury House, NC18/2/1121

37 Neville to Hilda, 15 Apr.1939, Chequers, in Self, ed., *The Neville Chamberlain Diary Letters*, IV, 405–7

38 Hilda to Neville, 14 Apr.1939, The Bury House, NC18/2/1122

welcomed her encouragement. He believed that his policy was bearing fruit 'in the consolidation of world opinion and in the improvement of the military position of ourselves & France'.

What worried him about the sabre-rattling of the dictators was how it enabled his critics 'to mock me publicly and to weaken my authority in this country'. Neville suspected that his popular support was faltering. He was also aware of the poor debating skills of the ministers alongside him in the Commons, buffeted as they were by broadsides from Churchill. So when Churchill told the Chief Whip 'of his strong desire to join the Govt.' Neville hesitated to turn him down. 'The question is whether Winston, who would certainly help on the Treasury bench in the Commons, would help or hinder in Cabinet or in council.'

But springtime brought a lull in the international storms. 'It is curious,' Hilda remarked, 'how after another period of acute tension all the world is now beginning to say again: – somehow I don't believe there will be war though I don't see how it is to be avoided! I think I share their opinions.' She renewed her faith in Neville's policy: 'I feel with you that time is on our side. The dictators cannot go on indefinitely on their present lines, & maintain their armies & their peoples at war level forever, & probably we could stand it better than they can on account of our great wealth & the fact that we had not been in that state of tension for the same number of years. Surely if war can be staved off for a time – either one of the dictators will die or there will be a revulsion of feeling which will allow of another attempt to get back to more normal conditions.'[39] Ida was not so sure. 'I am struck,' she admitted, 'by the number of people ... who ... have stated that "somehow" they don't believe there is going to be war. I should share their feelings if Hitler were sane, but as he is not it is impossible to foretell what may happen.'[40] Still she treasured the evidence of her brother's achievement the previous autumn. 'I can't tell you how much we have enjoyed your Munich tulips. They at least have proved no disappointment.'[41]

Neville embraced Hilda's assessment of the outlook. He was encouraged by reports from British visitors to Berlin of conversations with the German leadership. He even found something to welcome in the speech in which Hitler repudiated the Anglo-German naval arms limitation agreement of 1935. Neville seized on the invitation Hitler issued in that speech for 'fresh discussions with us and Poland'. He took that as indicating that Hitler 'does not think the time favourable for a new challenge'. But he no longer trusted Hitler; and even had he wished to

---

39  Hilda to Neville, 28 Apr.1939, The Bury House, NC18/2/1124
40  Ida to Neville, 5 May 1939, The Bury House, NC18/2/1125
41  Ida to Neville, 18 May 1939, The Bury House, NC18/2/1127

reopen discussions with Hitler, Neville realised that parliamentary opinion would prevent him. He was therefore inclined 'to approach Musso again. From certain information which comes to me it would appear that Musso has been getting more and more irritated with Hitler ... I have a feeling that if he is now handled judiciously it might be possible to give the axis another twist and that this might be the best way of keeping Master Hitler quiet.'[42] Neville was further heartened by indications that his sisters' interpretation of public opinion in Hampshire applied elsewhere in the country. Now there was no need to invite Churchill into the government: 'the nearer we get to war the more his chances improve and vice versa'. Under present circumstances, 'I can snap my fingers at Winston.'[43] But Neville also used the springtime lull to introduce military conscription, welcoming an opportunity to do so without shaking his fist at another aggressive move by the dictators.

He celebrated his second anniversary as Prime Minister being cheered by the public but abused in the House of Commons. The uneasy calm that descended over Europe at Easter continued into the summer, deepening his commitment to the leading features of his policy: 'the longer war is put off the less likely it is to come at all as we go on perfecting our defences ... You don't need offensive forces sufficient to win a smashing victory. What you want are defensive forces sufficiently strong to make it impossible for the other side to win except at such a cost as to make it not worth while.'[44] He kept as much distance from Russia as his colleagues would allow. Even Halifax favoured strengthened ties to Russia and was willing to send Eden there to see what he could achieve, to Hilda's dismay. 'No doubt [Eden] or Churchill could have returned triumphantly with an Alliance in a very short time, but it would have meant exactly what you have tried so hard to avoid – the belief on the part of Russia that we are entirely in her hands, & also the rousing the fears & weakening the support we might receive from all the minor powers – Poland the Northern States, Roumania & Turkey. No,' she went on, exalting her brother, '... you are the only Statesman it seems to me in the whole Government ...

42  Neville to Hilda, 29 Apr.1939, Chequers, in Self, ed., *The Neville Chamberlain Diary Letters*, IV, 411–2
43  Neville to Ida, 23 Apr.1939, 10 Downing Street, in Self, ed., *The Neville Chamberlain Diary Letters*, IV, 409–10
44  Neville to Ida, 23 July 1939, Chequers, in Self, ed., *The Neville Chamberlain Diary Letters*, IV, 431

England <u>has</u> thrown up the man for the situation this time as we did against Napoleon with Pitt. He & you & possibly, at one moment, Wellington, are really the only British Statesmen who have really held Europe in the hollow of their hands.'[45]

Neville encouraged his sisters to head to France at the end of July for their annual cure, confident that 'Hitler now realizes that he can't grab anything else without a major war and has decided therefore to put Danzig into cold storage'.[46] Danzig, Poland's German-populated port on the Baltic, remained the focus of concern. But all reports suggested that a German attack was not imminent. Neville continued to insist that 'Hitler missed the bus last September' when he drew back from attacking Czechoslovakia: '... his generals won't let him risk a major war now'.[47] He added that Hitler 'is not such a fool as some hysterical people make out and that he would not be sorry to compromise if he could do so without what he would feel to be humiliation'.[48] Neville continued also to 'believe that our best plan is to keep up contacts with Rome where I am certain war is looked upon with terror'.[49] Even so, he insisted on meaningful responses from Mussolini. Hitler's springtime takeover of Czechoslovakia forced Neville to recognise the inadequacy of his achievement at Munich. Mussolini responded to his plea over Poland by saying, 'Let the Poles agree that Danzig goes to the Reich and I will do my best to get a peaceful agreed solution. But that is not good enough,' Neville insisted. 'That is just what we tried at Munich, but Hitler broke it up when it suited him.'[50]

Alarm bells began to ring in mid-August, calling Neville back from his Scottish holiday. Though he still saw no reason why his sisters should alter their plans, he promised that 'if at any time I think you ought to come back,' he would tell them by telegram. Hilda sent him anxious best wishes. She doubted now that war could be avoided: 'but anyway the year gained has put us in a very different position to that which we faced a year ago'.[51]

45  Hilda to Neville, 16 June 1939, The Bury House, NC18/2/1131

46  Neville to Hilda, 30 July 1939, Chequers, in Self, ed., *The Neville Chamberlain Diary Letters*, IV, 435

47  Neville to Hilda, 28 May 1939, Alresford, Hants., in Self, ed., *The Neville Chamberlain Diary Letters*, IV, 419

48  Neville to Hilda, 2 July 1939, 10 Downing Street, in Self, ed., *The Neville Chamberlain Diary Letters*, IV, 426

49  Neville to Ida, 10 June 1939, Westbourne, in Self, ed., *The Neville Chamberlain Diary Letters*, IV, 420

50  Neville to Hilda, 15 July 1939, Chequers, in Self, ed., *The Neville Chamberlain Diary Letters*, IV, 428

51  Hilda to Neville, 22 Aug.1939, Royat Palace Hotel, NC18/2/1141

The next day Germany signed a non-aggression pact with Russia. The sisters hurried home, and were astonished on arrival to receive a 'wonderful letter' from Neville. 'Phew! What a week,' he wrote:[52] '... the places buzzes with rumours and our own Secret Service continually reports information "derived from an absolutely reliable source" of the most alarming character. I don't know how many times we have been given the exact date and even hour when the Germans would march into Poland.' But the flood of reports only heightened Neville's scepticism: the Germans 'haven't marched yet and, as always, I count every hour that passes without a catastrophe as adding its might to the slowly accumulating anti-war forces'. He continued to place his trust in those forces, essentially the worldwide revulsion at any renewal of war.

To give them time to accumulate, he refused to hurry his own pace. The 'worst trial' occurred two days after Russia and Germany signed their agreement, when Hitler sent for Henderson, the British ambassador. Would Hitler confront Henderson with an ultimatum and tell him to leave the country? Neville 'sat with Annie in the drawing room' of 10 Downing Street awaiting Henderson's report, 'unable to read, unable to talk, just sitting with folded hands & a gnawing pain in the stomach'(a sign of his incipient illness?). But 'as hour after hour went by and nothing was heard I began to cheer up a little'. At last they learnt that Hitler had given Henderson a proposal and an aeroplane to deliver it swiftly. In the meantime Henderson 'was sending a record of his conversation in two long cipher telegrams. I got the first telegram at dinner that night and found it unilluminating.' Told that 'the second would not be deciphered till midnight I refused to sit up for it & went to bed and to sleep! Next morning it was on the breakfast table but I had my breakfast and read the papers before opening the box.'

Neville spent the rest of the day drafting a reply in consultation with Halifax and Henderson, once he arrived. 'I had a Cabinet in the late afternoon and then sat up again till long after midnight redrafting our reply.' Throughout that 'gruelling day,' the person whose support he found most helpful was Annie who 'as always in critical moments was calm & cheerful ... and [refrained] from worrying suggestions or enquiries'. When the next day also passed without an explosion, Neville interpreted it as 'a good omen for every postponement of the crisis serves to enable world opinion to show itself and to isolate the man or the nation that would disturb the peace'.

He found encouragement in the things that did not happen. The Russo-German

---

52 Neville to Hilda, 27 Aug.1939, 10 Downing Street, in Self, ed., *The Neville Chamberlain Diary Letters*, IV, 440–2

agreement did not 'destroy the peace front'. Neville was 'fairly certain' that Italy would 'not come in if Hitler goes to war over Poland'. And Hitler had not yet gone to war. The proposals that he sent Britain brushed 'Poland aside as a matter to be settled by Germany and *after that* (i.e. if we leave Germany alone) Hitler will make us a splendid offer which in effect will be an Anglo-German alliance'. Neville did not jump at the proposals because they consigned Poland to the tender mercy of the Germans and did not offer to negotiate a settlement like the one reached at Munich. But he was nonetheless struck by Hitler's offer. 'The mentality of that extraordinary man would be incredible to anyone who had not seen and talked with him. I believe that in his excitement over the prospect of this Anglo German alliance ... he has almost forgotten Poland! ... we can't forget it and so for the moment we are not further advanced. ... But on Friday the motto on my calendar was "Remember that the tide turns at the low as well as at the high level"!'

Once again, Hilda and Ida scarcely knew what to make of Neville's response. It helped Ida 'bear these days of suspense' to know 'that you have not yet given up all hope & that there are still possibilities of new development. ... How <u>could</u> you eat your breakfast & read your newspaper before opening the box with Hitler's message! & yet how wise of you! ... It looks as if at last Berlin & Rome were beginning to realise that war is really close upon them & they don't like the prospect.'[53] Neville's letter made Hilda almost ecstatic. 'Oh, may you be rewarded for all that you have borne & suffered by drawing Europe out of the maelstrom of war & armaments to a new vision of a United states of Europe.'[54]

At dawn three days later the Germans invaded Poland. Before midnight Britain found itself at war.

❦

Ida and Hilda dealt with the outbreak of the war without guidance from Neville. They knew that he would not have time to write them at the moment of the explosion. Doubting that he could even look at letters from them, they wrote to Annie. 'So the blow has fallen at last,' wrote Ida, '& the war which Neville has spent so many efforts to avert, has been brought upon us by the folly & wickedness of one small group of men.'[55] She still wanted to assure her brother that 'his efforts have not been in vain', that they had 'united the nation & given the world time to appreciate

53  Ida to Neville, 28 Aug.1939, The Bury House, NC18/2/1142
54  Hilda to Neville, 29 Aug.1939, The Bury House, NC1/15/3/161
55  Ida to Annie, 1 Sept.1939, The Bury House, NC18/2/1143

the true nature of Germany's claims'. But the force of national and world opinion had not kept war from breaking out. Now 'nothing can serve but to oppose our force against theirs'. Ida retained some illusions: she did not expect 'that this war can last as long as the last one. I don't believe human nature could stand it.' Nor did she lose her faith in Neville: she prayed God to give him 'strength to carry on. I feel his sane & steady judgment will be needed every bit as much when the war is over as at the present juncture.' Amplifying her reaction in a letter to Mary, Ida faced up to 'the failure of all the efforts [Neville] has made to avoid this awful catastrophe'.[56] She viewed the situation in the starkest terms: 'Hitler has set up the Gospel of Force & only force can defeat him.' Her response was similarly harsh: 'I can't help hoping that the Germans may this time get their share of the bombing, & that their civilian population may know something of what they are making others suffer.'

Hilda reached out to her brother in 'this bitter hour' more sympathetically. She encouraged him to find strength in the fact that 'from the first moment that you took office, you have given of your best to the cause of peace, that you have left no stone unturned, that you have again & again opened a way which could have been accepted with honour & safety by Germany'.[57] She was reluctant to face the failure and sought compensation, which Ida too had found, in the popular support Neville had won: 'if you have failed ... yet you have succeeded in winning the support, not only of all our people, but of the Empire, & of all the neutral countries'. Hilda narrowed Neville's failure down to his misunderstanding of Hitler individually: 'his bad faith & lust of domination is clear to all & there can be no end until his power is broken'. Still she could not resist the conclusion which Neville had refused to accept: 'everything that has happened in these last days shows more than ever that this war was inevitable'. Like Ida, Hilda added further rearmament to the benefits Britain gained at Munich: 'your action last Sept. by giving time for world opinion to be formed & for defence preparations to be made, has put us in an immeasurably stronger position'.

The response that Neville at last sent them two weeks later was very different. His sisters had said nothing about his delay in declaring war on Germany after the invasion of Poland, a delay that brought the House of Commons close to mutiny. Neville now explained that the 'long drawn out agonies that preceded the actual declaration of war' were due to 'three complications':[58] firstly, secret communica-

---

56  Ida to Mary, 3 Sept.1939, The Bury House, BC4/2/242
57  Hilda to Annie & Neville, 3 Sept.1939, The Bury House, NC1/15/4/4
58  Neville to Ida, 10 Sept.1939, Chequers, in Self, ed., *The Neville Chamberlain Diary Letters*, IV, 443–5

tions that a neutral intermediary had conducted between Hitler and Goering with Neville and Halifax; secondly, Mussolini's last minute proposal for a Munich-style conference; and thirdly, French demands for time to mobilise. The only one of the three that mattered for Neville was the first. He had found the 'communications with Hitler and Goering ... rather promising'. They 'didn't really go much beyond friendly expressions ... they gave the impression, probably with intention, that it was possible to persuade Hitler to accept a peaceful & reasonable solution of the Polish question in order to get an Anglo German agreement which he continually declared to be his greatest ambition.' Neville could not make out what destroyed this chance. He could not believe that Hitler was deliberately deceiving the British 'while he matured his schemes ... There is good evidence that orders for the invasion on the 25th August were actually given and then cancelled at the last moment because H. wavered.' Neville was sure that Hitler 'worked seriously at proposals' for an agreement with the British: '... But at the last moment some brainstorm took possession of him'. His interpretation of Hitler remained fundamentally psychological. Neville described him as 'a paranoiac', and could not credit that all along Hitler wanted war.

The German forces swept across Poland faster than expected. Attention turned back toward the western front where Ida thought 'nothing can serve but to oppose our force against theirs'. Neville challenged her assumption. 'There is such a wide spread desire to avoid war & it is so deeply rooted that it must surely find expression somehow.' He had at last lost faith in Hitler: 'Until he disappears and his system collapses there can be no peace.' But Neville refused to believe that the time had come to fight: 'what I hope for is not a military victory – I very much doubt the possibility of that – but a collapse of the German home front.' He disagreed entirely with Ida's desire to see German civilians experience 'something of what they are making others suffer'. Neville did not even want to bomb military targets in urban areas: 'to convince the Germans that they cannot win ... one must weigh every action in the light of its probable effect on German mentality. I hope myself we shall not start to bomb their munition centres and objectives in towns unless they begin it.' He reacted impatiently to his sisters' assurance that his efforts had not been unavailing. 'It was of course a grievous disappointment that peace could not be saved but I know that my persistent efforts *have* convinced the world that no part of the blame can lie here. That consciousness of moral right, which it is impossible for the Germans to feel, *must* be a tremendous force on our side.'

Far from accepting the now almost universal impression that his policy had failed, Neville simply adapted it to the situation created by the German invasion of Poland. 'My policy continues to be the same,' he told Ida a month later, 'Hold on tight. Keep up the economic pressure, push on with munitions production & military preparations with the utmost energy, take no offensive unless Hitler begins it. I reckon that if we are allowed to carry on this policy we shall have won the war by the Spring.'[59] He refused to believe what his military advisers told him, that the Germans meant to launch an all-out attack westwards, either across the heavily fortified Maginot line constructed by the French or through the neutral Low Countries. Neville argued that the losses Germany would incur in an assault on the Maginot line 'would be too severe to make it worth while'.[60] As for the Low Countries, he relied on public outrage at 'a breach of neutrality so flagrant and unscrupulous' to deter Hitler from invasion, though it had not deterred the Kaiser in 1914: 'If any doubt remained in the mind of anyone that [Hitler] was the enemy of the human race surely such an action would remove it.' The superiority of British radar and fighter planes made an air attack on England also unlikely: 'London is now the best defended place in Europe ... no reasonably prudent air force would go near it.'

Instead Neville expected Hitler to launch a peace offensive, keeping military pressure on the western powers to a level that would maximise public irritation at the privations of war without rousing the popular will to fight. Once the public was fed up, Hitler would 'put out a very reasonable offer' saying, in effect, 'It's no use crying over spilt milk. ... We have no quarrel with you and are quite ready to settle down as good Europeans without further territorial ambitions. Why spill good men's blood for something you can never get. Why not sit down to table with us like sensible men & good fellows.' Neville felt that 'such a specious appeal might be most difficult to resist'. Not that he was willing to entertain it; he refused to contemplate any settlement that allowed Germany to hang on to what it had gained by invading Poland. Nor could Neville contemplate any settlement with Hitler: he would have to be removed from office. The only way, in Neville's estimation, to deal with the kind of offensive he expected would be 'to throw back the peace offer and continue the blockade. In a waiting war of that kind I believe we could outlast the Germans. ... The way to win the war is to convince the Germans that they cannot win. If we can do that without bloodshed I shall rejoice.'

He still could not credit that Hitler actually wanted war. True to his father's essentially economic understanding of the world order, Neville continued to believe that the standard of living was of fundamental importance to ordinary

---

59 Neville to Ida, 8 Oct.1939, Chequers, in Self, ed., *The Neville Chamberlain Diary Letters*, IV, 456
60 Neville to Ida, 23 Sept.1939, 10 Downing Street, in Self, ed., *The Neville Chamberlain Diary Letters*, IV, 450–1

people. He could not believe that the Germans would put up readily with the privations of conflict, let alone take stoic pride in them. Nor could Neville understand the attraction of war. 'How I do hate and loathe this war,' he exclaimed: '... Even the triumph of U-boats destroyed gives me a very uncomfortable feeling. If they called in at our ports in peace time we should probably say what good fellows the officer & crew were.'[61] The force on which he continued to rely was public opinion, abroad as at home. He expected German revulsion at the cost of all-out war and the prospect of retaliatory bombing of German cities to deter Hitler from attacking to the west. 'I am more than ever convinced that his weakest point is the home front.' Neville lost faith also in Mussolini, and now based his 'hopes & indeed my confidence on the attitude of the Italian King, Church, and People. I do not believe that they will fight us on behalf of Germany.'[62]

He knew that his assumptions might soon be put to the test. At the beginning of October the 'soldiers, French and British, [were] all convinced that [Hitler] will begin with an air attack on the Maginot line & follow it up with a rush through the Low Countries. With the approach of winter there is not a lot of time for such manoeuvres', so Neville warned Hilda that October was likely to be 'the critical month'.[63] But after three weeks of German comparative inactivity he reported with satisfaction that 'the weather is deteriorating, we grow stronger in the defence', and 'although troops move, the great offensive does not come. ... Instead of great and decisive battles we have minor engagements, half hearted attacks on our fleet or convoys, and instead of soldiers it is ambassadors and Gauleiters that Hitler summons to Berlin.'[64] Neville's military advisers changed their tune in November, telling him that the 'testing time will be in the spring, in March or in April ... Well it may be so, but I have a "hunch" that the war will be over before the spring. It won't be by defeat in the field but by German realisation that they *can't* win and that it isn't worth their while to go on getting thinner & poorer when they might have instant relief and perhaps not have to give up anything they really care about.'[65]

---

61  Neville to Hilda, 15 Oct.1939, 10 Downing Street, in Self, ed., *The Neville Chamberlain Diary Letters*, IV, 458

62  Neville to Hilda, 17 Sept.1939, Chequers, in Self, ed., *The Neville Chamberlain Diary Letters*, IV, 446–7

63  Neville to Hilda, 1 Oct.1939, Chequers, in Self, ed., *The Neville Chamberlain Diary Letters*, IV, 454

64  Neville to Ida, 22 Oct.1939, Chequers, in Self, ed., *The Neville Chamberlain Diary Letters*, IV, 460

65  Neville to Ida, 5 Nov.1939, 10 Downing Street, in Self, ed., *The Neville Chamberlain Diary Letters*, IV, 466–7

He continued also to account for the behaviour of the dictators in psychological terms. Mussolini was reported 'to be in a state of great depression'. Hitler's silence could be explained only 'by the state of "abject depression" in which I believe he has been plunged owing to his inability to find any opportunity of doing anything'. The peace offensive that Neville expected failed to materialise, but that did not prompt him to revise his calculations. Nor did his deepening isolation: he admitted that he was 'almost alone' in denying the likelihood of a German invasion of Holland. 'But we have already passed some of the dates that were so confidently named ... I cannot believe that if the Germans had intended an invasion they would have let every one know beforehand so that a surprise is now impossible.'[66]

&

Neville moved into a world of his own, little affected by even the faintest, friendliest disagreement. He accepted Hilda's reiteration of his arguments, but did not notice Ida's uneasiness. 'I wonder,' she asked him, 'how much longer we shall go on sitting on the top of the volcano waiting for the eruption.'[67] She expressed herself more openly to Mary, questioning Neville's assumption that the German people could be induced to overthrow Hitler before he experienced 'a spectacular defeat' on the western front.[68]

The sisters dealt with the national emergency in the ways they understood best. 'Sometimes we step out & look at ourselves & are surprised to find what an amount of expert knowledge we have acquired in so many different directions in the course of a long & not inactive life!'[69] Ida chaired District and County Council committees on public health and housing when their male chairmen were called up for active service. She found out how local food production could replace imported produce cut off by German submarines. Hilda marshalled the Women's Institutes in the neighbourhood to increase production. As chair of the agricultural committee of the Women's Institutes nationally, she persuaded the Ministry of Food to allow the women enough sugar to make jam. More forward-looking than her siblings, she wondered 'whether this state of war will lead to family allowances. ... this is a reform with which I have always had a great deal of sympathy ... Certainly

---

66 Neville to Hilda, 12 Nov.1939, 10 Downing Street, in Self, ed., *The Neville Chamberlain Diary Letters*, IV, 469
67 Ida to Neville, 6 Oct.1939, The Bury House, NC18/2/1148
68 Ida to Mary, 9 Oct.1939, The Bury House, BC4/2/244
69 Ida to Neville, 5 Jan.1940, The Bury House, NC18/2/1161

the longer I live the more I feel that for the sake of the nation & the characters of the children larger families should be encouraged.'[70]

Neville was oppressed by more immediate issues. In December he sensed that the year ahead was likely to be 'rougher & grimmer ... than anything we have experienced up to now'.[71] Popular revulsion at the prospect of war broke down, at least in Germany. The crowds that cheered him on his way to Berchtesgaden had now swallowed Goebbels' propaganda and hardened in their devotion to Hitler. Neville was also disconcerted by the way that the pact between Germany and Russia – 'this pernicious pair' – was working as they carved up Poland and Rumania between them. Occasionally he questioned his reliance on diplomacy. Ida prompted him at last 'to wonder whether we shall do any good with [the Germans] unless they first get a real hard punch in the stomach'. Still he saw 'no reason to change the belief I have expressed all along, that Hitler will abstain from any action which would entail real bad fighting with heavy losses whether among soldiers or civilians'.[72] Neville reacted with similar ambivalence when shown over the Maginot line. 'I don't see how the Germans could ever break through.'[73] Yet 'it sickened me to see the barbed wire & pill boxes and guns & anti tank obstacles, remembering what they meant in the last war'.[74] He closed the old year with a ringing reaffirmation of the value of the Munich agreement: 'Hitler missed the bus in Sept.1938. He could have dealt France and ourselves a terrible, perhaps a mortal, blow then. The opportunity will not recur.'

Neville's body, however, had its own messages to deliver. Soon after war was declared, he came down with gout. It grew increasingly severe, and in November he had to be 'carried in a chair to the lift [in 10 Downing Street] & from the lift to the Cabinet room'.[75] By the end of the year he was 'much better' but still wore a snow shoe on his gouty foot and used crutches wherever possible. In retrospect he detected something much more serious than gout. Physically he was running out of time.

Paradoxically his grip on his place at the head of the government grew slightly stronger. The Labour opposition bayed louder than ever for his removal. Their cries were fortified by carping from the press and by demands among Conservative

70  Hilda to Neville, 12 Jan.1940, The Bury House, NC18/2/1162

71  Neville to Hilda, 30 Dec.1939, 10 Downing Street, in Self, ed., *The Neville Chamberlain Diary Letters*, IV, 483

72  Neville to Ida, 3 Dec.1939, Chequers, in Self, ed., *The Neville Chamberlain Diary Letters*, IV, 475

73  Neville to Dorothy, 23 Dec.1939, Chequers, NC1/23/75

74  Neville to Ida, 20 Dec.1939, in Self, ed., *The Neville Chamberlain Diary Letters*, IV, 481

75  Neville to Dorothy, 15 Nov.1939, 10 Downing Street, NC1/23/74

malcontents for the creation of a small War Cabinet. That essentially meant giving more power to Churchill. Neville had at last brought him into the Cabinet as First Lord of the Admiralty at the outbreak of war. But the two men then worked together surprisingly well: the acquisition of Churchill brought more strength than dissension to Neville's ministry. Their different interpretations of the conflict with Germany produced disagreements, of course. But whenever Churchill went his own way and Neville called him to account, Churchill fell into line, anxious to overcome his reputation for self-seeking and lack of collegiality. The two men differed from each other as much in style as in substance. But here too they complemented each other. What Ida called Neville's 'predilection for under-statements'[76] reassured those who would have welcomed such restraint in Churchill. On the other hand, said Ida, 'after all we <u>are</u> at war & it may be useful to have someone who rouses the fighting spirit'.[77]

The only issue over which the differences between the two men grew serious was the treatment of the neutral states, mainly the Scandinavians. Churchill was infuriated by their refusal to take even the weakest stand against Germany; and he said so publicly in terms that only made matters worse, damage that Neville had to repair. The difference between them grew acute when Churchill pressed for the laying of a minefield in Norway's coastal waters. Neville rejected the proposal as inopportune, a decision Churchill termed 'disastrous'. But in the end he 'took it admirably & fully recognised that with my special responsibilities I must be the final judge'. Neville responded by paying Churchill 'warm compliments'. Privately, however, he put Churchill's acceptance down to delight at being back in high office. Neville preferred Halifax to Churchill as a possible successor, but still thought of himself as indispensable.

His confidence in himself and in his policy was not ruffled by a note of alarm from Hilda. She had read a recently-published account by Hermann Rauschning of 'Conversations with Adolf Hitler on His Real Aims'.[78] It was not so much Hitler's willingness to repudiate any agreement that shocked Hilda. She was horrified by the barbaric policies which Rauschning quoted Hitler as willing to embrace, particularly the development of 'a technique of depopulation ... the removal of

76 Ida to Neville, 15 Dec.1939, The Bury House, NC18/2/1159
77 Ida to Neville, 18 Nov.1939, The Bury House, NC18/2/1155
78 Hermann Rauschning, *Hitler Speaks: A series of political conversations with Adolf Hitler on His Real Aims* (London: Thornton Butterworth, 1939, republished in the United States in 2006 by Kessinger Publishing)

entire racial units', of 'millions of an inferior race that breeds like vermin!'[79] 'It really is unbelievable,' Hilda exclaimed, '& yet everything in it is born [sic] out by all Hitler's actions. Once again one is faced by the emergence of a whole attitude to civilisation & humanity so crude, so utterly opposed to all Christian feeling as to be almost inconceivable, & yet one can see faintly that it has an idea at the back of it which you can persuade men to accept, provided you have a visionary to teach it & a degradation of all independence of thought & speech to work on.'[80]

Rauschning's revelations overturned Neville's assumptions at Munich. 'As I read,' Hilda continued, 'I said to myself: – if you had read this before you went to Munich could you have gone? Thank Heaven it was not published then, for without your visit where should we have been; – faced with an enormously stronger enemy & quite clearly the neutrals not only unwilling to risk war on their own account, but still far from being in sympathy with us.' Her faith in the benefits of Munich remained unshaken. Brushing aside Rauschning's revelations, Hilda built up Neville's already overweening self-confidence in her next letter, an exultation on his seventy-first birthday. 'I often think what would your mother have felt if she could have seen your future career! To have given birth to such a son would be worth anything ... I ... can only repeat that whilst literally millions bless the day you were born, you are the pride, the joy & the treasure of your sisters to whom you have been so perfect a brother, & whose lives you have filled with interest & love.'[81]

The protracted delay of the German assault to the west deepened Neville's doubt that it would ever come. But the deteriorating situation in the Baltic quickened the demand for a livelier military response from Britain, a demand to which Churchill was well suited and eager to respond. Though the two men wished to work together effectively in the national emergency, their contrasting instincts and reputation made their relationship toward each other delicate, a situation Churchill handled more astutely than Neville. Neville resisted Churchill's evident desire 'to become Minister of Defence with authority over the War Office and Air Ministry.'[82] Churchill advanced his cause with gestures of cooperation and expressions of loyalty designed for Neville's ears, which Neville accepted at face value. 'Winston, in spite of his violence and impulsiveness, is very responsive to sympathetic handling,' he told Ida. 'To me personally he is absolutely loyal and I am

---

79  Rauschning, *Hitler Speaks*, p. 140
80  Hilda to Neville, 8 Mary [1940], The Bury House, NC18/2/1171
81  Hilda to Neville, 17 Mar.1940, The Bury House, NC18/2/1173
82  Neville to Hilda, 10 Mar.1940, 10 Downing Street, in Self, ed., *The Neville Chamberlain Diary Letters*, IV, 508

continually hearing from others of the admiration he expresses for the P.M. This week I had an hour's talk alone with him. The best talk with the P.M. he had ever had, he told a friend'.[83]

Thereupon Neville made him chairman of the Military Coordination Committee, a significant step towards his goal. Neville was now confident that 'there is no misunderstanding between us. [Churchill] has told me that he deeply appreciates the confidence I have given him and that he will endeavour to respond to it'.[84] But Hilda was sceptical. 'America & Italy are both beginning to speculate on whether his star is not in the ascendant & yours on the decline', she noted; 'but though many people will be pleased & are convinced that he possesses the greatest driving force, yet they don't really trust him, and would be in consternation if they thought you were not there to keep a watch upon him. I feel rather that way myself.'[85]

Neville's confidence in his crucial colleague was not entirely misplaced. That could not be said of the greater confidence he placed in the policy he had pursued since Munich. He remained sure that German military superiority was at its peak back then, and hence that Hitler would not risk all-out war now. He expressed this confidence early in April when he declared for the first time in public that Hitler 'missed the bus' at Munich. Neville thought 'the informality and "jauntiness"' of the remark went down well. But it exposed him to ridicule.

Four days later, Hitler marched his troops through Denmark towards Norway.

ͽ

That movement brought the armed forces of Germany and Britain into direct conflict with each other. The phoney war was over. The real war was about to begin. It confronted Neville with a twofold challenge, to his political position at home as well as from the war in the Baltic. It took barely a month to bring him down. A further personal anxiety clouded that month. His daughter Dorothy underwent surgery in Oxford to alleviate a back problem. He could communicate with her only by letter, though here again letters to his family helped him order his thoughts.

The pace that month was frantic, doubly accelerated by the swiftness of the German advance and by Churchill's equally swift but chaotic responses. Churchill's

---

83 Neville to Ida, 30 Mar.1940, Chequers, in Self, ed., *The Neville Chamberlain Diary Letters*, IV, 513

84 Neville to Hilda, 6 Apr.1940, 10 Downing Street, in Self, ed., *The Neville Chamberlain Diary Letters*, IV, 515–6

85 Hilda to Neville, 5 Apr.1940, The Bury House, NC18/2/1176

understanding of war was appreciated in Parliament and among the public. Neville knew that his government needed Churchill's popularity, but he recognised Churchill's genius for war only grudgingly, and he found Churchill's mercurial approach to government exhausting. Neville was not alone in this. The service chiefs resented dictation from Churchill; and the Military Coordination Committee was paralysed rather than energised under his chairmanship. 'It was getting into a sad mess,' Neville told Hilda, 'quarrelling and sulking, with ... a general conviction that Winston had smashed the machine we had so carefully built up to ensure that all projects should be thought out or examined by a planning staff drawn from all three services. ... Winston himself fully recognised that he was getting into an impossible position and himself asked me to take the chair, remarking "They'll take from you what they won't take from me". So I did ... The result was magical. ... Instead of spending hours in arguing over details as I am told the Committee had been doing we finished in about 35 minutes. ... Everyone wore a smile ... W.C. himself is in the best of humour & tells his friends that he and the P.M. are working admirably together.'[86]

Even so, Churchill could not resist 'complaining bitterly' to his friends 'of being "thwarted" and not having sufficient powers.' His friends in turn endorsed Churchill's ambition to take charge of the war effort as Minister of Defence. But Neville refused to 'accept a proposal which would make him sole director of military policy without safeguards which would ensure the Cabinet getting the independent advice of the Chiefs of Staff before taking decisions'.[87] The service chiefs pleaded with Neville to reject Churchill's proposal, which 'would give Winston the power without the open responsibility & would so fasten on them the blame for decisions which were his'.[88] Neville hammered out a compromise which Churchill accepted more readily than did the service chiefs.

But it was already too late. The speed with which the Germans seized control of Norway confounded the efforts of Winston as well as Neville to hold them at bay. But the blame for this poor performance fell on Neville, who continued to question the likelihood of a German invasion of the Low Countries. He argued that the German need for iron ore and oil would keep them focused on the Baltic and Rumania. He also thought that the outlook in Norway favoured the British. 'I don't

---

86  Neville to Hilda, 20 Apr.1940, Chequers, in Self, ed., *The Neville Chamberlain Diary Letters*, IV, 519–21

87  Neville to Ida, 27 Apr.1940, 10 Downing Street, in Self, ed., *The Neville Chamberlain Diary Letters*, IV 522–4

88  Neville to Hilda, 4 May 1940, Chequers, in Self, ed., *The Neville Chamberlain Diary Letters*, IV, 524–8

pretend to have studied strategy sufficiently to be dogmatic about it, but it does not seem clear to me what advantage Hitler has yet gained or is likely to gain from his Scandinavian adventure to set off against the disadvantages of having come out from behind his defences and dispersed his forces along the coast without having command of the sea. Of course if he got possession of the ore fields that might be a prize worth having but the chances don't look too good.'[89] A week later he noted with satisfaction that 'the great offensive' against the Low Countries 'hasn't come off yet'.[90] But by the end of the month he had to confess that 'we hadn't reckoned on the way in which the Germans had poured in reinforcements of men guns tanks & aeroplanes' toward the Norwegian coast. The British were forced to abandon the footholds they attempted to seize there.

All too late Neville sensed that he might have made inadequate use of the time he had gained at Munich to rearm. Faced with a rising cry of, 'Why are we always too late?' he replied privately, 'Because we are not yet strong enough. ... We have plenty of manpower but it is neither trained nor equipped. We are short of many weapons of offence and defence. Above all we are short of air power.' He estimated that it would take another year 'to remove our worst deficiencies'. But to admit that publicly would amount to a confession of failure. Churchill bore much of the responsibility for the defeat in Norway, and he did not deny it. But he was 'too apt', Neville noted, 'to look the other way while his friends exalt him as the War Genius & hint that if only he had not been thwarted things would have gone very differently'. The scale of the rebellion in the Commons that forced Neville to resign a few days later still took him by surprise. Churchill was installed as Prime Minister before Neville could send his next weekly report to his sisters.

Ida and Hilda followed the proceedings in the House of Commons with anxiety, which turned to anger. Before the debate on the Norway debacle began, Hilda saw 'from the Times that opinion in the House of Commons remains critical'. So far, however, Neville's presentation of his case had impressed her as 'not only a vindication of all you have done, but a proof of the foresight, decision & courage with which the Govt. has acted'.[91] The first day of the debate in the Commons changed the outlook ominously. When the House divided at the end of debate the following day, the handsome majority that the National Government had enjoyed throughout the 1930s fell to a humiliating 81. 'Well!' Ida exclaimed, '... a pretty

---

89  Neville to Dorothy, 14 Apr.1940, 10 Downing Street, NC1/23/79

90  Neville to Hilda, 20 Apr.1940, Chequers, in Self, ed., *The Neville Chamberlain Diary Letters*, IV, 519–21

91  Hilda to Neville, 2 May 1940, The Bury House, NC18/2/1180

spectacle our democracy has made of itself! It is too sickening for words & the personal feeling shown in such a national crisis is positively degrading.' She could not but recognise that the Opposition and Conservative rebels 'made it a personal attack on you. ... I might even be glad for your own sake,' she struggled to convince herself, 'if you were freed from your responsibility, but I shudder to think of what would happen to the country if your guiding & steadying hand were withdrawn. Of course what people want is a spectacular success somewhere ... and as you cannot publish loudly to the world that ... we aren't strong enough your hands are tied & you can't defend yourself. ... I feel ashamed of my country which can't stand a disappointment without crying for a scapegoat.'[92]

Neville told Annie the next morning that the vote 'was a mortal blow'.[93] He did not, however, tender his resignation until the following day. The change of government was quickened by Germany's immediate invasion of the Low Countries and bombardment of Britain. Neville recognised that only a truly national government could meet the emergency. He abandoned his lingering hope of retaining his position. He was more reluctant to give up Halifax as his preferred successor. But Halifax ruled himself out because his seat in the Lords removed him from the crucial theatre of the Commons; and Labour opted for Churchill. Neville then resigned, agreed to serve under Churchill, and announced the change of government on the radio, asking for the country's support of Churchill and pledging his own.

Annie hurried to forewarn the sisters. Ida responded with reassurance: 'we feel prouder than ever of him for his sacrifice of all personal feelings to the great cause ... in the future (probably when we are all gone) his actions will be fully known & he will rank amongst England's greatest men.'[94] On hearing his announcement on the radio, Mary wrote to Neville, 'Your noble words & the ring of your voice bore witness to the courage & high endeavour which have guided you through these three years of unexampled anxiety & strain.' In accepting office under Churchill, she said, 'you have given another proof of your readiness to serve your country without thought of self & have set a great example of unswerving patriotism.'[95] Hilda strove to say more. She expressed the bittersweet hope 'in this time of peril that the good foundation which you have laid through these last 3 years with such unremitting force, & energy & farsightedness, will bear its fruits & enable us to stand up to the onslaught even though the credit goes to others'. She knew what

92  Ida to Neville, 9 May 1940, The Bury House, NC18/2/1181
93  As he relayed to Mary, 11 May 1940, 10 Downing Street, NC1/20/1/198
94  Ida to Annie, 10 May 19[40], The Bury House, NC1/16
95  Mary to Neville, 10 May 1940, 41 Lennox Gardens, NC1/20/2/51

Neville would miss: 'my heart is wrung for the loss of Chequers ... the only spot where you could get free even for a moment to breathe the fresh air & peace of the country'. She could not forgive his enemies: 'it is sad,' she concluded, 'that the cunning of wicked men should prevail but nothing can alter the fact which will stand out clearly in the future, that you & you alone have saved this country'.[96]

Neville responded with an account of the past three days that muted his anguish. 'At present everything is overshadowed by the new aggression,' he insisted.[97] His bitterness flashed out only at the partisanship of the lesser Labour leaders and the jockeying for position among Churchill's Conservative acolytes. Otherwise he emphasised the cordiality of his own relationship with Churchill. They had learned to work together remarkably well since the war was declared. Once Churchill became Prime Minister, Neville served Churchill as well as Churchill had him. Both men recognised that fact. 'Winston has been most handsome in his appreciation of my willingness to help and my ability to do so,' Neville insisted. Churchill told him, '"My fate depends largely on you".'

Ida accepted the situation reluctantly: 'I suppose that Winston has some qualities, – like Lloyd George – that are particularly valuable in war time.' She understood what Neville supplied to the partnership that Churchill lacked. 'It is his judgment that I & many others mistrust, & it is on <u>your</u> judgment & strength of character that we shall have to rely to keep him from indulging in wildcat schemes, & to try to oil the wheels of the machinery.'[98] She was reassured by Churchill's insistence that Neville stay in 10 Downing Street for at least another month. Neville declined to become Chancellor again. He knew full well that, 'With Labour's set at me I should soon have seemed the obstacle to all they wanted & they would quickly have been making my position untenable.' Instead he became Lord President of the Council, to live at 11 Downing Street. There, as Ida put it, 'he will be in constant touch with Churchill & able to do something to counteract the influence of the extreme men'.[99] 'But Chequers!' Neville sighed: 'I shall have to go there some time to collect my things & say goodbye. It will be a bad wrench to part with that place where I have been so happy.'

The terrible weeks of war which ensued made the situation easier for Neville than for his sisters. He was 'rather stunned at first by the suddenness of the change'

---

96  Hilda to Neville, 10 May 1940, The Bury House, NC18/2/1182
97  Neville to Ida, 11 May 1940, 10 Downing Street, in Self, ed., *The Neville Chamberlain Diary Letters*, IV, 528–30
98  Ida to Neville, 11 May 1940, The Bury House, NC18/2/1183
99  Ida to Mary, 12 May 1940, The Bury House, BC4/2/248

in his position.[100] But the national emergency 'swamped all personal feelings', as did the demands upon him as Churchill's leading adjutant on the home front. Neville next wrote to his sisters at the beginning rather than the end of the weekend, 'as in these days I never know from minute to minute that I shant be called on to hear some fresh news, which always seems to be bad and to take some decision which at best is a choice between desperate risks'.[101] Ida and Hilda could not, however, distract themselves from the accompanying drama in Parliament. Though Hilda echoed Neville in observing that 'everything is overshadowed by the great offensive', she found Churchill's oratory hard to stomach: 'W's speech in the House of Commons ... made me sick! ... I try to bury my own personal feelings for this is not the time to foster any bitterness or criticism & I do believe that Churchill was loyal to you – up to the standard of Churchill loyalty, but that is not & never has been the Chamberlain standard.'[102]

Neville challenged her reaction. He felt none of Churchill's relish for war and was relieved 'to hand over to someone else'. He knew 'what agony of mind' it would mean for him 'to give directions that would bring death & mutilation & misery to so many ... perhaps it was providential that the revolution which overturned me coincided with the entry of the real thing. ... Winston has shown up well so far. After one or two hectic nights when we were kept up till the small hours he has reverted to morning sittings of the Cabinet. He does take the opinions of the staff and doesn't attempt ... to shoulder off his colleagues.' Neville put it more succinctly to Dorothy: 'Winston is the right man for the head in view of his experience & study of war.' Churchill in turn recognised that Neville must continue as leader of the Conservative party. That was 'essential if Winston was to have whole hearted support'. Hilda reflected the resentment still felt among party regulars at the way Neville had been treated, resentment that 'would certainly have broken out if there had been any change in the Leadership'. Ida was more willing to agree with Neville that the main burden of responsibility was better shouldered by 'one who can feel the thrill & excitement of war' than by one 'to whom the whole idea has always been a nightmare'.[103] As for herself, she could not 'help feeling that those who have gone, before this second Armageddon began, are rather to be envied. All the same, since I am here I should like to live to see the forces of evil defeated.'[104]

---

100  Neville to Dorothy, 18 May 1940, 10 Downing Street, NC1/23/80

101  Neville to Hilda, 17 May 1940, 10 Downing Street, in Self, ed., *The Neville Chamberlain Diary Letters*, IV, 531–2

102  Hilda to Neville, 15 May 1940, Randolph Hotel, Oxford, NC18/2/1184

103  Ida to Neville, 24 May 1940, The Bury House, NC18/2/1185

104  Ida to Mary, 27 May 1940, The Bury House, BC4/2/249

Old Joe's three surviving children still had no idea how swiftly the family story that they had been telling each other for the past half century was drawing to a close. Its termination was obscured by the pace of the war. The 'forces of evil' drove west toward the Channel with devastating speed. Neville was shocked but also stiffened by the news. In St James's Park, he found it 'heartbreaking to see the people enjoying the sunshine as they lolled in their chairs or watched the little ducklings darting about in the water'. The King of the Belgians surrendered, the forces of France crumbled, and the British were driven back to the sea at Dunkirk. Ministers were told 'that there was small likelihood of our being able to evacuate any substantial number'. But Neville was soon able to report that, 'Thanks to the prodigious feats of the R.A.F. and the Navy and the dogged courage of the Army I doubt if we shall lose more than about 10%, though of course we have had to abandon the equipment and the losses at sea have been considerable.'[105] He worked contentedly alongside Churchill, 'leaving him free to look after the military aspect of the war', while Neville pushed the Defence Emergency Powers bill through Parliament. He took sardonic pleasure when the Act was hailed as 'a refreshing demonstration of the energy of the new Government'.[106]

But he received little, if any, credit. Those who had languished on the back benches because of their opposition to appeasement but had gained office in the new government sought to get rid of the 'Men of Munich' entirely. None of the angriest malcontents was at Cabinet level. Neville was gratified by the respect he won from Labour leaders at close quarters. But he was galled to find that his most venomous critics were Conservatives: Harold Macmillan, Robert Boothby, Leo Amery. 'Amery!' Neville was staggered at the blows he received from the man he had helped to make MP for South Birmingham, godfather of his son, once one of his 'rather particular friends'.[107] Amery, Macmillan, Boothby and their associates gathered nightly to conspire against Neville at the Reform Club, where they sought the help of Lloyd George.

Churchill backed Neville up against the malcontents. When Amery kept up his machinations, Churchill sent for him '& said if he was dissatisfied he should

105 Neville to Hilda, 1 June 1940, 10 Downing Street, in Self, ed., *The Neville Chamberlain Diary Letters*, IV, 534–6
106 Neville to Ida, 25 May 1940, 10 Downing Street, in Self, ed., *The Neville Chamberlain Diary Letters*, IV, 533
107 Neville to Ida, 24 June 1923, 35 Egerton Crescent, in Self, ed., *The Neville Chamberlain Diary Letters*, II, 169

resign', the sooner the better – at which Amery backed off.[108] At Neville's request, Churchill persuaded the Labour leadership to silence the attacks on him in the pro-Labour press. But at the same time Churchill pressed Neville to permit the recruitment of Lloyd George to strengthen the ministry. When Neville refused to serve with Lloyd George and obliged Churchill to choose between them, Churchill 'said at once that there was no question of any comparison between Ll.G. & myself. We had gone in together & would if necessary go down together.' Still he reiterated his request. Eventually Neville complied, 'saying that I could not resist his appeal, difficult though I found it to accept'.[109] In the event, Neville was spared this bitter medicine by Lloyd George himself. He left Churchill's invitation unanswered, waiting, so Lord Beaverbrook told Neville, to see how the war developed: 'if there is a good chance of our winning he will come in and get his share of the glory. If it goes the other way he will stay out' to make peace with the Germans.[110]

While Lloyd George procrastinated, the war strengthened the bonds between Churchill and Neville. 'Blow after blow came upon us', Neville reported after the fall of France: 'Turkey has run out of her obligations, Egypt the same, Iraq wavering, Spain on the point of coming in. American opinion is clearly veering in our direction, but it will be long before they can give us much material help.' In those circumstances Neville heralded the speech in which Churchill announced the beginning of the Battle of Britain as 'a real tonic' which 'had done much to keep up morale'. Neville himself spoke out in words that came to be identified with Churchill about fighting the Germans in air and sea and if need be on the beaches. Conversely, when 'the great invasion' predicted 'with great precision and confidence' for the beginning of July did not occur, Churchill joined Neville in doubting 'whether Hitler will risk it'.[111]

Ida and Hilda rallied to the war in their own way. They focused on the promotion of war savings and local food production. They found a kindred spirit in the Minister of Food, Lord Woolton, who 'seems to know his own mind & to stick to it & ... is getting things done'. They admired the businesslike approach of this newly created office. As Hilda put it, 'The Food ministry having, as it were, no

---

108 Neville to Ida, 21 June 1940, 11 Downing Street, in Self, ed., *The Neville Chamberlain Diary Letters*, IV, 541–3

109 Neville to Ida, 8 June 1940, 10 Downing Street, in Self, ed., *The Neville Chamberlain Diary Letters*, IV, 537–8

110 Neville to Hilda, 15 June 1940, 11 Downing Street, in Self, ed., *The Neville Chamberlain Diary Letters*, IV, 540

111 Neville to Ida, 7 July 1940, 11 Downing Street, in Self, ed., *The Neville Chamberlain Diary Letters*, IV, 546–8

past & possibly no future, does not mind cutting through the red tape', and 'we get on much faster than under the Minister for Agriculture'.[112] She cooperated with Woolton at a national level through the Women's Institutes. Ida convened a conference in Hampshire among 'the <u>four</u> bodies that are now supposed to be dealing with Food Economy & Food Production so that the work may be coordinated & overlapping avoided. – It is often extraordinarily convenient to have Hilda carrying on the Voluntary Work whilst I do Public Work.'[113] German aerial bombardment came close to the Bury House before it affected Downing Street. The sisters refused to be disconcerted. 'We had our first air raid alarm last night ... & had all to get up & go down to the dining room where we sat & talked & knitted for an hour till the all clear signal was given'.[114]

The three Chamberlains were in comparatively good heart by the middle of July. Neville 'got so tired of waiting for Hitler to begin his invasion that I set to with Annie this morning on the pictures' to be hung in 11 Downing Street. Every passing week made invasion more difficult for the Germans: as Neville told Hilda, 'you yourself have seen evidence of the ground defences which grow in strength every day'.[115] Even so, his outlook was darkening: 'I have lost my spring & my spirits,' he confessed. 'All my recreations, flowers, fishing & shooting, country life, have been taken from me and there is nothing to look forward to.' Later in the month he revealed more: 'I am in considerable trouble with my inside which hasn't been working properly for a long time & is getting worse.'[116]

His sisters did not grasp the seriousness of this news. 'I am very sorry to hear that you have been having physical discomfort in addition to all your other worries,' Hilda replied; '...it is exactly what one ought to have expected ... the strain you have been upon since Xmas has been awful.' She built him up to face the surge in denunciations of his post-Munich rearmament policy as Germany deployed massive might on land. 'I do so feel that the magnificent success of the R.A.F. & the navy <u>are</u> due almost entirely to you. Nobody will publicly give you credit for it now, but it is as I say the <u>man</u> of Munich who made those exploits possible.'[117] But the deterioration in Neville's health moved as fast as the German army. He was

---

112  Hilda to Neville, 11 July 1940, The Bury House, NC18/2/1192
113  Ida to Neville, 19 July 1940, The Bury House, NC18/2/1193
114  Ida to Neville, 7 June 1940, The Bury House, NC18/2/1187
115  Neville to Hilda, 14 July 1940, 11 Downing Street, in Self, ed., *The Neville Chamberlain Diary Letters*, IV, 550–1
116  Neville to Ida, 20 July 1940, 11 Downing Street, in Self, ed., *The Neville Chamberlain Diary Letters*, IV, 553
117  Hilda to Neville, 25 July 1940, The Bury House, NC18/2/1194

X-rayed at the end of July and immediately underwent surgery. Still he disguised the gravity of the situation from his sisters, which he did not fully realise himself. 'It is not in itself a serious operation and I should be out again in a fortnight but the consequences will not be altogether pleasant and I shall have to adjust myself to a new condition of things.'[118]

He did not report again to his sisters for six weeks; and that letter was his last to them. Their correspondence, weekly since the death of their father, was no longer pivotal to the family. The central letter-writing shifted to Annie, Mary and Dorothy. Ida and Hilda kept in touch with Annie and Mary by telephone as well as by letter, but both forms of communication were subject to wartime interruption. Hilda drew close to Dorothy, whom she had come to love as the child she never had. The sisters also saw more of Neville once he moved to convalesce at Highfield Park near Odiham. 'I have been over this morning at Highfield to see the staff there about arrangements for next week,' Hilda told him in her last letter, '... the place is so attractive & just now is so peaceful ... it will be a real joy to you to get there & breathe the fresh air for some little time before resuming your activities.'[119]

Though Neville suffered 'a lot of minor miseries & discomforts', he longed to get back to work. 'My surgeon ... says I am 500% ahead of the average patient,' he reported hopefully to Mary. Even Duff Cooper, who had resigned from Neville's Cabinet over Munich, encouraged him now to return: 'You were never more needed in the Cabinet than you are today,' he wrote, to Neville's astonishment.[120] Toward the end of August Neville reported that he was 'getting stronger every day. I can walk over a mile now.'[121] On September 9th, he was called back to London.

By that time the German bombers had shifted their attention from the air fields near Odiham to London. Ida and Hilda could hear the planes passing overhead. Neville found his first week back on Downing Street 'nightmarish'. He and Annie spent their nights in an underground shelter, 'getting up when the all clear sounded mostly about 5–6 a.m. and snatching an hour or so for sleep in our beds before rising again at 8. ... I wonder what I shall have to write about next week!'[122] He never wrote to his sisters again. He was in worse straits than he let on. Annie reported

---

118  Neville to Hilda, 27 July 1940, 11 Downing Street, in Self, ed., *The Neville Chamberlain Diary Letters*, IV, 554

119  Hilda to Neville, Thursday, NC18/2/1197

120  As reported by Neville to Mary, 23 Aug.1940, Highfield Park, NC1/20/1/200

121  Neville to Dorothy, 24 Aug.1940, NC1/23/81

122  Neville to Ida, 15 Sept.1940, 11 Downing Street, in Self, ed., *The Neville Chamberlain Diary Letters*, IV, 555–6

that the hours for meetings to which he was called were 'constantly changed, & added to this a terrific noise from guns at 50 yds. either side of us going all night'. After ten days in these conditions, Neville was exhausted. 'Winston suddenly ... said why didn't N. get away for a few days,' and Neville left straightaway for High- field. 'It is awfully depressing for N,' Annie observed. 'He started out so well, so delighted to be back, taking Cabinets in Winston's absence, planning & discussing etc etc. & with 2 special bits of work on hand.'[123]

Neville slept through his first two days back at Highfield. 'By then I realised what I must do,' he told Mary, '... I wrote to Winston & proffered my resignation. As I had rather expected, he replied at once saying in effect carry on. You came back too soon. Stop where you are till you can build up your strength.'[124] The two men had worked together well. But Neville had to remain close at hand to bring his talents to bear. Though grateful for Churchill's request to remain in office, he felt 'that there must be a limit to the time I could stay away' from London. 'So I replied that I would do as Winston suggested on the understanding that he was free at any time to change his mind if he thought it desirable.'

Churchill did not take long. A British expedition to Dakar to strengthen resistance to Germany among the French colonies along the Atlantic coast failed badly. Churchill learned at the same time that Kingsley Wood, who had served in Neville's Cabinet and now in Churchill's, was about to visit Neville in Highfield; and Churchill suggested 'that he should take some soundings as to [Neville's] views for the future'. Kingsley Wood told Neville that 'Winston was very worried at the prospect of the criticism of the Dakar fiasco' and 'was thinking of distract- ing attention from that issue by making a number of changes in the Government'. It was thus 'evident' to Neville that Churchill 'was revolving [sic] a change in my office. I told K.W. that my attitude was as I had already written to the P.M.'. Neville was 'therefore not surprised' three days later 'to receive another letter from Winston ... saying that he was reconstructing his Govt and wished now to accept my resignation. This letter was quite nicely worded and I have no complaint to make.' He thought Churchill 'right to face up now to the fact that he cannot have my help'.

Ida was standing beside Neville 'when Winston's second letter accepting his resignation arrived, & [she] could see that the final decision came to him really as a relief'.[125] She knew that he would nevertheless 'feel the reaction very much a little

---

123  Annie to Mary, 24 Sept.1940, Highfield, Annie Chamberlain correspondence
124  Neville to Mary, 1 Oct.1940, Highfield Park, NC1/20/1/202
125  Ida to Mary, 4 Oct.1940, The Bury House, BC4/2/255

later, when he [found] himself cut off not only from all his work but from all inside knowledge of what is going on'. That reaction came fast; Ida felt it herself. Within three days of rejecting Neville's resignation, Churchill had 'with his usual instability ... changed his mind ... for reasons which to my mind only confirm my distrust of him. He is too easily swayed by political motives & momentary advantages. I grieve for the country,' she went on, 'for I believed that as long as Neville remained at his side he would be saved from his worst faults & the two supplemented each other in a most useful way. ... It is a tragedy that his career should be closed so suddenly & unexpectedly ... At present he has neither work nor health nor home.'

Neville could not hide his bitterness. He warned his daughter that the press would treat his departure less kindly than they had most former Prime Ministers. 'I won't let the papers bother me, if they don't do you justice,' Dorothy replied. 'I know from talks with many people of different classes ...that they appreciate all you've done & haven't got such short memories as the journalists.' She hoped but was not confident that, 'when this hectic period is over there will be some thinking done perhaps, & then they will realise rather more clearly the true course of events'. She could not repress a swipe at the man who accepted her father's resignation: 'I can't see that Winston has done so marvellously myself, what about Dakar?'[126] Neville's son Frank reacted similarly. He found 'some good bits in the papers about you but my God they've got short memories'.[127]

The blow to the family intensified when Frank was ordered to leave at the head of his battery for the Mediterranean. 'You can guess our mixed feelings,' Annie told Mary. 'He hopes to get 48 hours leave & get here first.'[128] Annie bore up well as she always did in a crisis. But she saw how Neville was pulled down. 'It is so hard to give up all you care for, & then not to be equal to getting long walks or drives to distract one's mind.' She found consolation in the 'Hundreds of <u>most</u> wonderful letters' that continued 'to pour in, from dockers to Kings'. All made the same point: 'how N. made the Country & Empire know that there was no alternative left but war'.

The war struck ever closer. Odiham was 'strafed and bombed & four poor women were killed – but no damage to the Bury House apart from five broken windows & a punctured gable roof'.[129] Ida and Hilda were away at the time, Ida

---

126  Dorothy to Neville, 2 Oct.1940, 57 Calthorpe Road, NC1/23/22
127  Frank to Neville, 5 Oct.1940, 191 AA Battery R.A., Oakland Recreation Ground, Yardley, NC1/23/16
128  Annie to Mary, 9 Oct.1940, Highfield, Annie Chamberlain correspondence
129  Ida to Mary, 20 Oct.1940, The Bury House, BC4/2/256

at Highfield close enough to hear the bomb, Hilda at the headquarters of the Women's Institute in London. Neville's digestive system was in collapse when Frank came to bid farewell. 'It was very hard saying Goodbye,' he wrote on embarkation. 'But I do want to say this Papa. I shall always see you and always have seen you as far away above any other person we've ever known or read about in all the qualities which are worth while and all the principles which are worth striving for. ... it's some pride to me to think that it was my father who saved England and that so many people love and admire him. ... it is so cruel that you should be ill now and have to hand over all your plans and ideas to those small-minded men who are out for their names. But it <u>does</u> all come out in the end and it's really what you know you've done that matters.'[130]

Toward the end of October Neville was diagnosed definitely to have advanced bowel cancer. His physicians thought the disease could have begun eighteen months earlier, in other words after Hitler's takeover of Czechoslovakia. Though they said that Neville did not have long to live, they overestimated how long. There was some consolation in the rapid advance of his illness, as Neville reminded Mary: 'my cross is not as heavy as Father's & I hope I may not have to wait so long as he to be relieved of it'. Ida discouraged Dorothy from seeking a second opinion. Ten days later Ida reported, 'It has proved impossible to control the sickness' and 'he is getting weaker & weaker'. Annie, encouraged by Hilda, told Neville that the end might be near. Lord Halifax came to pay his last respects. Dorothy hurried down from Birmingham, Mary over from London. Ida reopened her report next morning to say that the doctor 'expects the end to be quite peaceful. It is all we can hope for now'.[131] Neville died on November 9th, barely forty days after his resignation.

---

130  Frank to Neville, 21 Oct.1940, 191 AA Battery RA, NC1/23/17
131  Ida to Mary, 6 Nov.1940, The Bury House, BC4/2/258

*Hilda in the 1950s*

*Epilogue*

# From Litany to Lament

Stunned by the speed of Neville's fall and his death, his sisters took time to think over the story that the family had been telling each other about their lives for more than half a century. Hilda had summed it up in the litany which reached its climax at Munich. But after Hitler swallowed up what the Munich agreement had left of Czechoslovakia, Neville's weekly letters disconcerted his sisters by denying the inevitability of war and even, after war broke out, of an armed showdown with Germany. Neville was loath to recognise what Austen had sensed: that under Hitler's leadership Germany wanted war, war rather than improvement in the standard of living, the assumption upon which the rest of the Chamberlain family based its commitment to public service. Only after Germany launched its blitzkrieg to the west and Neville was dismissed as Prime Minister did he accept his sisters' lower estimate of the benefits of Munich, namely that it had gained nineteen more months for Britain to rearm and cordial support from the British Commonwealth for the war effort, support which otherwise would have been lacking.

Regardless of their uneasiness at Neville's protracted refusal to modify the policy he had pursued at Munich, Ida and Hilda remained nonetheless confident that 'there will be sufficient evidence in your letters to us to put you right with posterity'.[1] After Neville's death, they relied entirely on those letters to do him this service. They never recognised the damagingly ambivalent message that these letters would convey to subsequent readers, an ambivalence that their responses unmistakeably exposed.

Controversy about the verdict that history would pronounce on Neville

---

1 Ida to Neville, 15 Dec.1940, The Bury House, NC18/2/1159

intensified as he died. That dispute affected the entire family. Joseph's dazzling though disruptive career in public life had continued to elevate the reputation of the family long after his death. But that memory was overshadowed by the short-lived fame and long-lived notoriety of Neville's achievement at Munich, a fleeting agreement that discredited peacemaking diplomacy for the rest of the century. The attempts by the Chamberlains to secure creditable biographies of the statesmen in the family failed again and again. And they were finally engulfed by the meta-narrative of the Second World War written afterwards by Neville's triumphant rival, Churchill. Hilda lived long enough to read that account to its close. It turned her family litany into a lament on the transience of political glory.

❧

Neville did not rely upon his letters to his sisters to put the record straight. Though he knew that it would be 'rash to prophesy the verdict of history', he remained confident after his fall that 'if full access is obtained to all the records',[2] his policies as Prime Minister would be vindicated. Hilda reinforced his confidence: 'the voice of history is not the voice of the present day,' she assured him, '& we may confidently await the ultimate judgement.'[3]

But the Chamberlains had good reason to be apprehensive. 'Our family are not fortunate in their biographers,' Ida recalled.[4] After Joseph's death, his children commissioned the tariff reformer who edited *The Observer*, J.L. Garvin, to write his biography. Garvin made little headway with it during the Great War. By 1918 the family had lost patience, but reluctantly they agreed to leave the task in his hands. A decade later Neville exploded at Garvin's endless delays. Apart from family piety, he wanted to reinforce his campaign for tariff reform by securing a good account of his father's last crusade. Neville prevailed upon Austen to join him in interviewing Garvin. 'It was rather a painful affair,' Neville reported afterwards. Garvin 'poured out for 20 minutes such a spate of extravagant & complacent eulogy of himself as I have never heard from any man before. ... At last I rapped out "Haven't you a contract?" He ... shouted that that was wiped out long since, and turning to the silent Austen he began his song of self praise again. As soon as I saw an opening I said "You have done irreparable injury to my father's memory". It stung him like

2 Neville to Ida, 25 May 1940, 10 Downing Street, in Self, ed., *The Neville Chamberlain Diary Letters*, IV, 533

3 Hilda to Annie, 14 June 1940, The Bury House, NC1/15/4/7

4 Ida to Neville, 5 July 1940, The Bury House, NC18/2/1191

a whiplash and he fairly foamed at the mouth, saying he would not tolerate such insults from any man.' Neville and Austen finally 'extracted from him a definite promise that if by the end of January he had not completed the life down to 1903 he would revise the first two volumes for publication.'[5]

Another two years later Garvin produced two volumes for Austen's inspection. They were certainly monumental. The first volume took six hundred pages to tell the story only up until 1885. Neville declared it 'far too detailed ... Still, the tremendous personality of the subject can't fail to excite & retain interest ... surely there can never have been any public man whose whole career from start to finish, private as well as public, was so startlingly original and arresting.'[6] The second volume, which brought the biography to the eve of Joseph's tenure as Colonial Secretary, gave Neville 'the same sort of feeling' that he experienced 'in reading a book on astronomy: I have felt myself growing smaller & smaller until I became insignificance itself'[7] – often Joseph's impact on his sons. Neville found it 'difficult to wait patiently for the new volume.'[8]

He did not have to wait long. Garvin delivered the third volume within another year and a half. It took the story to the turn of the century. The crusade for imperial preference lay ahead. Austen thought that the opening pages dragged, but after that he 'could not put them down.'[9] Neville was even more enthusiastic. He found 'the story of the Jameson Raid, of the attempt at an Anglo-German Alliance, of the Partition of West Africa and of the Boer war ... at times thrilling'. Garvin's account of Joseph's abortive bid for an alliance with Germany gave Neville a moment of anxiety: 'I hope I too shall not be finally bowled out by the duplicity of the foreigner.'[10]

His contentment with his father's biographer did not endure. Garvin devoted all his remaining attention to the deteriorating situation in Europe, which he interpreted quite differently from Neville. By the summer of 1939 Neville was fed up.

5 Neville to Ida, 12 July 1930, Westbourne, in Self, ed., *The Neville Chamberlain Diary Letters*, III, 194–5

6 Neville to Hilda, 26 Nov.1932, Westbourne, in Self, ed., *The Neville Chamberlain Diary Letters*, III, 361–2

7 Austen to Hilda, 7 Dec.1932, 58 Rutland Gate, in Self, ed., *The Austen Chamberlain Diary Letters*, 420

8 Neville to Hilda, 10 Dec.1932, Faringdon, Berkshire, in Self, ed., *The Neville Chamberlain Diary Letters*, III, 368

9 Austen to Neville, 29 Aug.1934, NC1/27/117

10 Neville to Ida, 13 Oct.1934, Westbourne, in Self, ed., *The Neville Chamberlain Diary Letters*, IV, 91

'When I think of the way in which he has behaved over this Life, my blood boils'.[11] Ida resigned herself to the situation: 'I fear we shall have to wait for [Garvin's] demise & then put the work into other hands.' She concluded prophetically, 'we may all be dead first'.[12]

The family had to select a biographer again, this time for Austen after his death. First they approached G.M. Trevelyan, biographer of Sir Edward Grey. Ida offered help, letting Grey know that she and Hilda had 'a series of weekly letters' from Austen 'beginning after Beatrice's death, & we shall try as soon as possible to ... sort them out a bit'.[13] But Trevelyan turned the invitation down. With hesitant approval from Neville, Ivy opened negotiations with Sir Charles Petrie, a popular historian with Fascist leanings who had written an admiring biography of Mussolini. Petrie produced a two-volume work on Austen in short order. But the first volume left the family apprehensive. The *Times Literary Supplement* said that it 'tells the story no more than adequately'.[14] Neville found it 'undoubtedly a dull book'. The second volume was even worse. Neville wrote it off as 'a terribly pedestrian narrative' which 'gives no real picture of Austen'.[15]

Churchill's entry into the Cabinet at the beginning of World War II roused Neville's concern about how his own life story would be told. Churchill had a better reputation as a historian than as a Cabinet minister. Neville recognised the popularity of Churchill's books, and was wary of the account he would write of their now shared responsibilities. 'We are getting along quite well in the Cabinet,' he told Hilda, but Churchill 'continually writes me letters many pages long. ... for the purpose of quotation in the Book that he will write hereafter. Hitherto I haven't answered them, but the one I got yesterday was so obviously recording his foresight and embodied warnings so plainly for purposes of future allusion that I thought I must get something on the record too which would have to be quoted in the Book.'[16]

But Neville failed to act accordingly, partly because his sisters undertook to fill the gap in the historical record from his point of view. Ida assured him that 'Hilda has gone out to deposit your last four letters in the tin box we have stored in the

---

11  Neville to Mary, 14 June 1939, 10 Downing Street, NC1/20/1/191

12  Ida to Neville, 21 July 1939, The Bury House, NC18/2/1135

13  Ida to Neville, 1 Apr.1937, The Bury House, NC18/2/1012

14  Ida to Neville, 3 Nov.1939, The Bury House, NC18/2/1152

15  Neville to Hilda, 26 Nov.1939, and to Ida, 8 June 1940, 10 Downing Street, in Self, ed., *The Neville Chamberlain Diary Letters*, IV, 474 & 539

16  Neville to Hilda, 17 Sept.1939, Chequers, in Self, ed., *The Neville Chamberlain Diary Letters*, IV, 448

[local] Bank's strong room.'[17] When 'the barrage of letters from Winston' continued unabated, Neville 'sent for him and had a very frank talk.' Churchill responded disarmingly. He 'withdrew his letter and promised to write no more and swore vehemently that he had no desire or intention of intrigue. That he was quite satisfied with the responsibility he had & wanted no more and that his sole desire was to help me to win the war. I believe all this was quite genuine, though Winston is in some respects such a child that he neither knows his own motives nor sees where his actions are carrying him.'[18] It was Neville's trust in Churchill's protestations that was naïve.

Neville remained uneasy about Churchill until Churchill replaced him as Prime Minister. But then they worked together so well that the embers of Neville's suspicion died down. They glowed again at the speed with which Churchill finally accepted his resignation. Yet Neville never foresaw how damagingly Churchill would tell the story of their former duel. He was more concerned at the attack on the men of Munich by anonymous Labour authors in *Guilty Men*[19]. That broadside made Neville regret that during the 'anxious months' before Munich he had 'kept no papers or notes ... no diary even in the most abbreviated form'. He nevertheless remained confident that, 'although history may go wrong in details ... the broad line of the story will be plain enough'. 'So far as my personal reputation is concerned, I am not in the least disturbed about it. The letters which I am still receiving in such vast quantities so unanimously dwell on the same point, namely that without Munich the war would have been lost and the Empire destroyed in 1938, that I do not feel the opposite view expressed I understand by "guilty men" and elsewhere has a chance of survival. Even if nothing further were to be published giving the true inside story of the past two years, I should not fear the historians' verdict.'[20]

After Neville's death, Dorothy turned to his sisters for help in preparing for a Life of her father. They responded by 're-reading his letters starting in 1917'. Hilda found them 'absolutely enthralling & more revealing of his character, his interests & his marvellous fertility of mind than even I had thought'.[21] As for a biographer, Hilda thought first of Blanche Dugdale, who had written a Life of her uncle, Arthur Balfour. 'Of course it is much too early to write the historians account of

17  Ida to Neville, 6 Oct.1939, The Bury House, NC18/2/1148
18  Neville to Ida, 8 Oct.1939, Chequers, in Self, ed., *The Neville Chamberlain Diary Letters*, IV, 457
19  *Guilty Men* by 'Cato' (London: Victor Gollancz, 1940)
20  Neville to Sir Joseph Ball, 28 Oct.1940, Kenneth W. Rendell World War II Collection, Boston
21  Hilda to Dorothy, 18 Jan.1941, The Bury House, BC4/8/1

[your father's] life but she knew him slightly & had a very great admiration for him'. Furthermore, 'Her intimate association with the political life of the day ... would prevent her from making mistakes in her presentment [sic] of the facts & she would know already all the people from whom personal impressions could be gathered.' Fearful that male historians might not take correspondence with sisters seriously, Hilda added that Mrs Dugdale 'would be more likely than a man to read through our twenty years of letters, & would then get a really intimate knowledge of your Father which could be obtained in no other way.'

Annie opened discussion with the man the family eventually chose to write the Life of Neville, Keith Feiling. Though unanimous about the choice, they were not enthusiastic. Ivy described Feiling's style as 'hardly popular'. Ida was less charitable: 'his style is not only not good but makes him difficult to read'. But that was 'a secondary consideration. If the facts are stated & the character of the man brought out some one else can come along later on & produce something more literary. One can at least be sure that Mr. Feiling will spare himself no trouble to get at the truth in everything & that [Neville's] reputation will not suffer at his hands.'[22] Annie did not want Feiling to pay much attention to Neville's years in Birmingham before moving on to the national stage. She insisted that Neville 'towered like a giant' over the other leading men of Birmingham, men from families like the Lloyds, Martineaus and Cadburys, who were 'just parochial.'[23] She also feared the effect that reliance on the letters Neville had written to his sisters would have on Feiling. With some jealousy she worried that he might carry away a perspective in which 'the female side will only be uppermost ... in a possessive manner'.

But Feiling had little else to work with. Churchill took care to restrict access to the records in government custody to himself. Ida had good reason to doubt that 'Mr Feiling can get permission to see Cabinet records, even if he promised to publish nothing except with special permission'. She also warned Annie against consultation with former enemies. Little 'would be gained by seeing Attlee. It is true that he was impressed by what he saw of Neville's methods in the Cabinet, but I wonder how lasting that impression has been, & whether he may not by now have reverted to his former opinion. ... Mr. Feiling should not try to see Lloyd George. ... after all, why should L.G. give any help to the biographer of a man whom he hated & feared.'[24] Fellow Conservatives posed a more difficult question, particularly when they cast aspersions on Neville's record over rearmament.

---

22  Ida to Dorothy, 24 Oct.1942, The Bury House, BC4/7/9a
23  Annie to Mary, 3 Oct.1941, Chaddesley Corbett, Annie Chamberlain correspondence
24  Ida to Annie, 7 Jan.1942, The Bury House, NC1/16/4/18

Yet Ida remained remarkably unconcerned about Churchill, whom she regarded by now as politically indispensable. 'We all know Winston's weak points, but we have no alternative & the House [of Commons] ought to try & make things easy for him instead of badgering & harassing him as it does. ... It is tragic that there is no one to whom he can turn for support & good counsel' as he had to Neville.[25] Towards the rest of the Cabinet the sisters felt much less charitable: 'the present ministers never acknowledge the debt they owed [Neville], for which always bear them a grudge,' Hilda counselled Dorothy.[26]

The lack of accessible and trustworthy documentation on the controversies of Neville's final five years placed the family and the biographer in a quandary. When Feiling proposed writing 'a "provisional" Life of one volume only', the sisters did not warm to the suggestion: 'but we still more dislike the idea of doing nothing for ten years during which time [Neville's] opponents will continue to build up a legend entirely contrary to the real facts'.[27] They suggested that Feiling 'give a pretty full picture of the later years ... without documentation.' Ida knew that 'this would be abhorrent to an historian'; but she could not 'see why other people should be allowed to make assertions which we know are false & which go by default because we can't prove our counter assertions at the present time.' Neville's letters showed 'that from the beginning he was in favour of rearmament & that he was mainly instrumental in getting the Govt to take it up', that it was Neville who pushed for the build-up of the air arm, that it was 'he who insisted that all efforts should be concentrated on producing the latest types of planes, like Spitfires & Hurricanes'. She said nothing of his refusal to recognise Hitler's appetite for war. Confident that Neville's correspondence with his sisters would speak for itself, they granted Feiling complete and unconditional access to it.

❦

The course of the war bore out some but not all of Churchill's pre-war prophecies. His assessment of Hitler was right and Neville's egregiously wrong. But on rearmament the contrast was not so clear. The agreement Neville gained from Hitler at Munich gave Britain much-needed time to rearm, though Neville refused even then to make the all-out effort Churchill called for. Neville's focus on air power, and particularly on fighter planes, had been sharper than Churchill's, and proved

---

25  Ida to Dorothy, 25 July 1942, The Bury House, BC4/7/7
26  Hilda to Dorothy, 31 Dec.1942, The Bury House, BC4/18/12f
27  Ida to Annie, 9 Jan.1943, The Bury House, NC1/16/4/22

vital in the Battle of Britain. The inability of the Germans to invade Britain was in part a vindication of the policies Neville pursued. Even so, the terrible war that Hitler unleashed upon Europe exposed, indeed exaggerated, the folly of appeasement. The Second World War turned 'Chamberlain' into a synonym for weakness and 'Munich' into a precedent to avoid at all costs. Ida and Hilda clung to their conviction that, 'The great mass of people now living are ... still intensely grateful to Neville for all he did & saved us from'. But they did not 'want the younger generation to be brought up on the legend of either a good weak man who was tricked & taken in by Hitler, or of a Fascist at heart'.

To Dorothy's dismay, Churchill began during the war to impose his interpretation of the past few years on a receptive public. Hilda too could see that Churchill forgot all he owed to Neville in the summer of 1940: 'in his own mind it has probably all faded away & all that remains is a belief that he was always right & that if he had been P.M. earlier he would have smashed the Germans much sooner. It is hard to possess one's soul in patience but one knows it is inevitable in times like these ... Winston does not care if he gets his effect if it is true or not.' Politically, nevertheless, Hilda admitted that, 'as matters stand he is a great asset & we must not forget that'.[28]

Churchill's reading of history won more ardent endorsement in the United States than in Britain. The 'travesty of [Neville's] aims & actions presented to Americans by their press' made Hilda more than ever anxious 'that Feiling should get his book written & published as soon as possible, even if it is necessarily incomplete'. She yearned to challenge the tale told by the critics of appeasement: 'until people take note of what really happened & what were the conditions under which [Neville] took office, we can't squash this hopelessly false presentment'.[29]

The ranks of the family were thinning fast. Ivy died three months after Neville. Ida's health also weakened that winter, and she never quite recovered. Undaunted, she threw herself back into public service. 'My Public Health work is getting more exacting again,' she reported to Dorothy in the spring of 1943, 'as not only have we all the evacuees to deal with which means constantly starting new Maternity Homes & Hostels & Day Nurseries but we are now having to consider post-war problems & developments.'[30] After a meeting two weeks later in Winchester, she hurried back to the Bury House and her beloved garden, where she died suddenly of a heart attack.

Severed from her companion of nearly seventy years, Hilda reached out to Dorothy. 'I long hoped to have children & a husband of my own, but I always feel

---

28　Hilda to Dorothy, 2 July 1943, The Bury House, BC4/8/20
29　Hilda to Dorothy, 15 Jan.1944, The Bury House, BC4/8/29
30　Ida to Dorothy, 20 Mar.1943, The Bury House, BC4/7/14

as if the children were given to me in you & Frank, whom I loved so much first for [Neville's] sake, & now for your own as well as his.'[31] Later that summer Hilda told Dorothy, 'you alone can give me something of the feeling of that inner communion which I shared with Aunt Ida.'[32]

Hilda was now Joseph's sole surviving child and custodian of the family legacy. With war raging all around the world, her appreciation of Churchill deepened. She came to regard him as 'indispensable at this time & the contacts he has made with both Roosevelt & Stalin will be quite as valuable when it comes to settling peace terms, as even for the present conduct of the war.'[33] Even so, like Neville, she was fundamentally less interested in developments abroad than at home. The Beveridge report came out shortly before Ida died, recommending generous social security to cover old age, illness and unemployment. Hilda was 'thrilled' by the report: 'I like the fact that it applies to <u>everyone</u> [with] no income limitations. I hate the "class" distinction, which was often so unjust with regard to old age pensions & insurance up to now.' Yet on the unemployed she thought that Beveridge was 'too easy, particularly with regard to the six months before they can be made to work'; and she feared that these provisions were 'more likely to be weakened than strengthened' because 'the labour members of the ministry have not an ounce of courage when it comes to asking the working classes to accept anything unpleasant.'[34]

Hilda interpreted Beveridge as building upon foundations that Neville had constructed at the Ministry of Health. She was proud also of Ida's achievement in local government as well as of her own in the voluntary sector. She was accordingly appalled when the government thought of 'removing the Health services from the local authorities & forming large Regional committees to administer them directly under the Ministry'. This she denounced as 'totalitarian govt. with a vengeance'; and she predicted that the voluntary associations would also be 'wiped out'.[35]

When the Allies invaded Normandy, Hilda and Dorothy agreed that for the moment 'it would not be a good thing to publish' Neville's biography. However, 'when the war is over it will not be long before old controversies come to the surface & it will then be very desirable to have it published'.[36] Hilda contacted Feiling when Women's Institute business took her to Oxford. She was encouraged

31  Hilda to Dorothy, 10 Apr.1943, The Bury House, BC4/8/18
32  Hilda to Dorothy, 17 July 1943, The Bury House, BC4/8/20a
33  Hilda to Dorothy, 28 Feb.1943, The Bury House, BC4/8/15
34  Hilda to Dorothy, 31 Dec.1942, The Bury House, BC4/8/12f
35  Hilda to Dorothy, 27 Nov.1943, The Bury House, BC4/8/26
36  Hilda to Dorothy, 15 July 1944, The Bury House, BC4/8/40

to find that he had acquired 'a much greater appreciation of [Neville's] character & whole outlook' and was 'making very good progress'. She used the occasion 'to put my point of view – with regard to one or two things – notably the non-inclusion of Churchill in the Cabinet long before Munich'. Feiling in return told her 'some of the things which he thought the extremists Labour & Churchillite would say & wanted to know my answer'.

The Allied victory in Europe in the spring of 1945 removed the reason for delay in publishing Neville's biography. The ensuing general election also underscored how profoundly things had changed in Britain since the Chamberlain era. Labour destroyed the ascendancy that the Unionists had maintained in Birmingham for two-thirds of a century. Conservatives went down to defeat all over the country. 'What a crash!' Hilda exclaimed to Dorothy. 'There has been nothing like it since 1906 when Balfour & all the principal Cabinet members were defeated & only Grandpa & Uncle Austen survived!'[37]

Feiling's *Life of Neville Chamberlain* came out the next year. Feiling based his treatment of Neville's years as Prime Minister almost entirely on Neville's letters to his sisters. And he used them to paint Neville warts and all. He included the passages that documented Neville's endless denial of the inevitability of armed confrontation with Hitler. Hilda was nevertheless content with the biography, as she told Dorothy. 'Feiling has proved himself a much better writer than I thought he could be, & ... has produced a biography which ... really does do justice to your father's character & to a large extent to his work.' She thought the book 'very well proportioned', surveying the whole of Neville's life instead of being preoccupied with his three years as Prime Minister. Of course she had criticisms to make. She wished that 'in the earlier part' Feiling had better 'realized the buoyancy which made [Neville] so captivating a companion', one who 'always made one's spirits rise when he was in the house'. She also wished that Feiling 'could have pronounced more emphatically on the great fertility of your father's mind & the originality of his work', particularly at the Ministry of Health and in the Ottawa agreements. She took issue with Feiling's criticism of Neville's harshness towards the Labour opposition in the 1930s and his refusal to bring Churchill into the government before war was declared. But she concluded laughingly, 'of course we are biased & though we say we want people to form their own judgement yet naturally unless it means that they think [Neville] was always right we can't agree!' It was nonetheless 'the kind of Life we wanted & one that your Father would, himself, have approved'.[38]

---

37 Hilda to Dorothy, 27 July 1945, The Bury House, BC4/8/53
38 Hilda to Dorothy, 21 Dec.1946, The Bury House, BC4/8/62

Hilda failed to see how Feiling's quotations from Neville's letters to his sisters could be used by critics of his version of appeasement. She failed also to foresee the avalanche that overran Feiling's Life of Neville over the next eight years as Churchill published his six-volume history of *The Second World War*. In riveting prose, Churchill hammered out what immediately became for the English-speaking world the master narrative of the twentieth century. Particularly in the United States, it left Neville to be remembered only for Munich, just as Pontius Pilate is remembered only for the crucifixion.

Churchill was gratified by the idolising reception he received in the United States. But he had overriding concerns in the United Kingdom which softened the treatment of Neville in his history. During his struggle in the late 1930s against Neville's misunderstanding of Hitler and underestimate of the need to catch up with German rearmament, Churchill was made acutely aware of the bonds of loyalty within the Conservative party to Neville as its leader. He felt the painful force of the division that he exacerbated among Conservatives over Neville's policy of appeasement 'to a degree the like of which I have never seen'. He also recognised the 'widespread and sincere admiration for Mr. Chamberlain's persevering and unflinching efforts to maintain peace, and for the personal exertions he had made. It is impossible,' Churchill went on, '... to avoid marking the long series of miscalculations and misjudgments of men and facts, on which he based himself, but the motives which inspired him have never been impugned, and the course he followed required the highest degree of moral courage.'[39]

Nor did Churchill forget that when Neville first entered the House of Commons after his removal as Prime Minister, 'the whole of his party – the large majority of the House – rose and received him in a vehement demonstration of sympathy and regard. ... it was from the Labour benches that I was mainly greeted.'[40] Churchill furthermore recognised the common ground that all Conservatives had found between themselves and 'the Labour and Liberal Opposition' who 'had never missed an opportunity of gaining popularity by resisting and denouncing even the half-measures for defence which [Neville's] Government had taken'.

There was another common bond between the two men which they learned to appreciate working together in the War Cabinet. However much Churchill enjoyed his own oratory, he shared to the full Neville's desire to *do* things rather than just talk about them; hence Churchill's persistent wish to return to government under

---

39 *The Gathering Storm*, vol. I of *The Second World War* (London: Penguin Books, 1985), 290 & 292

40 *Their Finest Hour*, vol. II of *The Second World*, 9

the man he was so fiercely criticising. And Churchill found much to admire in Neville at close quarters. It was a measure of Neville's social chilliness that the two men and their wives never dined together until November 1939. 'By happy chance' Churchill turned the conversation that evening to Neville's life in the Bahamas. He 'was fascinated by the way Mr. Chamberlain warmed as he talked, and by the tale itself, which was one of gallant endeavour. I thought to myself, "What a pity Hitler did not know when he met this sober English politician with his umbrella at Berchtesgaden, Godesberg, and Munich that he was actually talking to a hard-bitten pioneer from the outer marches of the British Empire!"'[41] Churchill never shared the illusion of Hitler and the Americans that Neville was weak.

In his account of *The Second World War* Churchill accordingly treated Neville was considerable respect. That respect was genuine. But it was also politically necessary if Churchill was to overcome the sharp division in sentiment among Conservatives about Munich and Neville's fall from power, a division that lingered on after the war while Churchill was writing its history.

His expressions of respect for Neville had the further, unanticipated benefit of enabling Hilda to assimilate the rest of what Churchill had to say. His massive history hence induced her to reappraise the achievement not just of her most beloved brother but of all three statesmen in the family. Hitherto she had celebrated the story of the three in a set of repetitive sentences about cumulative accomplishment, each man overcoming the setbacks of his predecessor and standing on his shoulders to reach ever higher. Her litany celebrated Austen and Neville's gradual fulfilment of Joseph's crusade for imperial preference. It soared to its height when Neville brought the work of European pacification which Austen began at Locarno to a triumphant climax at Munich. Hilda was forced, however, to sing a different song, not so much by the Second World War as by the way in which Churchill imposed his interpretation of that war on the English-reading public.

In the summer of 1956, now in her eighties, Hilda turned her exultant litany into a solemn meditation on the rhythm common to political life where accomplishment is so often followed by failure. She delivered a brief 'Portrait of the three Chamberlains' for transmission by radio.[42] She could no longer recapture the thrill she had voiced for nearly seventy years at the way in which the men in her family mounted ever higher. Instead, she closed her broadcast with a sombre summary: 'though each man had, in his own life, his day of glory, each man appeared to have failed in what he set out to perform'.

---

41  *The Gathering Storm*, 444
42  NCI/1895

# Chronology

| Year | UK and British Imperial Politics | International History |
|------|----------------------------------|----------------------|
| 1870 | Elementary Education Act passed.<br>Irish Land Act.<br>Red River Rebellion in Canada ends; Manitoba becomes Canadian province.<br>Western Australia granted representative government. | Franco-Prussian War: France declares war on Prussia, Napoleon III defeated at Sedan.<br>Revolt in Paris: Third Republic proclaimed, Prussians besiege Paris.<br>Italians enter Rome, declare it capital of Italy. |
| 1871 | Treaty of Washington settles existing difficulties between Britain and US.<br>Basutoland becomes part of Cape Colony; Britain annexes Kimberley diamond fields in South Africa.<br>Act of Parliament legalizes labour unions.<br>British Columbia joins Dominion of Canada.<br>Bank holidays introduced in England and Wales.<br>Stanley meets Livingstone in Ujiji. | Franco-Prussian War ends: Wilhelm I of Prussia declared German Emperor at Versailles, Paris capitulates, Peace of Frankfurt ends war ceding Alsace-Lorraine to Germany.<br>Paris Commune rules for two months.<br>Italian law guarantees Pope possession of Vatican.<br>Great Fire in Chicago. |
| 1872 | Ballot Act: voting by secret ballot.<br>C P Scott becomes editor of *Manchester Guardian*. | Civil war in Spain begins.<br>Three Emperors' League (German, Russian, Austro-Hungarian) established in Berlin.<br>Ulysses S Grant re-elected US President. |

| Year | UK and British Imperial Politics | International History |
|------|----------------------------------|----------------------|
| 1873 | William Gladstone's Liberal government begins to crumble.<br>Famine in Bengal.<br>Second Anglo-Ashanti War begins. | Republic proclaimed in Spain.<br>Financial panic in Vienna (May) and New York (Sept).<br>Abolition of slave markets and exports in Zanzibar.<br>Germans evacuate last troops from France. |
| 1874 | General Election; Disraeli becomes Prime Minister, succeeding William Gladstone<br>Second Anglo-Ashanti War ends.<br>Britain annexes Fiji Islands. | |
| 1875 | Prince of Wales visits India.<br>Britain buys Suez Canal shares from Khedive of Egypt.<br>Public Health Act passed.<br>London's main sewerage system completed.<br>Captain Matthew Webb first man to swim English Channel. | Risings in Bosnia and Herzegovina against Turkish rule.<br>Rebellion in Cuba. |
| 1876 | Disraeli made Earl Beaconsfield.<br>Gladstone launches campaign about the Bulgarian atrocities | Korea becomes independent nation.<br>Ethiopians defeat Egyptians at Gura.<br>Turkish troops massacre Bulgarians.<br>Ottoman Sultan deposed, successor deposed, succeeded by Abdul Hamid II.<br>Serbia and Montenegro declare war on Ottoman Empire.<br>New Ottoman constitution proclaimed.<br>Alexander Graham Bell invents telephone.<br>Rutherford B Hayes elected US President. |
| 1877 | National Liberal Federation formed.<br>Queen Victoria proclaimed Empress of India.<br>Famine in Bengal. | Russo-Turkish War begins.<br>Satsuma rebellion suppressed in Japan.<br>First Kaffir War.<br>Thomas A Edison invents the phonograph. |
| 1878 | British fleet arrives off Constantinople.<br>Lord Salisbury becomes Foreign Secretary.<br>Electric street lighting introduced in London.<br>CID, New Scotland Yard established in London. | Russo-Turkish War: Ottoman Empire seeks armistice, armistice signed.<br>Greece declares war on Turkey.<br>Attempt to assassinate Kaiser I of Germany.<br>Congress of Berlin discusses Eastern Question. |

| Year | UK and British Imperial Politics | International History |
|------|----------------------------------|----------------------|
| 1879 | Gladstone launches Midlothian campaign. Zulu War; peace signed with Zulu chiefs. British occupy Khyber Pass on North-West Frontier of India: British legation in Kabul massacred. First London telephone exchange opens. | Alsace-Lorraine declared integral part of Germany. |
| 1880 | General Election; Disraeli defeated; William Gladstone becomes Prime Minister again Transvaal Republic declares independence from Britain; Boers under Kruger declare republic. Parcel post introduced. | France annexes Tahiti. Pacific War: Chile vs Bolivia and Peru (-1884). James Garfield elected US President. |
| 1881 | Disraeli dies. Second Irish Land Act. First Boer War: British defeated at Majuba Hill, Treaty of Pretoria recognises independence of Transvaal. | US President James Garfield assassinated; Chester A Arthur succeeds him. Austro-Serbian treaty of alliance signed. Pogroms against Jews in Russia. Freedom of press established in France. |
| 1882 | Kilmainham Agreement between Parnell and British government; Fenians murder Lord Cavendish and T H Burke in Dublin; terrorist massacres in Maamtrasne. British occupy Cairo. | US government bans Chinese immigrants for ten years. Triple Alliance between Italy, Germany and Austria-Hungary. Hiram Maxim patents his machine gun. |
| 1883 | British decide to evacuate the Sudan. | French gain control of Tunis. Bismarck introduces sickness insurance in Germany. Orient Express (Paris-Constantinople) makes first run. |
| 1884 | General Gordon reaches Khartoum. Third Reform Act. London Convention on Transvaal. First deep underground railroad (Tube), London. | Germans occupy South-West Africa. Berlin Conference of 14 nations on African affairs. Gold discovered in the Transvaal. Grover Cleveland elected US President. |

| Year | UK and British Imperial Politics | International History |
|------|----------------------------------|----------------------|
| 1885 | General Charles G Gordon killed in fall of Khartoum to the Mahdi; British evacuate Sudan; Mahdi dies; leads to Gladstone's resignation, Lord Salisbury becomes Prime Minister.<br>Britain establishes protectorate over North Bechuanaland, Niger River region, South New Guinea; occupy Port Hamilton, Korea.<br>General Election leaves a minority Conservative government in office. | The Congo becomes personal possession of King Léopold II of Belgium.<br>Germany annexes Tanganyika and Zanzibar. |
| 1886 | Gladstone becomes Prime Minister for third time; introduces Irish Home Rule Bill, defeated in the House of Commons.<br>Liberal party splits.<br>General Election; Liberals defeated; Lord Salisbury again becomes Prime Minister. | Bonaparte and Orléans families banished from France.<br>First Indian National Congress meets.<br>American Federation of Labor founded.<br>Canadian-Pacific Railway completed. |
| 1887 | Suppression of riots in Ireland; prosecutions under the Crimes Act.<br>First Colonial Conference in London.<br>Queen Victoria celebrates Golden Jubilee. | General Georges Boulanger's coup fails in Paris. |
| 1888 | Local Government Act; establishment of the London County Council.<br>Lobengula, King of Matabele, accepts British protection, grants Cecil Rhodes mining rights, Rhodes amalgamates Kimberley diamond companies.<br>Suez Canal Convention.<br>'Jack the Ripper' murders in London.<br>*The Financial Times* first published. | Kaiser Wilhelm II accedes to German throne.<br>Benjamin Harrison, grandson of ninth President, elected US President. |
| 1889 | London Dock Strike.<br>Rhodes' British South Africa Company granted royal charter. | Austro-Hungarian Crown Prince Rudolf commits suicide at Mayerling.<br>Pedro II abdicates: Brazil proclaimed republic. |
| 1890 | Britain exchanges Helgoland with Germany for Zanzibar and Pemba.<br>Parnell cited as co-respondent in divorce case; adultery proven; loses leadership of the Irish Nationalists | Germany's Kaiser Wilhelm II dismisses Otto von Bismarck.<br>First general election in Japan.<br>German Social Democrats adopt Marxist Programme at Erfurt Congress.<br>Luxembourg separated from Netherlands.<br>Global influenza epidemics. |

| Year | UK and British Imperial Politics | International History |
|------|----------------------------------|----------------------|
| 1891 | Irish Land Purchase Act.<br>German Kaiser Wilhelm II visits London.<br>In libel action Gordon v Lycett, concerning cheating at cards, Prince of Wales admits playing baccarat for high stakes. | Triple Alliance (Austria-Hungary, Germany, Italy) renewed for 12 years.<br>Franco-Russian entente.<br>Young Turk Movement founded in Vienna.<br>Widespread famine in Russia.<br>Japanese earthquake kills as many as 10,000. |
| 1892 | General Election; Gladstone becomes Prime Minister for fourth and final time.<br>Keir Hardy becomes first Labour MP.<br>Britain and Germany agree on Cameroons. | Pan-Slav Conference in Cracow.<br>Grover Cleveland elected US President again. |
| 1893 | Independent Labour Party formed under Hardy.<br>House of Lords rejects second Irish Home Rule Bill.<br>Natal granted self-government.<br>Revolt against British South Africa Company in Matabeleland, crushed by Starr Jameson, occupation of Bulawayo.<br>Swaziland annexed by Transvaal. | Franco-Russian alliance signed.<br>Trial over Panama Canal corruption in Paris.<br>France acquires protectorate over Laos.<br>Benz constructs his four-wheel car; Henry Ford builds his first car. |
| 1894 | Jameson completes occupation of Matabeleland.<br>Uganda becomes protectorate.<br>Death duties (inheritance tax) introduced.<br>Gladstone resigns; succeeded as Prime Minister by Lord Rosebery. | German-Russian commercial treaty.<br>Sino-Japanese War begins: Japan and Korea declare war on China; defeat Chinese at Port Arthur.<br>Dreyfus Case begins in France.<br>Russian Tsar Alexander III dies, succeeded by son Nicholas II. |
| 1895 | General Election; Lord Salisbury becomes Prime Minister in alliance with the Liberal Unionists.<br>British South Africa Company territory south of Zambezi becomes Rhodesia.<br>Jameson Raid into Transvaal.<br>Oscar Wilde loses libel action against Marquis of Queensberry and is jailed. | Sino-Japanese War ends in Chinese defeat.<br>Armenians massacred in Turkey.<br>Abyssinians defeat Italy at Amba Alagi.<br>Cuba rebels against Spanish rule.<br>Guglielmo Marconi invents radio telegraphy. |

| Year | UK and British Imperial Politics | International History |
|------|----------------------------------|----------------------|
| 1896 | General Kitchener begins re-conquest of the Sudan. Jameson Raid fails in Transvaal: German Kaiser Wilhelm II congratulates President Kruger. Tsar Nicholas II visits London and Paris. Alfred Harmsworth issues the *London Daily Mail*. | Abyssinians defeat Italian army at Adowa; Italy sues for peace, withdraws protectorate from Abyssinia. New evidence of Dreyfus' innocence suppressed in France. France annexes Madagascar. Firther Armenian massacres in Turkey. Russia and China sign Manchurian Convention. William McKinley elected US President. First modern Olympics held in Athens. |
| 1897 | Queen Victoria celebrates Diamond Jubilee. Severe famine in India. Britain obtains lease of Kowloon. | Klondike (Yukon, Alaska) Gold Rush begins. Crete proclaims union with Greece: Ottoman Empire declares war, defeated in Thessaly; Peace of Constantinople. Russia occupies Port Arthur, China. Germany occupies Kiao-chow, China. Zionist Congress in Basel, Switzerland. |
| 1898 | General Kitchener defeats Mahdists at Omdurman. Kruger re-elected President of Transvaal. William Gladstone dies. | Dreyfus case: Émile Zola publishes J'Accuse letter. Spanish-American War: US gains Cuba, Puerto Rico, Guam and the Philippines for $20 million. Russia obtains lease of Port Arthur, China. Paris Métro opens. Germany's Otto von Bismarck dies. |
| 1899 | Anglo-Egyptian Sudan Convention. Second Boer War begins: British defeats at Stormberg, Magersfontein and Colenso ('Black Week'). German Emperor William II visits England. London borough councils established. | Philippines demand independence from US. First Peace Conference at the Hague. Alfred Dreyfus pardoned by presidential decree. Germany secures Baghdad railway contract. |

| Year | UK and British Imperial Politics | International History |
|------|----------------------------------|------------------------|
| *1900* | Boer War: Lord Roberts named Commander-in-Chief of British armed forces in South Africa, Kitchener Chief of Staff; Bloemfontein captured, Mafeking relieved, Orange Free State and Transvaal annexed, Pretoria and Johannesburg taken.<br>General Election; Lord Salisbury's Unionist government retains majority<br>Ramsay MacDonald appointed secretary of Labour Party.<br>Australia becomes Commonwealth. | King Umberto I of Italy murdered by anarchist; succeeded by son Victor Emmanuel III.<br>Max Planck formulates Quantum Theory.<br>Boxer Risings in China.<br>US President William McKinley re-elected. |
| *1901* | Queen Victoria dies; succeeded by son Edward VII.<br>Boers begin organised guerrilla warfare; Kitchener and Botha negotiate on amnesty of Cape rebels.<br>Negotiations for Anglo-German alliance end without agreement. | Cuba Convention: makes Cuba US protectorate.<br>US President McKinley assassinated by anarchist; succeeded by Theodore Roosevelt.<br>Treaty on building Panama Canal under US supervision.<br>Social Revolutionary Party founded in Russia.<br>First transatlantic radio signal transmitted. |
| *1902* | Anglo-Japanese treaty recognises independence of China and Korea.<br>Treaty of Vereenigung ends Boer War; Orange Free State becomes British Crown Colony.<br>Lord Salisbury leaves office and dies shortly thereafter; Arthur James Balfour succeeds his uncle as Prime Minister.<br>Colonial Conference meets in London.<br>First meeting of Committee of Imperial Defence.<br>Rhodes dies.<br>Leon Trotsky escapes Siberian prison, settles in London.<br>Education Act brings in first truly national education system. | Triple Alliance between Austria, Germany and Italy renewed for another six years.<br>US acquires perpetual control over Panama Canal.<br>Aswan Dam opens. |

| Year | UK and British Imperial Politics | International History |
|------|----------------------------------|------------------------|
| 1903 | Joseph Chamberlain begins tariff reform campaign. Five ministers, including Chamberlain, resign from Cabinet over proposed tariff reforms. Wyndham Act: government to buy Irish landlords' land and sell it to tenants on low-rate, long-term mortgages. Beginning of Entente Cordiale: King Edward VII visits Paris, French President Loubet visits London. | King Alexander I of Serbia murdered. At its London Congress, the Russian Social Democratic Party splits into Mensheviks (led by Plechanoff) and Bolsheviks (led by Lenin and Trotsky). Wright Brothers' first flight. |
| 1904 | Entente Cordiale settles British-French differences in Morocco, Egypt and Newfoundland fisheries. Britain recognises Suez Canal Convention; surrenders claim to Madagascar. | Russo-Japanese War begins in February, Japanese defeat Russians in September. Roosevelt wins US Presidential election. Photoelectric cell is invented. |
| 1905 | Unemployed Workmen's Act: local authorities to provide work for seasonally unemployed. Aliens Act: first piece of immigration legislation in 20th century Britain; first to define some groups of migrants 'undesirable', thereby making entry to UK discretionary rather than automatic. Anglo-Japanese alliance renewed for ten years. Balfour leaves office, succeeded by Sir Henry Campbell-Bannerman. | Port Arthur surrenders to Japanese. 'Bloody Sunday' – Russian demonstration broken-up by police. Sailors' mutiny on the battleship Potemkin. Tsar Nicholas II issues the 'October Manifesto'. Sinn Fein Party founded in Dublin. Albert Einstein develops his Special Theory of Relativity. |
| 1906 | Liberals win landslide victory at General Election. Edward VII of England and Kaiser Wilhelm II of Germany meet. Britain grants self-government to Transvaal and Orange River Colonies. British ultimatum forces Turkey to cede Sinai Peninsula to Egypt. Education (Provision of Meals) Act: permitted local authorities to provide school meals. | Armand Fallieres elected President of France. Joao Franco becomes Prime Minister of Spain. In France, Dreyfus rehabilitated. Major earthquake in San Francisco USA kills over 1,000. |
| 1907 | British and French agree on Siamese independence. New Zealand granted Dominion status. King Edward VII in Rome, Paris and Marienbad, meets Russian Foreign Minister Izvolski. | Rasputin gains influence at the court of Tsar Nicholas II. Peace Conference held in The Hague. |

| Year | UK and British Imperial Politics | International History |
|------|----------------------------------|----------------------|
| *1908* | Campbell-Bannerman resigns, passes away at 10 Downing Street, the last Prime Minister to die 'on the premises'; Herbert Henry Asquith summoned by King to holiday home at Biarritz to 'kiss hands', returns next day list of Cabinet ministers already approved.<br>*The Daily Telegraph* publishes German Kaiser Wilhelm II's hostile remarks towards England.<br>Union of South Africa established.<br>King Edward VII and Tsar Nicholas II meet at Reval. | King Carlos I of Portugal and the crown prince assassinated. Manuel II becomes King.<br>Ferdinand I declares Bulgaria's independence and assumes the title of Tsar.<br>William Howard Taft elected US President. |
| *1909* | Lloyd George proposes People's Budget to raise money for defence and social expenditure; rejected by House of Lords<br>King Edward VII makes state visits to Berlin and Rome.<br>Anglo-German discussions on control of Baghdad railway. | Kiamil Pasha, grand vizier of Turkey, forced to resign by Turkish nationalists.<br>Plastic (Bakelite) is invented in US. |
| *1910* | King Edward VII dies, succeeded by George V.<br>House of Commons resolves House of Lords should have no power to veto money bills.<br>Liberals win narrowly in two General Elections.<br>South Africa becomes Dominion within British Empire with Botha as Premier. | Egyptian Premier Butros Ghali assassinated.<br>King Manuel II flees Portugal to England. Portugal is proclaimed a republic.<br>Marie Curie publishes Treatise on Radiography. |
| *1911* | Lloyd George introduces National Health Insurance bill in Parliament.<br>Coronation of King George V.<br>Winston Churchill appointed First Lord of the Admiralty.<br>A J Balfour resigns leadership of Conservative Party.<br>Ramsey MacDonald elected chairman of Labour Party.<br>Anglo-Japanese Commercial Treaty signed. | US-Japanese Commercial Treaty signed.<br>Arrival of German gunboat *Panther* in Agadir; triggers international crisis.<br>Peter Stolypyn, Russian Premier, assassinated.<br>Italy declares war on Turkey. |

| Year | UK and British Imperial Politics | International History |
|------|----------------------------------|----------------------|
| 1912 | Ulster Unionists repudiate authority of any Irish parliament set up under Home Rule Bill.<br>British coal strike; London dock strike; transport workers' strike.<br>House of Commons rejects women's franchise bill.<br>*Titanic* sinks: 1,513 die. | First Balkan War begins: Montenegro declares war on Turkey, Turkey declares war on Bulgaria and Serbia, Turkey asks Great Powers to intervene to end Balkan War, Armistice between Turkey, Bulgaria, Serbia and Montenegro.<br>Woodrow Wilson is elected US President.<br>Lenin establishes connection with Stalin and takes over editorship of *Pravda*. |
| 1913 | Suffragette demonstrations in London; House of Commons again rejects a women's franchise bill; first woman magistrate is sworn in. | London Ambassadors Conference ends 1st Balkan War: establishes independent Albania.<br>Bulgarians renew Turkish War.<br>King George I of Greece assassinated and succeeded by Constantine I.<br>Second Balkan war opens.<br>US Federal Reserve System is established.<br>Mahatma Ghandi, leader of the Indian Passive Resistance Movement, is arrested. |
| 1914 | Liberal Unionists unite with Conservatives.<br>Britain declares war on Germany, Austria and Turkey. | Archduke Franz Ferdinand of Austria-Hungary and wife assassinated in Sarajevo.<br>First World War begins: Battles of Mons, the Marne and First Ypres; trench warfare on Western Front; Russians defeated in Battles of Tannenberg and Masurian Lakes. |
| 1915 | Asquith forms a coalition government with A J Balfour, Reginald McKenna; Winston Churchill leaves Admiralty for Chancellorship of Duchy of Lancaster; new Ministry of Munitions created with Lloyd George as Minister.<br>U-boat sinks the British liner *Lusitania*, killing 1,198.<br>'Shells Scandal'.<br>Germans execute British nurse Edith Cavell in Brussels for harbouring British prisoners and aiding escapes. | First World War: Battles of Neuve Chapelle and Loos, Gallipoli campaign<br>Erich Münter plants bomb that destroys US Senate reception room. |
| 1916 | Asquith leaves office, David Lloyd George becomes Prime Minister; forms War Cabinet, including Balfour, Curzon, Milner, Henderson.<br>'Summertime' (daylight saving time) introduced. | First World War: Battles of Verdun, the Somme and Jutland.<br>US President Woodrow Wilson is re-elected.<br>Wilson issues Peace Note to belligerents in European war.<br>Development and use of first effective tanks. |

| Year | UK and British Imperial Politics | International History |
|------|----------------------------------|----------------------|
| 1917 | Lloyd George forces Admiralty to accept convoy system; sets up new Ministries of Food and of Shipping.<br>British and Commonwealth forces take Jerusalem.<br>Balfour Declaration favouring establishment of national home for Jewish People in Palestine.<br>Royal family renounces German names, titles. | First World War: Battle of Passchendaele (Third Ypres); USA declares war on Germany; China declares war on Germany and Russia.<br>February Revolution in Russia.<br>US Senate rejects Wilson's suffrage bill.<br>German and Russian delegates sign Armistice at Brest-Litovsk. |
| 1918 | Lloyd George persuades French to appoint Foch Supreme Allied Commander on Western Front, sacks CIGS Robertson; imposes martial law in Ireland; supplies fresh troops to meet Ludendorff's Spring Offensive; defends record in Maurice debate; oversees Education Act and Representation of the People Act. Haig launches massive offensive; Germany surrenders. Lloyd George receives Order of Merit and hailed as 'the man who won the war'. Wins massive majority in general ('coupon') election for continuation of Coalition Government.<br>Woman over 30 get right to vote.<br>Food shortages lead to national food kitchens and rationing. | First World War: Peace Treaty of Brest-Litovsk signed between Russia and Central Powers; German Spring offensives on Western Front fail; Romania signs Peace of Bucharest with Germany and Austria-Hungary; Allied offensives on Western Front have German army in full retreat; Armistice signed between Allies and Germany; German Fleet surrenders.<br>Ex-Tsar Nicholas II and family executed.<br>German Chancellor Hertling resigns.<br>Revolution in Berlin: William II abdicates.<br>Worldwide influenza epidemic strikes; by 1920 nearly 22 million dead. |
| 1919 | Lloyd George attends Peace Conference in Paris; returns with Treaty of Versailles; passes the Emergency Powers Act to deal with industrial unrest; sets up Sankey Commission on Coalmines; ends wartime Cabinet system.<br>The War of Independence begins in Ireland; Lloyd George calls for volunteers ('Black and Tans') to aid Royal Irish Constabulary.<br>Lady Astor is first British woman to be elected as MP.<br>Britain and France authorise resumption of commercial relations with Germany.<br>British-Persian agreement at Tehran to preserve integrity of Persia. | Communist Revolt in Berlin.<br>Paris Peace Conference adopts principle to found League of Nations.<br>Benito Mussolini founds fascist movement in Italy.<br>Peace Treaty of Versailles signed.<br>US Senate votes against ratification of Versailles Treaty, leaving the USA outside the League of Nations. |

| Year | UK and British Imperial Politics | International History |
|------|----------------------------------|-----------------------|
| 1920 | Lloyd George attends San Remo Conference; heads off Churchill's wish for war with Russia; attempts to form new centre party by fusing Coalition Liberals with moderate Conservatives. Government of Ireland Act passed: Ireland divided into two territories, each with own Parliament. Receives Palestine Mandate. Conscription abolished. | League of Nations comes into existence; US Senate votes against joining. The Hague is selected as seat of Permanent Court of International Justice. League of Nations headquarters moved to Geneva. Warren G Harding wins US Presidential election; 18th Amendment (Prohibition) goes into effect, 19th Amendment gives women right to vote. Bolsheviks win Russian Civil War. Adolf Hitler announces his 25-point programme in Munich. |
| 1921 | Lloyd George averts major strike demanded by Triple Alliance of miners, dockers and railwaymen; dismayed by Andrew Bonar Law resignation as leader of Conservative Party; negotiates Anglo-Irish Agreement: paves way for Irish Free State. | Paris Conference of wartime allies fixes Germany's reparation payments. Peace treaty signed between Russia and Germany. State of emergency proclaimed in Germany in the face of economic crisis. Washington Naval Treaty signed (British Empire, US, France, Japan). |
| 1922 | Lloyd George receives huge criticism in press for Honours scandal, 'Geddes' axe'; almost causes war over Chanak in Turkey. Bonar Law writes in *The Times* that Britain alone cannot act as 'policeman of the world'. Coalition is voted out by Conservative backbenchers; Lloyd George resigns, Bonar Law becomes Prime Minister, Irish Treaty passed creating Irish Free State. Bonar Law meets with Raymond Poincaré, Georges Theunis and Benito Mussolini in London to attempt to resolve French aggression over Germany defaulting on reparations. Britain recognises Kingdom of Egypt under Fuad I. League of Nations Council approves British Mandates for former German colonies Togo, the Cameroons, Tanzania, and Palestine. British mandate proclaimed in Palestine while Arabs declare day of mourning. | Gandhi sentenced to six years in prison for civil disobedience. Election in Irish Free State gives majority to Pro-Treaty candidates; IRA takes large areas under its control. |

| Year | UK and British Imperial Politics | International History |
|------|----------------------------------|----------------------|
| 1923 | Delegation sent to New York to negotiate British repayment of US war loans, including Stanley Baldwin; Chancellor of Exchequer recalled after Bonar Law refuses to accept US terms.<br>Government loses three seats: Mitcham, Willesden East and Liverpool Edge Hill.<br>Baldwin's budget proposes limited tax-cuts.<br>Bonar Law resigns; Stanley Baldwin becomes Prime Minister; Conservatives lose heavily in general election.<br>British Mandate in Palestine begins. | French and Belgian troops occupy the Ruhr when Germany fails to make reparation payments.<br>USSR formally comes into existence.<br>Severe earthquake in Japan destroys all of Yokohama and most of Tokyo.<br>Miguel Primo de Rivera assumes dictatorship of Spain.<br>Wilhelm Marx succeeds Stresemann as German Chancellor.<br>State of emergency declared in Germany.<br>Adolf Hitler's coup d'état (The Beer Hall Putsch) fails. |
| 1924 | James Ramsay MacDonald becomes first Labour Prime Minister.<br>MacDonald convenes London Conference: settles reparations crisis.<br>Wheatley Housing Act: massive programme of house building to provide Britain's working class with decent housing at affordable rents.<br>Two draft treaties concluded with Soviet Union, including controversial provisions for possible Soviet loan.<br>MacDonald first British Prime Minister to address League of Nations.<br>Geneva Protocol.<br>Government loses vote of confidence in the Commons and general election after *Daily Mail* publishes Zinoviev Letter; MacDonald leaves office for first time; Baldwin becomes Prime Minister for second time with his own mandate on programme of 'social idealism tied to sound finance'. | Lenin dies.<br>Dawes Plan published.<br>Turkish National Assembly expels Ottoman dynasty.<br>Greece proclaimed republic.<br>Nazi Party enters the Reichstag with 32 seats for first time, after elections.<br>Calvin Coolidge elected US President. |
| 1925 | Churchill, Chancellor of Exchequer, returns £ to Gold Standard at pre-war parity; Keynes warns of deflationary impact on pay; also leads to tight constraints on defence budget.<br>'Red Friday': government capitulates to threats of general strike and pays subsidy to support miners' pay.<br>Unemployment Insurance Act passed. | Christiania, Norwegian capital, renamed Oslo.<br>In Italy, Mussolini announces that he will take dictatorial powers.<br>Paul von Hindenburg elected President of Germany.<br>Hitler reorganises Nazi Party in Germany.<br>Locarno Conference discusses question of security pact; Locarno Treaty later signed in London. |

| Year | UK and British Imperial Politics | International History |
|------|----------------------------------|----------------------|
| 1926 | General Strike in support of miners' pay claim; after government victory, Baldwin brings back eight-hour day in pits, seen as vindictive.<br>Imperial Conference in London decides Britain and Dominions autonomous communities, equal in status. | Germany applies for admission to League of Nations but is blocked by Spain and Brazil.<br>France proclaims the Lebanon republic.<br>Germany is admitted to League of Nations; Spain leaves as result.<br>Fascist youth organisation Ballilla in Italy and Hitler Jugend in Germany are founded.<br>Leon Trotsky and Grigory Zinoviev expelled from Politburo of Communist Party following Stalin's victory in USSR. |
| 1927 | Trade Disputes Bill ends contracting-out, outlaws strikes threatening state.<br>Baldwin travels to Canada with Prince of Wales.<br>India Commission under Sir John Simon established to review Montagu-Chelmsford Act.<br>Britain recognises rule of Ibn Saud in the Hejaz.<br>Britain recognises Iraq's independence and promises to support its application for membership of the League of Nations. | Inter-Allied military control of Germany ends.<br>'Black Friday' in Germany – the economic system collapses.<br>President Hindenburg of Germany repudiates Germany's responsibility for the First World War.<br>Trotsky and Zinoviev are ultimately expelled from the Communist Party. |
| 1928 | Lloyd George's 'Yellow Book' makes radical proposals for dealing with Depression and unemployment.<br>Equal Franchise Act: all women over 21 obtain right to vote.<br>Transjordan becomes self-governing under the British Mandate.<br>Alexander Fleming discovers penicillin. | Italian electorate is reduced from ten million to three million.<br>Herman Müller is appointed German Chancellor.<br>Kellogg-Briand Pact outlawing war and providing for peaceful settlement of disputes signed.<br>Herbert Hoover elected US President.<br>Albania is proclaimed Kingdom.<br>Plebiscite in Germany against building new battleships fails. |
| 1929 | Lord Irwin tells Baldwin Dominion status for India essential amid fears of terrible communal violence.<br>'Safety First' election campaign built round Baldwin; ends in failure; Baldwin leaves office a second time; Ramsay MacDonald becomes head of Labour government.<br>Anglo-Egyptian Treaty.<br>MacDonald visits United States; first British Prime Minister to do so in official capacity.<br>Round Table Conference: Viceroy and Indian leaders discuss Dominion status. | Dictatorship established in Yugoslavia under King Alexander I; constitution suppressed.<br>St Valentine's Day Massacre of Chicago gangsters.<br>Fascists win single-party elections in Italy.<br>Germany accepts Young Plan at Reparations Conference in the Hague: Allies agree to evacuate Rhineland.<br>Arabs attack Jews in Palestine following dispute over Jewish use of Wailing Wall.<br>Wall Street Crash; world economic crisis begins. Cessation of loans to Europe. |

| Year | UK and British Imperial Politics | International History |
|------|----------------------------------|------------------------|
| 1930 | MacDonald establishes Economic Advisory Council, comprising expert advisers to deal with rising unemployment.<br>Coal Mines Act: seeks to balance commitments on working hours with owners' desire for quotas.<br>Housing Act ('Greenwood Act'): encourages mass slum clearance.<br>UK, France, Italy, Japan and US sign London Naval Treaty regulating naval expansion.<br>MacDonald's friend and colleague Lord Thomson killed with 47 others when airship R 101 crashes in France.<br>Indian Round Table Conference opens. | Nazi politician Wilhelm Frick becomes minister in Thuringia.<br>Nazi party in Germany gains 107 seats.<br>Constantinople's name changed to Istanbul.<br>Acrylic plastics invented. |
| 1931 | British Imperial Conference London: Statute of Westminster approved.<br>Oswald Mosley breaks away from Labour Party to form New Party along fascist lines.<br>Government appoints Economy Committee chaired by Sir George May: findings propose economies of £96 million.<br>MacDonald forms National Government.<br>Britain abandons gold standard; Pound Sterling falls drastically.<br>National Government wins comprehensive victory in general election.<br>Naval force at Invergordon mutinies over pay cuts. | Delhi Pact between Viceroy of India and Gandhi suspends civil disobedience campaign.<br>Austrian Credit-Anstalt bankruptcy begins Central Europe's financial collapse.<br>Nazi leader Adolf Hitler and Alfred Hugenberg of German National Party agree to co-operate.<br>Bankruptcy of German Danatbank leads to closure of all German banks. |
| 1932 | Oswald Mosley founds British Union of Fascists.<br>Government decides not to support US Stimson Doctrine (urges countries not to recognise acts violating Kellogg-Briand Pact).<br>Anglo-French Pact of Friendship signed in Lausanne.<br>Ottawa Agreements introduce tariffs, provoking Snowden's resignation from Cabinet.<br>Britain, France, Germany and Italy make 'No Force Declaration', renouncing use of force for settling differences. | Gandhi returns to India; later arrested.<br>Chancellor Heinrich Brüning declares Germany cannot and will not resume reparation payments.<br>Germany withdraws temporarily from Geneva Disarmament Conference, demanding permission for armaments equal to those of other powers.<br>Franklin D Roosevelt wins US Presidential election.<br>German Kurt von Schleicher attempts to conciliate Centre and Left. |

| Year | UK and British Imperial Politics | International History |
|---|---|---|
| 1933 | MacDonald's proposed cuts in troop numbers fail despite endorsement from US.<br>Government responds to economic crisis in Newfoundland by setting up Royal Commission to investigate financial state of Empire.<br>Anglo-German Trade Agreement.<br>Britain, France, Germany and Italy sign diluted version of Mussolini's proposed Four-Power Pact. | Kurt von Schleicher falls; Adolf Hitler appointed Chancellor of Germany.<br>Fire destroys Reichstag in Berlin.<br>Enabling Act gives Hitler dictatorial powers in Germany.<br>Japan announces it will leave League of Nations.<br>Geneva Disarmament Conference collapses.<br>Start of official persecution of Jews in Germany.<br>Germany withdraws from League of Nations and Disarmament Conference.<br>Germany opens concentration camps for enemies of Nazi regime.<br>In US, 21st Amendment repeals 18th Amendment: Prohibition ends. |
| 1934 | Anglo-Russian Trade Agreement.<br>Road Traffic Act introduces driving tests.<br>Depressed Areas Bill introduced. | General strike staged in France.<br>Germany: 'Night of the Long Knives'; role of German President and Chancellor merged, Hitler becomes Führer after German President Paul von Hindenburg dies.<br>USSR admitted to League of Nations.<br>Kirov assassinated in USSR.<br>Japan repudiates Washington treaties of 1922 and 1930. |

| Year | UK and British Imperial Politics | International History |
|------|----------------------------------|----------------------|
| 1935 | Despite ongoing tariff war, Britain and Ireland sign Coal-Cattle Pact to promote trade.<br>British and French governments meet in London to discuss German rearmament.<br>British government announces expansion and modernisation of national defences, focusing on Royal Navy.<br>Stresa Conference.<br>King George V's Silver Jubilee.<br>Ramsay MacDonald leaves office; Baldwin returns office third time as head of National Government.<br>General election: another landslide for National Government/ Conservatives which Baldwin treats as mandate for rearmament.<br>Baldwin's close political ally, Sam Hoare, Foreign Secretary, negotiates Hoare-Laval pact with France dismembering Abyssinia and undermines League of Nations; uproar forces Hoare's resignation; sanctions applied but have no effect.<br>Baldwin makes disastrous 'lips are sealed' speech.<br>Anglo-Indian Trade Pact signed.<br>Prime Ministers of Italy, France and Britain issue protest at German rearmament and agree to act together against Germany. | Saarland incorporated into Germany following plebiscite.<br>Hitler announces anti-Jewish 'Nuremberg Laws', Swastika to become Germany's official flag.<br>League of Nations imposes sanctions against Italy following invasion of Abyssinia. |

| Year | UK and British Imperial Politics | International History |
|------|----------------------------------|----------------------|
| **1936** | British King George V dies: succeeded by Edward VIII, who abdicates at end of year to marry Wallis Simpson; succeeded by George VI. | German troops occupy Rhineland violating Treaty of Versailles. |
| | Churchill passed over for new role of Minister for Defence in favour of Sir Thomas Inskip. | Franco mutiny in Morocco and throughout Spain starting civil war. |
| | Major programmes of social reform, largely guided by Neville Chamberlain as Chancellor, instigated. | Franco appointed nationalist chief of Spanish state. |
| | School leaving age raised to 15; slum clearance begun; unemployment benefit reformed (not successfully). | Mussolini proclaims the Rome-Berlin Axis. |
| | | Roosevelt re-elected US President. |
| | Public Order Act outlaws wearing of political uniforms. | Germany and Japan sign Anti-Comintern Pact against international communism. |
| | Baldwin hopes Hitler will fight in East rather than West. | |
| | Baldwin shows signs of severe nervous strain, takes August–October off for complete rest. | |
| | British end Egyptian Protectorate. | |
| | Mosley leads anti-Jewish march in London. | |
| | Amy Johnson flies from England to Cape Town. | |
| | Crystal Palace destroyed by fire. | |
| **1937** | King George VI crowned. | Japan invades China, captures Shanghai, Rape of Nanjing (250,000 Chinese killed). |
| | Baldwin leaves office, Neville Chamberlain becomes Prime Minister. | Italy joins German-Japanese Anti-Comintern Pact. |
| | Lord Halifax attempts settlement of Sudetenland problem with Hitler. | Irish Free State becomes Eire under de Valera's Irish Constitution. |
| | Factory Act: seeks to improve working conditions by limiting working hours for women and children, and setting standard working regulations. | |
| | Physical Training Act. | |
| | UK Royal Commission on Palestine recommends partition into British and Arab areas and Jewish state. | |
| | Frank Whittle invents jet engine. | |

| Year | UK and British Imperial Politics | International History |
|------|----------------------------------|----------------------|
| 1938 | Eden resigns as Foreign Secretary.<br>Anglo-Italian Agreement: recognises Mussolini's conquest of Abyssinia in return for withdrawal of 'volunteers' from Spain.<br>Chamberlain, on third trip to Germany for talks to avert war, signs Munich Agreement ('Peace in our time.'); hands Sudetenland to Germany.<br>Housing Act: subsidies to encourage slum clearance, as well as maintaining rent control.<br>Coal Act: coal deposits nationalised and Coal Commission established to administer them.<br>Holidays with Pay Act. | German troops enter Austria declaring it part of German Reich.<br>Japanese puppet government of China at Nanjing.<br>Anti-Semitic legislation in Italy: no public employment or property.<br>Kristallnacht in Germany: Jewish houses, synagogues and schools burnt for a week.<br>US introduces minimum wage, age and maximum hours for employment.<br>Nuclear fission discovered in Germany. |
| 1939 | Chamberlain guarantees Polish sovereignty.<br>Conscription introduced.<br>Britain declares war on Germany following invasion of Poland.<br>Churchill appointed First Lord of Admiralty.<br>British Expeditionary Force sent to France.<br>First German air raid on Britain.<br>Battle of River Plate: Graf Spee scuttled. | Germans troops enter Prague.<br>Italy invades Albania.<br>Germany demands Danzig and Polish Corridor: Poland refuses.<br>Spanish Civil War ends as Nationalists take Madrid.<br>Japanese-Soviet clashes in Manchuria.<br>Hitler and Mussolini sign Pact of Steel.<br>Nazi-Soviet Pact agrees no fighting, partition of Poland: Japanese withdraw from Anti-Comintern Pact in protest.<br>Second World War begins: Germany invades Poland; France declares war; Soviets invade Finland. |

| Year | UK and British Imperial Politics | International History |
|------|----------------------------------|------------------------|
| 1940 | Allied troops sent to Narvik.<br>Government majority in vote of confidence on Norway debate drops to only 81 votes.<br>Norwegian campaign failure causes Chamberlain to resign on same day Germany invades Holland and Belgium; Winston Churchill becomes Prime Minister.<br>British Expeditionary Force evacuated from Dunkirk.<br>Churchill makes 'fight on the beaches' speech; orders destruction of Vichy French fleet at Oran.<br>Battle of Britain.<br>Failed Free French and British attack on Dakar.<br>Italian fleet crippled by British carrier aircraft at Taranto.<br>Wavell defeats Italians in Libya.<br>Italy declares war on Britain.<br>British victories against Italians in Western Desert. | Second World War: Germany invades Norway, Holland, Belgium, Luxembourg,; Italy declares war on France; France divided into German-occupied north and Vichy south; Hungary and Romania join Axis; Italy invades Greece.<br>Roosevelt re-elected US president for unprecedented third term. |

# Index